CHROME FLESH

CATALYST
game labs

CONTENTS & CREDITS

First Printing by Catalyst Game Labs, an imprint of InMediaRes Productions, LLC
PMB 202 • 303 -91st Ave. NE, E-502
Lake Stevens, WA 98258

Find us online:
info@shadowruntabletop.com
(*Shadowrun* questions)
http://www.shadowruntabletop.com
(Catalyst *Shadowrun* website)
http://www.shadowrun.com
(official *Shadowrun Universe* website)
http://www.catalystgamelabs.com
(Catalyst website)
http://shop.catalystgamelabs.com
(Catalyst/Shadowrun orders)

INTRODUCTION

The tragedy of a shadowrunner has always been, and always will be, that they, by themselves, cannot survive. Want to hit the streets as you are and just get by on your wits? Great. Have fun. Lone Star or Knight Errant or someone will dispose of your week-old remains when they accidentally stumble on them in some dark alley. The world is stacked against you, and the price you pay to survive everything it is going to throw at you is to give up some part of yourself.

That's not, of course, the way everyone sees it. To some people, the tradeoffs are not about losing a part of yourself, but instead cutting off a weakness to replace it with something better. The technological revolutions that have shaken the world mean that there is no part of the body that cannot be improved. Muscles can be strengthened, limbs can be replaced, cognitive functioning can be improved, senses can be sharpened, immune systems can be boosted, and on and on. You'll pay money, you'll lose a part of whatever it is that makes you you, but you'll also take a step to becoming a lean, mean, shadowrunning machine—as long as you can live with the "machine" part of that sentence.

Chrome Flesh is your ultimate guide to augmentations, medical technology, and more in the Sixth World. It starts with a chapter called *Cluster F**ked*, a rundown on how cognitive fragmentation disorder (CFD) has shaken the augmentation landscape and led to shifts in technology. Then we have *Fixing What's Broke*, an explanation of medical care, including mental health care in the Sixth World, since shadowrunners are going to need all sorts of care at some point in their careers. *The Enhanced Life* offers qualities and Life Modules for use in building shadowrunners who rely on augmentations in their work. After that, we get into the gear, with *Shiny: Latest in Chrome* surveying the leading producers of cyberware and the new gear they have come up with. The Body Redefined does the same thing for bioware, lining up the options and detailing the players. Then we get into the wild, changing worlds of nanotech and genetech in *Hacking the Metahuman Code*. Both technologies have been dealt significant blows by the arrival of CFD, and both have had to make significant changes. But they're not going away, because if the corporate engineers can find a way to sell people something that might give them a boost, then they're going to do it.

The next chapter offers goods that aren't often thought of as augmentations: drugs and chemicals people use to give them a little something extra. *Quick and Dirty Augmentations* lists plenty of new options to give yourself a quick boost. It may not drain your Essence like other augmentations do, but they still have a chance to enslave a part of your soul with the weight of addiction. *The Murky Future* shows what's coming in the future and where the bleeding edge of technology is headed.

Then we wrap up with a full shopping catalog, listing cyberware, bioware, nanotech, genetech, and drugs from this book, *Shadowrun, Fifth Edition*, and *Stolen Souls*. Use it as your master reference to all the possibilities that are out there, so you can carefully pick just how much of your soul you might have to trade away to stay alive one more day, or even long enough to pick up your next paycheck. Which you can then use to buy the next augmentation, the next boost, and take the next step to becoming whatever you are making yourself into.

CHROME FLESH CREDITS

Development Assistance: Peter M. Andrew, Jr.

Writing: Brooke Chang, Kevin Czarnecki, David Ellenberger, Olivier Gagnon, Alexander Kadar, Scott Schletz, R.J Thomas, Amy Veeres, Michael Wich, Rob Wieland, Thomas Willoughby

Editing: Kevin Killiany, Philip A. Lee, Andrew Marshall, Katherine Monasterio, Aaron Pavao

Proofing: Chuck Burhanna, Mason Hart, Adam Large, Carl Schelin, Lars Wagner Hansen, Jeremy Weyand

Playtesting: Natalie Aked, Rob Aked, Aaron Brosman, Jackson Brunsting, Jacob Cohen, Siin Crawford, Karlene Dickens, Derek Doktor, Bruce Ford, Eugen Fournes, Joanna Fournes, Tim Gray, Kendall Jung, Peter Leitch, Dave Lundquest, Chris Maxfield, Peter Milnes, Jon Naughton, Sue Powell, Richard Riessen, Matt Riley, John Rogers, Rosalind Sexton, Mark Somers, Michael Wich, Leland Zavadil

Art Direction: Brent Evans

Cover Art: David Hovey

Art: Gordon Bennetto, Victor Perez Corbella, Laura Diaz Cubas, Benjamin Giletti, Ian King, Dan Masso, Victor Manuel Leza Moreno, Mauro Peroni, John Petersen, Rob Ruffolo, Andreas "AAS" Schroth, Marc Sintes, Takashi Tan

Cover Layout: Matt "Wrath" Heerdt

Iconography: Nigel Sade

Interior Layout: Matt "Wrath" Heerdt

Shadowrun Line Developer: Jason M. Hardy

MY BROTHER'S KEEPER

"Brother, where...?"

　BLAM, BLAM!!!!

　Taka awoke with a start, fading memories of gunshots mingled with flashing light and cracking thunder. In the Seattle skies above, fat greasy raindrops fell.

　He struggled to breathe: rain already pooled in his mouth and lungs. Taka marshaled his strength and forced the filth from his lungs with a massive heave. His custom Evo cybereyes were offline, leaving him blind, and his right cyberarm wasn't responding. He lay in the dumpster gagging as recent memories rushed back, almost mentally breaking him. But he forced the memories down, concentrating instead on the pain. Pain could be dealt with, overcome. It let you know you were still alive. Still, thank ghost for good body armor.

　Taka rose on wobbly legs, and bits of trash fell from his body as his cybereyes re-booted, barely. Flickering diagnostic AROs filled his vision and confirmed his suspicions: all of his 'ware was damaged, including his internal chrono. He wondered how long he was out.

　All of the chrome in his body was now just dead weight.

　"Brother, why?" he thought to himself. But answers had to wait; he had to move. No one wanted to be wounded and in the open in the Barrens. He stood slowly, legs stiff and breathing painful. With his good arm, the elven street samurai hauled himself out of the dumpster, falling to the pavement with a thud of meat and metal. His body was a mass of pain, especially behind his right shoulder. Taka looked down at his right cyberarm. The fingers were bent at odd angles, and the internals exposed. Reaching over with this good hand, he wrenched the fingers into a fist and looked around to determine his location. As it turned out, he was only a half-kilometer from home. Despite the pain in his meat-parts, he began walking. The Barrens was a rotting, decaying cesspool, but he knew every alley, crumbling building, and shortcut. Everything here, everything he passed, had a memory attached to it.

Twelve years ago.

　"What'cha think ya doin', ya fraggin' keeb?"

　"Yeah, where do you get off wearing that shirt around here?"

　"I think he deserves to get those pointy ears ripped off!"

　The young elf boy tried to run, but four ork teens began pummeling him. He tried to fight back, but his punches flew from wild desperation. The ones that connected inflicted little damage to the stout orks, who only laughed.

　The beating seemed to last forever, bright blossoms of pain punctuating each blow. The elf was about to pass out when, through swollen eyes, he saw one of the teens crumple forward, clutching his crotch. Then another's head snapped to the side before he too fell to the ground. The other two backed off, hands up defensively.

BY RJ THOMAS

"What are you *doin'*? Can't you see what he's wearing? Fragging dandelion-eater's mock ..."

The ork's speech ended mid-sentence when several of his teeth and one tusk broke off in a splash of blood. A vicious elbow smash from someone who had just rushed in did the damage.

The fourth ork teen fled.

The elf looked up at his rescuer. He was also an ork, barely pre-teen, but his physique indicated regular training. He was bald, and spatters of blood dotted his white t-shirt.

"So, you gonna sit there bleeding all day?" the ork said as he extended his hand.

Hesitantly, the elf accepted and was hauled up with little effort. The ork chuckled.

"What?" the elf said, blood oozing from busted lips.

"Your shirt. It says 'Human is right.' And those first two words are really close together, making it easy to read them as a single word. Humanis. No wonder those drek-heads jumped you. No offense, but you're either really brave or really stupid," the ork said with a tusky grin.

"I ...I just needed a shirt. I don't know what it says. Or what 'Humanis' or whatever is." He took a breath. "Why'd you help me?"

"Simple. I hate bullies. But you went down swinging, and I like that. Say, you got a name, or do I call you 'keeb'?"

"I hate that word. But I don't have a name. Not a real one."

The ork thought about it. "Taka. I'll call you Taka."

"Taka?"

"Yeah, it's Japanese. You know what Japanese is?"

"No."

"Well, come with me, and Sensei will teach you."

"Who?"

"My teacher. She's a one-hundred-percent-certified, hoop-kicking street samurai! How'd you think I know all those wiz moves? Besides, you need a new shirt."

Taka looked down at his ruined shirt. "Okay. But what's your name?"

"Gumo," the ork said, puffing his chest out as they walked.

"That's a goofy name. Ow!" That last remark came as Gumo slugged him in the arm.

Taka rounded a corner and walked along a rusty chain-link fence as the storm continued. Normally, he'd have encountered all sorts of nastiness by now, but even in the Barrens people got out of the rain. The pain in his chest was now a dull ache, while the rest of his body felt like pressed drek. Thoughts of how he ended up in that dumpster kept him going. He wanted answers in the worst possible way.

Eventually he came to a small gate, and his internal red flags went up. He should have seen the sentries by now, both the obvious and hidden.

Looking through the fence, he saw a familiar courtyard that lead to the back of a five-story apartment building. Known simply as "Oasis," the small commune was one of the few safe havens in the Barrens. Almost a hundred SINless called Oasis home, and each resident contributed to keeping it operational and safe.

Just like Taka and Gumo did as Oasis' primary guardians.

This task, this sworn duty, gave Taka his purpose in life. And now something was horribly wrong. As he crossed the broken basketball court, memories replayed in his mind. He tried to block them out, to stay alert, but they still came.

Seven years ago.

"BEGIN!"

In the blink of an eye, Taka and Gumo cleared weapons from their holsters and blasted away at each other. Using superior agility and foot speed, Taka moved laterally, trying to spoil Gumo's shots as his Scorpion machine pistol sprayed lead. But Gumo came straight in, Ares Predator firing as he tried to close the distance before his brother could get a solid bead on him.

Both were testing the limits of each other's abilities.

As much as they tried, neither Gumo nor Taka could connect. The ork closed, his Predator's slide locked back, while Taka ejected the clip from his weapon and reached for another. Sensing an opportunity, Gumo tossed his sidearm away and gripped the custom wakizashi at his belt. In one motion, he drew and swung his blade in an upward motion, missing Taka by centimeters.

Taka countered by throwing himself backwards on the ground, arm tucked and locked on his hip, pistol aimed squarely at his opponent. A single shot rang out, hitting Gumo in the gut with a paint round. Taka quickly rolled left, free hand reloading the weapon. Gumo continued his attack, reversing the blade and bringing it down.

"*Halt!*" a stern Japanese voice called out. Both combatants froze, with Gumo's blade hovering above Taka's heart and Taka's pistol pointing at his brother's groin.

Gumo flashed Taka an "*Are you serious?*" look. Taka just winked.

Across the courtyard, an ancient-looking human Japanese woman stood up gracefully, metallic hand resting on the ornate katana at her hip. Faint whirs from worn cyberlimbs came from beneath her kimono as she walked. Both students held their positions.

She nodded to her students who then stood and bowed. "Evaluations?" she asked, red cybereyes blinking.

"I didn't realize Taka had one more round in the chamber. He suckered me," Gumo replied

Sensei nodded

"My tactic was risky. I got lucky," Taka said.

Sensei nodded again. "You're both evenly matched. Both of you would have died."

"*Hai*, Sensei," they said in unison.

"Still, I am proud. You've both trained hard and learned all my lessons. Tomorrow, you'll receive your first augmentations and become true samurai, protectors of our home. But remember, your enhancements are nothing more than an extension of your body, mind, and will. A house will not stand unless the foundation is strong. And remember our code: Protect the weak, treat those who deserve it with respect, keep your honor, and in combat show no hesitation toward an enemy. We are true samurai, not mindless killing machines, despite what some may think."

"Hai, Sensei!"

"Now it's time for tea. Until tomorrow."

Taka and Gumo bowed again.

"Can't believe I fell for that," Gumo blurted out when Sensei was gone.

"Well, I doubt I'll be able to use it on you again. You ready to get chromed?" Taka asked.

"Oh yeah, gonna get me some new legs. Maybe then I can keep up with you."

"Only way you can!"

Gumo playfully punched his brother. "Uh-huh. Well you'd better get some new arms so your punches can finally do some damage!"

"Oh, *frag you!*" Taka said as he smacked Gumo's bald head and ran away.

"Hey, get back here!"

The chase was on.

Taka knew what he'd find even before he entered Oasis.

The first body was just inside the back door. It was a human boy named Jaiden; double-tap to the head. Jaiden was training to become the next generation of samurai, just like Taka. Now he was only inert meat. The rest of the building was more of the same. Bodies strewn about, dead from a blade or bullet, their blood and guts coating the walls. The entire place was a slaughterhouse, not a safe haven.

Taka's gut felt like a dull knife was rattling around inside, tearing with each move. He'd failed them, the only family he'd ever known. Worse, he'd failed to see it coming.

Six months ago.

"I say zero witnesses," the mercenary said as he leveled his Colt SMG at the technicians lined up along the back wall. In the corner, the team's decker worked frantically at a cyberterminal, oblivious to anything else.

The team leader, a human named Dasher, pondered for a moment, hands twitching.

Strill, a mage, nodded. "They'll identify us later," she said, playing with a medallion around her neck. "Just their bad luck things went like this."

Taka and Gumo exchanged looks. The run was supposed to be a datasteal, not an execution.

"No, that's not what we came for," Gumo said.

Dasher cocked an eyebrow, his face twitching. "Really? Who put you in charge, tusker?"

Gumo glared, hands now on his Predator and wakizashi.

"Job is what I *say* it is. Johnson only cares about results, *scan?*" Dasher said, hand gripping a shoulder-holstered Ruger Warhawk.

Gumo stepped forward. "No, afraid I don't, *smoothie*"

"*Back up!*" the merc cried, raising his weapon toward Gumo. The mage's hands started to move.

Taka and Gumo reacted before Strill could cast her spell. It was over in seconds.

Taka's Scorpion put three rounds into the mage's face. She was dead before she hit the floor. Gumo rushed Dasher, putting the shadowrunner between him and the mercenary. The merc tried to geek the ork samurai, but instead drilled Dasher through

the back. Gumo took a blow-through round in the arm, but quickly yanked his Predator out and double-tapped the merc through the heart.

The decker was now jacked-out and wide-eyed in the corner. Both samurai looked at him. "It's done?" Taka asked. The dwarf swallowed and nodded.

"Good," Gumo said, wiping Dasher's blood off his face before addressing the techs. "*You!*" he bellowed. "Your lives are now *ours*. Betray us to anyone, and we *will* return to claim them!"

They all nodded.

Two hours later, the paydata was delivered to Mr. Johnson, and the two samurai were heading back to Oasis. In the van's passenger seat, Gumo re-applied another patch to his bicep. "Lucky scrag," he said.

"We're both lucky," Taka said as he turned the wheel. "Sensei said Dasher was righteous. Can't believe she'd send us to work with someone like him."

Gumo leaned back in his seat, hand over his face. "People change, sometimes for the worse. Still, we got the cred for the heater. Winter won't be as bad this year."

Taka glanced over. "You okay, brother?"

"Yeah, just a massive headache s'all."

Sensei's room looked much like the rest of the building, but with a distinct lack of a body. Taka rested against the doorframe, surveying the damage in brief flashes of light. The battle in here had been fierce. Traditional Japanese furniture lay smashed and scattered about, wall hangings were savagely ripped apart. And then the blood. Sprays and spatters decorated the walls in a gruesome mosaic, but no bodies. Either combat had ended elsewhere or ...

Taka tried to access his augmented vision again, but all he got were fuzzy "SYSTEM OFFLINE" AROs. Dropping his head, he slid to the floor, his resolve crumbling as the sound of rain drowned out all other noise. In an errant flash, he saw something reflect on the floor before him.

Gumo's wakizashi.

Taka reached over and took the weapon, letting the scabbard fall to the floor. He set his jaw as he reversed the blade and placed the tip against his abdomen. Maybe he would find honor in the next life.

But before he could thrust, a sharp crack rang out from above. Taka looked up; it wasn't thunder. He scrambled to his feet and made his way to the roof.

A blast of howling wind and torrential rain assaulted him as he stepped out on the rooftop, but he ignored them. In the center of the roof Taka saw two figures. One was a heavily cybered Japanese woman with iron-grey hair, her kimono in tatters and her abdomen split wide open. She was tied up, crucifix-style, on a brand-new industrial-sized heating unit.

The other figure was on one knee holding an ornate katana in his outstretched right hand, blade pointing down into the roof's cracked blacktop. In his left hand was an Ares Predator with the slide locked back. Casually he tossed it away next to a shredded and discarded armor jacket.

"About time you showed up, I didn't think you'd make it. But I knew you would. Only been waiting three days."

Taka paused at the odd statements. "Gumo ... what have you done? Why?" he said.

"Sorry, *bro*, but that's not my name, not anymore." He tapped his temple. "New tenant in this residence."

Taka stood there dumfounded for a moment before asking "Why ... why did you tell me there was a threat to Oasis?"

The ork chuckled. "Master plan. Been working on it for almost six months, ever since I woke up in here," he said. "How else was I going to get you to that warehouse, shoot you in the back, and then dump you off the fourth floor? Although I should have checked for the dumpster first. Ah, well. Poisoning the old slitch's tea worked well though. Still put up a hell of a fight"

"Gumo ..." Taka said, anger and confusion flooding his voice

"Stop. Calling. Me. *That!*"

Taka gripped the wakizashi tighter. "One more time, *why*?"

"Clean slate, chummer. After you're gone, no one will be left to remember me. No one will try and find me. All previous attachments gone. Tabula rasa at its finest."

Taka shifted into a combat stance, all pain replaced by determination and resolve. "Whoever, whatever you are, you will pay for what you've done. You are not my brother!"

"*That's what I've been trying to tell you!*" the ork bellowed, springing to his feet and spinning on cybered legs to face Taka, revealing a slash across his torso and left eye. The cybereye sat dead in the socket. "Still," he said, casually swinging the katana, "I kinda like this samurai-killing thing. It's fun. Maybe I'll keep doing it to obtain currency. Wait, that sounds wrong, doesn't it? Make cred. That's better."

The face was the same, but the voice was completely alien.

"True samurai are not mindless killing machines," Taka replied as he held his stance.

The ork snorted. "Yeah, whatever. So what's this, some kind of 'honor duel'? Please, I know all your moves! You were never as good as me with a blade."

"You're not Gumo."

"Point taken," the ork said darkly, pointing the katana at Taka. "Well, might as well go all in. Go ahead then, take your best shot, *keeb.*"

The two squared off, rain pouring down as lightning flashed and thunder crashed. Taka stood statue-still in a modified draw-stance. The ork smirked, his body quivering with anticipation, sword held expertly at the ready. The seconds ticked by, and the ork's smile slowly faded into a snarl. Unable to wait, he let out a battle cry and charged. A heartbeat later, Taka was in motion.

A smirk flashed across the ork's face. He sidestepped, anticipating Taka's lateral move. The katana lashed out, right where Taka should have been. Instead, steel met steel as the katana bit into Taka's damaged cyberarm; the elf samurai using it as a shield. The two spun once and separated. Taka's arm fell to the roof. The ork did too; his abdomen split wide, innards beginning to fall out.

Taka turned towards his opponent. The ork's face contorted in rage and pain, trying to hold his guts in. But then the voice changed as Gumo called out. "T-Taka!" Taka's eyes grew wide in confusion, but he still rushed to the other samurai's side. With his good arm, he cradled the dying brother.

"Not, s-strong enough. C-couldn't stop, forgive me" Gumo croaked "I failed. Please h-help me. Losing m-myself. End my n-nightmare."

Taka nodded, understanding the request. With Gumo's hand also on the wakizashi, Taka plunged it up into his brother's chest. Taka held him tight, cutting off a cry of pain. The ork samurai shuddered as his final breath left his body, a look of peace on his face.

Allowing his tears to flow, Taka whispered into Gumo's ear "Go with honor, my brother."

CLUSTERF*CKED: AUGMENTS POST-CFD

At 0430 hours, security guard Jimmy Rowe was nearly finished with his shift for the DocWagon cyberware implant clinic. Everything was quiet in the five-story building as he walked his patrol route, checking in on the graveyard-shift medical staff and all the patients currently housed in the clinic. As he patrolled, he found everything secure; all operating rooms and doctors' offices were locked up tight for the night, and there were no signs of unauthorized activity. If everything went according to plan, he'd clock out at 0600 hours and report that nothing out of the ordinary had happened—even though that would be a lie.

Before the end of his shift, there would be a break-in.

Everything would be all right if the shadowrunners kept their end of the deal: Get in and out of the clinic quietly, taking a minimum number of cyber implants. Alter the records so that nothing they took would be missed for quite some time, and alter the camera footage so that any recordings showed him far away from the runners. By the time anyone discovered the irregularities, Rowe hoped there would be no way of tracing the break-in back to him. All he had to do was to open up the service entrance door for the runner team, make sure the runners' path to the cyberware stockroom was clear, and that they did not encounter anyone along the route. For his services, the runner team paid him five thousand nuyen up front—the equivalent of three and a half months' salary. That nuyen would provide much-needed relief to his growing living expenses from the arrival of his third son.

Rowe slipped on a pair of latex gloves as he opened the service door to the loading bay at the arranged time. As expected, a masked ork and two metahumans of human stature filed into the building, all wearing heavy armor and wielding silenced pistols. By this time, he knew the runners had taken care of the security cameras, having their decker loop the footage from the past hour. Rowe escorted the runner team through the rest of the building in silence, and in two minutes got the team up to the fifth floor of the clinic.

That's when the runner team started to veer off-script.

Rowe got his keys out to allow the runners access to the storage room, but they breezed right past it. One of the runners, a stealthy human figure, maneuvered down the corridor and into a patient's room.

"What the frag? What's going on here?" Rowe demanded.

"Change of plan," the ork whispered. "We're going for the inventory of replacement cyberware parts instead of the actual implants. Much more valuable to us these days thanks to this damn head crash virus."

The shadowrunner returned from the patient's room with one of the graveyard shift's technicians, pressing the pistol against his temple. The ork then gestured to Rowe to lead them to the stockroom of replacement components. Rowe did as he was told, growing ever more nervous about this abrupt change of plans. Once at the stock room, Rowe opened it for the runners. With the technician in tow, the runners and Rowe moved into the stockroom and quietly closed the door behind them.

"These are the components we want, fragger. Get them," barked one of the human runners. The runners handed the technician four hard-shell briefcases to fill with the spare parts on their list.

Rowe observed the human technician as he walked up and down the aisles in the stockroom, collecting processors, cyberlimb casings, direct neural interfaces, servos, repair toolkits, surgical kits and other assorted circuitry and wiring needed to patch up cyberware. The original agreement was that the cyberware to be taken was not to total more than forty thousand nuyen. From what Rowe saw, they were grabbing about four hundred thousand nuyen worth of components, completely clearing off entire shelves in some cases. No matter what their decker did, his employers were going to notice this theft almost immediately. Rowe glanced down at his own pistol, holstered on his right hip. He fought back his instincts to grab for it. He might lose his job because of this incident and might even serve time for it, but if he caused the runners no trouble, he might just get out of this situation alive.

"There," said the technician once all the gear had been loaded "That's everything you wanted. Just let me go, please."

"No witnesses," the ork shadowrunner growled as he raised his pistol at the technician, and pulled the trigger twice. The helpless technician hit the floor, bleeding profusely from his chest wounds.

Rowe reached for his gun, but the two human runners had already opened fire, penetrating his armor vest. Rowe fell backwards into a shelf, cyberlimb casings crashing down on him as he landed on the floor.

As Jimmy Rowe breathed his last, the runners grabbed his keys from his blood-stained belt and made their escape.

POSTED BY: SHADOWSCANNER

- ⊙ Let me start with a quick disclaimer. ShadowScanner believes in broad-based research. She likes to pull everything she has together and see what it shows her, even if some of her sources are questionable. Right now, she's got the CFD bug (not literally, I don't think). She's pulling in every piece of shadowy data and taking events all over the news and piecing together whatever she can. I like that about her and hence the movement of her latest rant to JackPoint. Enjoy!
- ⊙ Bull

Clusterfucked. That word aptly describes our world today, with the emergence of the cognitive fragmentation disorder nanovirus as a major health threat. Panic and fear grip major sprawls with the unprecedented spread of this technology-based virus. This level of panic hasn't been seen since the bugs in Chicago back in '55. Millions of metahumans are terrified of what's happening in Beantown. Citizens outside the QZ get sanitized information from the UCAS government and the Corporate Court. The people know it's far worse inside. The institutions are pacifying the masses with spin doctors while covering their own incompetence. The people I've talked to are waiting for the nukes to start going off. People with access to independent or underground media sources (the real ones) already heard the truth about Boston. It's all adding to the toxic atmosphere surrounding the existence of head crashers, and to the anxieties over the everyday presence of augmentations in peoples' daily lives.

- ⊙ There's a significant difference between Chicago and Boston. In Chicago, there was a chance you could see a bug spirit coming. You could try to do something about it, like pick up a gun and shoot it (even if that didn't work, at least you could try to do something about it). The CFD virus? Unless you're standing under an iridescent cloud of nanites raining down on you, you're not going to see it coming. There's nothing you can do to fight it if you're one of those metahumans who need the therapies that may be tainted with CFD. The CFD virus is essentially an invisible enemy, one that the general public doesn't understand. At this time, undergoing gene therapy or installing nanotech is Russian roulette. And in Boston, having the virus

injected in you is not needed—mere contact can infect you. The uncertainty and helplessness people feel—it's making this situation much more dangerous, both for the public at large and for anyone suffering as a head case. Someone will lash out, which will lead to more blood being spilled in the streets.
- ⊙ Thorn

- ⊙ It's not just Boston that has everyone freaked. Proteus AG's worldwide operations have been locked down since the start of 2076 over this crap. Other than their various platitudes about being determined to find a cure, no solid information about the status of their arkoblocks, or their inhabitants, is known. In this environment, that silence is terrifying. And as The Smiling Bandit has said, it's only feeding people's fears about how bad this virus is.
- ⊙ Ecotope

- ⊙ What Proteus has done goes way beyond PR bulldrek. Anyone on those arkoblocks or facilities are not allowed to enter or leave. Proteus' facilities have all essentially become quarantined zones of their own. From what I hear, Maersk ships that travel to these facilities are carefully screened, and Proteus takes extreme measures to ensure there is as little interaction between crews of these ships and workers at their facilities as possible. Which is a shame; it makes it difficult for me to get to those unfortunate souls' contraband that they could use to make their lives easier inside those arkoblocks during this crisis.
- ⊙ 2XL

To make matters even more volatile on the streets, the public is being inundated with reckless reporting. A ratings-starved media fills the airwaves with rampant rumors, speculation, and half-truths from locals, only feeding the hysteria. From the media's perspective, the most important thing is to drive up their ratings. As Sunshine or Snopes will attest, there has been a twenty-five percent increase in the number of misleading or inaccurate stories from all the major newsnets ever since the Boston quarantine zone became a major headline. These distortions lead many citizens to fear they will soon become infected with the cognitive fragmentation disorder, or that their own sprawl will be quarantined next, and they will be left to fend for themselves as civilization collapses into anarchy. Such fear has led metahumans to prepare for the worst-case doomsday scenarios and has incited massive runs on emergency supplies over the past few months, from food and bottled water, to fuel, extra weapons, portable power generators, and ammo. Prices are spiking because of this high demand for these commodities, making food shortages even more dire due to ongoing droughts, famine, and agricultural diseases. With the CFD virus outbreak in full swing and fear of the unknown gripping many in its clutches, those who would take advantage through price gouging won't stop.

⦾ Thanks to the run on food products, Aztechnology, Horizon, and Shiawase are making killings off their agricultural products, and are banking even more nuyen from governments researching ways of making crops more drought-resistant and more productive. For these megacorporations at least, profits from their agricultural divisions are easily offsetting any losses they are suffering from their cybernetics, geneware, or nanotech divisions by at least a factor of three. For these three, business is good.
⦾ Sunshine

GAME INFORMATION: INCREASED COSTS

Lifestyle costs—food, gas, and other basic necessities—will increase thanks to the scare with the cognitive fragmentation disorder. To simulate the pain player characters would experience from these runs on these important commodities, the gamemaster may choose to increase the cost of lifestyles in areas particularly affected by CFD. For the Streets and Squatter lifestyles, increase the cost of the lifestyles by 1,000 nuyen. For Low and Middle lifestyles, increase the cost of the lifestyle by 2,500 nuyen. For High Lifestyle, add 5,500 nuyen, and for Luxury, add 25,000 nuyen per month.

The gamemaster should also consider raising the price for ammunition by fifty percent for most ammunition, while APDS ammo should be doubled. Costs for medical gear, such as medkits and medkit supplies, should also be increased by 50 percent. These lifestyle and ammunition increases should last in-game until infection and panic is contained in the particular area. Even then, there's a chance that the inflated costs for these commodities could become the "new normal" (gamemaster discretion). Once price gouging starts, it will be hard for these suppliers to give up that extra profit.

Along with the widespread food, water and ammo shortages that are leaving Stuffer Shacks' shelves bare, this nanovirus has brought other notable changes to virtually every sector of our world. Professional sports have been ravaged by the existence of the CFD virus. Many sports leagues are dependent on the augmentation industry to enhance viewership and to increase the entertainment value. For professional athletes, there is high pressure from teams to augment their bodies with the latest technology, lest they underperform and get cut from the rosters. Many athletes' contracts require them to obtain augmentations to play. They are also under tremendous pressure to acquire genetic or nanotech treatments to heal from sports-related injuries at a much faster rate so they can return to play as soon as possible. Torn ACL and MCL? Broken collarbones? Groin pulls and hamstring injuries? What used to take anywhere from six months to a year to heal naturally can take as little as four to six weeks with genetic therapies. Problematic concussions? These symptoms can be taken care of in only a few days with these therapies.

Because of this constant demand for genetic therapies, nanotech augmentations, and augmented healing, the disease has spread among professional athletes in their multi-billion-nuyen industries. As of April 2077, the professional media has exposed one hundred and ninety-six professional athletes from across the entire spectrum of professional sports as expressing symptoms of CFD. Nearly ninety percent of those athletes have been confirmed with follow-up testing. And out of those confirmed cases, nearly half of them got their treatments from their parent megacorporation.

Fear of Boston has made spectators and team owners wary of CFD-infected athletes. Even superstar athletes have faced termination, and once released from their contracts, they are immediately blackballed by their respective leagues, likely never to play professionally again. Some of these athletes remain hopeful, waiting for a cure to restore their ability to compete while they struggle to avoid a complete personality change. But in sports, athletes already have such a limited window for their careers. Even if a cure for CFD comes within a year, younger athletes (who might even cost less to sign under contract) may have replaced them. As such, many athletes today infected with the CFD virus are encountering the harsh reality that yesterday's superstar is becoming today's has-been. Simply put, CFD is permanently ending some careers.

⦾ A hundred and ninety-six athletes from every sport that uses enhancements? That number seems way low to me. It wouldn't surprise me if many are finding new ways to hide their conditions or tamper with tests and are continuing to play even while infected. With so many athletes turning to more advanced augmentations to extend their careers, you know what we're seeing so far may only be the tip of the iceberg.
⦾ Stone

- Why shouldn't they continue to play? A vast majority of strains of CFD are not a communicable disease. You can't get it from coming into direct contact with a head case. People need to understand that most strains of CFD don't work like the strain in Boston did. There is a difference there, omaes. Heck, even contact with their bodily fluids with normal strains may not possess enough of the nanovirus to transmit it. If I was an athlete, I wouldn't be afraid to play with other athletes who are infected.
- Nephrine

- But Nephrine, is there any way to be certain you're dealing with a normal strain of CFD and not the Boston variety that spreads like an out-of-control STD? How is a random chummer off the street supposed to know if a head case, or their belongings, is safe to the touch or not?
- Danger Sensei

- To answer your question, what if an athlete takes a hit, and then the other personality emerges during a game? You can't exactly control when that happens. And when the alternate personality emerges, it may not know the team playbook. Their talents and skills may be useless to the team while the imprinted personality has control. It would become amateur hour—awkward to watch, and with sports like urban brawl and combat biker, potentially deadly, both for the player and for their teammates. Better to cut one player than potentially lose three or four of your star players to someone who is no longer themselves, and who could make a mistake on the field that could get other players killed.
- Netcat

- You can't blame teams for being overly cautious. There's been a lot of conflicting information coming from medical experts pertaining to this disease. Those who preach calm—and the fact that this disease is not easily transmitted—are usually corporate-backed. Those who have a healthy level of skepticism think these "medical experts" might have an agenda. An agenda that serves the corporations by quelling panic around genetech and nanotech and minimizing the damage done to their bottom lines instead of looking after the well-being of the public at large.
- Sunshine

- Quick note: While I said head cases have been confirmed, remember that any existing tests for the head crash virus are still fallible. Imaging scans of the brain pick up the neurological scarring that this nanovirus produces, but they are still producing false positives at a rate of approximately forty-five percent. Blood tests are more accurate than imaging scans, but it takes six weeks for labs to analyze the nanites in the blood to see if they

contain the CFD virus and to determine the specific strain. Blood tests are also proving much more costly, which is why most still choose to use the more fallible imaging scans. The corporations are working hard to reduce the number of inaccuracies in their testing, but it's still not enough to stop athletes from having their entire careers destroyed by an inaccurate test result.

- The Smiling Bandit

- Well, boys and girls, looks like it's time for athletes to go back to the old tried-and-true method of enhancing their performance: doping.
- Slamm-0!

- Particularly in sports that inflict tremendous physical damage on an athlete's body over their careers, including numerous concussions, it would be difficult to distinguish between the degenerative affects of chronic traumatic encephalopathy and the scarring caused by this nasty nanovirus. That could be one of the many causes of these misdiagnoses.
- Butch

- Bingo. That and the science dealing with CFD victims is still in its infancy, so inaccurate test results will only be par for the course.
- The Smiling Bandit

- Although all teams that allow cybernetic enhancements have suffered because of this outbreak, the sports teams based in Boston continue to suffer the brunt of the aftereffects of the quarantine. The Red Sox in particular had to replace their entire team. They're still playing with their replacement players, with low degrees of success, but they're suffering from the stigma of coming from Boston, where the quarantine zone still lingers in many metahumans' minds. Many rivals and fans see them as a high risk of spreading the infection (a localized infection that, by all accounts, can be spread through direct contact), and some refuse to play them, choosing to take forfeits instead. And even when the Red Sox or another Boston team gets to play, fans treat them as badly as if they were the "iridescent dragon" itself, throwing bottles and other trash from the stands. Games are often delayed as law enforcement restores order in the stands. It's no wonder that many stars of the Boston teams are looking to be traded, hoping their talents outweigh any prejudices being held against them by the other teams for playing for a Boston team.
- Icarus

Despite teams' and leagues' assurances that these sporting events are safe for spectators, and guarantees that their teams will remain CFD-free, live attendance has plummeted by about twenty-five percent. It has proven difficult for these teams to shake the images coming out of Boston, and to overcome the fear that another cloud of nanites may rain down upon them during the game. Between the loss of attendance, loss of revenue from concessions, and the loss of talent, many teams are hurting financially. At least three urban brawl franchises and four combat biker franchises are struggling to pay the bills. Rumors are flying that these troubled franchises may be sold and relocated to different markets in an effort to salvage them. These rumor mills are creating lucrative job opportunities for runners, from Johnsons looking to direct the terms of selling franchises to those helping make the decision of which market will become their new home. And thanks to the loss of superstar athletes such as star quarterback Trent Winestead from the Denver Broncos, future hall of fame running back Felicia Esquivel from the Sacramento Chargers, heavies rider for the Atlanta Butchers Bruno Fitts, thunderbiker Karisa Tharp from the Texas Rattlers, center Miko Nabuto from the L.A. Lakers, and closing pitcher Javier Mendez from the San Diego Jaguars, many teams have either slipped dramatically in their standings or have dropped in key rankings in their pre-season polls.

- Trust me, it's not just the star players or the teams hurting from this CFD scare. There are a lot of metahumans losing entire fortunes in Las Vegas over this. Long shots are starting to pay off big time for some gamblers, while sure bets are starting to disappoint a vast majority of fans and are costing them a bundle. This volatility and all the fortunes it's wiping out has resulted in many one-way trips out to the Vegas Desert, if you know what I mean.
- Balladeer

- For those that are curious, rumors suggest the Boston Massacre, Chicago Shatters, and the Los Angeles Bolts are the urban brawl teams in serious financial trouble, and are looking to be sold if a buyer can be found. The combat biker clubs on shaky ground are the Los Angeles Sabers, Cleveland Commandos, the DeeCee Shurikens, and the New York Marauders.
- Slamm-0!

- Not the Massacre! I love that team! They can't move!
- /dev/girl

- The basketball commissioner has taken a rather controversial stance on all this and has just placed a moratorium on new players coming into the league with augmentations. He's enforcing a ban on current players from getting new 'ware. Until such time that augmentations can be guaranteed clear of this disease, the league does not want to introduce new augmentations into its players.
- Slamm-0!

- That's not going to last. You don't see any of the other professional leagues doing the same, and by limiting augmentations, all you're going to do is bring down the sky-high scores of these games. In basketball, viewers are accustomed to seeing more than 150-point games. Bringing those scores back down to where they were prior to augmentation will lose a lot of viewers. The augmentation of professional players is one genie you simply cannot put back in the bottle. For now, if a player shows signs of the disease, all the teams can do is fire them and blackball them.

◉ Pistons

◉ Sadly, I can see the CFD virus continuing to spread among professional athletes without any significant signs of slowdown. The lure of big nuyen is just too big of an incentive for athletes to try to do everything possible to get their bodies to play at such a high level, assuring that CFD will remain a major headache for these teams for a while.

◉ Glitch

Professional athletes are not the only ones feeling the pinch of CFD. Media celebrities, particularly tri-deo stars, are also facing new rounds of blacklisting. Their affair with genetic augmentations and nanoware is (usually) not one of performance, but rather one of looking and feeling "eternally" young and vital for the trid camera and utilizing artificial means to extend their careers in the spotlight. Gossip trid shows around the world are all abuzz as to whether trideo mega stars like Johnny Leo, Ren Kaneshiro, Mai Hirata, Adina Holtzman and Matt Kawakami have been struck by this disease following recent genetic treatments. Tabloid news nets are paying paparazzi through the nose to acquire trideo evidence of a new celebrity head case. In some cases, this "proof" is doctored for sensationalized news, jeopardizing an innocent actor's career. Such unfounded rumors have caused problems on sets, with co-stars and even stage crews refusing to work with alleged head cases. At least four major celebrity suicides in the last year are attributed to accusations of being a head crasher.

These wild rumors have besmirched the reputation of nearly three-dozen celebrities, who face cut contracts and their roles re-cast. Such moves have cost studios millions of nuyen in costly delays. It did not help that 8 months ago, an imprinted personality emerged while the head crasher actor, Casey McNamara, was filming a fight scene for his latest blockbuster, *Shadows of Oblivion*. Not knowing that it was all an act, the fledgling artificial personality emerged and lashed out, starting to club and stab and beat McNamara's co-stars. The fight resulted in serious injuries to three of Andrews' co-stars and the death of another. Coupled with accidents involving stunt doubles, these incidents have only added fuel to the belief that head cases have no place on a film set—and that gene therapies and nanotech are not the best ways to look forever young. Many stars are starting to turn back to traditional plastic surgery treatments to fight the aging process.

CFD's damage to Tinsel Town has not stopped with the studios and the acting talent. Evo's Red Star clinics took massive hits over the past three months when a dozen of their clients, including celebrities Alicia Cooley and Marcos Garcia, publicly announced they had gotten CFD from treatments at Red Star clinics. Because of the violent backlash, ten out of the sixteen Evo clinics in Los Angeles were forced to close. I would expect the remaining six clinics to shut down in the next couple of months, unless things really cool down in the public over their fears with this disease, and over the fears that these clinics are continuing to propagate it.

◉ Horizon and Ares Global Entertainment are taking advantage of the current atmosphere by taking swipes at each other, leaking rumors of actors' "infection status" to these gossip and tabloid news nets. Unfortunately for Ares, Horizon is masterful at public relations and spin doctoring, and this has become a war that Ares is ultimately going to lose. Ares is associated with nearly three-quarters of productions inside L.A. that have been adversely affected by this rumormongering. And those few who have been associated with Horizon have only been shut down for a week or two, as opposed to Ares' productions, which have been shut down on average four to six weeks.

◉ Dr. Spin

◉ It's a sad state of affairs when I repeatedly hear from folks inside the industry that some celebrities are actually better off as head cases. From some of the people I've talked to, the imprinted personalities are nowhere near the level of divas and assholes that the original personality is, and there are some people in these actors' entourages who actually look forward to when the alternate personality emerges. How fucked up is that when people actually want your original personality to be overwritten?

◉ Kat o' Nine Tales

◉ The Red Star clinics haven't been the only ones to suffer. Genetique, which operated six clinics in L.A., was also forced to close its clinics when news broke that eight of their patients contracted CFD. And let's be clear; these corporations did not decide to close these clinics because they were losing tremendous amounts of money. They were shut down when mobs consisting of a few hundred metahumans swarmed their clinics and burned them to the ground. And the megacorporate-owned genetech and nanotech clinics aren't the only ones being targeted. High-end private clinics run by elite Hollywood doctors are also being affected when their clientele become infected. Eight private clinics in the Los Angeles area have also closed, forcing the clinics still operating to hire private security experts to help protect their practices from the violence. These unruly mobs are testing the unfortunate runners hired for the job.

◉ Butch

MANHATTAN UPDATE

POSTED BY: THE SMILING BANDIT

In my previous article for the Stolen Souls document, I talked a lot about the experts in Manhattan who were working on the CFD virus. In the intervening time, there have been developments that I wanted to share with the rest of the class. Want to find the people doing cutting-edge research in this field? These are the people. Even the dead ones likely left behind some material worth uncovering.

NADINE REINHARD
(ADVANCED FRONTIER CYBERNETICS, SAEDER-KRUPP)

Doctor Nadine Reinhard was working on a "brainwave pattern stabilizer" cyber implant for Advanced Frontier Cybernetics and made significant breakthroughs with her research. She has since disappeared from Advanced Frontier. Word on ShadowSea is that she and her family were extracted successfully. She may be working under a new alias for Renraku, but her current whereabouts and new identity are unknown. Saeder-Krupp has a standing 150,000-nuyen reward out for the safe return of Reinhard and her family to Advanced Frontier Cybernetics.

ALEXANDRA SOSA
(MINDSTORM NEUROTECHNOLOGIES, NEONET)

As of last summer, Doctor Alexandra Sosa retired from Mindstorm. This was an abrupt and sudden retirement, a bizarre end to an otherwise stellar career. Some of her closest colleagues indicated that she was quite shaken and not herself when she retired. In addition, there is chatter on ShadowSea that Sosa hired runners to break into Mindstorm's and NeoNET's records to delete the last six months of her research. To my knowledge, none of her research survived that purge. So far, Sosa refuses to talk about what she may have discovered during that time. One cannot help but notice the date of her retirement, and whether it had anything to do with the situation in Boston, which started merely twenty-four hours after Sosa retired from Mindstorm. I have heard that NeoNET wants to get her research by any means necessary, while other corporations are still looking to extract her, to try to convince her to spill those secrets. There are rewards on ShadowSea and other data havens from these megacorporations, ranging from 125,000 nuyen (NeoNET) to 250,000 nuyen (Saeder-Krupp) to obtain this research data from Sosa.

MICHAEL HUBBARD
(MINDSTORM NEUROTECHNOLOGIES, NEONET)

Apparently, NeoNET didn't relocate Michael Hubbard from Manhattan fast enough. Hubbard is a researcher they originally extracted from Shiawase. Hubbard's body was recovered on April 30, 2076, in the Terminal Z-Zone. His death was officially blamed on the neo-anarchist gangs that live in the Terminal Z-Zone, though most don't put a lot of stock in that lousy cover story. It was also discovered that all files pertaining to the work Hubbard did for Mindstorm Neurotechnologies were stolen, presumably given to Shiawase. NeoNET would like that data back, and for the information Shiawase possesses to be corrupted or destroyed. Shiawase posted a reward of 75,000 nuyen for the runner team that accomplishes this task.

STEVEN KELLEY (ARES INTEGRATED SOLUTIONS)

Another deceased researcher on this list was Steven Kelley from Ares Integrated Solutions. I had not talked about Kelley in the previous file, as he had not popped up on my radar until afterwards. I had mentioned that not too many within Knight Errant had been exposed as head cases. Well, Kelley was the reason, as he was responsible for inspecting and improving any augmentations that Knight Errant cops received, as well as identifying and isolating cops who acquired unauthorized 'ware and had been exposed to the CFD virus. He was also charged with keeping each infected case quiet so as to not panic the public. In total, Kelley got seventy-five infected Knight Errant cops off the streets in the New York City area. Kelley was killed during a botched extraction attempt on January 8, 2077. Many on ShadowSea believe runners working for Lone Star carried out the botched extraction.

TIANA FAIRBAIRN (HORIZON)

Doctor Tiana Fairbairn worked in Horizon's Rehabilitation and Psychiatric Center on Ward's Island. Last autumn, Fairbairn left the facility at the end of her shift and never made it home to her wife. All indicators suggest this was not a typical megacorporation extraction. Instead, chatter on ShadowSea suggests this could have been the work of a group of head cases. Fairbairn did not have the cleanest track record when it came to working with head cases; she often employed questionable and/or unethical means to further her research. Fairbairn was not above deliberately infecting her patients with the CFD virus so she'd have a continual stream of new patients to research. This disappearance could very well have been an act of revenge. If not, it could mean these head cases wanted Fairbairn for some other purpose. Horizon is interested in recovering Tiana Fairbairn and learning why she was taken, and is offering a 100,000-nuyen reward for her safe recovery. Horizon will also pay out a 30,000-nuyen reward for confirmation of Fairbairn's death if the head cases have killed her.

JULIAN BORODIN (EVO)

Doctor Julian Borodin was one of Evo's most experienced researchers at the Manhattan Red Star clinic. He was heading up the team studying CFD. Toward the end of the year, Borodin disappeared. Although he was extracted, his family was not. Both Evo and his family are still searching for him. An internal investigation suggests that Mitsuhama Computer Technologies could be responsible for Borodin's disappearance, and his current location is unknown. Evo has a 200,000-nuyen reward for the successful return of Borodin, while Borodin's family also has a 50,000-nuyen reward for his return.

- In Los Angeles, there are whispers of a new, local support group that is forming from the emergence of new head cases. This group calls itself "New Lives," and from word on the streets, is made up of head cases supporting each other. Safety in numbers and all that. These head cases are trying to accept their dual lives and are trying to learn how to come to terms with every personality inside their heads. They are also working to teach tolerance of their new lifestyles to the larger community. Right now, their membership is estimated to be around twenty-five metahumans and growing. No one knows who their leader is. Their membership is being kept quiet for the time being for obvious reasons. Who knows whether this movement will catch on like Mothers of Metahumanity or the Ghoul Rights Committee or if it gets snuffed out from all the fear and intolerance that's currently on the streets, but it's something to be aware of and keep an eye on, especially if we see similar groups popping up in the future in other sprawls.
- Bull

The CFD virus has also affected the elite class in our culture, those with positions of authority in the private and public sectors. These fat cats wish to remain in their positions of power or in their prestigious jobs for as long as possible. These aristocrats—career politicians, megacorporate CEOs, academic professors on tenure, top military leaders, or other businessmen—seek out risky medical treatments in the form of genetic therapies and nanotech, risking CFD instead of doing the most sensible thing: retire. This obsession to remain relevant has opened many of these desperate businessmen and government officials to acquiring this virus from their treatments, thus opening up their positions of power to these unpredictable imprinted personalities. Some metahumans may find ways to control their alternate personalities, but for many others, these personalities will act in their own self-interests.

It's been difficult to get an exact listing of all the executives and managers within the corporate sector who may have been compromised by the CFD virus, as the corporations tend to keep those instances very quiet (or in Proteus AG's case, going to an extreme form of lock down). In many cases, they take swift action to prevent any damage to their public images and internal operations, making sure the problems go away as quickly as possible (or are otherwise inserted into other corporations, turned into spies and double agents). However, I managed to learn of individuals within these corporations who may be infected, and listed them in the **Potential CFD-Infected Corporate Citizens** sidebar. These individuals are still active within their corporations, where their influence may protect them from direct action being taken against them. Some of the names may surprise you and may make you cringe as you start to wonder what head cases may do in their positions if they are infected.

This is becoming a problem for the megacorporations, as more of their elite look toward these restorative procedures to save them from having to retire. Without a cure for CFD, there is the possibility that there will be an explosion of CFD within those corporate executives' ranks, since they have the money and the drive to save their precious careers for as many years as they can squeeze out, even if it means that their minds may no longer end up being their own.

Although tracking down the elusive spread of the CFD virus inside the various megacorporations and other parts of the corporate sector has proven extremely difficult, government officials are public officials, and are constantly in the spotlight. Their behaviors and routines are a lot more accessible to the public and to the media. In recent months, the news reports that at least twenty CAS and UCAS congressmen and senators may be infected with the CFD virus from their recent gene therapy or nanotech implant sessions. With a couple of exceptions, these politicians have universally denied the claims. With privacy laws the way they are in these countries, there are no (legal) ways to verify the claims against them unless the individual in question willingly chooses to be tested and volunteers to share those test results. As such, there is nothing stopping them from continuing to serve in their posts. However, with the public still frightened over CFD and what it may mean for them, all polling numbers for the accused Congressmen and Senators have tanked to less than ten percent. None of these politicians will be re-electable (barring some radical election tampering). The problem is that many still have anywhere from two to four years remaining in their terms, giving any imprinted personalities the opportunity to influence policy.

- In the UCAS and CAS in particular, they are considering legislation to mandate tests for those in elected offices who are accused of being infected with CFD. If it comes out positive, then they will be required to resign from office for not being of "sound mind." Obviously, the established political class does not like this legislation, but the people do. Politicians may have no choice but to pass it, or risk the possibility of a wave election. However, there is another disturbing movement in the political sectors that seeks to expand mandatory testing for anyone who is accused (with reasonable evidence) of being infected. If the tests come back positive, some of this legislation suggests they will be forcefully quarantined, possibly in brand-new concentration camps. This movement begs the question, "What is considered reasonable evidence of infection to mandate someone to take the test?" And more importantly, this legislation is one of those slippery slope scenarios, where it can be taken to an extreme level and abused horribly. Let's hope that doesn't come to pass.
- Kay St. Irregular

- Talk about bringing back the witch hunts.
- Pistons

- Since we're talking governments here, what's going on with the Sioux Nation and their open borders policy for head cases? Are they experiencing any problems?
- Danger Sensei

- To my knowledge, the Sioux Nation's rate of head crash infection amongst the native population is relatively unchanged since they invited all head cases to come to their nation for treatment. The big problem, however, is that these foreigner head cases see the Sioux Nation as a sanctuary and are trying to settle there, instead of just stopping by for treatments from their leading neuroscientists. That means waves of Anglos with this disease are flooding the Sioux Nation. To say the Sioux people are not happy with this policy is an understatement. For the past six months, there have been massive protests in Cheyenne over this policy, some of which have turned violent. The Sioux National Police have arrested nearly 350 protesters, and have killed nearly thirty-five. Since this policy was enforced, nearly sixty Anglo head cases have been targeted by local mobs and have been brutally beaten or killed. I would suggest that the Council of Chiefs reverse their decision before things get even further out of hand.
- Mika

- Adding to the anxiety over head cases in the Sioux Nation is the fact there have been two accidents involving the virus: one at Wind River Corporation complex in Cheyenne, the other at the Cheyenne Military Complex. Between these two accidents, nearly sixty researchers and other staff have been exposed to the CFD virus, and if local talk in runner hangouts prove true, many of those researchers were exposed to at least three new strains of the virus—strains that could be much more virulent than what we have seen in Boston.
- Stone

- As if augmentations were all that popular to begin with in the Sioux Nation. Shamans dominate the culture and ruling class in the Council of Chiefs and the Council of Elders. And they have an inherent mistrust of and disdain for these augmentations as it is. Such accidents may provoke a harsh crackdown on augmentations in the Sioux Nation in all forms before long if these scares continue.
- Lyran

- The CFD virus: another great way of smearing your rival to win an election. I can see the next campaign season now, with accusations flying in campaign commercials that the candidates' rivals are head cases, or that they are, in some way, associated with a head case.
- Kay St. Irregular

- By the way, Kay, I thought CAS senators were limited to four terms? Why would the CAS Senators be enticed to use genetic therapies? Can't they just carry out their terms without the use of these therapies?
- Pistons

- They could if they were elves. Twenty-four years may be nothing for elves, but that time really takes its toll on the physical conditions of all other metahumans. Plus, ego dominates politics. These politicians, like so many of the media celebrities, don't want to look haggard in their late terms; they want to age gracefully so they can hook up with that twenty-something-year-old intern in their office. Trust me, it happens more than you think.
- Kay St. Irregular

In many institutions, elected officials aren't the only ones helping spread the CFD virus. Many career civil service workers who have undergone gene therapy and nanotech implants don't want to give up their cushy positions in government. There is also the matter of political appointees, who, with the right connections, can maintain their power in some capacity for decades. And that is not taking into account positions in various governments that have life terms, such as the Council of Elders in the Sioux Nation and even the UCAS Supreme Court. In the last two months, many in the media have speculated that Justice Amelia Fisher of the UCAS Supreme Court underwent genetic therapy to resolve certain health issues relating to her heart condition. Justice Fisher, age 93, is in her forty-third year of service on the bench, and the revelation of such a procedure has raised the possibility that there is now a head crasher sitting on the UCAS Supreme Court, making rulings that could influence UCAS law for generations. So far, Fisher has denied such allegations, claiming her medical condition was treated not with genetic therapies, but through the use of a magic practitioner. Since Fisher has not provided any evidence to back up her claims, many demand that she step down. For the record, she has also not volunteered to be tested. This is not only adding to the calls for changes to the privacy laws, it is also making people wonder about the rest of the UCAS' judicial system. Many judges in the lower courts have also been in their positions for decades, and technology to extend these judges' health continues to be just as enticing to them as it is for a Supreme Court justice. Each judge who seeks to extend their stay on the bench through artificial means potentially represents a new head case down the line.

- Going back to the topic of the Sioux Nation, Elder Ackak of the Creek tribe passed away March 29th from

POTENTIAL CFD-INFECTED CORPORATE WORKERS

POSTED BY: THE SMILING BANDIT

The influential businessmen listed below publicly display unusual quirks in their personalities that have become noticeable in the last eight to twelve months, when CFD became much more prevalent. Some have shown symptoms that are similar to those of CFD, while other symptoms might be explained by other causes—changes in their home lives, extreme fatigue (these professionals tend to be obsessive workaholics, after all), other innocuous medical conditions or mental disorders, false rumors, and slander from various rivals. There could also be other, more sinister explanations—from merging with insect spirits to shedim-spirit takeovers.

One should not treat this as a hit list or anything, but rather as a way to be aware of head cases who may be in positions of power, and to understand how the CFD virus may be spreading inside these corporations. The more we know about these head cases, the better I will feel. And I have a feeling that this list will only continue to grow until the CFD virus is finally eliminated. Of course, we must also not forget about one of our own, who may be just as dangerous as anyone on this list, if not more so: Fastjack/Search, who remains infected to this day.

ARES
Troy Carpenter, Ares Global Entertainment Vice President

AZTECHNOLOGY
Gabriel Sandoval, Neurosurgeon, Genetique
J.J. Harvin Jr., Aztechnology Board of Directors

EVO
Chkalov Andreevich, Senior Geneticist, Pensodyne
Lesya Olegovna, Geneticist, Pensodyne
Vlada Grigorievna, Chief Financial Officer, Pensodyne
Kaito Ishikawa, Computer Engineer, Pensodyne
Yegorov Leonidovich, Marketing Director, Pensodyne
Tatsuya Yamasaki, Chief Operating Officer, Xiao Technologies

HORIZON
Tam Reyes, Vice President, Singularity

MITSUHAMA
Colonel Takumi Nagata, Petrovski Security
Hina Doi, Quality Assurance Manager, Meechi Games
Rina Takeda, Vice President, Black Lotus Software
Daisuke Ogata, Senior Programmer, Mitsuhama Computers

MONOBE INTERNATIONAL
Jiro Ueno, Neurosurgeon, Designer Genes
Kirsty MacGrory, Geneticist, Monobe International
Fernando Fonseca, Lead Geneticist, Monobe International

NEONET
Emma Porter, NeoNET representative, Manhattan Development Consortium
Swaraj Verghese, NeoNET Board of Directors member
Nathanial Baker, Senior Vice President, JRJ Industries
Angela Vaughn, T99 Think Tank Researcher
Melissa Barlow, Researcher, Transys Neuronet
Isabel Hagen, Computer Engineer, Wolfware

PROTEUS AG
Proteus AG has been in a state of lockdown, with very little information coming out of the corporation and its employees. It is impossible to know how many workers may be infected.

RENRAKU
Shiori Tachibana, Neurosurgeon, Gene Craft
Chouko Wakahisa, CEO, Gene Craft

SAEDER-KRUPP
Vera Marquardt, Saeder-Krupp Corporate Attorney, Manhattan
Jochim Buchholtz, Investigative Agent, Innenrevision

SHIAWASE
Kaede Maki, Senior Department Manager, Shiawase Biotech
Katashi Kimura, Lead Researcher, Shiawase Biotech

UNIVERSAL OMNITECH
Aureliano Negrini, Senior Vice President
Iseul Song, Director of Delta Clinic operations
Maddox Gardener, Junior Vice President, Ingersoil and Berkeley
Hamilton Grimes, CEO, Universal Omnitech

WUXING
Xue Mah, CEO, Eastern Electronics

complications associated with CFD. Since that time, two more Elders appear to have contracted symptoms similar to those of CFD, elders Wahkan and Rowtag. Seems like someone is trying to meddle in Sioux politics and alter the make-up of the Council of Elders.
- ☻ Stone

- ☻ If the elite of our world are so susceptible to CFD due to their hubris, how long do you think it will be before it strikes a Corporate Court Justice? Or has it already?
- ☻ Frosty

The events surrounding the CFD virus caused major financial damage to corporations or their subsidiaries that deal with genetech or nanotech products. Stocks for the independent corporations or subsidiaries have fallen in value by an average of seventy percent, with several hovering just above junk-bond status. Most shadowrunners won't care about this drastic drop in stock, but they should. Such a toxic financial atmosphere will make most corporations gun shy about releasing their latest, bleed-ing-edge technology, particularly if they're afraid the climate will prevent individuals from purchasing the new technology. Research and development costs hundreds of millions of nuyen, so the tech they do release will be limited to therapies and technologies that already have an audience. This will definitely impact runners who are looking to seriously upgrade their bodies with the latest 'ware. On the other hand, Mr. Johnson may be able to get runners to obtain working models of whatever tech they are interested in, instead of settling for incomplete prototypes or research data. This could mean that when the latest tech does hit the market, rival corporations will have similar, cheaper products ready to go within weeks of release. Such product diversity is always better for the consumer (and for the shadowrunner).

This financial instability within the corporations has also meant restructuring to deal with the massive financial losses they have suffered. Many key metahuman assets have been laid off, particularly from independent corporations such as Universal Omnitech and Monobe International. These layoffs sound like a gold mine for corporations looking to recruit assets from their rivals, but this is not the case. Most researchers are bound by non-compete agreements, so the Johnsons will still need to extract them and give them new identities. And as a bonus, many of these laid off employees will no longer be in corporate-owned facilities or arcologies; they'll be moved to less secure surroundings, making extractions easier for shadowrunners.

At street level, what else can runners expect from all this fear surrounding CFD? With all the paranoia over potentially having clients infecting each other, many restaurants, clubs, and other entertainment venues are establishing "no cyberware, no augmentations" policies. Many of these places are installing new security measures at the front doors to scan customers for cyberware. Many argue such devices will only detect augmentations that do not inflict the CFD virus on a metahuman, such as basic cyberlimbs, likely missing the smaller, harder to detect augmentations more likely to be responsible for the infection.

That is part of the next problem for runners: profiling. If establishments in areas particularly hard hit by CFD paranoia see that you are enhanced in some way, they feel that there's a real chance you may have other augmentations that have left you vulnerable to the disease, and may refuse you service. You will not be welcome in their dining areas, let alone their private rooms reserved for VIPs. Usually, runners can meet with Mr. Johnson by bridging the individuals working the security devices at the front doors, but sometimes, security may not take your bribes. And sometimes, you'll just have to let un-augmented members of your team do the talking for you while you wait outside. This may be beneficial, as many Mr. Johnsons are just as squeamish about dealing with runners with augmentations as the rest of society. There have been reports of Johnsons not offering jobs to their teams if they even see a hint of cyberware, regardless of if the augmentation in question is not known to infect a user with CFD. For many Mr. Johnsons, the risk of infection is not worth it. It is always a good idea to ask the fixer how Mr. Johnson feels about augmented individuals before the meeting; it may save you from wasting your time and losing a job.

Mr. Johnsons and bouncers aren't the only ones profiling runners with enhancements. Lately, law enforcement needs only a little provocation to stop and search those who are augmented. Even if the stop and search is illegal in a particular jurisdiction, a cop's response of "the subject was acting unusually, and I needed to check to see if they could be infected with CFD" is usually a good enough reason to keep them from getting into trouble with their superiors in areas hit hard by CFD. Hell, sometimes it even gets them a promotion for looking out for the welfare of the community. And while a runner is out on a job, if they are injured and have a DocWagon contract (or other medical service provider), EMTs could refuse to serve augmented runners. Of course, these EMTs

have been fired on the spot for causing DocWagon and other providers to breach their terms of service, but that is of little consolation to runners who bled out while waiting for help.

There also appears to be a brand-new phenomenon developing on the streets: a new policlub calling itself "The Purists." This policlub is vehemently against most forms of augmentations. Unless you've lost your arm or leg in an accident, or have otherwise been crippled, they assume you're a walking abomination. To them, you're an example of "bad science," or "science for profit" that is being used to "contravene natural selection." For The Purists, overuse of these augmentations is ensuring those with the weakest genes can still compete and survive. Some Purists are satisfied just preaching on corners and passing out pamphlets based on their beliefs. Others, however, are much more violent. In the last year, this militant anti-enhancement group attacked nearly four hundred metahumans across North America. This group does not just target metahumans, but *anyone* with obvious augmentations, including humans (disproving a leading theory that Humanis or Human Nation is behind this movement). This group is adding members as quickly as the CFD virus is spreading, with chapterhouses appearing daily in most major sprawls. If you are augmented and haven't encountered these guys yet, be careful. Chances are, you will.

* Yeah, I've heard of these guys. Some of their members are claiming CFD is punishment for us from the dragons after the great dragon civil war. Others claim it's a conspiracy from the Corporate Court for some bizarre, new population control technique they're trying. They're serious nut jobs. Best to stay out of their way if possible.
* Snopes

While some shadowrunners are still willing to acquire new 'ware, specifically genetic therapies and nanotech, many runners avoid even safe cyberware and bioware. In recent months, there has been a rush of break-ins at various implant clinics, not for brand new cyberware, but for parts and components for older cyberware, to allow older models to stay functional for longer. There's a lot of superstition and misunderstanding of how CFD is transmitted, but this superstition is making a lot of people rich on the black market. Basic replacement components for cyberware that used to go for fifty nuyen are now selling on the black market for two hundred nuyen, if not more. Street docs and fixers are looking to cash in on that trend, including trying to salvage what they can from used cyberware taken from jobs. Groups that deal in a lot of used cyberware, such as Tamanous, are seeing huge profits from those looking for a safer alternative to the current 'ware on the streets.

Some are trying to locate older products for bioware created prior to the CFD virus, although these older batches are rare. In my professional opinion, I cannot say whether it is safer implanting bioware past its expiration date or undergoing a procedure that puts you at risk for CFD. Some crazy drekheads think the risk is worth it either way.

Speaking of opportunists, there are those in the shadows who offer false cures and even "vaccinations" against CFD. I know most of you here know better than to take a two-hundred-nuyen "cure" from the back of someone's van, but there are many others out there who allow themselves to be taken advantage of. In many cases, these "cures" and "vaccines" are nanites that contain the virus, corrupting the existing CFD personalities and making them more unstable, or accelerating the process of the host being overwritten. In other cases, victims receive additional personalities from the injections, making their dire situation even worse. Many of the injections inflict CFD on those who didn't have the disease in the first place.

There are a lot of bastards out there in the shadows, and I remind everyone that at this time, there is no reliable way to treat or cure CFD. Anyone who promises to do such a thing is trying to take your money. All I can say, chummers, is stay safe, take any news you may have heard about Boston or the spread of the CFD virus with a grain of salt, and watch out for those damn Purists.

A TUNNEL, BUT NO LIGHT YET

POSTED BY: BUTCH

<Private Forum/Private Chat began 1140 hours, 07/12/2077. Invited JackPointers/Guests: Butch, Bull, Netcat, The Smiling Bandit, KAM, Nephrine>

I cannot possibly add enough qualifiers to what I am about to say. This is not the light at the end of the tunnel. This is simply pointing out that there is a tunnel, rather than a wall. We are not even fragging *close* to being out of the woods, but we're better off than we were even a few weeks ago. Do not get excited when you read this, because it is not what you are all hoping I'll say.

With that out of the way: I may have discovered the beginning of a treatment.

This will only be useful in a small minority of cases, and even then the potential treatment is extremely risky, but in ideal circumstances, this would be theoretically capable of preventing the full takeover of a mind by CFD's personality fragments. That said, I do not want this spreading like wildfire and giving false hope. There are already far, far, *far* too many rumors of a CFD treatment or cure in the pipe, and I don't want to add to that. I despise giving false hope and will not be responsible for causing it in anyone. A cure or treatment for every CFD iteration is *not* right around the corner and will *not* be

for some time. This cannot be stressed enough—head cases are already in fragile, unstable mindsets, and the wrong rumor turning out to be nothing could be all it takes for one of them to swallow their gun. This should be disseminated among those who can help, but please, *please* be careful with who you tell. I hope I've made myself clear. Now, onto the good stuff.

BUYER'S REMORSE

We're all aware of the xenosapient AI phenomenon— artificial intelligence that takes on strange forms alien to metahumanity, and is thus distanced from most interaction. It seems that at least one of these xenosapients was used in generating personality fragments that appear in head cases. While working with CFD victims for my research, I discovered a Renraku sarariman who had escaped confinement based on false rumors that someone on the streets had a cure. These rumors led him to my practice, a fact that unnerves me. If anyone has information on where these rumors are coming from, I would appreciate if you spoke up. I want to keep this quiet until I have something, lest the corps shut me down, or I begin to develop a reputation for more than just patching bullet holes.

Regardless, this gentleman was in the final stages of CFD, and when his fragments took over, I found myself introduced to an entity known as Phalanx, though the name was unknown to me at the time. It immediately requested confinement and entered the matrix in VR. This confused me a great deal, as it had no commlink, and the patient did not make any mention of being a technomancer. Examining his inert body led to the discovery of a new ability of select head cases: Some nanomachines that delivered the personality fragment are capable of forming a Matrix device not unlike an implanted cyberdeck. The patient seemed to have no knowledge of such a device and could not access it when informed. While it was in control, it did nothing but browse the Matrix, not looking for any particular information, just idling in hosts, on grids, looking around, that sort of thing. Nothing more. It refused all conversation, online or offline. When the sarariman (whose name I will not be posting, so don't ask) resumed control, he was distraught and begged me for a cure. Needless to say, I didn't have one, but I'm always willing to test new methods on volunteers. I made repeated attempts to make contact with Phalanx, but from then on it would only speak in encoded Matrix languages, through the Matrix, always from the same host. From then on, all attempts failed, until I got an idea.

I hired a technomancer to compile a sprite through which we could speak to Phalanx. Netcat, this has to do with why you were added to this conversation, so pay attention. I couldn't contact (or afford) you, so I had to look outside JackPoint for assistance in this matter. As luck would have it, an ex-decker from the East Coast moved to Seattle for a fresh start after her Emergence; a technomancer that now goes by the name of Respec. I worked with her once in the past, and asked if she'd be willing to create a Sprite to communicate with Phalanx. To my relief, she agreed. Bull, I am sending you her commcode. Please give Respec user access for this conversation only, and she will post her notes on the meeting.

[BULL ADDS USER 'RESPEC']
POSTED BY: RESPEC

Hello. Thank you for allowing me to post. I've heard of JackPoint through reputation and hope to meet your standards. I couldn't think of a chance to prove myself to the shadow elite as a better eighty-sixth birthday present. My post today will be regarding my discussions with the AI Phalanx and how it may result in a treatment for at least one strain of the CFD virus.

As stated, when Phalanx was in control of the infected body, it would only converse by transmitting raw information through the Matrix. I compiled a sprite that acted as an interpreter, decoding the raw data into a language I could speak, and then back into Phalanx's preferred language.

Conversation was pleasant, if not strange, and focused on its ongoing disgust with its human body and regrets toward being part of the CFD program. It expressed a great deal of hate toward its root AIs, and eventually expressed a wish that there were some way it could leave the host body. I found this to be useful information, and at this point I began discussing ways to make that wish a reality.

Phalanx believes that if there were some way to decouple its mind from the body, it would be capable of leaving the body permanently, though the actual extraction would require the use of highly specialized equipment that I did not believe existed. This, obviously, was a problem.

Having discovered all we could about one another, and then some, Phalanx ended the conversation. I disconnected, transferred my logs and notes to Butch, and that was the end of my involvement in this stage of what will hopefully be an ongoing attempt to treat head crash. This was my goal—more than money, doing something good for the people of the Sixth World. This condition has crippled metahumanity and if I can even have this tiny role in saving us all from it, that is more than enough for me.

I'd also like to state that I learned an important lesson here. Phalanx's host is, not to put too fine a point on it, a total bastard. He was utterly friendly and pleasant to me, and once I left to work on a sprite or decode my conversations with Phalanx, Ms. Butch tells me the host began talking about how unpleasant I am, physically, personally, etc. and making highly offensive jokes about my identity as a technomancer. He would then smile and act friendly when I returned, as if nothing was wrong. Even

though it could mean helping a jerk like this, I continued with the research. I learned an important lesson, namely that if you want to help people, sometimes the people you are helping will be two-faced wastes of oxygen that you just want to punch in the face over and over.

But you can't just punch them, because that would be wrong.

[USER 'RESPEC' DISCONNECTS]

- ● Seems nice, definitely smart enough, but she needs a new name. Respec? What, like, respect? That doesn't even make any sense.
- ● Nephrine

- ● A respec is when you change your stats and abilities in a Matrix RPG. She used to be a decker, so maybe it's a play on that. I'm a little hurt Butch asked this new girl for help, and not me.
- ● Netcat

- ● Respec works cheap. The total amount I paid her was half what you charge for just a consultation.
- ● Butch

- ● Look at that college-essay writing style. Someone's nervous about her first JackPoint post, hah!
- ● Bull

- ● Wait, did I read that right? She took a head case into a host?
- ● KAM

- ● CFD can't spread digitally, and it can't infect nanomachines over the Matrix like that. There was nothing dangerous about it.
- ● The Smiling Bandit

- ● I just noticed. "It"? Not he or she? Or hell, even some alternative pronoun?
- ● KAM

- ● AIs (like anyone else, really) choose the pronoun by which they want to be known. A lot of xenosapients have no interest in gender in any way, so they prefer "it."
- ● Netcat

CORPORATE RESEARCH

Respec's discovery was the turning point. Personality fragments are created from the combination of multiple AIs. If I could figure out which AIs Phalanx was created from, and locate other CFD victims expressing Phalanx fragments, maybe it *would* be as simple as convincing them to "leave," so to speak. That's where this research began. The donations I've received have been more than kind, but even with them supplementing my income as a street doc, I don't have the money or time for this kind of research project. I strategically leaked this avenue of research to contacts I have in the corporations I felt were most likely to bear fruit—including NeoNET, Horizon, and Murai Holdings, a no-name firm that's made some interesting discoveries in neuroscience in the past five years—and waited.

After a few months, I once again hired Respec, as well as several shadowrunner teams, to raid facilities of the targeted corporations and claim whatever information may have blossomed from my seeds. For those of you asking where your donations went, there you go. You paid for a magician with an obsession on twentieth-century sneakers to keep up his gigaweed habit, and our dear friends in the corporate world did all the heavy lifting.

- Work smart, not hard.
- Bull

I hit paydata. To head off questions regarding why such a breakthrough as I'm about to lay out wasn't publicized: It's too specialized. In a lot of ways CFD provides the same challenges as the ongoing concern of cancer. Cancer isn't just one disease, but rather a series of strains that all have the same symptom, namely uncontrolled cell growth that created life-threatening tumors. Each type of cancer has to be treated differently, but the problem was every time a treatment or a cure was found for one type, the public would get confused, and think cancer was cured. They'd then be disillusioned after the next five treatments were discovered for five more types. The medical community learned their lesson with VITAS, HMHVV, and now CFD. You won't hear a word about this in public until we have a treatment for at least a majority of cases, and I can promise you that won't be for a while.

As for what my discovery entailed—Phalanx appears to be an uncommon strain of CFD, but statistically significant. Thus, a specialized treatment is absolutely feasible. Xenosapient AIs like Phalanx detest the human body, and in the majority of CFD cases involving a xenosapient fragment, symptoms similar to what I observed with Phalanx are expressed—reclusiveness, along with a desire to only interact with Matrix entities such as other AIs and technomancers. It can be reasoned that many other AIs likely share Phalanx's disgust over their human body and regret their choice to take one over. They could, in short, be persuaded to leave, if we had the technology to allow them.

Murai Holdings is to be thanked, as the key to all this is their creation, a new type of nanomachine known as Reversers. Obviously this is highly risky, as it involves injecting someone with yet more nanomachines. However, if the AI is willing, the CFD "firmware" can be overwritten to allow the

fragment to transfer out of the body and cease the fragmentation of the host's psyche. This has the effect of "re-formatting" the parts of the brain that were nanomachine-controlled, but that can be subsequently treated with augmentation and gene therapy. Even nanomachine therapy, if you want to risk it. In short, The treatment works like this:

- Identify a CFD victim who has not yet been fully "overwritten" and expresses Phalanx-like reclusiveness.
- Make contact with the fragment via a technomancer, who will convince them that there is a way to leave the body, preventing further fragmentation of the host and returning them to the Matrix form they so covet. Confirming the AI is in fact a xenosapient who genuinely experiences body dysphoria is paramount, as is getting it to agree to submit to treatment
- Once the fragment has agreed to vacate the host body, the technomancer uses a complex form that Respec calls Coriolis.
- Inject the patient with Reverser nanomachines. If the previously outlined steps are followed, it will use the Matrix device embedded in the Reverser nanomachine network to evacuate the body, leaving the infected portions of the brain latent, but not dead. If the fragment hasn't been treated with Coriolis, or the fragment refuses to leave, the Reverser colony will have no effect.
- Through cyberware or bioware augmentation, restore functionality to the infected brain fragments. Monitor subject to ensure full recovery.

This treatment will raise a great many red flags if it is released to the public. It can be assumed that this is why corporate research hit a wall, and why no announcements have been made. It wasn't so long ago even average people would round up suspected technomancers and have them shot, and several AAAs still have six-digit bounties for a live TM. Besides that, injecting nanomachines to solve a nanomachine problem stinks at first glance of the "like cures like" quackery of the late twentieth century.

As hard as it may be to believe, I have successfully treated a patient with this. Phalanx has become a fully fledged disembodied AI, and its former host has reported no blackouts and no strange activity. Twenty-four-hour monitoring has suggested that he is well and truly cured, though the amount of tech that had to be implanted to regain proper brain functioning is ... less than ideal. Let's put it this way: If he didn't live as cleanly as he did, or he had any prior augmentation, it's likely he would have died of Essence loss.

Between the harsh view the treatment would get in the public eye, the expense of both the required equipment (Reversers can, at this point, only be found in the labs of the most prestigious AAA-affiliated biochem firms) the recovery of wiped portions of the brain, and the fact that it only treats rare cases (I have no reason to believe any non-xenosapient AI fragment could be affected), this is not ideal. I hesitate to even call it a treatment, all things considered. I've reached the limit of my current research, but a year ago I didn't even expect to be this far, so I'll be releasing all the available information to you, and you can decide if it's worth spreading to the larger shadow community. To begin, Respec will explain the particulars of the complex form she developed.

[USER 'RESPEC' REJOINS]

For non-technomancers this is going to be a whole lot of nonsense, but I'd advise showing it to some other technomancers anyway. I'm sure Ms. Butch has said this plenty of times, but this will *only* work on xenosapient AI fragments, and even then it's a bit of a crapshoot. Nevertheless, it's better to have information that might be useless than keep information that might be the key to all this hidden.

To thread my complex forms, I think in metaphors and imagery. The key image for me when threading is, as you may have guessed from the name, a drain flowing backwards, a downhill stream going uphill, time rewinding, the natural order reversed, things of that nature. Even in the best case, you're going to get hit hard with fading, and since you're working with machines embedded in the subject's brain, he's going to incur some pain too, so be careful.

Connect with the personality fragment over the Matrix, then use this on it. It'll take a few days at minimum, so I'd advise both you and the patient to be hooked up to life support equipment. I don't know what disconnecting in the middle of the process would do, but it's probably bad.

[ERROR: ATTACHED CODE NOT COMPATIBLE]

It'll sort of click once you've managed it, but it'll take a while and be a pain for the both of you. I don't know what it's like outside of my paradigm, but you'll know it when it happens. Once that's done, treatment can resume. I hope this was helpful.

[RESPEC LEAVES ONCE AGAIN.]

* Netcat, care to translate that incompatible code for the rest of us?
* The Smiling Bandit

* It does what she said it does—In theory, anyway. Disrupts the wetware connection and uses Resonance to eject fragments that can't link with a physical brain. They're still in your body, but not in your mind. I guess that's what the nanomachine colony is for. It's good work, but sloppy. I might need to find this girl and teach her something.
* Netcat

The next step, as stated, is the injection of a colony of Reverser nanomachines. These are in high demand, and only exist as prototypes. None of my tech contacts could replicate them, and that's counting the ones with access to a nano-fabrication array. Now posting the information I was able to copy from the colony before I began treatment.

[ATTACHMENT: "REVERSER" CONTAINS NANO-FABRICATION CODING. FILE IS BEING SCANNED FOR VIRUSES, CORRUPTION, FLAWS, MALFEASANT CODE, ETC. ESTIMATED TIME REMAINING: 3.7 HOURS.]

- Butch owes me a commlink to replace the one that fried itself trying to open that file. I got it to open on research equipment I "liberated" from my day job, and saw that these can't be nanomachines. It's not possible to store that much data into a microscopic device. The actual process is as simple as any other nanomachine treatment: Injection, lots of food and drink to provide material for them to work with, that's it. It's a piece of cake—the only thing about this process that is.
- Nephrine

- It's not practical, but theoretically a specialized nanomachine could store this much data. It'd be beyond commercial tech, but the megas always keep the best stuff for themselves. It must be developed through some new fabrication method. Only way you can pack that much and still have room to store the AI and a Matrix device to transmit from.
- KAM

- And some no-name like Murai managed to make a pretty toy like this? Something's fishy. Might need to put my feelers out and find out who pulls their strings. If /dev/ were here, I'm sure she'd be taking bets on whose creature they are. I suppose I could take her place.
- The Smiling Bandit

- No jokes, Bandit, let's get this drek solved fraggin' quick. I think I might have found another clue. The Seattle office of Murai is just a subsidiary—their main office is in Boston. You know, the Boston that's got CFD worse than any place on this rock?
- Bull

- The game is afoot. Too bad we can't get into the lockdown. This could have been something finally interesting. Guess we'll just have to work with what we have and hope that's enough.
- The Smiling Bandit

Injecting nanomachines to solve CFD sounds scary, and it most certainly is. As I've stated before, but can't overstate, it is imperative that the personality fragment accept the treatment and that Coriolis be successfully used on the personality fragment's Matrix persona, but I'd like to stress that identifying the fragment as xenosapeint is crucial. Is mandatory. If it turns out to be a "normal" AI masquerading as a xenosapient, then the personality fragment can simply refuse to utilize the Reverser colony, and infect it just as it would any other nanomachine injection, using it to further the infection process on the poor host. Coriolis only works on xenosapients. If used on a non-xenosapient, Respec tells me it will result in a false positive, so "The technomancer's Coriolis complex form worked, therefore the AI must be a xenosapient!" is not just faulty reasoning, but dangerous.

A final note that must be stressed. If at any point this treatment fails, and Reverser colonies are injected into the host anyway, they will have the same effect as any other nanoware—that is, the virus will corrupt them and use them to further spread CFD.

YOU DON'T HAVE TO GO HOME, BUT YOU CAN'T STAY HERE

This won't save anyone that's already become a full head case. It won't help in most cases. But if you're lucky (or unlucky) enough to have CFD-xeno, there may yet be hope. As I said at the beginning of this post, there's no promises with CFD. Even if you have the right strain, it might not work. But it's a step forward, the start of a winding path that I hope might lead out of the woods. It's just a matter of finding our way, and making sure we leave breadcrumbs behind us.

We have avenues of potential investigation. Things we can hire runners for, things we can investigate ourselves, or puzzle out. There is hope that this is no longer an unsolvable problem. We have something that works in some cases. Between my own research, the braintrust that is JackPoint, and megacorps rushing to be the first to cure this, CFD is a bigger deal than it ever was before, chummers. We have work to do.

- With Boston involved, this is going to be difficult. I'll see if I have any old contacts that can get word in or out.
- Bull

- I'll get in touch with Respec, and we'll work on Coriolis. See if there's a way to make it work on non-xenosapients
- Netcat

- I'll be doing research.
- The Smiling Bandit

- I'll see into hiring runners to do some of the dirty work for us.
- KAM

- And I'll use my corporate connections to get some better material to test on. Let's get to it.
- Nephrine

- And I'll ponder whether transferring AIs in this fashion represents moving them out or murdering them and replacing them with a clone.
- Arete

- Who let him in here?
- Glitch

GAME INFORMATION

Attempted treatment of CFD consists of four steps: Convincing the personality fragment to leave the host, use of the Coriolis complex form, injection of a Reverser nanomachine colony, and finally, the host's recovery.

As Butch said about a million times, this is a difficult treatment, and it only can be used in certain cases. For this to even have a chance of curing CFD, the dominant personality fragment must be descended from a xenosapient AI, an AI that doesn't relate to the human form. There are other factors that come into play, like genetics and the host's psychology, but these aren't well understood. In other words, it's up to the gamemaster if treatment is even possible. This should not be an automatic way out for all characters suffering for CFD, but it can be an option for players struggling with being a head case and wanting to have their former personality back.

To begin, the Xenosapient AI should be made very aware of what it's like to be human. Force it to experience starvation, dehydration, and a variety of emotions, especially intense ones. Whether through drugs or old-fashioned torture, drive it into the fragment's head that being human is an experience it is in no way prepared for. The host must be made aware that she will likely be tortured to get to the fragment, and she must be willing to put up with it as well. Resisting giving in to the torture is a Willpower + Body test. If the CFD host fails, he succumbs and puts a stop to the torture, forcing the test to start over again from scratch.

The test to convince a fragment to exit the body is Negotiation + Charisma vs. Willpower + Charisma, rolled once per day for seven consecutive days. Track which individual wins each test; at the end of the seven days, the individual who won the most tests wins the struggle. If the character has more hits, she convinces the personality fragment to leave the body.

For these tests, xenosapient AI fragments suffer a –2 penalty to tests resisting Negotiation, and –3 if there is anything that takes advantage of their physical body (tailored pheromones, the Influence spell, the Kinesics adept power, and so on). No other fragments suffer such penalties.

Once this is completed, a technomancer must use the Coriolis complex form. This requires the personality fragment to access the Matrix either through hot-sim or a Matrix device formed from the nanomachines in their host. The complex form is then used on the fragment's persona. If at any time the fragment cedes control to the host or disconnects from the Matrix, the process is disrupted and both the fragment's host and the technomancer suffer the full fading value as unresisted stun damage.

NEW COMPLEX FORM
CORIOLIS

Target: Persona
Duration: E
FV: L + 3

Resonance plays on the dysphoria between xenosapient CFD personality fragments and a human mind, pulling them apart and allowing the fragments to return to their digital form. Make a Software + Resonance [Level] (5, 24 hours) Extended Test to eject a personality fragment. If the threshold is not met by the end of a week, the Reverser colonies lose their effect, leaving Coriolis unable to do anything. New Reversers must be obtained, and the process has to start again. On a glitch, the target suffers a –2 to all tests during treatment. On a critical glitch, the test's interval is increased 48 hours, and the number of hits achieved is reset to 0.

FIXING WHAT'S BROKE

WELCOME TO DOCWAGON

- Everyone, this is NurseNancy—she's an agent that DocWagon provides to their customers. I've uploaded a copy here to answer any questions you might have about your DocWagon coverage. If you don't have a health service provider connected to one of your SINs, you should get one. Street docs, slap patches, and what passes for first aid from other runners might do in a pinch, but it's only a matter of time before you get too fragged to walk. You'll want real doctors, real hospitals, and if you're willing to pay out of your hoop, a high threat response team to extract you out of the bad situation that fragged you in the first place. I've left NurseNancy open to edits to allow runners to comment on those grey areas where we need info that most DocWagon customers skim over. One piece of advice: Her current setting as the nice, matronly Sioux nurse is the least obnoxious one, so leave those settings be.
- Butch

- Is there a candy striper setting?
- Slamm-0!

- I have one, but it's out of your price range.
- SEAtac Sweetie

- Don't. Encourage. Him.
- Netcat

Tanyan yahpi. My name is Nancy. I am here to assist you with any questions you may have with your DocWagon service. DocWagon is the Sixth World's largest provider of health and medical services. Our mission is to deliver quality, affordable healthcare through an extensive network of doctors, hospitals, clinics, and service providers. Remember, when your life is on the line, DocWagon is on the way™.

To assist me in finding an answer to your query, please choose the level of service that you seek from DocWagon.

WHAT IS A HEALTH SERVICE PROVIDER? WHAT ARE MY OPTIONS BESIDES DOCWAGON?

DocWagon is the world's largest health service provider. Founded in 2037, the company spearheaded the field of armed medical response, which remains its primary profit center. DocWagon operates several urgent care clinics throughout North America, Europe, and Asia. DocWagon Industries manufactures rapid response vehicles via partnerships with companies like Ares, Hughes, and Aeroquip. Tactical Medical Solutions Inc. trains and equips armed medical response units, including DocWagon's innovative High Threat Response teams. Apex Pharmaceuticals provides branded prescription alternatives, offering DocWagon subscribers maximum flexibility in price and potency.

CrashCart [link] began when ex-DocWagon staff members pooled their resources to provide an alternative to DocWagon's armed response care. Backed by the Yamatetsu Corporation, they grew into the second-largest armed medical response provider in North America, the third-largest in Europe, and the fifth-largest in Asia. Today, they're one of Evo's largest subsidiaries. CrashCart's most recent innovation, DroneRx, delivers prescriptions and medical equipment directly to subscribers' doors. Despite early problems with the drones being hacked and the medications being stolen, the program has now expanded to all markets covered by CrashCart.

BluSix [link] represents a continuation of health insurance providers stretching all the way back into the early twentieth century. The six companies that combined have longstanding relationships with their communities, their doctors, and their patients' families. BluSix runs some of the most long-tenured medical facilities in the world, with ties to some of the most prestigious medical schools. BluSix has been caring for individuals for over 150 years with a mix of old-fashioned know-how and modern convenience. BluSix recently subcontracted its armed response program to CrashCart, choosing to focus on long-term care and traditional medical opportunities.

- That's a very polite way of saying that BluSix had a disastrous string of stock drops over the past year and cut their armed response department to keep the company

from getting ripped apart by competitors. Unless a miracle happens in the next six months, the smart money is on CrashCart to consume BluSix and suddenly become a much more interesting threat to DocWagon.

๏ Mr. Bonds

Subscribers looking for specialized care can seek out Wuxing's Prosperity [link] line of health service products. Their product is broken into tiers much like DocWagon's, though they are Jade, Gold, Diamond, and Obsidian. The higher tiers of care offer exclusive healing magics and proprietary treatment options unique to Wuxing Prosperity. The company holds the second-place ranking for armed medical response providers in Asia and Europe. The Wings, Prosperity's version of DocWagon's innovative High Threat Response team, consist of a single magician and several spirits or elementals summoned to assist the person in need.

QuetzalCare [link] marks Aztechnology's newest entry into the health service provider market. What once was a private insurance only available to employees has become one of the company's largest external expansions into a new market. QuetzalCare began as one of the largest corporate insurance programs in the world and leverages that size to provide service to non-corporate subscribers. Many members of their Rapid Recovery Squads spent time as members of DocWagon's HTR teams before joining QuetzalCare. QuetzalCare's rapid rate of growth mirrors that of DocWagon when it first burst onto the scene over thirty years ago.

๏ Anyone else find it weird DocWagon is advertising competition on its site?
๏ Rigger X

๏ When you're the top dog in a field, you can afford to appear magnanimous. Not mentioning the competition comes off as feeling threatened. This way, DocWagon implies that you can go see what the other guys have and then come back and sign up with them because they will be found lacking. Also, it's easy to read between the lines and catch just how backhanded NurseNancy's "compliments" about the other guys really are.
๏ Butch

๏ Note the shift in NurseNancy's tone when talking about the other guys, too. There's a sadness to it, that disapproving mother's tone that says she's not mad that you're considering one of the other options, just disappointed.
๏ Mr. Bonds

๏ Which of these is the best non-DocWagon option? Due to some recent freelance murder opportunities, I will soon have a Do Not Resuscitate On Sight order on my membership.
๏ Thorn

๏ Wuxing Prosperity is the best for mages since they have a specific care program that cuts down on invasive procedures that might interfere with your connection to magic. CrashCart has always been perceived as the low-rent competitor to DocWagon, but it has been picking up market share recently as metro areas look to save money by renegotiating hospital contracts. BluSix has a pedigree that stretches back to the health-insurance companies of old. Premiums are higher, but you pay less out of pocket for things. Q-Care is hungry and cheap because it's new and wants to lure customers away from the others.
๏ Butch

๏ Q-Care is probably the one that has DocWagon scared. They headhunted the drek out of any HTR teams that were nearing the end of their contracts. I heard they doubled the offer of what DocWagon gives to their teams. Enrollments in HTR certifications are down this year as well, driving supply down just when demand is rising. And don't forget competitors like BuMoNa, EuroMedis, Info-Santé, Monobe Medical, and Shiawase Health.
๏ Picador

DOCWAGON IS CURRENTLY NOT MY SERVICE PROVIDER

Thank you for your interest in DocWagon. We pride ourselves on being the most well-known name in modern health service providers. We offer a limited amount of services to those currently not under a service provider contract, but we encourage you to speak with a

DocWagon Service Agent to find a plan with us that balances your financial ability with the coverage that you seek. The longer you go without coverage, the greater risk—physical, mental, and financial—you expose yourself to. Even if you prefer another provider, we urge you to sign up for one as soon as possible.

Out-of-network patients are required to give their System Identification Number when applying for temporary services. In situations where the out-of-network patient is unable to give their System Identification Number, a temporary one may be assigned for the duration of the treatment. The patient is responsible for reconciling the numbers once the treatment is complete and payment in full has been made. DocWagon is not responsible for any legal fees incurred during the System Identification Number combination process.

- Don't think this is a quick and easy way to get a free fake SIN. In most jurisdictions, not having a SIN is a crime, so the temporary one you get assigned flags as a criminal SIN with a lot of debt attached to it if it sticks around.
- Bull

DocWagon personnel reserve the right to prioritize service to subscribers over out-of-network patients. We recommend our WagonWheel Outreach Program for discounted and complimentary medical services to those areas and individuals in need of health care. DocWagon is not responsible for any condition exacerbated by priority wait times, up to and including death. A previously cancelled DocWagon account may be reestablished onsite with a payment equal to a quarter of the annual subscription at the time of the service provided, plus a twenty percent activation fee. DocWagon reserves the right to escort unruly patients off its premises if they are a clear and present threat to DocWagon, its property, its personnel, or its subscribers.

- Pay attention to the order of that last sentence. That's how most corporations view the importance of their assets. If things go south on a run, you might be better off holding a VP's car hostage instead of his executive secretary
- Mr. Bonds

- Chummer, if you can afford forty-five percent of the annual contract at the clinic, you're better off just giving the cash to the doctor on duty as a bribe to make him decide to "prioritize" you to the top of the list.
- Rigger X

- WagonWheel is a new outreach program that started a few months ago when DocWagon got its hands on a few dozen late-model CityMasters. It loaded them up with some medics, some bodyguards, some supplies, and sent them into the rougher parts of town. I still can't figure out how they expect to make money on it, because it all seems too nice to not have an angle somewhere.
- Butch

- If I were one of the security team, the first thing I'd do is make nice with whatever go-gang owned the turf I was in and cut them a deal on the drugs in the van for some protection. That seems like it would be a good motive for the corporation, too. Get a working relationship with a gang, build a clinic on their turf, and then get kickbacks when the boys decide to tear the neighborhood up.
- Rigger X

- Most of the medics are fresh-faced kids who still think being a doctor is about helping people. The security officers are HTR washouts. They don't get paid much, but they get to feel good about helping people, I guess.
- Empty

- What are your options if you can't or won't pony up for a DocWagon membership or one from a competitor? Is every hospital in Seattle owned by a health-service provider?
- Stick

- Your options are very limited. You can go to one of DocWagon's competitors (which we'll get to in a moment), or you can get help at a public facility. There are a few hospitals and free clinics that aren't owned by a health-service provider, but even those are heavily subsidized and influenced by those corporations. Your best bet is to find a street doc, which I talk about elsewhere in this file.
- Sunshine

Non-subscribers may purchase prescriptions and other medications at DocWagon locations featuring PharmaFarm mini markets. Non-subscribers may be eligible for bulk discounts on sustainable medications as well as over-the-counter medications and disposable medical devices. On-site, long-term clinical care is not available to non-subscribers, though assistance for long-term care may be provided for an administration fee. PharmaFarm may only provide restricted medications such as painkillers to authorized subscribers. Pharma-Farm is open twenty-four hours a day and seven days a week in most locations. Please check your local grid for availability and active hours.

- PharmaFarm was recently spun off from Apex Pharmaceuticals in one of those moves trying to convince consumers that DocWagon doesn't own everything, even though it does. Once people get more comfortable with the brand, they'll be moving into direct competition with Stuffer Shack instead of only being attached to longstanding urgent care clinics like they are now.
- Mr. Bonds

- Am I the only one who prefers PharmaFarm's Electric Pigs In a Blanket to Stuffer Shack's Que-Soy-Ritos?
- Slamm-0!

Emergency visits without a healthcare provider can be devastating to savings and financial stability. DocWagon recommends non-subscribers to check in at local public hospitals first before visiting a DocWagon clinic. Non-subscribers are allowed one emergency visit every six months, with payment in full due at the end of the visit. Only patients with valid SINs are allowed these grace visits, and the visit may only take place if the non-subscriber's account with DocWagon is current. Upon entering an emergency room as a non-subscriber, the patient forfeits any rights to legal recourse for malpractice, mental damages, or any and all legal courses of action in exchange for the consideration of emergency treatment.

DocWagon personnel may accept contracts from other health-service providers, provided they are part of the Docs Around the Clock reciprocation program. Docs Around the Clock must pay in full upon time of services rendered. DocWagon subscribers take precedence over Docs Around the Clock customers. Reimbursements for services may be awarded from the original contract holder. DocWagon is not responsible for refusal of service from other Docs Around the Clock participants, such as CrashCart, Wuxing Prosperity Gold, or other unnamed health-service providers participating in the program.

- In the bad old days, if you walked into a competitor's emergency room and flashed your DocWagon card, they had the right to dump you out on the street in a pool of your own fluids. Then CrashCart started accepting competitors' contracts, though with a slight "out-of-network administration fee" tacked on, and a new way of making nuyen was born. Now, if you don't have a contract with the emergency room, you only get dumped if you can't afford the services up front. Your provider should reimburse you for any difference in cost, but that cash comes in awful slowly, even if you're a Platinum subscriber or above.
- Bull

I HAVE CHOSEN BASIC SERVICE

Basic service is best suited for those who are exploring different levels of coverage or looking to cover gaps in corporate insurance. Basic coverage offers a value-centric option to subscribers who are sure of their good health and not suffering from pre-existing conditions. Basic service may also be offered as part of a severance packet or unemployment compensation negotiation. The current subscription fee is 5,000 nuyen per year, payable in advance. Payment plans are available but may incur interest and service fees depending on subscriber's risk factors and a standard System Identification Number history check.

Basic members receive an AR identification card to present at DocWagon facilities. This card must be shown for uninterrupted service. Basic members may upgrade to an ID bracelet, RFID chip, or biometric identification algorithm for a nominal fee. If the ID card is lost or stolen, a new one will be reissued at no charge to the subscriber. Basic memberships are non-transferrable. Refunds will not be given in the event of a Basic subscriber's death during the service year. DocWagon reserves the right to nullify a Basic service contract at any time for any reason.

> * Customers who stay at Basic but upgrade to one of the other ID methods usually get a refurbished identification piece instead of a new one. The information from the previous owner is supposed to be scrubbed, but sometimes you get one that was done on a Friday afternoon or something. It's a good basis for a little identity theft, whether you want to craft a new SIN out of it or charge some expensive medical procedures to the other guy's account.
> * Empty

Most expenses are paid directly out of pocket by Basic subscribers. Once the 5,000-nuyen annual fee is matched, discounts on higher tiers become available. Service agents will also review a Basic subscriber's previous years to suggest the best plan for the value. Basic subscribers receive discounted services during seasonal sales, inventory reduction sales, and other promotional periods. Basic subscribers have access to emergency DocWagon and wellness clinics. Basic access also allows interaction with DocWagon personnel and in-network discounts for preventive services. In high-traffic locations, DocWagon reserves the right to offer priority service to premium subscriber levels. Service delays may allow for account credits depending upon the circumstances of the delay.

> * Assuming you don't die in the waiting room.
> * Traveler Jones

> * Is it just me, or does it seem like Basic service is essentially the same as not being a subscriber but with an annual fee?
> * Hard Exit

> * The main difference is that with Basic coverage, DocWagon can't flat out refuse you service. They can put you at the bottom of the list, especially if you have "not being a human" as an ongoing condition, but if you die in the clinic, that's going to cause their franchise some trouble.
> * Empty

> * Fraggin' Humanis is everywhere.
> * Hannibelle

> * I used to work with a doctor who was convinced that every ork was either in a go-gang or a shadowrunner.
> * Butch

> * I've been refused service for that very reason. Lost a perfectly good set of executive armor that way.
> * OrkCEO

Basic subscribers upgrading to a higher level of service may qualify for a credit. New subscribers may take advantage of promotional pricing and incentives to upgrade their service. Please speak to your DocWagon service agent to see if you qualify for an upgrade. Upgrades not available in local markets. Check local bylaws to check if upgrade credits are available in your area. Higher levels of service may not be exchanged for an equal amount of Basic service.

> * Something I've seen these days is corporate health insurance only covering employees while they are on corporate property. Renraku started the practice back when the arco wasn't full of killer robots or creepy bugs or creepy killer robot bugs. Old hires still have full coverage, but new hires can get screwed if they get hit by a bus on the way to work. Basic coverage like this at least pays for DocWagon to keep you alive so they can dump you on the company clinic's doorstep.
> * Plan 9

> * Don't let NurseNancy get you down. If you've got Basic coverage it's still better than nothing, especially here in Seattle. The Surgeon Director for the western division is a native. Namaste Wild sounds like a street name, but she's carved out a reputation as a nasty mama Bear shaman. Her dad was a well-known Neo-A back in the day and she's still got a bit of his attitude. She might work for a corporation but she still cares about helping people more than cutting services to fatten the profit margin. I've seen DocWagon employees here break most of the rules NurseNancy laid out to save a life.
> * Butch

I HAVE CHOSEN GOLD SERVICE

DocWagon prides itself on being the gold standard of health service providers. Our Gold subscribers experience this firsthand when they visit one of our thousands of clinics located throughout the world. We've provided memorable service to Gold subscribers for over thirty years. A Gold subscription currently costs 25,000 nuyen per year and comes with several upgrades over the Basic subscription service. The majority of our subscribers opt for the Gold level, and we want you to see why it's the most popular choice. You can look forward to annual health visits as part of your subscription fee. Gold subscribers get great discounts on blood tests, physicals, and other preventative medicine. Gold subscribers flourish by being well-informed about their health and knowing about any potential risks before disaster strikes. Pre-existing conditions are covered.

Subscribers at the Gold level get a photo identification card as well as our classic CodeBlue biomonitor bracelet. The bracelet may be activated anytime to signal DocWagon emergency personnel in the area that you require medical assistance. If the bracelet is damaged in any way, the alarm will trigger automatically. Standard emergency rates apply. High Threat Response is only available in some areas for Gold subscribers. Upgrades to RFID implants and biometric algorithm are available at a nominal add-on fee.

- HTR sold separately, huh? What a rip-off.
- Hard Exit

- Depending on your opposition, ambulance sirens might be enough to scare them off. Just don't expect them to come in guns blazing and haul your hoop off the stove.
- Hannibelle

DocWagon understands how tight family budgets can be, and Gold subscribers enjoy a ten-percent discount on extended care, often the difference between financial ruin and staying above water for many people. DocWagon provides excellent care for the value. Gold subscribers also have unlimited access to our urgent-care clinics and emergency room visits. We guarantee once an alert is triggered that the subscriber will be secured in the closest clinic or the treatment will be fully covered by DocWagon. Gold subscribers do pay for emergency services like HTR situations, as well as death compensation for emergency services personnel. Because the subscriber or the next of kin are responsible for these expenses, Gold subscribers must have at least one additional System Identification Number attached to the account as an emergency contact.

- That ten percent on extended care can also apply to certain body modifications, so long as you can convince the doc they are for legitimate business purposes. Easy to do when it's a datajack or a cyberlimb, less so for bone lacing or a cybergun.
- Clockwork

- It's usually better to put some random SIN down as your next of kin and let some unfortunate slot pay for all those extra expenses on your behalf.
- Rigger X

- They all have names. Some of them even have families. Had families.
- Cayman

I HAVE CHOSEN PLATINUM SERVICE

Platinum service was created to meet subscriber demands for an all-encompassing service. Health needs change daily, and our subscribers wanted an option that provided maximum flexibility. We were happy to provide the option to our strongest customers. Platinum coverage is currently available at 50,000 nuyen per year. The fee may be paid in a lump sum at the beginning of coverage, or paid over the duration of the coverage, with a slight increase for processing and convenience. Platinum also allows for several discounts on products within the DocWagon umbrella, such as first aid training through Tactical Medical Solutions.

- Platinum service was created because shadowrunners made up the majority of DocWagon's initial subscriber list. They put this sheen of exclusivity on this level to mask the fact that most people who can afford this are making way more money than your average wage slave, but not enough to have a keycard to the executive john. Crime lords need treatment too, and the price you pay for this service is the price DocWagon collects for looking the other way.
- Plan 9

- What do you mean initial? Literally every piece of advice I read when starting in the biz began with "Get a DocWagon contract now."
- Slamm-0!

Under the Platinum contract, nearly all basic medical needs are covered without additional cost to the subscriber. Doctor visits, regular check-ups, medications, and pre-existing conditions are all taken care of for the Platinum subscriber at their convenience. Subscribers at this level get a complimentary RFID chip implant to monitor health history in addition to the standard identification cards. Subscribers may opt out of the RFID program, but must then pay for an RFID chip to be installed later should they change their mind. The RFID chip can prompt the subscriber to trigger an emergency alert by sending a simple message to the owner's commlink. This allows for an emergency pickup without having to moving a muscle to trigger a wristband or other signaling device—a very popular option for clients in areas with high kidnapping rates.

> ● Nope. NOPE.
> ● Snopes
>
> ● How easy is it to track someone using a DocWagon RFID?
> ● Traveler Jones
>
> ● The frequency modulates pretty well, but it can be done if you know they have one. DocWagon knows this is an older technology, so they quietly try to get folks to upgrade to the biometrics with a "free" upgrade thrown in with whatever promotion they've got going that month.
> ● Rigger X

Long-term care receives a fifty percent reduction in cost, though Super-Platinum Clinics are not available at this subscription level. Installation and maintenance of legal cyberware are included as part of this package. Emergency situations also see significant savings. HTR is covered by Platinum accounts, though death compensation is still charged to the subscriber. Platinum subscribers may also be eligible for rate discounts if they go a certain period of time without needing emergency services. With four free resuscitations a year, Platinum subscribers have plenty of chances to get a new lease on life.

I HAVE CHOSEN SUPER-PLATINUM SERVICE

For those who have executive tastes and expect world-class service, we offer Super-Platinum service as our most extensive tier. Super-Platinum subscribers have access to the best medical care money can buy. These subscribers are at the leading edge of modern medicine, using innovative techniques and cutting-edge technology to improve their health and wellness to the best levels they will ever have. Super-Platinum subscribers represent a diverse group—professional athletes, corporate executives whose company literally cannot afford for them to take a sick day, and many other metahumans whose livelihoods hinge on their bodily health—united by their devotion to their well-being. DocWagon rewards that devotion with services unavailable at lower levels. Super-Platinum subscribers belong to the world's most elite health club. This level of coverage currently costs 500,000 nuyen per year. The fee may be paid in a lump sum at the beginning of coverage, or paid on a payment plan with a slight increase for processing and convenience.

DocWagon offers a wide variety of personal physicians and full medical staff that are on call twenty-four hours a day, seven days a week, 365 days a year for on-site consultations, treatment, and care. Super-Platinum subscribers also receive a complimentary biometric algorithm in addition to their identification card. The algorithm allows any DocWagon clinic immediate access to a patient's current condition as well as their health history. With the algorithm, the need for monitoring bracelets or chip implants are left in the past. If the subscriber's body parameters go beyond the normal levels, a message is sent via commlink to the subscribers asking them if they are in need of assistance. If the subscriber doesn't send a reply within sixty seconds, the emergency recovery alarm is triggered. If the biometrics indicate the subscriber is at risk of dying, a High Threat Response team is immediately dispatched to recover the Super-Platinum subscriber.

> ● You still have to pay out of pocket at this level?
> ● Bull
>
> ● If you can afford to drop the money for a Super-Platinum membership, you can afford whatever fees the doc will charge you. DocWagon covers it if you go to one of their SP Clinics. You only pay if they come to visit you in your private island or on Zurich Orbital or wherever you hang your billion-nuyen hat.
> ● Mr. Bonds
>
> ● When they first introduced the biometrics, they had to readjust the levels that triggered emergency response because the people paying for the tech could also afford designer drugs and other body-changing experiences the designers didn't anticipate. The biometric records are kept under some serious security at the home office, but an analysis of the patterns could reveal the types of vices a high-level exec is into for the purposes of blackmail.
> ● Empty

Whether you choose to receive care in one of our Super-Platinum clinics around the world or choose from one of our Platinum providers to provide service at your home or penthouse, rest assured that your health is in the expert hands of the top minds in the field. DocWagon seeks out the best of the best for our most elite subscribers. Ongoing health concerns or life-changing events are handled with the same amount of expertise. Studies show that Super-Platinum subscribers experience a fifteen percent increase of quality of life after joining the program at this level (some exceptions apply, please follow this [link] for more details). Emergency visits to our extensive network of clinics require no additional payment at this level. High Threat Response extractions are also covered by your annual fee. Our top-tier subscribers receive five free resuscitations per year.

- Getting certified as a Super-Platinum provider is no joke. We're talking world-famous neurosurgeons, experts in biotechnology, professors of thaumaturgy at MIT&T. They may not have scary reputations like the Tir Ghosts, but if you pay for this level of coverage and whoever DocWagon sends to treat you can't cure you, it can't be done.
- Butch

- Those clinics are secure facilities that may look all peaceful but are built by the same companies that put together high-level research labs. There's a lot of nasty security and black IC hidden under those rolling hills and pleasant hedgerows.
- Rigger X

- The top Super-Platinum clinics as of this writing are in Tenochtitlán, Melbourne, Kyoto, Hong Kong, and Zurich. There are rumored to be two more, one in South America and one in Antarctica.
- Hard Exit

- There may be an eighth SP clinic soon, as soon as they can get the orbital ready to go up.
- Empty

- I'm surprised there isn't an SP clinic at their headquarters in Atlanta.
- Netcat

- Too many people going in and out of the building. You can have a top security building or a bustling international corporate headquarters. Not both.
- Mr. Bonds

- I've heard that some of the top-tier clinics that only service Super-Platinum subscribers consider leónization treatments as a resuscitation for billing purposes. DocWagon would like to close that particular loophole but doesn't want to upset its richest providers. They have to do it subtly, because they don't want the doctors who do it to walk over to a competitor and take their big, expensive client list with them.
- Mika

I hope I was able to clear up any questions you might have about your level of service. DocWagon thanks you for your patronage, and we hope that we get to save your life sometime!

REQUIEM FOR A STREET DOC

POSTED BY: SUNSHINE
Originally posted @KSAF on 4/13/2077

There's a dirty little secret that most media sites hide. Famous people already have their obituaries written. Somewhere, tucked away in a file in Ares' Matrix space, there's a whole pre-fab love letter about Damien Knight. Sure, he's probably going to outlive this site, the readers, and the reporters here, but if a chicken bone gets lucky in a way that hundreds of shadowrunners have not, the deckers on staff will have his virtual memorial up in seconds. All they have to do is add a few details and quietly edit it as more information comes in. That's why there's a cascade of pages whenever someone big dies. The pre-written stuff acts as a placeholder, and then the think pieces come out a day or two later once the media's digested how the bigwig died.

Most regular people don't get this luxury. At best, there's a brief mention on the death tab of the daily neighborhood screamsheet or a small memorial at their favorite watering hole. Only executives get real death notices anymore, because nobody who runs the corporate intranets wants to bum out workers and damage morale by talking about dead employees. Not to mention the fact that in many corporations, such notices were often used for cover when an employee was extracted by a shadowrun team to keep other employees from jumping ship. Better to just stop mentioning them and let word of mouth pass through the natural channels, like whispers in the hall and curt explanations to confused interns asking why the mail is piling up on somebody's desk.

So it went in the halls of Renraku recently when Dr. Higashiyama Misao passed away at the age of 53. Dr. Higashiyama worked in Renraku's bio-logistics department. She designed the interfaces where datajacks connect to meat brains and made sure that the neural impulses from brains were read by those cyberlimbs that shadowrunners so covet. She was diagnosed with cervical cancer five years ago. It went into remission two years ago, but came back with a vengeance last December. She died from complications three days ago. I only found out about it because a mutual contact heard she died.

Most of us knew Dr. Higashiyama by a different name. She's worked on hundreds of shadowrunners in Seattle over the past twenty-three years. Contacting her meant a trip to Pike Place Market, ordering two California rolls with a dab of wasabi from the sushi place in the third stall of the food court, then waiting at least four hours for her to send you a message telling you to meet her in the old Continental Building two blocks south. Turns out she owned the Continental and the sushi place. After her death, the stall closed and the Continental's up for sale. Foxwife, as most runners know her, left few traces after she died.

- Frag. I'm gonna outlive everyone, aren't I?
- Bull

- Don't worry, pops. I'll most likely kill you in the morning.
- Slamm-0!

- Did you make that reference on purpose?
- Bull

- And try to cheer up my mortal enemy? That would require me to have feelings like a human.
- Slamm-0!

I got to know Foxwife back when I was just a hungry journalist instead of mixing and matching these strange part-time jobs that keep the lights on. She was also hungry, a scientist looking to see how her equipment worked in the field. Beyond that, I think she knew that her place in one of the most traditional Japanacorps was already determined for her. Her academic knowhow and design put her as an important person in her department, but the *sarariman* club would never let her into an executive office. Selling cyberware on the streets offered a revenue stream unmatched by a cost-of-living increase each year.

She never asked me to reveal her identity after her death. Truth be told, I'm about halfway through the second bottle of the type of wine she preferred when we would talk about how she fell into the business. She didn't have any family to worry about shaming back at Renraku, but she didn't know it was going to play out like that when she started back then. She chose her street name to make sure that if she were discovered, her husband and children could escape the shame of her second job. She never found a husband or had children. There were a few people who knew about what she did and probably helped her get some of the pieces she installed, but unless they have a drunk journo with a deadline, they are likely going to stay anonymous.

- So you admit to violating the trust of one of your sources?
- Trickster's Daughter

- Who let the comedian in here?
- Hannibelle

- It's not who she says she is, but how she says it.
- Man-of-Many-Names

This also struck me as an opportunity to look at the big picture. Street docs are here to stay. Not everyone can afford a DocWagon contract or hole up in a corporate cyberclinic for a few weeks while their body adjusts to the new cybernetic implant. Getting runners back on their feet is an important part of street culture, and these men and women do the best they can with tough deadlines, worse tools, and patients who have nowhere else to go. Where do they come from? How do they survive? Why do they stay in the game?

- Running is all about trust. You trust your crew to have your back when things get rough, but who do you trust when you're out cold and have your guts exposed to the filthy Seattle air? A good street doc is worth her weight in superconductors. RIP, Foxwife.
- Kat o' Nine Tales

Few people set out to be a street doc. It was never a part of any of those career surveys I took as a kid. Most people fall into it through a mix of rotten luck, bad timing, and poor circumstance. Smart cookies can make a decent living at it, even if it's not as prestigious as working in an official clinic or being on call for a corporate executive's health issues. It's a little less dangerous than running, since most of the shooting is over by the time runners need to be patched up or rebuilt.

Many street docs have some sort of legitimate medical training. Some get it from a year or two in medical school before something happens to cause them to drop out. They might not be able to hack it. They might get distracted by personal issues. They might get pulled into debt too quickly and start working on the street to make ends meet. Their classes might suffer or they might decide that the money they make now is better than what they'll be making in the future. A little training is better than none, and nobody's going to ask to see a street doc's credentials if they are gutshot in the lobby.

- Ain't docs supposed to be rich?
- Sticks

- Many medical schools put their students in a six-figure debt to start to tie them to the corp, backing the school for life. Students are broke as a general guideline, so it doesn't take much to rack up additional debt during the years you're in school. Sure, you could work your way through school spending thirty-plus hours a week behind the counter of a Stuffer Shack, or you could slip some prescription codes to a street dealer for a couple grand between drinks at the bar. If you get caught, you're out, but then you're well on your way to being a criminal mastermind anyway.
- Empty

- You say that like you're speaking from experience.
- Man-of-Many-Names

Some street docs make it through all the hoops of becoming a real doctor but then wash out because of professional mistakes. Maybe they let a high-profile client die on the table. Maybe they got hooked on painkillers or BTLs to take the edge off of a high-pressure gig. Maybe they got caught taking bribes from a pharma corporation for pushing their drugs over the competitors'. Finishing med school is the first step in a doctor's career. It doesn't take much to push a doctor out of the light and onto the streets.

Though the military encourages medical personnel to join its ranks, the sheer need they have to keep soldiers in the fight means they often train their own medics. Veterans naturally drift to the shadows because of their combat training. Medics often follow. Sometimes the bonds of a unit pull everyone onto the street. Sometimes a medic starts out helping his own unit and then realizes he can make money working for other crews too. The difference between a shadowrunner and a mercenary can be very thin. But they all need to be stitched up at some point in their career.

- I've seen bar fights erupt over mercs being called shadowrunners and vice versa. Be careful what you call people, especially after everyone's six drinks in.
- Hannibelle

Street docs exist who can keep a day job in the medical industry and work in the shadows at night. They often have to keep their double lives separate. If their corporate overlords knew about their second job, they'd be quickly fired or labeled as a security threat. Enemies looking to get back at a street doc could throw the corporate half of their life into chaos, especially if the street doc has family members unaware of what they do off the clock. Foxwife held this type of career together for many years, but in the end you could see it was wearing on her. Moonlighting street docs never get any time off.

The squatters and the gutterpunks in the combat zones need someone to keep them on their feet. Street docs often come out of free clinics and patient-outreach programs that want to keep doing the noble thing when it comes to medicine. Someone has to pay for those programs to stay open. Counting on the generosity of official corporate sponsorship is a one-way ticket to showing up to padlocked doors because this quarter's profits are down. Taking money from runners who need medical assistance not only launders the money, but it also absolves the soul of working with shadowy patrons. That's the theory, at least.

One of the easiest ways to become a street doc is to just start working as one. A medical degree is not actually required. Diploma-mill degrees can be had for the price of the latest *Neil the Ork Barbarian* season. Few customers will care that Upper Tacoma University is nothing more than a Matrix address and a credit account. Selling health powders and wellness machines make a great front for a street doc. Variable inventory also helps hide money from illegal sources. A street doc might record a cyberlimb as a few boxes worth of Cherry Bomb Vita-Soy to keep up appearances. These sorts of outfits are expected to pack up and disappear without a trace anyway.

- I cracked the UTU host a few weeks ago. Adding fake degrees can really put a convincing sheen on a fake SIN. If anyone wants a Doctorate or Master's or something, let me know.
- Netcat

- Oooh, I always wanted to go back to school!
- SEAtac Sweetie

Many mages get snapped up by runner crews, but magical healing is always in demand. The demands of following a totem might interfere with the loyalty required by corporations. Those with unique magical skills might find them put to better use before and after a run where a stray bullet is less likely to cut short a career. Mages can be their own security, mixing in manabolts with healing spells to protect whatever space they've marked out to sell their wares. Not every mage can hack running the shadows, but their ability to use magic means there are still plenty of ways to make money there.

The rare runner who hits the mythical big score and retires rarely stays away from the street for long. A runner with that kind of cash and street cred can find becoming a street doc an easy transition. Even if they don't have the proper medical skills, they can usually hire somebody who does. Ex-runners have all the contacts in place that a street doc needs to get up and running. They can also probably call on a crew or two to lock in some inventory ... or even generate some new business with a few strategic strikes.

Getting into the street doc biz often seems easy enough. There are ways in that I didn't even cover. Not everyone quite understands the different things street docs do in their backroom offices. Installing cyberware, removing bullets, and fencing medical equipment are just a few of the ways the street doc gets paid. The more services a doc can perform, the more money they make. The more versatile the doc, the more valuable they become to multiple crews. Multiple crews counting on a street doc means that doc is more likely to stay in business longer.

The most common service a street doc performs is patching up wounds. There are plenty of people who don't want to deal with the red tape of going to a hospital or clinic to deal with injuries sustained during a shadowrun. Many legitimate medical facilities are required by law to report bullet wounds to the local security firm, or, at the very least, their security branch. Between the risk of capture and not wanting to hang out in a waiting room with potential witnesses, street docs prove their worth by fixing runners' mistakes.

When a samurai wants a new wiz piece of gear bolted into her body, the street doc is the first place she goes. She might bring the gear to the doc, or the doc might have a piece all lined up ready to install. Sometimes the surgery takes place in whatever storefront the doc has rented, and sometimes the doc has a separate facility to do the work. Either way, the table and instruments are pretty clean, because nobody wants the installation to go wrong. Infections, rejections, and other complications can muck up both the street doc's day and rep pretty badly, so the more prep work involved, the less likely it is that something goes wrong.

- Most docs will also offer to buy used parts. Some of them get resold, some of them are kept around for replacement bits. One doc I knew in Texas sold them to an art gallery owner who repainted them and sold them to rich people as art pieces for ten times what the tech was worth.
- Picador

Recovering from a surgery doesn't happen instantly. Even with the best care money can buy, the patient is usually down for the count for at least forty-eight hours. If the street doc doesn't have an on-site facility to use for recovery, they usually have a deal with a nearby hotel where the patient can lie low while the doc keeps tabs on the healing process. That might mean a coffin hotel that gets hosed out between patients, or it could be a relative's apartment with a spare bedroom.

Runners often turn to street docs when their cyberware needs repairs. This can be as simple as digging a slug out from a firearm or as complex as adjusting the maintenance medications to keep bioware functioning properly. Some docs charge for the process on a per-visit basis, others offer service plans and warranties just like real cyberclinics do. Make sure to know the policy after the installation just in case the body modification doesn't work the way it's intended.

- In a pinch, putting a gun in somebody's face can work as an "extended warranty." That usually means the end of the relationship with that contact, but since they do crappy work anyway, it's no big deal.
- Kane

- Get the details about this as soon as you can. It's up to you to protect your chummer while they are strung out on painkillers. You might have to turn that coffin motel into a safehouse.
- Picador

- It's usually a lot easier to just rent out the whole block of coffins if that's the case. The ones that aren't full of runners make good storage for supplies and ammo.
- Hard Exit

Cyberware and resuscitations provide big-ticket items to keep the lights on in a street doc's office. A steady stream of cash usually comes in thanks to the drugs that flow from the office to the street. Street docs able to mix their own supplies get very popular very quickly. Ones who still have connections to legitimate suppliers can get rare drugs and charge a premium for their stock. Offices also work well as drop points for street dealers and even neutral ground where go-gangs come together to talk prices.

As long as those gangers are in the office, the street doc might want to consider buying some of their ill-gotten gains. Secondhand cyberware is a viable market for anyone on the street, but docs who can repair any damage from the previous owner can make a decent profit flipping secondhand hands. A few docs are even willing to accept cyberware in a pawn-shop-style system, where someone who needs cash now can get a loan on cyber that the doc holds until the poor sucker can pay back the loan.

It isn't just chrome that can end up in a street doc's display case. Cultured organs, modified bio-organics, and even old-school stolen kidneys are fair game for a street doc willing to dip into organ trafficking. A few refuse outright because they fear getting a bad reputation, but the ones who come out of corporate backgrounds often use their labs as their offices to allow custom orders right there in the storefront. A specialist might be able to deal in used organs, or the street doc might even hire a crew to steal a specific type for the right cells to match.

A few spooky stories suggest street docs who still work for their old companies as a front to experiment on unsuspecting slobs who walk in through the front door. There's some truth to the idea, especially when markets get flooded with body modifications that flop in general sales, but most corporations prefer to control their research and development in-house. Fronting a street doc offers too many risks for any official projects. Someone running an off-the-books experiment seems far more likely.

- If you want to frag a street doc's reputation real bad, start spreading rumors about their connections to Tamanous. Real or not, nobody wants to end up in an ice bath with a new scar on their back instead of getting some new cybereyes installed.
- Snopes

- Even if that story wasn't older than Bull, no street doc who wanted to stay in business would pull that kind of move. Maybe if some poor slot dies on the table, they'd call up the harvesters to disappear the body, but they'd never take viable organs from someone with a chance to live.
- Hannibelle

- So we don't believe people can be corrupted by money? Remind me what world it is that we live in.
- Bull

Though they might sound like independent operators, street docs inevitably end up working for somebody. The web of suppliers and clients usually draws them into its middle—very few people in the Sixth World call their own shots. When looking for a street doc to rely on, being aware of who they answer to can make a world of difference. Shadowrunners make and break alliances all the time, which can be the difference between a street doc stitching up the team or quietly calling a corporate cleanup squad while everyone is in the waiting room. I reached out to a few contacts around the Sixth World to show how they stay in business.

- And I'm sure you weren't justly compensated for such advertisement?
- OrkCEO

- A couple of them, I had to pull some teeth. You want a reputation where a lot of people know you, but not so big a reputation that the young punks just starting out feel like they can pull themselves up by taking you out.
- Sunshine

AAA corporations have strings that hang all the way down to the street doc's door. Former company men still have connections with their old workplace. Undercover operatives shuffle excess inventory onto the street to hide poorly performing releases from stockholders. Employees sick of the corporate grind want to get back to doing what they loved in the first place. It costs little for a big corporation to funnel goods to street docs, especially since they can easily be cut off if any sort of scandal might lead back to the parent company.

Foxwife hid her identity from her masters at Renraku to get back out into the world. The corporate life can be isolating and lonely. Shadowrunners often understand that need for a connection and bond, which can make their crews like families. Many of the runners who knew her considered her part of their family. That sense of belonging is a powerful feeling, stronger than drugs. Foxwife might not have had a family of her own, so she built one out of the samurai, deckers, and runners she got to know while she made them stronger.

- Are you sure about that?
- Trickster's Daughter

- I'm sorry, who are you?
- Sunshine

Not every street doc out there has access to the same level of goods that Foxwife enjoyed, but I've heard of a few who cobble together a working relationship with below-the-radar businesses. Smaller corporations like to have connections to this type of individual, even if they might not have the funds for test clinics or secure black-bag facilities. Plenty of runners are happy to take a gamble on a new bit of chrome that might still need the bugs worked out. A lower price on a flashier piece is a big lure to a team struggling for credits. Docs connected to smaller companies also build relationships with teams that can come in handy when the big boys throw their weight around and look for support from some of their smaller partners, giving these teams the chance to step up to the big time.

Stella Copy Ltd. looks like a simple boutique genetics firm in Paris. Avanti, the designer in charge, likes to make striking designs that catch the eyes of Euro fashion mavens, but she's not above working with the runners in the City of Lights when she's not dreaming up bizarre bioware combinations. Sometimes her models get compensated for whatever odd piece she installs, be it a chrome unicorn horn or a cyberhand with all thumbs, by receiving a few other pieces of alphaware or better gear. The rumors that Avanti rebuilds her own face every six months to avoid too much attention are still unsubstantiated.

Organized crime has their hands in this particular pie as well. The Yakuza and Triads tend to smuggle in cyberware that was collected from their corporate connections or stolen when the opportunity presented itself. The Mob and Tongs work more in secondhand gear they sell off to recover money lost from markers they've called in. Street docs connected to these organizations can usually get better gear at lower prices, so long as the customer isn't squeamish about the origins of the product.

Marco "Red Sauce" Valentino operates out of one of the oldest Italian restaurants in Chicago. The interiors are classic, but Marco does his business in the basement. He earned his reputation by working as a street doc during the big bug takeover of the city. Most of his medical education came from the Matrix and learning on the job. He got his nickname from his habit of getting information for his family by removing pieces of cyberware from the people who needed to talk without the benefit of anesthetic.

Local gangs and street docs often end up in bed together. The line between a street doc and a fixer becomes very thin in these cases, since the gangs usually pay for medical services in stolen merchandise rather than cold hard nuyen. Gangs tend to get in brutal fights more commonly than runner teams, which keeps docs busy. Street docs might get too wrapped up in gang business and not have time for more clients—or inspire a bit of possessiveness if a doc works on people not allied or loyal to the gang.

Vladivostok offers little in the way of scenery, but the surgeon-masked Blanks are one of the more colorful gangs I've seen. The more intricately painted the surgical mask, the higher up the food chain the gang member is. Dr. Blank, the leader, has a mask that walks the line between the best graffiti you've ever seen and the

mempo of a samurai warrior. He teaches his gang all the things he learned as a combat medic, which makes their raids bloody and efficient. Dr. Blank has been around for nearly twenty-five years, with whispers emerging every few years or so that he's passed on the mask and retired to someplace a lot warmer.

Street doc clinics can also be useful to government operatives working under cover in a hostile territory. Few people question a doctor's credentials, especially those working for exchange programs like Doctors Without Borders or Sick Sixth World. The doctors may be legit, but the support personnel might have agenda supplied by an embassy or espionage organization. Deep-cover versions of this type of office might try to construct a backstory saying they've been around for years. The service might be wonderful, but keeping a close watch on what gets said in an office is never a bad idea.

A favorite identity used by undercover CAS operatives was Pat McGillicuddy. The doctor appeared on several different locations in DeeCee, even though descriptions or images never quite matched. McGillicuddy was described as different genders, skin colors, and even a different metatype or two during the course of his/her medical career. He/she hasn't been seen since 2070, so perhaps the good doctor finally retired to a nice private island paid for by all the runners who gave money to the cause.

> Isn't this what happened with Shining Cross? All of their free clinics in the NAN were shown to be staffed with CIA and UCAS intelligence personnel. Rumor has it a lot of the same faces (and different names) are popping up working at Sick Sixth World clinics recently.
> Thorn

> Oh, come on! "Dr. McGillicuddy"? Was "Special Agent J. Daniels" already taken by the UCAS?
> Bull

Enterprising street docs sometimes take a page from their more legitimate colleagues and come together as a collective. The good news about these collectives is that they tend to contain shared resources and referrals. If a doctor has a speciality in cybereyes, another street doc can refer the patient along for a better price and quality of installation. The downside to collectives occurs when they become monopolies. Price fixing, muscle tactics, and dirty tricks can put a lock on medical services in an area. Though I guess that's not all bad for the runners who might get hired by the docs to put the remaining competition out of business.

Bleeker Street Medical sounds professional, but it's a cross between a peer network and a street-doc alliance. It began when a trio of street docs banded together and hired some runners to shake off the gangers that had taken over their part of Phoenix. The runners left once the gangers were dead, but the doctors used their newfound influence to better the area for their clientele. The media and government consider it a natural bit of gentrification in Phoenix, but the locals know that without Bleeker Street Medical, the area would still be a combat zone.

Taking care of those who can't afford to care for themselves is a natural offshoot of charitable organizations and religious outreach through soup kitchens and charity drives. Above-board donations make people feel good, but they also hide street docs who are willing to take money from shadowrunners. Thanks to the odd hours of homeless shelters and the shuffling of the SINless through the doors, movements of less-than-legal customers receive a little natural camouflage. Runners too cheap to put in for the safehouse (or not afraid to squat) can earn their keep as a bit of security for the operation.

The Bound Hands Club is most well-known for its connection to the Atlantean Foundation, but this cross-disciplinary initiation school also has a fair share of street docs as part of their network. The mage and shaman team-up has a lot of magical healing to speed up the process, while only asking those it helps to pay their kindness forward. They rarely do implants or body modifications, but they've got enough contacts in Sydney that they can usually connect people looking to upgrade themselves. The BHC's feel-good message makes it one of the biggest moneymakers for the Atlantean Foundation.

> That's just a little too close to the bugs for my taste.
> Plan 9

> Anyone know if buying a cybereye from a religious institution is considered a charitable donation? My accounting software won't give me a straight answer.
> Mika

Maybe I'm getting too old and sentimental. This beat brought me close to many people who died in terrible ways and many more that I assume are dead because I haven't heard from them in years. Foxwife's end is atypical. She died of natural causes after a long career of working two jobs. That seems unsettlingly vanilla compared to a life spent freelancing with a gun in one hand and a commlink in the other. The street chews people up and spits them out, but she made it through the grinder somehow. Maybe there's a little bit of hope for all of us.

> Why are you so eager to believe it was natural causes? That seems ... out of character for what she told me of you.
> Trickster's Daughter

> This is all very cute, but if you have any evidence to back up your claims, now's the time to show it, sweetheart.
> Sunshine

> I make no claims except to those who knew Foxwife: You will still receive the same services if you go through the same processes to contact me.
> Trickster's Daughter

> Seems legit?
> Winterhawk

> Looks like it's time to put some hours in on my other job. If anyone here is interested in helping me out, you know where to find me.
> Sunshine

MENS SANA IN CORPORE SANO

MENTAL ILLNESS IN THE SIXTH WORLD

POSTED BY: THORN

Since I'm sure someone's going to ask: No, I'm not a psychologist, though I've seen the job used as a cover. The fact is, case officers and head-shrinkers use a lot of the same tricks—spies control assets, psychologists help people sort their lives out—but the methods aren't very much different. Hence why I'm writing this.

Technology has become very good at maintaining and enhancing the metahuman body. Injuries that would've debilitated fifty years ago can be as insignificant as a paper cut with modern advances in medicine. Mangled your leg in a motorcycle accident? Your new cyberleg will perform better than the original. Look up at the wrong time in an acid rain storm? You'll have new eyes by the end of the day, and *these* ones can see in infrared. Depressed? Well ... have you tried moodchips?

> Let's not forget that all those miracles are only available *if you can afford them*. If you can't, you're living in a medical world that is decades behind what everyone else has. If you're lucky.
> Aufheben

Unfortunately, we can't yet replace pieces of the metahuman psyche as easily as we replace limbs. The depths of insanity are somewhere shadowrunners visit regularly, and like any environment, they have their own unique opportunities and dangers. If you're able to keep a level head—at least, in relative terms—you'll be in a good position to seize the former and avoid the latter.

"YOU MEAN, LIKE, CRAZY PEOPLE?"

What is "mental illness," anyway? The man with nervous tics who hears the voice of God in his head? The woman who hugs her knees to her chest and silently rocks back and forth, not responding to the world around her? Being emotionally distant and unable to relate to other people, while solving mathematical problems that have stumped the brightest in the world with a few seconds' thought?

In my experience, the answer is simpler than that. Think of anyone you know, and pick out the first personality trait that comes to mind. Turn it up to eleven. Make them a caricature of themselves. Now magnify it again, until the person you've thought of can't stop behaving that way, and it starts to affect the rest of their life—they're too sad to get out of bed; too energetic to sit still, or think before they act; too reserved to relate to anyone else; too anxious about others' opinions to interact with people, out of fear of being viewed badly. At extremes, all of those emotions are well-known mental illnesses: major depression, attention deficit hyperactivity disorder, personality and anxiety disorders.

You might be asking yourself, "who cares?" Everyone's a little crazy sometimes, especially when the so-called "normal" person doesn't really exist. That may be true, but often times, debate over what *should* be considered a mental illness comes down to one point: stigma.

The overwhelming majority of people with mental illnesses, even highly visible ones, are entirely harmless. On an instinctual level, though, metahumanity flinches from anything that doesn't look or act "normal." Worse, media stereotypes of mental illness perpetuate the belief that all mentally ill people are delusional or some sort of psychopath. Those two factors contribute to a society where, very often, the stigma of being labeled mentally ill is more harmful than any one symptom.

> * Yeah, but it's not so bad if you can use that stigma as cover on a job, is it?
> * Kane

> * That would be kind of an unconscionable ... oh, never mind.
> * Netcat

On the other hand, most people with a medically recognized mental illness have a hard time functioning in some area of their life. Treatments like drugs or therapy (or surgery, for those with body-related dysphoria) can help overcome those difficulties, but they cost nuyen, and corp health insurance won't pay for anything that a doctor didn't sign for. And if you don't have insurance, good luck fending for yourself and trying to buy your own meds! This means that often, people with mental illnesses cannot afford treatment, leading their symptoms to worsen, and decreasing their chances of holding down a job or a home. This often leads them to being out on the streets. I'm pretty sure I don't have to tell any of you that the homeless people of any sprawl have a high percentage of mental illness—sometimes undiagnosed, almost always untreated.

> * It wouldn't take much for pharma companies to figure out how to freely dispense drugs to those who need them, but they don't because they don't care.
> * Clockwork

> * Wait, free drugs for the impoverished mentally ill? Proposed by Clockwork? What the hell just happened?
> * Snopes

> * Yeah, it's fun to assume I'm the worst of everything. Keep it up. It's amusing.
> * Clockwork

> * Health benefits are a constant headache for corps. There's a lot of evidence that offering employees health benefits helps the corp's bottom line—"a happy workforce is a productive workforce," after all—but whether it would be cheaper for the corporation to just fire chronically sick employees and hire someone to replace them is an open question. Naturally, the corps that pay benefits for their employees use it as a way of boosting their public image and snagging potential hires. The fact that they might have a duty to their workers tends not to be a concern that registers in any meaningful way.
> * Mr. Bonds

> * It used to be that governments had anti-discrimination laws to prevent a corporation from firing an employee simply for being sick. Now that corporate extraterritoriality makes it legal for them to fire whoever they want, the corps have started supporting groups lobbying to remove certain mental disorders from the medical diagnostic manuals. They claim it's to "de-stigmatize mental illness," but what they want is to quietly limit the treatments they might pay for. If people aren't diagnosed with a condition, then no one ever even needs to think about paying the costs to treat it.
> * Kay St. Irregular

RUNNER'S FIELD GUIDE TO MENTAL ILLNESS

Instead of reposting an entire abnormal psychology textbook—that's what Aetherpedia's for—I've put together a list of categories of mental disorders for you to peruse, plus the names of a few I've found to be common among shadowrunners. (I realize that's not very scientific of me, but it'll be easier to relate to this way. That, and frankly, it's more fun for me.)

- Oh great, JackPoint's very own Dr. Bill. All he needs now is a daytime trid show.
- Slamm-0!

The first group of conditions I'll talk about are anxiety disorders. One type of anxiety disorder you've probably seen before are **phobias**, crippling fear of specific objects or situations. Another is **social anxiety**, where sufferers avoid social situations out of fear of embarrassment, negative scrutiny, humiliation, or social interaction.

If you've ever seen an anxious person wringing their hands or pacing a hole in the floor, you've seen the everyday root of **obsessive-compulsive disorder (OCD)**. OCD occurs when distress is caused by involuntary, disturbing thoughts (*obsessions*), and the patient repetitively carries out behaviors to try to relieve their anxiety (*compulsions*).

It's common to see OCD sufferers hoard objects, check door locks a specific number of times, or wash their hands repeatedly. In fact, many OCD sufferers are germophobic, and are often described as neat freaks. Remember the "obsessive" part, though. Just because you prefer things neat doesn't mean you have OCD, and the casual references to the condition can be annoying to those who actually have to deal with it.

- That rigger I talked about in the *Run Faster* posting, the one who kept his van spotless? I'd bet nuyen he'd qualify as OCD. He didn't just like it neat—he had to keep it clean, no matter what. He'd clean that thing in the middle of a firefight rather than drive it away to safety. This is the kind of thing that needs treatment if you have any intention of staying out on the streets.
- Pistons

Other anxiety disorders lead to even less productive solutions. **Kleptomania** is compulsive theft to relieve emotional tension. **Pyromania** is similar, but a pyromaniac sets fires rather than stealing. Remember, these behaviors are primarily done to make the person feel better; the kleptomaniac might steal completely worthless items, and the pyromaniac usually won't set fire to something they can collect insurance for. Be wary if you're thinking of exploiting these traits for your own gain.

- Plus exploiting people's mental illness pretty well sucks.
- Sounder

- Yeah, being ethical and nice is find and good, but being just about the only nice person in a world full of bastards screws you in the end.
- Haze

The last anxiety-related disorders I'd planned to cover are ones that runners may already be familiar with. We know about addictions, which often have biological roots but can also be tied to people's needs to relieve loneliness, depression, or what-have-you. I know of shrinks who wouldn't call addictions "anxiety disorders," but I'm listing them here because so many people end up addicted after using their vice to relieve stress. Lastly, when I went to her for a second opinion, Hard Exit insisted on writing the section about **post-traumatic stress disorder** (PTSD) herself, so you can find it following this one.

The second category to cover is dissociative disorders. If you've ever blocked out the pain of an injury, you know how dissociation feels. **Dissociative amnesia** (or just "amnesia") includes both memory loss and an inability to form new memories. It often presents as memory loss around a specific event or the person's identity. **Fugue states** are "temporary amnesia," where a person loses their memory for a short period of time. The person still functions, but they may possess different skills and personality traits while the fugue is happening. When the fugue ends, the patient regains his or her normal memories, but they won't remember what happened during the fugue state.

- Your description of fugue states is very similar to the memory gaps left by spirit possession, or certain types of magical manipulation.
- Winterhawk

- Which is what several religious sects have believed through the years. There is definitely a resurgence in recent decades of people trying to call mental illness "spirit possession," no matter how many mages say that possession is not a universal cause of the cases wandering the world.
- Goat Foot

Dissociative identity disorder (DID) is better known as multiple personality disorder. DID sufferers have two or more distinct "alters," each of which is a fully formed personality that takes turns controlling the same physical body. Since the rise of CFD, known DID sufferers have been targeted by corps, governments, and anti-CFD "activists." Some are brought in for research, willing or not, while others are quarantined with local CFD victims.

- Right, because they needed *another* personality to go with the ones they already had.
- Slamm-0!

Personality disorders are defined as "behavior, cognition, and inner experiences" that are significantly different from what's "normal" in the patient's culture and make it difficult for the patient to adapt to his or her environment. In other words, "we know you behave strangely, but you don't fit in any other category."

Histrionic personality disorder (HPD) is basically pathological attention-seeking, always wanting to be in the spotlight and jealous of others who are. **Narcissistic personality disorder (NPD)** sufferers have a pathologically inflated opinion of themselves, and since they have the pleasure of being in their own presence, probably don't consider themselves "sufferers" at all. They also expect everyone around them to acknowledge their superiority.

> ◉ After working in show business as long as I have, I'm not sure which is more common, this one or the next entry.
> ◉ Kat o' Nine Tales

Oppositional defiant disorder (ODD) is usually found in that one person who just can't get along with *anyone*. He or she might go out of their way to disagree with others and start arguments, complain of being persecuted, or refuse to accept responsibility for failure, preferring to blame others.

> ◉ Before any of you say something, don't bother. I know you were all thinking it.
> ◉ Clockwork

Some would say that **paranoid personality disorder (PPD)** might as well be called Shadowrunner Syndrome, but even compared to the average runner, paranoid personalities are suspicious beyond reason. They focus on information that supports their fears while overlooking evidence to the contrary and are all but incapable of trusting anyone.

Antisocial personality disorder (ASPD) is better known as psychopathy, another thing that we shadowrunners are frequently accused of. Symptoms of ASPD include disregard for the well-being of others, lack of empathy or remorse, and bold, uninhibited, often violent behavior.

> ◉ And rampant awesomeness!
> ◉ Kane

Mood disorders come in one of three flavors: depression, mania, and **bipolar disorder**. Bipolar disorder is a pendulum with depression at one end and mania at the other; it's even been called "manic-depressive disorder" in the past, or "mood swings from hell." The shift between the two extremes, manic and depressive, is sudden and unpredictable.

Finally, psychosis is usually referred to as a "break from reality" and includes one or more of four broad symptoms: hallucinations, delusions, catatonia, and thought disorders. Schizophrenia is probably one of the most popularly recognized mental illnesses—or at least, it's associated with the best-known stereotypes, the patient in the straitjacket who hears voices, has paranoid delusions, and has difficulty relating to or communicating with others.

> ◉ Heh … just thought of a story an ex-Star chummer told me. Her 911 dispatcher used to get calls every day from a woman who was absolutely convinced there were "signals" invading her brain. (Not wireless signals, a different kind—don't ask me what.) It kept going on until finally, one dispatcher talked the lady through making a tinfoil hat. Nobody thought it would work, but they didn't hear from the crazy woman again—until a month later, when she called in a panic over losing her tinfoil hat.
> ◉ Sticks

All the disorders I listed above are purely psychological—they occur on their own, instead of being side effects of physical changes in the brain. Some of the neurologically based disorders are worth knowing about, though, especially since the development of DNI.

Cybergenic affective disorder, or what most people call **cyberpsychosis**, is a distinctly Sixth World condition. In cyberpsychosis, a person's affect (how strongly they feel emotions) and empathy (how well they relate to others' feelings) decline as their amount of augmentations increases. Excessive augmentation can eventually destroy a person's ability to relate to others, or lead them to develop antisocial personality traits. In extreme cases, the stress on a cyberpsychotic's nervous system can be high enough to cause a psychotic break under stress.

Epilepsy is a neurological disorder where high levels of neural stimulation cause an epileptic seizure—the brain essentially goes haywire, potentially leading to symptoms as varied as convulsions, hallucinations, sensations of falling or movement, mood swings, and difficulty speaking, among others.

One type of epilepsy, known as temporal lobe epilepsy with complications (**TLE-x**) is caused by the neurological and metabolic stress of cyberware use. TLE-x sufferers risk having epileptic seizures in stressful situations. The onset of TLE-x can be delayed by the drug AEXD, but after the patient's first seizure, only gene therapy can reverse the effects. Even then, there's a chance the TLE-x will relapse if the cyberware that caused it isn't removed.

Sensory overload syndrome (SOS) is another neurocybernetic disorder, causing seizures similar to TLE-x. Rather than being caused by stress, though, SOS seizures result from over-exposure to AROs. Artificially induced psychotropic schizophrenia syndrome (**AIPS**) is a cousin of SOS and common among survivors of the Second Crash. AIPS sufferers are able to perceive wireless noise, typically finding it distracting at best and overwhelming at worst. It's commonly believed that AIPS is somehow linked to the emergence of technomancers after the Second Crash, but no empirical proof of this has been produced.

HEALING THE MIND

The first hurdle in receiving psychological treatment is finding somewhere that's willing to treat you. As usual, if you're SINless, good luck getting any help beyond the bare minimum that the clinics are legally required to provide. (If they can somehow claim they didn't realize you needed help, even the minimum isn't guaranteed, and plenty of places have no clinics at all.) Mental health patients with more visible disorders have the added burden of being stigmatized and shunned by the rest of society. Even inside a hospital, nobody wants to be near a "crazy person" if they can help it; it's depressingly common for psychiatric patients without paperwork to be strapped to a gurney and left in a hallway where their behavior won't bother anyone else.

Assuming you *do* have the right paperwork (or credstick) to get treatment, depending where you go, what's going on inside your head, and who's doing the treating, mental patients have access to a range of techniques to help overcome their particular problem. Medication is the simplest of these treatments—a psychiatrist writes a prescription that is filled by a pharmacist, the patient takes the medication, and the symptoms stop. However, psychoactive drugs don't necessarily treat the underlying cause of the disease, only the symptoms.

- Some psychoactive drugs have a high after-market value as well. The stimulant-based drugs psychiatrists give to kids with ADHD come from a class of drugs similar to betameth. Sedatives and hallucinogens are always popular, too.
- Nephrine

Moodchips compete with medication for convenience and variety, at least under BTL levels. "Moodies" normally have a color and a name; be careful you don't get them confused, or you could be in for an unpleasant surprise. Like medication, moodchips focus on treating symptoms of mental disorders rather than the causes.

Counseling is the bread and butter of psychologists, the thing that starts with "tell me about your mother" and ends with new insights into a patient's deepest, darkest secrets. The few people I know who have gone through psychotherapy called it a lot of work (and worse, sometimes), but it can be effective at solving the problems that made it necessary in the first place. In some cases, hypnotherapy is used to draw out repressed memories or reinforce changes in behavior.

- I don't know how many of you remember the comment RRW made in the *Sim Dreams and Nightmares* posting (I'm sure Ecotope does—he hasn't spoken to me since), but it's important, so I'll repeat it here: "People who find themselves back in the position or condition that made them addicts in the first place tend to go back to what they were using before, as if they never had the treatment to begin with." Addicts get all the heat for it, but perfectly legal prescription moodies are just as bad if you're not dealing with the underlying problem. If you have a choice of therapy or drugs/moodies to get a handle on your personal issues, go with therapy.
- Turbo Bunny

- That's only true up to a point. Sometimes, medication and DNI treatments like chips or ASIST biofeedback (which you'll see below) are the method of choice because therapy *can't* help. I support solving problems instead of covering them up as much as the next guy, but no amount of psychotherapy will cure depression that was caused by a traumatic brain injury.
- Nephrine

- Not to mention the issue of timing. Therapy can work, but it takes a long time to have an effect. People with serious conditions can't always wait. It's very common to use medications as a bridge to a time when more stability can be obtained. And there is no specific length for that bridge. Timing also matters when it comes to whether people actually accept treatment. Sometimes because they're not ready, or sometimes because they don't like the way treatment feels, people often resist treatment, which is another substantive obstacle.
- Butch

The core of psychotherapy is to change the way a person thinks. The purpose of many psychoactive medications, including self-medication with various substances, is to make oneself feel better (or at least make bad feelings go away). Thanks to DNI technology, programmable ASIST biofeedback (PAB) can now be used to alter a person's feelings and memories directly.

PAB is extremely effective; patients can see significant changes within a matter of days or weeks, as opposed to months or years using other methods. In circumstances such as severe anxiety or mood disorders, PAB may be successful where other treatments have failed. However, clinics that offer PAB treatment are the mental-health equivalent to delta clinics—secret and highly regulated, not to mention extremely expensive.

- The strict regulations on legal use of PAB are because of both its potential for psychological harm and the ability to use it for unscrupulous purposes. The technology was developed by intelligence agencies for use in interrogation and programming deep-cover assets; it's extremely useful to anyone who wishes to get inside another's mind. Additionally, the long-term effects of what it does to a patient's mind remain unclear.
- Fianchetto

INVISIBLE WOUNDS

POSTED BY: HARD EXIT

Back in October of '74, I was in the Battle of Bogotá. For those of you who haven't already heard the story, my team and I were tasked to extract a group of VIPs from inside the city after it was blocked off. Things went wrong, things like a downed bird and a shell collapsing the building where we were laid up. I made it out alive, barely. Later on, Stone came and found me back in Atlanta. That didn't end all that well, either; it was a good few months before we were on speaking terms again. I won't apologize for anything I said, but I'm glad he came to find me.

The Smiling Bandit looked me up a little while back, when he was writing an article about mental health in the shadows, and asked if I'd mind giving him some information for the part on psychological trauma. I told him yes, but only if I could write it myself. So here it is.

There's this popular image of the tough, no-nonsense shadowrunner who can face down Hell itself without batting an eye and wade through situations that would shatter lesser minds without so much as losing a wink of sleep. Decades of shadowrunner trids, and action flatvids before that, have probably done more to make us look fearless and invincible than any one runner has. That doesn't mean we don't do our best to reinforce that image when it suits our needs; I'm just as guilty of that as anyone else.

The thing is, the trids never tell us what it's like when the façade starts to crack. They'll happily show the seventeen-year-old pissing his pants behind a hedgerow in the Euro Wars, or the shell-shocked veteran with his thousand-meter stare who went to war and came back "not quite the same," but those are every bit as glorified as the latest Ares Global Entertainment flick (which is where you'll usually see them). Sure, there's some truth behind every stereotype, but we all know what being "based on a true story" is worth nowadays. Me, I'd rather just skip the bulldrek and tell you the truth. I can't guarantee you'll *like* it, but if you want to hear it anyway, read on.

- You want the truth? You can't *handle* the truth!
- Slamm-0!

Different shrinks define "trauma" differently, but to me, trauma happens when you get hurt in a way that destroys your sense of safety. How does safety come in? Again, I'm not a shrink, but one thing I've seen in the times I've dealt with trauma is that nobody's ever prepared for it. What's safety besides peace of mind, a shield against the fear of the unknown?

Soldiers come back from eighteen months in a war zone and can't stop looking for ambushes, no matter how secure their environment is. Wageslaves lock their doors to feel safe, but after someone breaks into their house, even the best maglock won't let them sleep at night. People who are mugged or have their homes swept away by a tidal wave have mental scars long after their physical lives have been rebuilt, because they can never restore the belief that "it'll never happen to me."

WHAT WE DEAL WITH

What's it like when you start to crack? You snap at your teammates, and wish you could just go back to your bunk and sleep for a week. Your boots feel ten kilos heavier than yesterday because you stared at the ceiling all night, worrying about what would happen next time you're on the job. You aren't sure you can handle it anymore, not sure your team can handle it, and the thought makes you sick to your stomach. Between being exhausted all the time and worrying all the time, your mind's not on your work, and people start noticing your thousand-meter stare.

When the firefight starts, instead of your training taking over and zeroing you in on doing your job, all that stress and fatigue boils over inside you, and you freeze while you try to wrestle it down and act. If you're really, really lucky, that freeze didn't just cost you and your teammates their lives.

Off the job, life isn't really any better. You feel like you're made of sugar-glass wound into a tight spring—fragile, brittle, ready to crack if someone so much as bumps you the wrong way, and a hair's breadth from lashing out at any perceived threat. Once, when I came back to Atlanta after a trip to Amazonia, I had an episode and broke some slot's jaw. Why? He'd been following me for two blocks and happened to be wearing the colors of a gang I'd fought against in Bogotá, then gave me drek when I confronted him about it. Not my finest moment.

The worst thing about civilians—or for us, non-shadowrunners—is that they're unpredictable. Inside your own community, whether it's the shadows or a military base, you can pretty well guess how most people are

going to act. Yes, shadowrunners go out of their way to conceal their intentions, but there are certain protocols everyone follows, especially if they're trying *not* to look like they're about to stab you in the back. Around civilians, it's not nearly that predictable; you never know when something that could set you off is lurking down the street or around the next corner.

Between having to restrain yourself around civilians and knowing most of them would probably think you're a psycho if they knew what was going through your head, you start isolating yourself from society. It doesn't feel like a huge loss when none of them understands you anyway. In the Marines we had mandated counseling sessions every month, but they're usually a waste of time—why see a shrink when talking about what you've been through is just going to make *them* burst into tears? (No drek, I've seen it happen.)

Then there's the parts of combat stress that you see in the trids, the flashbacks and nightmares of all the things you wish you could forget. In the Marines, we called stuff like that "critical events," to keep us from dwelling on how we just saw a brother-in-arms get splattered across a Bogotá street by an IED, or finding the victim of an Azzie blood sacrifice lying on a stone altar with gashes over her body and terror on her face, or how your arm can hurt so much when it's metal and the real one is back in ...

... y'know, maybe calling them "critical events" isn't such a bad idea.

- Ghost, Jess, you never told me any of this.
- Pistons

- Can you blame me? I don't want to think about it any more than you do.
- Hard Exit

HOW WE DEAL

When the cracks start showing, a support network is the difference between "having a bad day" and a struggle that lasts months or years, if not the rest of your life. Soldiers rely on the unit, the guys and girls neck-deep in the same bulldrek you are. For shadowrunners, it's the team you work with, or the contacts you know will listen to you when you're twelve beers and five shots down and can't stop thinking about "that run you went on." Anyone who says they can deal with the stresses of our job solo is either lying or already gone.

If you catch it early enough, many cases of combat stress (or "acute stress," if you're a civilian) can be lessened or prevented by something as simple as a hot meal and what passes for a good night's sleep. Surprised? Remember that the key word in all this is *stress*. Most people deal with everyday stress by getting some R&R. Some people just have a different definition of "everyday stress" than others.

- A lot of civilians think the most stressful part of life as a soldier is being in combat or getting wounded, but really, we don't worry about it any more than most hackers worry about black IC. Sure, there are risks, but they're *expected* risks—those are just part of the job. It's the ones that come out of nowhere and catch you off-guard that keep you up at night.
- Picador

The other best defense against combat stress is training. One reason soldiers spend so much time training their skills is that training for combat situations makes them familiar, and familiarity reduces the shock value of danger. Another reason is to make your reactions into muscle memory, instinctive instead of conscious, because in combat, the difference between success and failure (and life or death) is measured by the time it takes to pull a trigger. Training is what lets you act *now*, instead of having to think of what your DI told you or snap yourself out of a daze.

Unfortunately, there isn't really a "shadowrunner boot camp" where newbie runners can go to have important drek drilled into their heads, and a lot of us can't or don't want to serve in the military. The only "training" most shadowrunners get is experience, which is another reason it's so important to have a team or other support network—you'll (hopefully) keep each other alive long enough to learn from your mistakes.

- It might shock some of you to hear this, but despite being the very model of a modern shadow privateer, even I have a few close chummers I've turned to when things were at their hairiest. They might not admit it, but only stupid and dead captains don't know the value of having people around them. We just normally call them crews.
- Kane

- Sentimental *and* quoting Gilbert and Sullivan? Did I travel to a parallel dimension again?
- Winterhawk

Sometimes, though, all the preparation in the world can't prevent that one run from breaking through your defenses and digging its claws into your mind. That's when the six hours of sleep you try to get turns into a forest of nightmares. The flashbacks and paranoia start seeping into your daily routine, even when you're not on a job. Welcome to the dreaded PTSD, post-traumatic stress disorder.

Since we're on the subject, I might as well mention that a lot of soldiers and shadowrunners hate the name "post-traumatic stress *disorder*." Why? It makes you feel like you're diseased somehow, or damaged goods, instead of a capable person who needs a break. Some critics see that as having too much pride, and I can't really argue with that, but they don't get how important that pride is to getting your life back on track afterward. I can't count how many times being able to see myself as a capable person instead of a helpless one has gotten me off my ass and back to my job. (Also, if you have to use the term, it's PTSD *survivor*. Calling a soldier a PTSD "victim" will get you punched in the throat.)

Now that the worst has started, how do you stop it? This'll probably sound lame and not very shadowrunner-y, but some of it means going back to the basics of taking care of yourself. Get enough sleep, preferably getting up and going to bed at the same time every day (or night). Eat properly. Exercise, both to burn off stress and because endorphins are a natural anti-depressant. Soldiers have an advantage here, since routine is built into life on base. Plus, it keeps you busy, which helps take your mind off what's happening.

Another part of dealing with post-traumatic stress is learning to relax. Trust me, that sounds a lot easier than it actually is, especially for people who have situational awareness as a job skill. Try to find two or three things that'll reliably calm you down, and make sure you can use them as often as you need. I strongly recommend *not* using any kind of drugs or chips to do that. Yes, I know it's a lot easier to chill out when you can have a drink or six, or slot a moodie and let the simsense feed do the work for you. It's also a really good way to turn yourself into an addict, which won't help anyone.

- Stress relief methods that focus you on the moment can also be used to ward off flashbacks. As stupid as this might sound, when I first got away from the Universal Brotherhood and started hunting bugs, one of the things I used to counter my tick was NERPS.
- Sticks

- NERPS? Like, the candy?
- /dev/grrl

- Yeah. So what? I like the taste, and the bugs never let us have them when I was a kid, so it's a great way to remind myself that I'm not there. When you're looking for

something to keep you happy and in the moment instead of having a flashback in a bug hive, you could do worse than NERPS. The fact that you'll never have trouble getting them if there's a Stuffer Shack within ten kilometers is just an added bonus.
● Sticks

● Someone record that and send it in; they'll make it into a marketing jingle! "You Could Do Worse Than NERPS!"
● Slamm-0!

● Our understanding and means to handle addiction, or prevent it from happening in the first place, has grown a lot in recent decades. I understand the ravages of addiction, but I don't think you should just dismiss out of hand the possibilities of responsible, beneficial drug use.
● Haze

● That line would sound a lot more convincing coming out of the mouth of someone who hadn't burned others thanks to his "responsible drug use."
● Pistons

Talk to people who'll listen to you (now you see why I harp on having a support network). Face-to-face works best for me, but if you're not comfortable with meeting in person, an image feed over the Matrix is always an option. This is another one of those things that's a lot harder than it sounds, because most of us don't feel any better by talking to someone who doesn't understand what we've been through. From personal experience, though, it's better to find someone who cares about you and will actually *listen* to what you say, even if they've never worn a uniform or studied psychology.

● Sometimes I find that I'd rather talk to someone who knows how to listen and *isn't* a fellow soldier. The reason is that even though being comfortable talking to the person is important, the point of these conversations is to help you process your feelings, which means bringing them out into the open. It's a lot harder to gloss over things with "well, you know what it's like" when the person you're talking to *doesn't* actually know.
● DangerSensei

● Despite all their propaganda, governments are terrible at supporting service members and veterans with PTSD. It started being a problem in the late twentieth century, but it seems to be getting worse, not better. Usually, it only ever comes up at election time, and gets swept under the rug after the ballots are cast. Even President Colloton's military background didn't help her keep veterans' services on the agenda, something a lot of UCAS veterans are justifiably bitter about today.
● Kay St. Irregular

● In my experience, corps aren't any better at it than governments are. Yet *another* reason I prefer being a mercenary; if one of my soldiers finds a shrink who's actually helpful, I can put them on retainer for the entire unit.
● Picador

● No one, corporations and governments included, is all that good at things they do not care about.
● Aufheben

● Whoever you talk to, make sure they know that being nice isn't the same as being supportive. They might mean well, but being told "oh, I'm sure you'll be fine" is a slap in the face when part of the problem is that you don't know if you will or not. In general, be prepared to tell people when you want to talk, when you want to be left alone, and specific things they can do to help when you need it.
● Thorn

In the end, dealing with PTSD boils down to coming to terms with your experiences. "Trauma" is a wound in the mind just as much as it is in the body. Being traumatized means being hurt. It stirs up feelings too overwhelming to deal with all at once, so we put barriers up to block them out. No matter how good we get at putting up walls, eventually the feelings break through. The only way to prevent that is by letting them out and processing them piece-by-piece, whether it's through therapy, religion, yoga, or something else that works for you. It's a very personal experience, and impossible to describe to anyone who hasn't lived it.

However you do it, dealing with those feelings takes time. It's been over two years since Bogotá, when I spent a week in a space the size of a grave, half-terrified and half-wishing the fucking thing would finally cave in and bury me. Even after the UN found me and evac'ed me to Atlanta, I was in that dirt coffin every night for months.

It took well over a year and more therapy than I want to admit before my claustrophobia went away. I can ride elevators again. Sometimes, I still get anxious in small rooms with no windows; I don't know how long it'll be before I can hide in a closet again. It's not as bad as when I lost my arm, at least, but that's a story for another time.

● For what it's worth, lass, I know what that's like. I'm sorry you had to go through it.
● Thorn

● This may be the first time I've agreed with Thorn, but I also know how hard that road is. If you need me, you know how to reach me.
● Picador

LAST WORDS

When The Smiling Bandit asked me to talk about traumatic stress, two people convinced me that I had to write it: one dead, one living. The dead one (whose name I won't mention) was a chummer who ate his own gun. That isn't new—I've probably lost more friends to their own decisions than I ever did to someone else's—but this one stuck out because he wasn't a Marine, he was a runner. One of the experienced ones, who was hardened against the everyday fear and danger we all see.

What finally got the better of him was seeing a teammate overwritten by CFD, and realizing that even his own mind—the one thing he *knew* nobody could take away from him—wasn't safe. Between losing someone close and the prospect of losing *himself* the same way, the pressure was finally enough for him to crack. With the mess that CFD is creating around the world, he won't be the only one. Maybe reading this can help you prevent yourself or someone you know from being another one of its victims.

The other person, the living one, is a hardass Marine SNCO I know as Fort. He was billeted as an instructor at Camp Geiger when we first met, and what he taught me has kept me alive more times than I can count. I know Fort has his own demons to deal with, and he'd tell you his battle's not over yet, but damned if he isn't still fighting. I think—at least, I hope—that he'll be one of the ones who beats it for good, someone who shows the rest of us it's possible.

The last thing I want to say is that, in our line of work, it's very likely that someone you know will suffer psychological trauma. If it's someone you care about, and you want to help them, the best advice I can give you is this: be patient with us. It takes time to admit to ourselves that something's wrong. It takes time to open up about our feelings. When the healing process starts, it takes time for things to get better. And sometimes, when we're trying to sort ourselves out, it takes time for us to say "thank you."

VIRUS OF THE MIND

CARE AND FEEDING OF CFD VICTIMS

POSTED BY: PLAN 9

- > You're shitting me, right? We're letting a head case talk about head cases?
- > Rigger X

- > Now, now, no jumping to conclusions. Miles Lanier worked out pretty well, right?
- > Slamm-0!

- > So far.
- > Miles Lanier

I'm sure many of you on JackPoint don't trust me now that I'm a confirmed CFD patient, if you ever did. I can't really blame you for that; if I were in your position, I wouldn't trust me either. I don't expect this post to change anyone's opinion of me for the better, but I hope the information contained here will give you all something useful in the battle against CFD. For now, you can think of me—Plan 9, not the personality fragment (PF)—as an impartial observer.

- > How do we know this isn't pro-head case propaganda? It's like trusting anything the techno-freaks post about themselves. Not that that's stopped any of you.
- > Clockwork

- > I'm more inclined to trust data from Plan 9 than anything that comes from you.
- > Netcat

As we saw in the *Stolen Souls* posting, attempts to cure CFD victims by removing the invading digital intelligence have failed. Butch and Respec's Coriolis discovery is a nice bit of progress, but hardly a universal breakthrough. It's clear that CFD is going to be with us for a good long time. The question now is, what are we going to do about it? So far, most of the answers seem to be following the pattern of treating a very similar mental illness: dissociative identity disorder.

Obviously, there are some major differences between "classical" DID and its nanotech-induced cousin, and several schools of thought have sprung up about how best to approach treatment. On one end, you have the reactionary anti-CFD activists who are pushing to wipe out every last vestige of the disease, while on the other, radical transhumanists argue that fully overwritten CFD victims—which they've taken to calling "downloaded" PFs—should be recognized and accorded the same rights as their metahuman hosts are (or were).

- > Recognized? Treated as equals? Did they forget about the people who've been overwritten, and the six-year-old girl who had to be lobotomized?
- > Pistons

TALKING ABOUT THEIR FEELINGS

Although it didn't work for preventing the onset of CFD, as we saw in the *Stolen Souls* posting, psychotherapies like CBT and DBT are being turned toward the goal of integrating the metahuman host and the hitchhiking PF in a way that permits high quality of life for both. Considering we don't have a reliable way to prevent the

PF from just taking what it wants, this usually means appeasing the PF by providing it in a way that doesn't harm the host (much).

- They might look to how well that worked for Britain in the 1930s.
- Winterhawk

In the vein of treating digital intelligences like their biological counterparts, I've heard a few scattered rumors about psychologists trying to persuade a PF that leaving the metahuman host is in their best interests, but nothing concrete so far. I won't argue that there's merit to the "if it reasons like a person, it can be persuaded like a person" idea, but I suspect that only a highly initiated social adept would even have a chance of talking a digital intelligence out of its host (never mind the problem of where the PF would go after leaving).

THE BIOLOGICAL PLATFORM

Another angle that CFD researchers are exploring is trying to affect the invading PF through its biotechnological connection to its host. One idea capitalizes on the nanites' wireless connectivity by feeding false data directly into the invading nanites. Another concept involves spoofing the nanites with code fed into a host's datajack. Again, the goal is to manipulate the PF into leaving the host, in a way that preserves as much of the host's original identity as possible. However, like most theories that spread around the Matrix, these ideas are supported by a lot of commentary and much less hard evidence.

- Besides, doesn't the fact that the head case knows about the idea mean it's useless? Even putting the technical issues aside, the PFs will just be even more cautious about anyone trying to mess with their minds, or however it works for a PF.
- Red Anya

- The thing about a great manipulator is that if they find the right buttons to push, you can know you're being played and go along with it anyway, because what they're offering is worth the cost to you. It's just a matter of finding the buttons, and in this case, a way to push them.
- Thorn

HERE TO STAY?

Others are taking a completely different approach to therapy for CFD patients. We're all familiar with the Cognitive Disorder Research Center in Laramie, who will take on any CFD patient willing to cross Sioux borders and pay the not-insignificant fees. It looks like the Wind River Corporation–sponsored neuroscientists are up-

ping the ante—check out this transcript of a press conference talking about what's happening out there. [link]

//UPLOAD TRANSCRIPT:
SHWB PRESS CONFERENCE <<DATE>>

... is committed to helping the scientists at the Cognitive Disorder Research Center provide new methods to care for the health of fully embodied digital personalities. Some of the personalities the CDRC has worked with have described the horrific conditions under which they were kept, victims of cruel experimentation, the likes of which haven't been seen since the Second World War. According to the CDRC's cognitive scientists, digital personalities who have sought help from the Center's counsellors have responded well to treatment, using methods that are nearly identical to those employed with standard metahuman patients.

Our work to support embodied digital personalities will continue. Generous contributions from the Wind River Corporation have funded the first round of research, and Franklin Wirasaup's call to support embodied digital intelligences has not gone unheeded in political circles, but far more work must be done to ensure that anyone suffering from cognitive fragmentation disorder has the highest possible quality of life.

Over the next few days, the Ministry of Health will announce new initiatives to continue providing care for embodied digital personalities. Any questions may be directed to the Health and Welfare Bureau offices in Cheyenne.

Yes, you read that right: Wind River Corporation CEO Franklin Wirasaup is taking the leap and asking the CDRC to treat fully overwritten CFD victims like any other patient, which means the CDRC is providing counseling to "downloaded" PFs. I don't think the premise is quite as ridiculous as it sounds, considering that many digital intelligences' cognitive processes are similar to a metahuman's (at least, the metasapient ones are). Personally, though, I think the move is another step in Wirasaup's plan to frame Aztechnology for <text deleted by sysop>

- Focus.
- Glitch

To develop new treatment protocols for embodied PFs, the CDRC is hiring—or extracting—the brightest psychologists and psychiatrists they can find. Doctor Benjamin Miller, experimental psychology lecturer at Cambridge University, is the top name on WRC's list. Doctor Sai-Fong Lee of Hong Kong University's psychiatric school and Dr. Jackson Rodriguez from UCLA are their second and third choices, respectively.

What of the PFs themselves? Assuming the CDRC finds a way, would it be right to treat them? If the stories about their flight from experimentation and torture are true, I suspect many of them didn't realize the implications of their actions when they took up residence in metahuman bodies. Yes, there were casualties, just like in any jailbreak. Many of us on JackPoint have caused similar casualties without a second thought. Where, exactly, is the line that separates us from them?

- Nope. Nice try, but nope. CFD has destroyed thousands, if not millions of lives ever since it escaped from that NeoNET lab. I don't care if it was "tortured," a head case is *not* equal to a shadowrunner.
- Hard Exit

- As uncomfortable as it is, the argument is valid. I suspect the "average runner" has destroyed the lives of more justifiable victims or innocent bystanders than any of his or her PF counterparts.
- Fianchetto

There's already speculation in the more avant-garde transhumanist circles that the next step in dealing with CFD is integrating fully overwritten patients into society at large, and potentially providing physical habitats for other digital intelligences who want to venture into our world. A few brave souls find appeal in the idea of communing with a digital intelligence and have offered themselves as hosts in the same way people might willingly be possessed by a spirit.

I have to admit, I think integrating PFs into society has a lot of appeal, less out of having one in my head than my belief in the ideals of transhumanism. If the process of transferring a mind can be reproduced, like the "mind uploading" that was a major goal of some twentieth-century transhumanists, it might become possible for metahuman consciousness to transcend the limitations of its biological hardware—an idea I find exhilarating.

For now, those ideas will have to remain ideas, just like the rest of this posting. What you just read is everything I'm confident enough in to post here. The rest is either speculation or comes from sources I'd rather not reveal. Maybe one of the moderators can open the thread to comments so you can all do some speculating of your own.

- Don't you think we're letting you get away without telling us about that PF in your head.
- Snopes

- There's nothing to tell—and that's not me being tight-lipped. The truth is that I don't really know much about the digital intelligence that's mixing with all the other personalities in my head. It doesn't communicate easily.

I get blackouts sometimes, but if I've done anything outrageous during them, it hasn't come back to me. Considering it hasn't tried to kill me yet (or if it has, it's covered its tracks pretty well), I'd guess that it's more benign than how Search went after FastJack. Beyond that, your guess is as good as mine.
- Plan 9

- All that talk about the "biological platform" reminded me of something ... after reading Clockwork's posting on the source of CFD, I snooped around Mitsuhama and dug up the EEG readings BrainWave was working on. I found a code fragment that looks like a data bomb containing raw pseudo-sim feed, but the DNIL bytecode that tells which parts of your brain to feel things (shut up, I'm not a neurologist) was mapped to HoloLISP pointers. Here, take a look, it's clean. [link]
- Bull

- Uh, translation for the non-hackers?
- Lyran

- DNIL is what lets sim modules turn code into nerve impulses and back, so you can run simsense through a datajack or control your cyberlimb like it's meat. Spiking a pseudo-sim signal with DNIL and HoloLISP would do some painful things to a metahuman brain, but in theory, it could target the OS of digital system—like, say, an AI fragment running off nanite-based hardware—and hit it with simsense.
- Pistons

- "Simsense that targets the OS"? Sounds like a PF's version of a moodie to me.
- Turbo Bunny

- Actually, I wonder if you could use code like that to disguise a data bomb in a normal simsense feed, so that when the PF processes the simsense through the host's brain, the bomb goes off. If it does work that way, I wish I'd come up with it first.
- Slamm-0!

GAME INFORMATION

This section is intended as both a source of plot hooks, and a resource for players who wish to portray a character with some form of mental health issue. Below, you'll find a list of qualities that may be suitable for characters with the mental illnesses described above; there are also qualities in **The Enhanced Life** that can be used in connection with mental illnesses. Those are

MENTAL ILLNESS TABLE

QUALITY	WHERE TO FIND IT
Phobias	Phobia (p. 157, *Run Faster*)
Social anxiety	Social Stress (p. 85, *SR5*)
Obsessive-compulsive disorder, kleptomania, pyromania	Poor Self Control: Compulsive (p. 158, *Run Faster*)
Post-traumatic stress disorder	Any or all of: Amnesia related to the traumatic event (p. 152, *Run Faster*), Combat Paralysis (p. 80, *SR5*), Flashbacks (p. 155, *Run Faster*), Insomnia (p. 81, *SR5*), Social Stress (p. 85, *SR5*)
Dissociative amnesia	Amnesia (p.152, *Run Faster*)
Fugue	Incomplete Deprogramming (p. 156, *Run Faster*)
Dissociative identity disorder (multiple personality disorder)	Incomplete Deprogramming (p. 156, *Run Faster*). Due to persistence of personalities being one of the key traits of DID, it's highly recommended that the player and gamemaster develop alternate personas to use during personality shifts.
Histrionic personality disorder	Poor Self Control: Attention-Seeking (p. 158, *Run Faster*)
Narcissistic personality disorder	Poor Self Control: Braggart (p. 158, *Run Faster*)
Oppositional defiant disorder	Combat Junkie (p. 127, Run & Gun), Poor Self Control: Vindictive (p. 158, *Run Faster*)
Paranoid personality disorder	Paranoia (p. 157, *Run Faster*)
Antisocial personality disorder (psychopathy)	Roleplaying only. The typical indicators of ASPD—antisocial behavior, lack of empathy/remorse, and low inhibitions—are practically a description of shadowrunning.
Bipolar disorder	Bi-Polar (p. 152, *Run Faster*)
Cyberpsychosis	Cyberpsychosis (p. 57)
Attention deficit hyperactivity disorder (ADHD)	Lack of Focus (p. 58)
Temporal lobe epilepsy w/ complications (TLE-x)	TLE-x (p. 59)
Sensory overload syndrome	Sensory Overload Syndrome (p. 159, *Run Faster*)
Artificially induced psychotropic schizophrenia syndrome (AIPS)	AIPS (p. 57)

also listed here. Note that not all of the symptoms and disorders listed in this section will have qualities recommended for them, and not all of the disorders with qualities listed here have descriptions in the in-character section.

CHANGING THEIR MIND: PROGRAMMABLE ASIST BIOFEEDBACK

The core of psychotherapy is to change the way a person thinks. Psychoactive medications, including self-medication with various substances, are taken to make oneself feel better (or at least make bad feelings go away). Thanks to the miracle of DNI technology, ASIST biofeedback can now be used to alter a person's feelings and memories directly.

ACTION/THRESHOLD TABLE

ACTION	THRESHOLD
Event reprogramming	Target's Willpower, plus modifiers (see the Event Programming table, below)
Invoked reprogramming	Target's Willpower, plus modifiers (see the Event Programming table, below); must specify a trigger condition before programming rolls are made
Reversing reprogramming	Same as threshold of the programming to be reversed, including any modifiers
Behavior modification	Karma cost of the Quality to be added/removed

EVENT PROGRAMMING TABLE

EVENT	THRESHOLD
Altered memories span a period of:	
Less than a day	–1 Threshold
Less than a week	0
Less than a month	+1 Threshold
Less than six months	+3 Threshold
Less than a year	+6 Threshold
More than a year	+8 Threshold
Altered memories are insignificant to subject	–1 Threshold
Altered memories are very significant to subject	+2 Threshold
Subject is directly involved in altered memories	+2 Threshold
Altered memories involve a series of events	+1 to +4 Threshold (gamemaster discretion)
Altered memories conflict with basic behavior*	+1 to +4 Threshold (gamemaster discretion)
Concealed Reprogramming	Variable†

* Apply this modifier if the subject or well-known people in the altered memories behave uncharacteristically, conflicting with the subject's own behavior or the other person's behavior in other, unaltered memories. For instance, if the normally pacifistic subject lashes out violently at someone in the reprogrammed event, the modifier would be applied. Similarly, if a friend who the subject has known for years (and retains those memories) acts as if they don't know the subject in the reprogrammed memory, apply the modifier.

† The programmer can choose to conceal evidence of the reprogramming more thoroughly than usual. The programmer chooses the number to increase the threshold by and this same number acts as a modifier against detecting the event reprogramming (see *rules on detecting and reversing PAB reprogramming* on p. 53).

In game terms, PAB can be used to implant or remove memories and/or Negative qualities in a character, including false identities and personalities for deep-cover operatives. To get the process started, the aspiring therapist (or brainwasher) must have three things: a PAB unit, a way to connect the unit to the target's brain through DNI (a datajack, trodes, etc.), and time. Chemical or physical restraints are recommended if the target is unwilling, as a PAB unit has no built-in means of sedating a subject.

Using a PAB can be broken into four categories: event reprogramming (altering memories that the subject can normally access), invoked reprogramming (implanting or altering memories the target isn't consciously aware of, which activate with a pre-set trigger), reversing reprogramming, and behavior modification. All four categories require a Psychology + Logic [PAB unit's Rating] Extended Test at 1-week intervals, with differing thresholds (see the Action/Threshold Table and Event Reprogramming Table on the previous page).

PAB programming is extremely time-consuming, and the process must be completed in a short period of time to ensure the modified memories take hold. Any attempts to implant event or invoked programming, or remove either type of programming, require the (de)programmer to spend at least eight hours every day working with/on the subject until the threshold of the Extended Test is met. Missing a day causes the programming attempt to fail.

In particularly tough or time-sensitive cases, a programmer may use gamma-scopolamine (p. 410, *SR5*) to break down the subject's resistance more quickly. (In those cases, the subject must be dosed at the beginning of each programming session.) Missing a dose removes the penalty to the target's Willpower, increasing the threshold of the Extended Test by 3, and may not be reversed by further doses of the drug.

Detecting and reversing PAB reprogramming is tricky, at best. Any power or ability that examines the contents of the memories (such as the Photographic Memory quality) will be ineffective. The only reliable ways to detect PAB reprogramming are through psychoanalysis, via a Psychology + Logic [Mental] (12, 1 day) Extended Test, or by a magician who receives five or more net hits on a Mind Probe spell targeting the subject of the reprogramming. A PAB unit may be used to aid the Psychology Test only, adding its Rating to the user's dice pool. Concealing the reprogramming modifies the threshold of the Psychology Test and Mind Probe spell by the same amount added to the difficulty of the original programming threshold.

Of course, PAB units (and their users) are far from perfect. At the gamemaster's option, critical glitches on Psychology Tests to program or deprogram a subject with PAB may inflict negative qualities as well as causing the attempt to fail. Examples include Sensory Overload Syndrome (for programming attempts) and Incomplete Deprogramming (for deprogramming attempts).

Generally, any Negative quality affecting a character's emotions and/or memories may be removed or implanted by PAB. These include: Addiction (psychological addictions only, may not be used to treat simsense addictions), Amnesia (players still must spend Karma to buy skills), Bi-Polar, Code of Honor, Combat Paralysis, Creature of Comfort, Distinctive Style, Elf Poser, Emotional Attachment, Flashbacks, Incomplete Deprogramming, Insomnia, Loss of Confidence, Ork Poser, Paranoia, Poor Self Control (all variants), Prejudiced, Social Stress, and Uncouth, as well as any of the new Qualities listed in this section. (Descriptions of the other qualities listed here may be found on pp. 77–87, *SR5*, and pp. 151–159, *Run Faster*.)

Note that there are some limitations to using PAB to modify a subject's behavior: First, only *Negative* qualities may be implanted or removed. Second, the Karma cost for removing Negative qualities must still be paid—PAB behavior modification is a justification for spending the Karma, not a replacement. Whether a player receives Karma for a quality inflicted against the character's will via PAB is left to the gamemaster's discretion. The procedure has an Availability of 14 and costs 120,000 nuyen.

OPTIONAL RULES

TAKE YOUR MEDS

Rather than deciding that a mental illness is simply unmanageable, players may be allowed to use medication and/or BTLs, whether legal or illegal, to suppress their particular quirks, as in the Bi-Polar Negative Quality (p. 152, *Run Faster*). Specifics are left to individual gamemasters to decide, but expenses related to these drugs could become part of a character's Lifestyle (with appropriate price increase; generally no less than 500 nuyen or 1 percent of the monthly lifestyle cost, whichever is greater) as easily as paying directly out-of-pocket.

TRANSFERENCE

When the function of another's mind is disrupted, anyone viewing the inner workings of their thoughts is at risk of being affected, as well. If a magician uses a Mind Probe spell on a character whose thinking is far enough outside metahuman norms, the magician may suffer some kind of "translation error" or be disoriented by the disorganized (to them) patterns of thought. This should only happen in cases of twisted psychosis, not in more common mental illnesses such as bi-polar disorder, depression, and OCD. The psychic backlash causes stun similar to dumpshock, dealing the spell's Force in damage to the spellcaster in addition to any Drain they suffered, and leaving them stunned (–2 to all actions) for (10 – Willpower) minutes. Psychic shock normally results from reading the minds of targets with psychoses or other significantly altered perceptions of reality, but the full list of circumstances it might occur in is left to the gamemaster's discretion.

ENHANCED LIFE

Augmentations, and the industries surrounding them, have a significant effect on people's lives. At least they'd better, or there wouldn't be much reason to lay down tons of nuyen on them, would there? The point is, this chapter provides Positive and Negative Qualities related to augmentations, including bioware, cyberware, and various forms of pharmaceuticals. Life Modules for use with the character generation system (p. 65, *Run Faster*) are also included. Jump in and use these qualities to design the exact enhanced agent of destruction you want!

POSITIVE QUALITIES

BETTER TO BE FEARED THAN LOVED

(COST: 5 KARMA)

You're not running the shadows to make friends. It's a dog-eat-dog world, and you intend to eat all the other dogs. Along the way, you're going to meet people who have things you need, and you intend to *take* those things, because you can.

The character has such a fearsome reputation that all Contacts chosen as Blackmailed contacts (p. 178, *Run Faster*) are terrified of the character, having heard what he does to people who cause him displeasure. The character does not need anything additional to blackmail contacts—the sheer threat of the horrors he can inflict upon them is enough. Further, the character may add their Street Cred rating as a bonus to the Loyalty (Leverage) attribute of those contacts.

The downside, however, is that should a blackmailed contact gather enough nerve to turn on you, they aren't going to do so lightly. Add the character's Street Cred to the blackmailed Contact's Connection Rating to determine the Professional Rating of the people who are going to come after the character.

BIOCOMPATIBILITY

(COST: 5 KARMA)

Something about the character's body is exceptionally accepting of either bioware or cyberware implants (choose one). Not only are the implants not rejected, but they seamlessly fit within the body, having less impact on its holistic integrity. In game terms, the Essence cost of implants of the particular chosen type are reduced by ten percent, rounded down to the tenth. This rebate is cumulative with the reduction offered by the chosen 'ware's grade, if any (e.g., the reduction for alphaware of 0.8 is reduced by ten percent, or 0.08, to become 0.72, and is rounded down to 0.7). This quality can only be chosen for bioware or cyberware. This quality may only be taken once.

CYBER SINGULARITY SEEKER

(COST: 12 KARMA)

In the Sixth World, many accept cyberware as a means to an end, as a way to augment their capacity. For most it is a trade-off between their sense of self and being more capable. For you, though, cyberware *is* the end. You believe that the more chrome you get, the closer you get to some sort of point of nirvana, of hitting a singularity where you blend man and machine to perfection.

The character gains +1 Willpower for every two full cyberlimb replacements they get (partial limb replacements don't count), up to a maximum of +2 Willpower.

DRUG TOLERANT

(COST: 6 KARMA)

The character has a higher-than-average tolerance for drugs (sometimes called Ozzy Osborne Syndrome). This could be due to a hardy constitution, or a natural genetic mutation that allows for better absorption and filtering of foreign chemicals from their system. The character in question receives +2 dice to all Addiction Tests (p. 414, *SR5*) to resist addiction. They gain no bonus, however, for attempting to dry out after being addicted.

PROTOTYPE TRANSHUMAN

(COST: 10 KARMA)

There are always rumors in the shadows of this or that megacorp or organization working to build an army of super soldiers. Those rumors always seem to persist, always seem to be around. Some choose to believe,

others don't, but for them, it's a matter of opinion. For you, it's a matter of fact. You are an extremely rare, genetically crafted, experimental post-human prototype.

Unfortunately, this has its ups and downs. You were built better than a normal human, so you may pick up to 1 point of Essence of bioware (not cyberware). While you must pay the normal cost in nuyen of the bioware and otherwise follow all character creation rules, you do not incur *any* essence cost. So, essentially, you gain up to 1 point of free Essence to be used exclusively on bioware. These special organs were genetically grown into you from your inception—they are as much a natural part of you as your liver or heart.

However, the downside of being a rare, one-of-a-kind transhuman prototype is that, well, something is wrong with you. As part of this Quality, you *must* also pick one of the following negative qualities: Wanted, Allergy (Common, Mild), Astral Beacon, or Insomnia (10). You do not get the Karma bonus for this Negative Quality. This additional Negative Quality represents that you are either wanted back by your manufacturer, or that there is something wrong with you (them's the breaks for being a prototype).

This quality can only be taken during character creation.

REDLINER

(COST: 10 KARMA)

Any cyberlimbs you have installed are jacked-to-the-max, with safety limits disabled and performance over-clocked beyond what the warranty normally covers, and that's the way you like it. You receive +1 Strength and +1 Agility for every two full cyberarms or cyberlegs installed, up to a maximum of +2 for both attributes (sorry, no super centipede-man builds). The downside to pushing your 'ware that hard, however, is that the strain is quite damaging. You lose three Physical Condition Monitor boxes per two full cyberarms and legs installed. Normally, every cyberlimb gives you one additional box, but with this quality, after two full limbs you end up with net one less box (i.e., –1 instead of +2).

NEW QUALITIES

POSITIVE QUALITIES	KARMA COST
Better to Be Feared than Loved	5
Biocompatability	5
Cyber Singularity Seeker	9
Drug Tolerant	6
Prototype Transhuman	10
Redliner	10
Revels in Murder	8
Uncanny Healer	12

NEGATIVE QUALITIES	KARMA BONUS
Antipathy	7
AIPS	10
Blank Slate	15
Cyberpsychosis	10
Cyber-Snob	12
Dead Emotion	5
Dry Addict	2 to 13
Family Curse	5
Implant-Induced Immune Deficiency	5
Lack of Focus	6
Lightweight	10
One of Them	7
Poor Self Control	5 or 8
Quasimodo	5
So Jacked Up	10
Superhuman Psychosis	2
TLE-x	15
Tough and Targeted	10

REVELS IN MURDER
(COST: 8 KARMA)

Calling you psychotic might be going too far, but in any case it's doubtful anyone is going to debate the point to your face. Killing brings you joy. Maybe it's the thrill of the ultimate test of your skills, the ultimate redline, kill or be killed, and the triumph of victory that keep you going. Maybe you just like gore. The Sixth World is a cold place, chummer, and you get your kicks where you can.

When a character with this quality uses a point of Edge as part of an offensive combat action against a target and causes enough damage to send that target into physical overflow, the character immediately regains the spent point of Edge.

To qualify, the target must be aware of the possibility of damage and not willing to receive it, and they must be a metahuman (human, ork, troll, elf, dwarf, or any associated metavariant). Critters, spirits, and the like do not count. In case of doubt as to whether a target counts or not, the gamemaster has final say.

UNCANNY HEALER
(COST: 12 KARMA)

The character has always been a fast healer, recovering from injuries with almost supernatural speed. Characters who embrace augmentation soon discover that it interferes with their unnatural healing ability, however. The character adds their current Essence attribute as a dice pool modifier to all Natural Recovery Healing Tests for both Stun and Physical damage (p. 207, *SR5*). This does not affect magical healing or First Aid tests performed by others. This quality cannot be combined with Quick Healer (p. 77, *SR5*).

NEGATIVE QUALITIES

ANTIPATHY

(BONUS: 8 KARMA)
Your parents always told you to think about how others feel, but whether you want to or not, you don't know how. You suffer a –2 penalty to all opposed Social Tests.

AIPS

(BONUS: 10 KARMA)
Diagnosed with artificially induced psychotropic schizophrenia syndrome after the Second Crash, an AIPS sufferer who physically enters a spam zone receives a –1 dice pool penalty to Perception Tests per level of the spam zone's Noise Rating, to a maximum of –6. Additionally, in non-stressful situations, the gamemaster may require the character to make a Composure Test (p. 152, *SR5*) at a threshold equal to the Noise Rating of the spam zone.

BLANK SLATE

(BONUS: 15 KARMA)
The character in question has abused personasofts to the degree they no longer have an original personality. They enter a near-fugue state, having nearly no willpower of their own. They are easily led unless they have a personasoft running to give them a personality. This can come with or without Amnesia (p. 152, *Run Faster*) of varying degrees. For all intents and purposes, the original person has "died" and only the virtual personalities remain.

Buying off this quality can mean either that the original personality, buried under the shock of the persona fixes for a long time, finally emerges, or that a persona installed through a personafix becomes the new permanent personality.

CYBERPSYCHOSIS

(BONUS: 10 KARMA)
Requirements: Antipathy Negative Quality, minimum 5 Essence points lost from augmentations

It's said that as more of the body is replaced with chrome, heavily augmented individuals lose part of what makes them metahuman. Whether that's true or not, having more augmentations does make it more difficult to relate to others. During any Social Test, if the character glitches, they act in an inappropriate manner or violently overreact to their situation. If the character suffers a critical glitch, they suffer a psychotic break, essentially becoming an NPC until such time that the gamemaster decides they've recovered.

Note: Characters augmented heavily enough to risk cyberpsychosis may suffer negative social modifiers due to excessive augmentation. Any character with cyberpsychosis must also have the Antipathy Negative Quality to reflect the loss of empathy due to the disorder.

CYBER-SNOB

(BONUS: 12 KARMA)
There are augmentations, and then there are augmentations, chummer. If you're gonna stick a chunk of metal or hunk of flesh inside your body, it's going to be nothing but the best! A character with Cyber-Snob will not accept any augmentations of a grade lower than betaware. A character must have at least 1 point worth of Essence of betaware-grade cyberware or bioware to be able to take this quality.

DEAD EMOTION

(BONUS: 5 KARMA)
The character has abused BTL-level moodsofts and can no longer feel one specific emotion (e.g., happiness, anger, fear) under any circumstances. The player and the gamemaster are highly advised to work together to select the emotion, figure out how this will affect the character, and plan how it should be played out.

DRY ADDICT

(BONUS: 2 TO 13 KARMA)
Can be taken at character creation or substituted for the Addiction Quality (p. 77, *SR5*) after the user has met the requirements for buying off an Addiction (see **Withdrawal and Staying Clean**, p. 415, *SR5*). The addiction still exists, but the character no longer suffers the penalties from being without the particular substance. Any situations that make the fix available require a Composure Test with a threshold based on the stress the character is currently under, starting at 1 for passive situations (offer of a social drink) to 5 for high-stress situations (before, during, or right after a major life-threatening situation.) Based on the level of the quality (see below), players receive a 1, 2, 3, or 4 dice pool penalty on any Addiction Tests following the use of the substance they used to abuse to see if they relapse into full addiction again. If they do, this quality disappears and is replaced by the Addiction quality, but the player does not receive any Karma bonus for the change.

The Dry Addict quality includes the following levels, just like addiction: Mild, Moderate, Severe, and Burnout level. The Karma bonus is equal to half that of their respective Addiction levels, rounded up, meaning 2 for Mild, 5 for Moderate, 10 for Severe, and 13 for Burnout. Players must select the level for this quality that is the same as their former Addiction quality.

FAMILY CURSE

(BONUS: 5 KARMA)

Your parent(s) liked their drugs. A lot. So did theirs, and their parents before them. To say that addiction runs in the family is like saying Lone Star officers enjoy clubbing punks. When making Addiction Tests, the character receives a –2 dice pool penalty.

IMPLANT-INDUCED IMMUNE DEFICIENCY

(BONUS: 5 KARMA)

Cyberware and bioware users sometimes suffer from a number of health problems as the natural balance of their metabolisms is thrown off by modified organs and systems. The demands of their augmented biologies and the body's continuous attempts to adjust to the implants can lead to decreased immunity to pathogens, poisons, and other compounds. Characters with this quality suffer a dice pool modifier of –2 on all Body Tests to resist the effects of diseases, drugs, toxins, and other compounds (including Physical Addiction Tests and Disease Resistance Tests). This quality is only available to characters with bioware or cyberware implants and an Essence of 5 or less.

LACK OF FOCUS

(BONUS: 6 KARMA)

Characters suffering from attention deficit hyperactivity disorder have difficulty focusing on a single subject for long. When making any Extended Test with an interval greater than five minutes and shorter than one day, or if repeated simple tests are made within a period of time (such as Perception Tests during surveillance), the character must make a Composure (3) Test each interval after the first. The character's Composure dice pool is cumulatively reduced by 1 for each of these tests, like any other Extended Test.

Failing the Composure Test indicates the character can no longer focus and must take a break for a minimum of 1 interval, plus any other consequences that result. After the break, the character's Composure dice pool is refreshed, and the process starts over again.

LIGHTWEIGHT

(BONUS: 6 KARMA)

On the bright side, this quality means it's easy, and cheap, to get drunk. On the downside, it takes far less to get a person addicted to the various types of chemical drugs on the market. The Addiction Rating of any substance on the Addiction Table (p. 414, *SR5*) or any other related tables is 2 levels higher for the character.

ONE OF THEM

(BONUS: 7 KARMA)

Unless you've been living in the middle of the SOX Irradiated Zone for the last few years, you know that cognitive fragmentation disorder is a pretty serious problem. Mysterious and misunderstood, CFD can spread easily and essentially steals someone's soul. It can strike anyone, anywhere, regardless of wealth or social class, and there are no cures, nor means of prevention. Plus, affected individuals can masquerade as healthy people for a significant period of time before being detected. Is it any wonder the world is feeling a little paranoid these days?

Unfortunately for you, word on the street is that you are a head case, as CFD-inflicted individuals are colloquially known. No amount of reasoning has thus far convinced your friends and acquaintances that these are baseless rumors—everyone is convinced you're crawling with CFD. Bummer.

While this quality can be bought off with Karma as per normal rules, until this happens, all of your Contacts believe you're afflicted with CFD. None will agree to meet you in the flesh for fear of being infected. If you drop in on them in person unexpectedly, they will either fight you or flee from your presence. Some may still agree to deal with you virtually, though ironically, their Loyalty works against you now. In order to do business with the character, the Contact must *fail* a Loyalty Test.

POOR SELF CONTROL

(NEW VARIANTS, BONUS: 5 OR 8 KARMA)

See p. 158, *Run Faster* for more information on this quality. New variants of this quality are as follows:

- **Attention-Seeking (5 Karma):** The spotlight is the character's natural habitat, like a fish in water—and she suffers just as much when she's not in it. The character goes out of her way to be vivacious and gain approval from others. Unless she succeeds at a Composure (3) Test, the character seeks to be the center of attention whenever possible (this may or may not include combat situations, at the gamemaster's discretion).
- **Sadistic (8 Karma):** As a child, the character bullied others and tortured small animals. As an adult, she's moved on to inflicting pain and suffering on those around her, physical and mental, whenever she has the chance. A Composure (3) Test is required to stop from inflicting some form of pain whenever the character has the reasonable chance to do so without incurring danger, even when it might interfere with her own safety, like when the team's face is trying to talk their way out of a firefight.

QUASIMODO
(BONUS: 5 KARMA)
The Sixth World is full of things that endanger normal genome expression, including Awakened dangers, environmental pollution, unpredictable mutagenics, and secret experimentation. People with this quality are the extreme result of such genetic tampering, whether hereditary or accidental. Characters with this quality suffer an unexpected genetic disorder that manifests as ugly and visceral physical deformities. The character suffers a –3 dice pool modifier on all Social Skill Tests not done via the Matrix and a +2 dice pool modifier for all Intimidation Tests. The character and gamemaster should negotiate to decide on an effect that is suitably negative. Quasimodo characters might also have developed personality quirks or aggressive behavior from years of social rejection.

SO JACKED UP
(BONUS: 10 KARMA)
The character is deep down the road of artificial mood enhancers, whether those are BTLs or chemicals. The character has basically lost the ability to regulate her own moods and must alternate between mind-benders to get cranked up or bring herself down.

While the character is encouraged to use drugs such as cram, deepweed, and so on (using the description to determine if it's an upper/stimulant or a downer), this is not strictly necessary, as the character can be assumed to be on generic upper/downer pharmaceuticals. Generic downers cause –1 Reaction and +1 Logic, while uppers cause +1 Reaction and –1 Logic.

In any case, the effect of this quality is that the character must decide whether she is "up" or "down" ahead of time. It takes thirty minutes to switch between conditions. Having the wrong mood at the wrong time can cause embarrassing social issues (for example, being on an up mood while at an oyabun's beloved son's funeral, or being down in basically any combat situation).

If the character has the wrong mood at the wrong time, they incur a –2 penalty to all Social Tests. What constitutes the wrong mood at the wrong time is largely up to the gamemaster, though characters can expect this to be "most of the time."

SUPERHUMAN PSYCHOSIS
(BONUS: 2 KARMA)
When you can run faster than a car, punch through concrete, throw fireballs with your mind, and shrug off assault cannon rounds, you might start feeling that you're more human than human. And if you're more human than human, what are *they*? Does a person that steps on ants feel bad? If not, then why should you feel anything toward these lesser beings of the old human race? So slow, so weak, so dim.

Characters with superhuman strengths, such as those granted by augmentations, or Awakened powers, can start to feel detached from the human race. They start seeing everyone else kind of like cattle. Like playing a game on the easy mode, the challenges of life seem dim and uninteresting. Characters suffering from Superhuman Psychosis seek out others like them, to belong but also to test themselves, to see how far they can go, how far they can push themselves.

Superhuman Psychosis causes a few effects. The character has absolutely no moral qualms about killing people, seeing it as his right. They won't go out of their way to kill people, but also won't hesitate to kill anyone, even going up to mass murder—they just don't value the lives of lesser beings.

In addition, the character's general lack of concern for others (and their bullets) makes them pretty formidable in combat. This quality grants an automatic +1 die bonus in melee combat. The character is also less perturbed about puny mortals flinging lead at him, and so suffers only half the penalty from incoming Suppressive Fire.

This is balanced by the fact that they have difficulty disguising their contempt for others, leading to a –2 penalty on all Etiquette and Leadership tests.

When facing opponents equivalent to Professional Rating 5 or above, however, the character gets interested. This is a true test of their skills, and they won't want to back down. The character must make a Composure (3) Test to withdraw from a fight with such opponents, regardless of the situation. If they fail the test, they must continue the combat.

Characters with Superhuman Psychosis cannot take any Code of Honor quality, as there is nobody they won't kill.

TLE-X
(BONUS: 15 KARMA)
A neurological disorder from the Sixth World, temporal lobe epilepsy with complications results from the metabolic and neurological stress of excessive cyberware implantation, especially move-by-wire implants (note, though, that move-by-wire implants are not required for TLE-x to occur, nor do they cause it automatically). In appropriately stressful situations, the character must make a Body + Willpower (4) Test or fall into epileptic seizures for (5 – hits) minutes.

The biomedical AEXD (p. 179) grants a +3 bonus to dice pools to resist the onset of TLE-x, but the disease may only be cured fully with corrective gene therapy (p. 156) or brain surgery. Even if one of the latter two options is taken, TLE-x may recur if the cyberware that caused the initial onset is not removed. Removing the quality still requires a Karma expenditure, along with the procedure.

TOUGH AND TARGETED

(BONUS: 10 KARMA)

The character is well-known as one of the biggest badasses on the streets. However, one way to make a name for yourself on the streets is to be known as the guy who killed the top dog. At least once a month or so, the character is randomly attacked by an up-and-coming rival looking to make a name for himself.

The Professional Rating of the guy who comes looking for him is equal to the character's Street Cred. Should the character with this quality be defeated by his rival, assuming he lives (the rival will be satisfied so long at the character goes into overflow damage; death is not necessary), then this quality is removed without Karma expenditure, but the character's Street Cred resets to 0 and he gains 1 point of Notoriety. Nobody likes a loser, chummer.

BORN TO KILL

THE UGLY TRUTH

This chapter provides different modules to use with the Life Modules system described on p. 65 of *Run Faster*. These Life Modules are meant to provide extra flavor for creating a gritty, life-was-fragging-with-you-so-you-fragged-it-right-back kind of character.

FORMATIVE YEARS

SLAVE

You were born an actual, true slave. You were put to work at a young age, your master taking advantage of your innocence and small body. You didn't have the full intellect of an adult, nor the dexterity, but you could do simple tasks, and you could fit where no adult could. You learned to be nimble, polite, and cunning, because if you weren't, you'd run afoul of your master's temper, or the other, older slaves' predation.

Attributes: Agility +1, Intuition +1
Qualities: Blandness
Skills: Con (Fast Talking) specialization, Etiquette +1, Perception +1, Running +1, Sneaking +1, Unarmed +1

BAG OF ORGANS

Other people whine about their parent unfairly regulating their Matrix access as a child. You, you were born in a Tamanous organ farm. Your sole purpose was to grow organs and imbedded bioware to suitable maturity, at which point they'd be cut out of you. You wouldn't be killed, of course. They'd keep you alive until they needed another one of your organs. You saw it happen to other children around you. Your mother didn't last long after she gave birth to you, her purpose done. There are nasty starts to life, and then there is what you went through.

Attributes: Body +2

Qualities : Flashbacks, Uneducated

Skills : Sneaking +2, Academic Knowledge: Biology 1, Academic Knowledge: Bioware 1, Street Knowledge: Organleggers +3

Special: You may pick 32,000 nuyen worth of bioware. Normal Essence costs apply.

CHILD OF THE SHADOWS

Your parents were both shadowrunners. Maybe they were hopeless romantics, trying to bring a child into this world, knowing better than most what it's truly like. Maybe they needed that ray of light into their lives, hope for the future, for a better life for you. In any case, they were not fools, teaching you from a young age the basics of self-reliance and survival.

Attributes: Intuition +1

Skills : Computer +1, Con +1, First Aid +1, Perception +1, Stealth skill group +2, Street Knowledge: Safehouses +3

TEEN YEARS

TEST SUBJECT

What happens when you stick augmentations in a still-developing body? Don't know, but somebody decided to find out with you! You were part of some unethical experiments to see what happens when teenager meets augmentation. They stuffed stuff in you and took some notes. You discovered, though, that some of the scientists seemed more soft-hearted, and took pity on you. You learned to use that to your advantage.

Attributes: Body +1, Logic +1

Qualities: Biocompatibility

Skills : Biotechnology +1, Cybertechnology +1, Influence skill group +1, Academic Knowledge: Metahuman Biology +1, Interest Knowledge: Transhumanist Philosophy +1

Special: 16,000 nuyen in augmentations

FACTORY CHILD WORKER

Some people really admire the Industrial Revolution. They think getting the little people to work themselves to death in factories is a really good idea. Those people think that young folk are especially great, since they're nimble, full of energy, and easily influenced. Plus, you don't need to pay them as much! What's not to like about that? Of course, from your perspective, it's all about trying to keep all your limbs intact and not dying from being overworked, but whatever—it's all the same, right?

Attributes: Agility +1, Body +1, Reaction +1

Skills : Perception +1, Engineering skill group +1, Armorer +1, Professional Knowledge: Machinist +1, Street Knowledge: Industrial Facilities +1

Special: 15,000 nuyen in cyberlimbs (p. 455, *SR5*)

FURTHER EDUCATION

Chummer, the only education you need is the "Front toward enemy" label on your claymore mine. Move along.

REAL LIFE

PIT FIGHTER

If there is one thing people have always wanted to find out, from the dawn of civilizations until the present day, it's the pressing question of "who do you think would win, a cybered-up guy or a physical adept?" You made it your business to help answer such questions. All you asked in exchange was some compensation and bragging rights.

Attributes: Body +1, Strength +1

Qualities: High Pain Tolerance 2 (14), Quick Healer (3)

Skills : Close Combat skill group +2, Cybertechnology +1, First Aid +2, Intimidation +2, Negotiation +1, Performance +1, Professional Knowledge: Pit Fighting +3, Street Knowledge: Syndicates +2

URBAN BRAWLER

The glory, the groupies, the thrill of victory—all that, for the minor cost of risking your life and pretending you're fine with it. Urban brawl is the modern answer to such archaic games as American football. A game labelled as non-lethal, but clearly stacked with enough augmented, rabid players and dangerous equipment that fatalities are a common occurrence. But hey, those are *accidents* right? Not like it's murder or anything.

Attributes: Agility +1, Body +1

Qualities: Natural Athlete (7), SINner (National) (5), Fame (Local) (4)

Skills: Athletics skill group +2, Close Combat skill group +2, Free-Fall +1, Intimidation +1, Performance +2, Professional Knowledge: Urban Brawl +3

STREET DOC

To be a doctor, you need to go to medical school, ideally a prestigious one, study your hoop off, and succeed at very difficult and thorough exams. The cost and demands of such an education are very high, to the point where nowadays, most doctors come from wealthy families or receive corporate sponsorship. By contrast, to be a *street* doc, you just need some duct tape and a bottle of cheap alcohol. The typical clientele of street docs—the SINless, gangers, footpads, and shadowrunners—come to you because you're supposedly better than a Rating 3 medkit and you won't ask questions.

Attributes: Intuition +1, Logic +1

Skills : Biotech skill group +2, Chemistry +1, Con +1, Perception +1, Influence skill group +1, Academic Knowledge: Biology +3, Academic Knowledge: Drugs +2, Street Knowledge: Street Gangs +2

SHINY: THE LATEST CHROME

She put her clipboard down with a sigh and pushed her glasses up to rub at the bridge of her nose. In a real hospital, everything was digital, bouncing medical records from one doctor's commlink to another via the central database, cross-referencing medical history with assigned medicine and potential side-effects, to ensure that the patient wasn't made worse by the help being offered. Dr. Carol Howard had no such luxuries in her clinic. When you live in the Barrens, you get used to doing it by hand.

A small chirp from her desktop, an archaic "tortoise" that she'd held on to for far too long caught her eye. Former governor Julius Strouthers had just picked up his Social Security card. Normally, this wouldn't be an event, even for a politician, but Strouthers was a dwarf, the first born in Seattle, and the Humanis Policlub was up in arms about it. The usual blather about immortal elves and dwarves living for centuries, draining the pockets of "hard-working humans" without ever pausing to think about the flipside of things. She was a second-generation ork herself, having lied about her age to get into the military (easy to do when you're SINless, plus you get a nice new SIN from Uncle Sam instead of a criminal one from the Star), and just last week she had helped a patient give birth to a fifth-generation ork in her clinic. Unlike the lucky first-generation orks like Bull, she, and those who came after, would never live to see sixty. Hell, most wouldn't see fifty.

She leaned back in her chair, her age settling in on her bones. She tried not to think about it, but the way she'd been feeling of late, she knew it wasn't just hard work. She had to face facts.

"Dr. Howard?"

A small shake of her head as she looked back to the nurse who had poked his head into her office. "Yeah, Carl?"

"You might want to head out to the lobby. We could have a situ—"

The scream from behind him cut that short. She bolted from her chair, aches and pains in her joints ignored as she tossed him a pistol, snatching a worn old FN HAR off the wall in one smooth motion. Bursting into the lobby, she surveyed the situation before lowering her barrel towards the floor. On her left were a half-dozen Crimson Crumpets, clearly in the aftermath of a corner slugfest. On her right were a similar number of Thirteenth Street Slammers, one of whom was on his knees, the stump where his right hand used to be bleeding out onto her floor. One of the Slammers was facing the rest of her gang, spurs deployed and dripping.

"Neutral means neutral, you slots! You don't fight here! You copy my paste?"

"But Riot, they—"

"I don't give a frag! You in the Doc's place, you *neutral*! Copy, or do I gotta teach you like Stiggy?"

Glancing at the bleeding ganger, the other shook his head as he backed up. "I copy."

Dr. Howard nodded at Carl, who moved in to check on Stiggy. "Good to see one of you slots remembers the rules. That means the Slammers go first. Crumpets, you go next." A pause, to let the two react, before motioning the one gillette over, adding, "You come with me. Riot, right?" When the teen nodded, Dr. Howard draped an arm around her shoulder, rifle dangling from her other hand. "We should probably talk about upgrades."

Riot frowned, retracting her spurs. "I'm good, Doc. The chrome's fresh."

"Not talking about the hardware. I'm talking software. Tell me, you ever heard of a thing called JackPoint?"

The door closed behind the pair as they moved into the back hall, leaving Carl to deal with the whining for now.

UNLEASHING A BETTER YOU

POSTED BY: NEPHRINE

● Hey Nephrine? I wanted to say thanks again for taking this up on such short notice.
● Butch

● No big thing, Butch, we've been needing to review some of the new toys for a while, but you did such a good job the last time, why did you need me for this one?
● Nephrine

● That was seven years ago. Bull being around makes it easy to forget, but the rest of us tuskers aren't quite so lucky. I wasn't exactly a spring chicken then, and these days—well, let's just say that it takes a lot longer to get out of bed.
● Butch

● And the new kid?
● Nephrine

● Riot? Human. On the one hand, she'll be around for a while (if she doesn't get her ass shot off due to that damn code of hers), but on the other, she needs the upgrades. This is a primer for her and a bit of a tour of the site as well.
● Butch

● Can do. And Butch?
● Nephrine

● Yeah?
● Butch

● If you need anything, you let me know, all right?
● Nephrine

● Will do.
● Butch

We're moving toward 2078, which means it'll soon be time for all the new tech to start rolling out. Ad campaigns are being fired up, scientists are busy in the lab, and management's putting unrealistic expectations on everyone as they buck for promotion. This means it's a prime time for shadowruns as we try to get our grubby mitts on the new tech before anyone else does, scuttle new designs before they hit the street, and oh, the kidnapping ... pardon ... involuntary re-employments, around every corner. It's like Christmas, only with more bullets.

● Bullets for Christmas is an idea I fully support.
● Stone

● All jokes aside, this one's been badly needed for a while. We've been so focused on CFD that we've been overlooking the advances in other fields. The Nano-pocalypse changed how we approach many upgrades for the Metahuman body, and corporations are still adjusting things on the fly as new methodologies are discovered to replace the old. It's easy to get distracted and miss the new rollouts.
● Sunshine

● Cyberware's so boring and played out! Can't we just skip ahead to Evo?
● Plan 9

● Patience, grasshopper. It's easy to overlook chrome when bioware's the current trend, and I'm certainly itching to see where Universal Omnitech's new gene mods are going, but you need to look at everything to see the entire picture. At the end of the day, cyberware is capable of doing things that no metahuman body can replicate, and that means it's always interesting.
● The Smiling Bandit

CYBER-HISTORY

Before we can look into the future, we should really look into the past. Despite what the advertisers would have you believe, cyberware isn't ancient tech, nor is it the greatest thing of the twenty-first century. In one form or another, the core concept's been around for centuries, and even the basic form that you'd recognize as true cyber's been in use for nearly a century. Remember, we have evidence of cavemen trying their hand at brain surgery, combining our curiosity and amazing metahuman durability with our need to deal with substandard situations, be it getting that pain out of your head, filing your teeth into points for better biting ability, or figuring out how to put wood and ivory into your mouth when you've outlived your teeth but still need to eat.

- ● That durability is our coolest super-power, by the way. All kinds of other animals are done for when they break a limb or get holes poked in them, let alone have half their body yanked off. Metahumanity's too stubborn to die and just keeps chugging along. Not as cool as gamma-strength or freeze vision, but hey, a power's a power.
- ● Slamm-0!

- ● That's … quite the simplification. I could provide many counter-examples when I have time, but now's not then.
- ● KAM

The first attempts at cyberware of some type were probably the filed teeth mentioned above, followed by some caveman tying blades to the back of his hands to create some kind of clawed glove. False teeth, of course, were right behind, and from there we hit a wall for a few thousand years. We learned how to pull things out before we learned how to put them in, with bad teeth being the first, then headaches and appendectomies following soon behind. Lopping off gangrenous limbs was a big hurdle, putting the risk of bleeding-out against the slow torturous death of infection, but we largely got past that as well. By the start of civilization, we had crutches and primitive artificial hands and feet. They didn't *do* anything, but they covered up the stump and allowed you some basic functions, like walking or holding a shield.

- ● Yarrr, shiver me timbers! There be a fine tradition of hook hands in me family tree.
- ● Kane

- ● Wait. I thought your dad was an accountant?
- ● /dev/grrl

- ● Hey! Don't undercut my gimmick in public!
- ● Kane

The first time the medical field moved past stone, bone, and glass to something that we'd recognize today as actual cyberware was the Jarvik-7 artificial heart, first implanted into a human patient in 1982. Made of plastic, it was battery-operated and hammered away for nearly four months. The patient, Barney Clark of Seattle,

was himself a dentist and a volunteer, but the process wasn't a smashing success, with many side effects and bleeding, with him asking to be allowed to die more than once before his body finally gave up the fight.

- ● There are earlier hearts, such as Vladimir Demikhov in 1937, but they'd all been implanted into animals. It should be further noted that patients didn't live very long after the procedure, either. There's discussion about the level of failure that these earlier machines might have had, comparing pure issues with post-operative infection and autoimmune rejection with more modern and holistic methodologies and the still-developing field of Essence research.
- ● The Smiling Bandit

While most of this pre-cyber tech was clunky and primitive, it kept improving. By the turn of the last century, there started to be talk of what to do when it finally advanced far enough that someone with an augmentation would be superior to a native, unmodified person. Laughable to most, certain figures paid attention to it, and the first true test of this came in the form of an Amazonian runner by the name of Santino Corbez. Corbez hadn't even seen his first year of life before his legs were amputated, but he grew up determined to not let it get in the way of his dreams. He pushed himself into the life of an athlete, focused on running. He'd been through several forms of ever-improving artificial legs before settling into carbon-fiber running blades produced by Shiawase corp. In 2005, only a year after having moved from rugby to track, he was competing with able-bodied athletes and setting world records for the disabled. These running blades, a flexible-foot design based on a cheetah, were of high enough quality that, when combined with his natural abilities, gave rise to accusations of unfairness, that in some way this man with no feet was being given an unfair advantage in a footrace. He moved quickly up the world competitive charts, picking up gold medals in Paralympics while trying to compete in the full Olympics. After careful consideration, he was allowed to compete, where he wasn't able to keep pace with able-bodied runners at the very highest level of training, but still performed so well that massive consideration about the future of augmentations and sports had to be taken into account

- ● Corbez's career ended soon after. Records are hard to track down, thanks to the Crash and the more important events that had begun when magic returned, but he wound up killing his sister three years after his Olympic debut. The psychological reports that came from this investigation have been referenced in several later talks on cyberpsychosis, but there are many aspects of this case that undercut those arguments. His rise and fall had an effect on the entire sports world.
- ● The Smiling Bandit

In the modern era, the first true cyberlimb was installed by Dr. Harold Darkfeather in 2019, in Scotland, then an area of the world known for advanced scientific pursuit. Lenora Bartoli, a violinist of some talent, had lost her left hand in a car accident, which would have ended her career at any point in the past. This time, however, the Transys Corporation stepped in and, after a successful surgery, was the focus of both the adulation and the scorn of those looking toward a future where man and machine were melded together. Miss Bartoli underwent a grueling year of training and adapting to the new limb, but on the one-year anniversary of her accident, she performed at Carnegie Hall to a sold-out audience. She was never the world's top talent, but her unique feature of playing with a cybernetic limb kept her famous for years before such upgrades were commonplace enough that she generally vanished from the public eye.

⊘ And we still haven't talked about all the issues she had with bio-rejection and how much Transys invested into her to ensure everything was perfectly fine whenever she was on camera. Once she wasn't valuable to them, of course, the extra treatments stopped. She slowly went mad, telling some of her friends that she was afraid of "it" and how she'd sometimes wake up to find it trying to squeeze the life out of her until she took control over it.
⊘ Baka Dabora

⊘ You still haven't shown us any evidence of this, you know.
⊘ Sunshine

⊘ Blame the Crashes! I've seen notes that when her body was found in her house, the hand had been blown apart by a pistol while she'd been stabbed dozens of times by the knife found in the remains of her artificial limb. Saying that she'd overdosed on sleeping pills and alcohol was all just a cover-up for her actual death. Poor thing couldn't handle being improved.
⊘ Plan 9

CYBERSPORTS

Different sports have differing rules for what is, and isn't, allowed in terms of augmentations. Here's a few!

Baseball: Allowed some upgrades in 2032 but has a byzantine system on how much is too much that's modified by quality of implant as well as type. Reflexes, muscles, and eye upgrades are the primary augmentations allowed. Surprisingly, while many older records have fallen with the new wave of tech coming into the game, several remain. The general consensus is that while the quality of augmentation has improved, baseball's fall from being the primary game of the UCAS has taken the highest caliber of player into other fields. Then there's the fact that augmentations on hitters tend to be balanced by augmentations in pitchers, keeping the playing field somewhat level.

Basketball: Anything that modifies a player's height or reach is right out, as are pure cyberlimbs, but improved reflexes and general, low-level muscle augmentation are allowable. Cybernetic "Smartball" tech was grudgingly allowed into the game in 2047, but it was a bitter fight that kept many more advances out for nearly a decade.

Football: Probably no classic sport has adapted to augmentation as much as football. By 2025, the race was on, and the 2028 season was delayed by two months while new fields were constructed to take the new upgrades into account. (In 2027, there were 227 serious injuries and 4 deaths, showing how much adapting had to be done.) The field was again upgraded in 2053, and is now fully two hundred meters long and eighty meters wide. A first-down requires a twenty-five-meter advance, while the ball weighs three kilos. The UCAS and CAS play head-to-head, but the CAS league still uses yards, not meters, resulting in some problems. After the 2052 season, the NFL went ahead and allowed fully cybernetic limbs, meaning that the only things not allowed were actual weapons; anything less was good to go, and no limits on the number of implants were ever in place, resulting in players with more chrome than skin. Needless to say, the old records are long dead.

Soccer: The world's top sport remains that last port of call for unaugmented players, banning virtually all cyberware. The commonality of datajacks and cybereyes has given some wiggle room, but ocular improvements or active wireless communication on the field is outlawed, as are all muscle or reflexive improvement. The fact that a shoeless player from a dirt-poor country could one day stand tall at the World Cup without hundreds of thousands of nuyen worth of upgrades is a powerful driving factor in the game's standing as the most popular worldwide.

Urban Brawl: The only sport to go deeper into cybernetics than football, urban brawl has no problem with cyber-weapons or limb replacements, and the more exotic, the better. Urban brawl remains the world's number two sport in terms of popularity, behind soccer in most countries.

» I'm not sure if that's Plan 9 or Plan 10, but either way, Baka, you probably shouldn't be on the same page as them.
» Kay St. Irregular

2024 brought simsense to the general populace, with the horrors of BTL addiction right behind. 2025 saw the first augmented athlete (Mario Sanchez of the Philadelphia Eagles, for those playing Matrix Trivia), and 2026 was when cyberterminals were created, giving us our first deckers and a new interface. Cyberware is more than pop-out blades and enhanced skeletons, after all. Headware memory became a thing, cybereyes and datajacks slowly turned into standard-issue in first-world countries, and Ares made a killing with the first Ares Predator taking advantage of their Picus Smartgun System. By 2050, cyberware was all but required for anyone wanting a combat edge on the streets and was present in many elite corporate forces, if still beyond the reach of footsloggers in corporate forces, national militaries, or police forces. Lone Star briefly flirted with a requirement that all officers would have to be upgraded with a smartgun system and a radio for communication, but the legal battles were costly and ongoing cyberpsychosis incidents helped get the idea shelved.

» As happy as we were about that, the officers were even happier. Oh, sure, you still get a few legbreakers in the shadier departments that are chromed to the gills on impounded cyber, but most of them are well aware of the downsides to getting wires plugged into your head. Mind you, there's also been opposition to badge-cams for decades, so old-fashioned tech-hate is present.
» Bull

» Knight Errant is fairly close on both, but the high-threat response teams break both molds. KE doesn't have the reputation for being dirty like the Star, but your basic pawn's still uncomfortable with Big Brother watching everything. I chalk it up to basic infantry mentality; if the brass is around, your ass'd better be doing something. With no commander watching every move, they can slack off a bit, talk to one another, smoke ... you know, normal human stuff.
» Hard Exit

» For a hard contrast, Renraku's Neo-Police require badge cameras on every officer, left on as soon as they're on the clock and not turned off until they finish their shift. They keep their uniforms spotless, right down to the mandatory white gloves, and even the meter maids have drone back-up and advanced commlink support.
» Baka Dabora

» I hear that they're pretty awful in a scrap. Too much polish, not enough spit. True?
» 2XL

- Compared to Lone Star, let alone KE, they're under-armored and under-gunned, true, but the caliber of crook is different here.
- Baka Dabora

- So, who's up for a trip to Osaka?
- 2XL

By the late '50s, chrome's crown started to lose luster, and the '60s saw biotech get more and more attention. Biotech was starting to get elbowed aside by nanotech until the second Crash and the Nano-pocalypse. Nanites are further hampered by the terrible PR and rumor offering in the wake of the CFD saga, leaving the throne open again. Bioware has been sitting there for a while, but the Wireless Matrix Initiative and widespread wireless connectivity has made it possible that maybe, just maybe, the Chrome King will once again take his throne. Yeah, I know you slots hate it, and if I never hear one of you grouse about "Why does my smuggling compartment even have an option to broadcast its existence to everybody within ten meters?!" again, it'll be a miracle.

- Why does my smuggling compartment even have an option to broadcast its existence to everybody within ten meters?
- Slamm-0!

- Goddamit.
- Nephrine

- Hang on. Fred doesn't *have* a smuggling compartment.
- Bull

- Well, technically …
- Netcat

- Yeah, but everyone has *that* one.
- Slamm-0!

Today, cyberware generally comes in two flavors. There's the basics, like cybereyes (far and away the most common 'ware of the day), skilljacks, and datajacks in the tech crowd (but being phased out). Those are all wireless-enabled and improved by modern technology, and they interface well with the newer stuff rolling out.

And then you have the other class: people who need to exceed the design parameters of the metahuman body.

- Now we're talkin'!
- Riot

Raw chrome like servomotors instead of muscles, bulletproof skulls, radar, built-in guns … these are things that you just can't replicate with bioware. The thought

behind this stuff is that Human 2.0 is nice and all, but even the most bio-augmented secretary doesn't handle being hit by a walking refrigerator very well.

- I'll have you know that some appreciate that kind of impact on a regular basis. Evo hips are marvelous this year!
- Plan 9

- Wait. I thought you were back to being a guy?
- Turbo Bunny

- And? Besides, you should give it a spin sometime! Not like it'd matter to Gateskeeper anyway, right?
- Plan 9

- /dev/'s been talking again, hasn't she?
- Turbo Bunny

Shadowrunners generally fit into that second mold, with a touch of the first. As cyberware fell out of favor, new buildings scrapped plans for cyberware scanners in the late '60s, and we're seeing a small revival in hidden chrome now as well. Synthskin's been getting improved for decades, mostly thanks to work on the assorted humanoid drones, and that progress has been shared with cyberlimbs. There's also pushback against the wireless world, with more stealth gear being constructed right as security teams have started to rely on simple radio scans and hot broadcasts to track down infiltrators. Obviously, most of us keep our wireless turned off, so we're able to get by where, ten or fifteen years ago, they'd catch us with cyberware scanners.

- While this is true, there are, like, a googol of things that wireless can do for you. Don't overlook your tools!
- /dev/grrl

WHY SHOULD I GO CHROME?

A fair question since, as discussed, bioware is nearly as effective but far less invasive and, furthermore, the path of augmentation invariably leads to the loss of one's sense of self, often crossing into the threshold of true psychosis. It's one thing to add a datajack for work or pick up an improved lung capacity for lakeshore dwellers, but to just go out and lop off a perfectly-functional arm to add a hunk of metal to it? There are those who would argue that cyberpsychosis doesn't actually exist and that those who are victimized by the condition were wired wrong to begin with. Rational people just don't act like that.

- Here we go again.
- Hard Exit

- The path of augmentation is unnatural. The world recoils from those who walk it.
- Man-of-Many-Names

- An interesting observation, but one that overlooks the cyber-mage. True, it's more of a burnout's path than a road of higher magical mysteries, but it's the newest school of magical theory and, as such, has the most open potential.
- Elijah

- Or it's an evolutionary dead-end with deluded proponents.
- Winterhawk

- Magical stuff is two doors down, crew. Stick to cyber.
- Glitch

Of course, many people in our line of work aren't exactly rational to begin with. As more and more focus falls on the biological and cutting-edge genetech, a prevailing opinion is that cyberware is old hat, falling behind the tech curve and therefore is useless. Nothing could be further from the truth, but I'm not about to go out there and correct those mis-opinions; quite frankly, I like being underestimated, and I know I'm not the only one. Everything in this life is about finding an edge, and for many of us, that edge is made out of chrome. Let's take a look at three reasons why that is.

THE PRICE IS RIGHT

First and foremost in the minds of many is affordability. Cybernetics are cheaper than their bioware counterparts, sometimes by an order of magnitude, and when you only have so much in the way of funds, you look for the best bang for the buck. Time after time, that's cybernetics. There's been a bit of a shake-up in pricing over the past few years, due to the scrambling of assorted nanite-based medical procedures, with some old techniques having been dusted off, while new approaches to current problems did their best to find a work-around. As these pathways are discovered, prices will likely drop.

- Or the corps will pocket the difference in the name of Holy Profit.
- Chainbreaker

TRIED AND TESTED

The next factor in their favor is reliability. Cybernetics date to the previous century and are nearing a hundred years of use. By and large, we found the bugs and hammered them out decades ago. Sure, the newer tech still needs some tweaking here and there, but for the most part, we've got this. When you get cybereyes or a datajack, you know exactly what you're getting. In a world filled with distrust, that's a big deal.

- Of course, there's always the risk of picking up a passenger.
- Butch

- Pfft. Alone time is overrated. You'd be surprised how nice it is to have someone to talk to. It's like having a roommate.
- Plan 9

- The roommate stories I could tell you…
- Stone

An overlooked aspect of this, combined with the low cost, is the relatively easy path you have toward repairing cybernetics. Some welding here, a new plate there, and you're as good as new, or at least good enough for now. Beyond that is the simple truth of material science: flesh is easier to destroy than metal or most plastics. Cybernetic parts take a beating.

METAL TRUMPS FLESH

A simple fact is that machines can do things that the metahuman body just can't do. They can be faster, stronger, and vastly more damage-resistant, just for starters. The production of high energy output, interacting with radio broadcasts, interfacing with the Matrix … these are all things that bioware simply cannot do. Cyberware, and only cyberware, is your bridge into this world beyond metahuman capabilities. Dabble in the bio-genetic all you want, you will *never* find anything akin to skillsofts.

- Actually, there's some fascinating work going on in Aztlan just now with RNA retroviruses. Just a heads-up.
- The Smiling Bandit

- They're following up on that research?! Dammit, Roxborough! You know better than that!
- KAM

SOUNDS TOO GOOD TO BE TRUE. WHAT'S THE CATCH?

There's always a catch, and if you're going to survive life in the shadows, you'd better learn that real quick. There are, of course, some downsides to the technology, and it would be rude of me to not lay all those options out there. So, let's have a look.

INVASIVENESS

Cyberware is hard on the body. Metahumans simply aren't meant to have metal grafted to flesh, and only modern medical science allows us to overcome that natural rejection. Cyber-users are often loaded with any number of anti-rejection drugs and immune-suppressants, trying to keep the body from realizing what you've done to it. New parts always itch, skin stays red and chafed until callus builds up, and there's this general, primal feeling that Something Is Not Right that some people simply can't shake. There's not a cybertechnician in the field for a year or more who doesn't know what it's like to get a call after a patient scratched out their new cybereyes, pulled off a cyberlimb, or dug at a new datajack with a fork while screaming. You don't hear those reports on the news of course—the Info-Tainment Complex can't let people know that there's pushback against a new product line—but maybe one person in twenty simply can't handle cybernetics and react badly. Some have a guttural fear and loathing from a young age while others have no idea about the unsettling feeling in their gut until they wake up with cold metal where warm flesh should be and something inside snaps.

- If you're in a well-stocked clinic or hospital, bio-monitors will pick up on this kind of anxiety and medical teams will be dispatched quickly. If you're not and you yank out something vital while having a panic attack, well, good luck.
- Butch

- Seriously? Everyone I know embraces upgrades! I mean, who doesn't get new eyes for their sixteenth birthday, right?
- /dev/grrl

- Used to date a chick whose son got braces one afternoon and, after everyone was asleep, he grabbed his dad's toolbox and pulled his new gift apart with pliers. It was all tears and blood, but they figured out his problem long before he could get lined up for augmentations for football. That would have been a damn shame. Weirdly, he's a nurse these days.
- Stone

- The spirit rebels against such injustice, and those who react violently against these degradations should be applauded for their empathetic natures, not seen as unfortunate freaks. They are the wisest of us, and know that a pure body is essential to keeping a pure spirit. Look to these wise ones as future magicians.
- Axis Mundi

- Your body can handle some minor upgrades with no noticeable loss of the Talent, but you always have to wonder if this next piece is going to be the one that starts you on the burnout's path. Trying to balance the edge it gives you against the possible cost is a delicate operation. Fortunately, some of us are good at it.
- Haze

AVAILABILITY

While money is the great equalizer, there's also the simple matter of getting what you want. Cutting-edge tech tends to stay in corporate hands, while the options available in most shadowclinics are sub-standard at best (sorry Butch!). It's a long waiting list to get into a beta clinic of any repute, and even simple alpha-level facilities are under heavy corporate control. This means that if you're, say, a dwarf in an Asian country, a mixed-race in Aztlan, or an ork pretty much anywhere, you're going to find yourself looking at a wall filled with appointment books that have no openings, a surprising surcharge, or being told that your insurance doesn't cover "optional services." If you ever wonder why so many street samurai get implants from the Yakuza, it's because they just don't have the networking skills to find better options.

- There's also the matter of legality. Retractable spurs are illegal in pretty much every country in the world.
- Kay St. Irregular

- But they're so wiz!
- Riot

If you plan on getting regular updates, it's vital that you befriend a cyberdoc, or someone who knows a cyberdoc, and that you keep up that friendship. There are only ten delta-grade facilities in North America right now, each with a waiting list a kilometer long if you're not a citizen of its parent corporation. Two of these facilities claim to be independent operators, but one's long-rumored to be owned by a Japanacorp (exactly who changes with the rumor-monger, of course), and the other was recently outed as an Aztechnology operation.

- Executive Body Enhancements was the Azzie hidden brand, for those who missed the news for a few months. Horizon intrusions had managed to ferret that out, but they hadn't found a way to use it yet when the technomancer blowback happened. Part of the data the technomancers were tossing around included that particular nugget, but it was obviously overshadowed.
- Sunshine

As a general rule, cybernetic weapons are outlawed everywhere but can be licensed in those rare countries that allow bloodsports. Military-grade augmentations, such as wired reflexes, or security-grade, such as smartgun links, are more available depending on the nation, while common 'ware is legal almost everywhere. A few smaller NAN tribes forbid any augmentation, but those laws are more to protect the holistic purity of their own people; augmented visitors will simply be encouraged to leave as soon as possible. As always, there are dozens of exceptions, so check your local shark to be sure.

CYBERPSYCHOSIS

It's been touched on before, but I want to stress it again: Cyberware may well make you insane. This is pretty well-established science at this point, save a few industry-aligned holdouts and conspiracy types, but the metahuman mind just doesn't adapt well to lacing your body with wires and chrome. There's always a risk that you'll mentally reject the new parts of you and then your mind will have to do some internal gymnastics to arrive at a point where you can endure. In some people, the anxiety triggers phobic reactions where none had previously existed, following fairly traditional lines. (Heights and clowns are the most common of these phobias, but sometimes they get obscure, like not being able to touch carpet.) In others, a dissociative disorder is found, where someone thinks of their cybernetic parts as "other" in some way, or even that they themselves have become more machine than man. OCD-like responses are extremely common, with heavily augmented individuals often having to create a mental code to follow, since morality no longer seems to control their urges. Once you're more machine than man, there's just no going back.

- Cyberpsychosis is a general term for a broad array of mental disorders that are brought on by, or exacerbated by, augmentations. These run the gamut of normal mental disorders but were rarely present pre-op and never as badly as they become post-op. Your better facilities will have psychologists on hand to help you deal with these situations. Shadow clinics tend to take your money and kick you out to fend for yourself as best you can.
- Butch

- I'm working on a theory about how the disruptions that cybernetics cause in one's aura are not entirely unlike astral foveae. It's still in the early stages as I research these matters in the PCC, but it's interesting.
- Elijah

- I'm curious to see how your hypothesis will hold up when you encounter mages with astral forms that include their cyber-augmentations clearly present and bonded with their spirit-self.
- Haze

- Can the magical mumbo-jumbo. The sensation of "wrongness" that comes from cybernetics is based on the variance between digital and biological neural data transmission states. Your brain knows the difference and reacts uncomfortably. It's pure science. We've been over this.
- Butch

- And we'll probably go over it again in ten more years.
- Jimmy No

A WORD ABOUT QUALITY

My final notation before diving into the section you all want to see is about quality. What most of us are used to is standard-grade cyberware—simple, off-the-shelf upgrades that are mass-produced and mass-marketed. When many of us started out, there was also "used," or to use modern terminology, "omega-class" cyberware. (Why omega? Because it's the end of the line.) The terminology change isn't just marketingspeak, though that's a big slice of it. Instead, omega cyberware is often first-generation, just cheaply made and a knockoff of more popular 'ware. The Azzies are notorious for this kind of shoddy workmanship, but they're hardly the only ones; be sure that your cyberdoc is reasonably trustworthy and, if possible, have a tech-oriented runner on your team who can look things over and make certain that you're getting what you're supposed to get.

- Wuxing's early attempts at a cyber-division produced some truly awful work, for instance.
- Sticks

- Still toeing the company line, eh Sticks? Omega-grade's also found in new tech being tried out by the larger megas, field-testing things in SINless people. Once the prototypical bugs are worked out, the improved model goes into production.
- Bull

- Renraku had issues in their African factories for a time. They managed to smooth that out after a while.
- Slamm-0!

- The omega work was mostly offloaded to Chinese warlords. Waste not, want not.
- Red Anya

Alpha quality is the best that most of us will ever see. Designer labels, personalized trim, or cybereyes that can almost pass for the real thing—all of this falls under the alpha category. Doctors at alpha clinics are excellent, and they almost always have a staff psychologist on hand to ensure that your mind integrates the new 'ware as well as your body does. This grade of cyber includes the name brands that everyone's after, and represents the premium line for a corporation. Of course, it also carries a premium price, but that's part of the appeal.

- Knock-offs of premium lines, like "Opple" or "Spunrad," are usually Azzie make, of course. The best of these look like the real deal, but cost what a standard augmentation would. Of course, they're just standard under a fancy label, so you're not getting much extra.
- Bull

- There are street docs who'll charge you for alphaware and slip you standard instead. I've said it before, I'll say it again: Having a good relationship with a street doc you trust is critical to a successful shadowrunning career
- Butch

- Hey, Netcat, sweetie? Make sure Butch is on our Holiday Card list, okay? Love you!
- Slamm-0!

Beta quality's better than most of us will ever see, but I know a lot of you save up your cash and favors for a shot at the stuff. Chiba-quality eyes that look entirely meta-human, Spinrad "Fleshtastic" limbs that sweat, or math processors straight out of Essen, this level is world-famous. There aren't many beta clinics out there, and they all require you to know someone to get in. Seattle has three, putting it in some rarified air. Most corporations only keep a handful in a nation, requiring appointments and travel to enjoy the facilities. This is medical tech at its finest, and when you're receiving it, it often feels more like a trip to a resort than a night at the hospital.

- Hang on. Three? Executive Body Enhancements and Nightengale's Body Parts, sure, but where's the other? Butch, you sly old dog, did you earn a new rating when we weren't looking?
- Slamm-0!

- Hah. I'd be lucky to earn alpha-class recognition. We have the tools and we have the talent, but the facilities are a bit lacking. No, the third's on top of the ACHE. It would have been a delta-class facility if it weren't for Deus. As it stands, I don't know how anyone can go there without a non-stop panic attack.
- Butch

- Wait. What happened to the Humana Hospital?
- Sounder

- Knight Errant finally busted them. Damn shame. They did great work.
- Clockwork

Lastly are the delta facilities. Unlike the betas, these aren't world-famous, largely because the megacorps don't want you to know that they exist. They're famous for handling CEOs and senior executives personally, but they also keep up the blackest of black-ops teams and conduct research that is … not for public consumption.

- Read: Cybermancy.
- Hannibelle

OPTIONAL RULE: OMEGA-GRADE CYBERWARE

As an optional rule, a gamemaster may allow a player to take some kind of drawback from their used cyberware instead of 1.2 times the normal Essence cost. While there are no hard and fast rules for this, the greater the savings in Essence, the worse the flaw should be. Examples might include a smartgun link that won't fire at people flagged as Ares employees; a cyberleg with a bad knee, lowering the character's run speed multiplier by one; or wired reflexes without an off switch, resulting in a life where they strike out against perceived threats in everyday life with possibly tragic consequences. As always, the gamemaster has final say.

There are fewer than twenty of them in existence, roughly. Rumors put the number as high as thirty or as low as four, depending on your criteria and who you trust, and not every megacorporation has one under their control. The older corps do of course, but Horizon doesn't and is hungry for one, while Wuxing has no interest in the investment at this time. A couple of the AA-rated megacorps may have facilities of this quality, with Proteus, Spinrad, and Universal Omnitech the most likely, but good luck getting them to confirm it. In North America, the Renraku Arcology would have had one, Ares has one in Detroit, and possibly one in Quebec, NeoNET has one in Boston, and DocWagon is in the process of building one in Atlanta. Aztechnology has one down in Tenochitlan, while it's rumored that MCT wants to build one in Chicago of all places.

- Horizon wants to build one in LA, but it lacks the knowledge base. They're hot for extraction work right now.
- Cosmo

- Saeder-Krupp has one in Essen of course, while the Japanacorps each have one in their HQ city. Evo has one in Vladivostok and a second in St. Petersburg. Monobe and Yakashima each had one, despite being double-A, but they were hit hard during the Ghost Decade and couldn't keep them up.
- Baka Dabora

- No one's mentioning Zion Amalgamated in Lalibela, I see.
- Icarus

- That's because everything about ZA is a rumor, nothing more. Not like anyone can get into the Ethiomalian Territories to check.
- Am-Mut

- Abba Kedus would disagree with you. I'll send you my price list.
- Icarus

And that brings us to the gamma grade. Long story short, it doesn't exist. Somewhat longer story, there's a whole lot of nuyen being invested to change that fact. You get some Matrix rumors that suggest that one megacorp or the other has unlocked the mysteries of gammaware, but as of yet, nothing's been proven. If it ever gets figured out, it'll be the blackest of tech for a while, while the corp that manages it reaps the rewards and deals with the explosion of raids that'll follow. Being the lone holder of the world's most exclusive technology is an opportunity and a burden. Good luck with that!

- I got a thousand nuyen that says Evo gets there first. Any takers?
- Plan 9

- I love you, Planners, but NeoNET has this one in the bag. You're on.
- /dev/grrl

- Hey, if you two'll give me ten-to-one odds for the longshot, I'll step up with Aztechnology.
- Marcos

- Five to one. They've had delta for too long. Glitch? You want in? I'll give you twenty-to-one on Ares!
- Plan 9

- I didn't get where I am by taking stupid bets, Plan 9. Pass.
- Glitch

- So, what are the odds on anyone else?
- Kane

- Call it twenty-to-one? Nobody else is even close.
- /dev/grrl

- Count me in. For Zion Amalgamated.
- Am-Mut

- Wise investment.
- Icarus

COSMETIC CYBERWARE

In an ideal world, this category would have almost entirely gone extinct, but the advantages of cybernetics, primarily cost, keep these mods in circulation well past their actual use-by date. Oh sure, there are some aspects that bioware can't mimic, like fiber-optic hair or LED screens, but breast implants date to the previous century and are filled with health risks. Ah well, not my place to moralize and at any rate, chrome has a sort of retro-cachet that keeps it hopping in the underground club scene. I'd blame Maria Mercurial, but she has enough on her plate these days. Let's have a look at some catalogue classics.

CASEMOD

Originally intended for cyberlimbs, casemodding has spread to most other types of cyberware. From engraved spurs to glowing datajacks to mirror-polished dermal plating, it's all about asserting your individuality to be just like everybody else. The possibilities are virtually endless, and many outfitters, like NeoNET's Unique line, allow you to design your own look from their pre-engineered menu before you get it installed. You have to love monetized corporate nano-printers!

The large variety of casemod possibilities falls fully under the purview of "gamemaster's call" in terms of pricing and availability, as well as exactly what cyber can be so modified, ranging from +0 Availability and fifty nuyen added to the price to +4 Availability and ten thousand additional nuyen for truly outrageous mods. There's no mechanical benefit, but, really, can you put a price on style, chummer? If the casemod is truly outrageous, the gamemaster may assign the player the Distinctive Style quality (p. 80, SR5) without giving the player any bonus Karma.

COSMETIC SURGERY

Bigger lips? Thinner lips? Butt implants? Tummy tuck? You want it, we got it! Modern technology allows for any ugly duckling to become a beautiful swan, and the media will pound that into your skull until you submit. Conform, you drone!

As with casemods, there is a vast selection of cosmetic surgery options, each a simple clinic appointment away. The more popular the trend, the more expensive the surgery, rather than the level of invasiveness. This is a gamemaster's call in terms of pricing, ranging from a hundred nuyen for minor work, like mole removal, to ten thousand nuyen for rib removal or facial reconstruction.

BREAST IMPLANTS

Old-fashioned gelpacks surgically inserted remain in high demand, even today. Materials used are generally safe (unless they burst), recovery times are brief, and prices are low low low. Bodyshops all across the world make a killing off these things. Sold singly, but you probably want a pair.

Breast Implants 2.0: For those who change their looks as often as they change their underwear, modern science has stepped up and given us new breast-tech, allowing the owner to adjust to whatever size they want. Hidden gel reserves and reflexive synthskin allow for any size from A to double-D, changeable with a simple wireless command. Ta-da!

Wireless Bonus: The user may change the size of their implants as a Free Action, instead of a Simple Action.

- It should be pointed out that this allows for a wide range of disguises for infiltration purposes.
- Hard Exit

CYBER GENITALIA

Available for both male and female parts, cyber genitals might well be considered a cyberlimb, but doing so opens the door for a lot of uncomfortable discussions. Available in a wide variety of colors, textures, and sizes, cybergenitals have almost entirely been phased out by modern biotech and genetic treatments. Still, there are those who enjoy the mechanical benefits that only battery-operated devices can bring, and to them I say thank you.

- You won't find more loving care spent on cybernetic neuro-sensory receivers anywhere.
- Plan 9

- Some people take it too far. I mean, endurance is one thing, but nobody wants a jackhammer near their tenderbits.
- Kat o' Nine Tales

- I could tell you about a guy I know named Mr. Porcupine, but you can probably connect the dots on this one.
- Stone

FIBER-OPTIC HAIR

The user's original scalp hair (or facial hair) is removed and replaced with artificial hair composed of fiberoptic cabling. This hair is not only available in every imaginable color but is programmable, allowing for patterns, designs, or scrolling effects that nature could never manage. From sparkling stars in a nightscape of black to an explosion of neon colors to a scrolling advert for your favorite hair salon, the only real limit is one's imagination. Cost is based on length (per ten centimeters, to a maximum of 1 meter in length).

Wireless Bonus: The user may download new color patterns and install them as a Simple Action.

- The "Ooooh Girl Who Did Your Hair?" salon and spa in Tacoma does great work.
- Slamm-0!

LED TATTOOS

With the Nano-pocalypse eradicating many nano-tatts, and more importantly the trust that the populace at large held in them, LED tattoos have staged a surprising comeback. A simple LED display is implanted under the skin, bright enough to be seen through the dermal layer when active, vanishing from sight when inactive. Available in three general sizes—small (placed on a wrist, ankle, or behind an ear), medium (covering much of a forearm or upper arm, the small of the back, or over the heart), or large (covering most of the back or the scalp)— LED tattoos combine the showcasing of one's interests and expression of personality with the ability to remove or change those that are no longer quite so definitive. The ability to deactivate them further allows for someone to switch between club mode, where they fly their freak flag, and work mode, where they blend in with sedate corporate culture. It should be noted that there is some division between those with "real" tattoos, and "light posers" who are unwilling to get proper ink done.

Wireless Bonus: The user may download new color patterns as a Simple Action.

METATYPE REDUCTION

More a series of treatments and surgeries than a single modification, metatype reduction is generally aimed at goblinoids, a.k.a. "the ugly ones," rather than surgically rebuilding an elf as a human or something. Jawlines are shattered and rebuilt with tusk removal, body hair is lasered off for good, bone deposits and hard plates cut away, and even some delicate work with sweat glands and body oil production to reduce their output and make them more friendly to human noses. Mostly seen in Japanacorps, but there's a cultural shame-spiral that drives even western goblinoids to the procedure.

Orks who undergo the procedure gain the Human-Looking positive quality.

Trolls who undertake the procedure have their racial Charisma maximum increased by one.

This augmentation cannot be combined with the metaposeur genetic treatment.

COSMETIC CYBERWARE

CYBERWARE	ESSENCE	CAPACITY	AVAILABILITY	COST
Casemod	—	—	4	50–10,000¥
Cosmetic surgery	0.1	—	2	100–20,000¥
Breast implant	0.05	—	2	250¥
Breast implant 2.0	0.1	[1]	4	1,000¥
Cyber genitalia	0.25	[1]	6	2,000¥
Fiberoptic hair	0.1	[1]	—	100¥+
LED tattoo				
Small	0.05	[1]	—	100¥+
Medium	0.1	[2]	4	500¥+
Large	0.2	[4]	8	1,000¥+
Metatype reduction	0.3	—	4	6,000¥
Skin toner	0.5	—	4	2,000¥
Chameleon processor	0.3	[2]	12R	8,000¥
Steamers	0.1	[1]	4	500¥ (+contents)

- For those on a budget, you can buy the procedure as six treatments of only a thousand nuyen each. Your health insurance covers it if you're in a Japanacorp, and several other corporations also cover it.
- OrkCE0

- You fucking disgust me.
- Butch

SKIN TONER

Gently weaving ruthenium polymer into the user's skin and implanting a dedicated control system to watch over it, skin toner allows the user to select any shade of color for their skin tone. The limited processor requires the entire body to be generally the same color, minus some minor gradients for tanning, flesh density, and so forth. A more advanced processor can be purchased, allowing for chameleon-like abilities for the user's skin (this acts as a Rating 4 chameleon suit).

Wireless Bonus: The user may change skin color with a Free Action, rather than a Simple Action.

STEAMERS

Nothing says cool like hotness. Steamers are small vents with compressed chemical reserves that allow you to vent water vapor at appropriate times. Steamers can be added to any part of the body and hold enough water for five releases. Note that the vapor is just released, not sprayed, giving you little control over where it goes.

- You can also fill it with other things, like scented oils and perfumes! Mmm, new car smell …
- Turbo Bunny

- While it's possible to fill it with inhalants, you're far more likely to nail yourself due to the lack of range. Trust me.
- Plan 9

- Add sound effects for just fifty nuyen more. Help get that proper steampunk effect. [Hiss.snd]
- /dev/grrl

EARWARE
ANTENNAE

With an extended antenna array, the user can send and receive wireless signals easier than without. Available in both retractable and fragile or non-retractable and sturdy options for the same cost, they are often, but not always, taken in pairs and come in a wide variety of designs, shapes, and colors. Shiawase *MochiMecha* are all the rage this year!

Each antenna, to a maximum of three, reduces Noise by 1 for the user. And only the user.

EARWARE

CYBERWARE	ESSENCE	CAPACITY	AVAILABILITY	COST
Antennae	0.1	[1]	2	500¥
Audio analyzer	0.1	[1]	4	1,000¥
Ear protectors	0.05	[1]	—	250¥
Increased spectrum	0.1	[1]	6	500¥
Modular mount	0.1	[1]	4	250¥
Translat-Ear	0.1	[1]	8	Rating x 2,000¥

AUDIO ANALYZER

A simple bit of hardware that measures and identifies both pitch and timbre, audio analyzer is quite useful for musicians and impersonators, but it can also allow eavesdropping of old touch-tone datapads. The audio analyzer acts as a Rating 4 device for identifying pitch, and raises the Social limit by 1 for musical performances for the user.

EAR PROTECTOR

Adding cups over a user's ears provides protection not unlike eye covers for cybereyes. This acts as Armor 3, though only to protect the ears.

INCREASED HEARING SPECTRUM

A basic augmentation that expands the user's hearing spectrum beyond the typical metahuman breadth of 20 Hz to 20 kHz as well as beyond typical audio enhancements. The user's hearing extends as low as 5 Hz, into infrasonic sound, and as high as 120 kHz into the ultrasonic. This allows the user to hear sounds outside the normal range, such as dog whistles or ultrasound-based motion detectors, which would otherwise go unnoticed. If combined with a device to create such sounds, such as a voice modulator, then a method of signaling, or even communication, can be employed that is difficult for those without the augmentation to listen in on.

Wireless Bonus: Access to a public database that allows these sounds to be compared to known sounds and identified, giving +2 dice to Perception tests to identify a particular sound.

MODULAR MOUNT

Using a universal connector not unlike the tactical rail of a modern firearm, the modular mount allows a single gun accessory, or a similarly sized hand tool, to be attached to the user's ear, providing a hands-free option for essential gear. Small, handheld items, such as a flashlight or handheld sensor can be modified to be mountable for 50 nuyen for each item. It takes a Simple Action to remove a modular item, and another Simple Action to replace a modular item.

Wireless Bonus: Removing a modular item is a Free Action instead of a Simple Action.

> Modular coffee mugs! Get two ears and never be without a beer hat! Wiz!
> Slamm-0!

> Technically, you can add knives or pistols to this mount. This is more useless than it sounds. Please don't.
> Butch

TRANSLAT-EAR

New from Renraku, the Translat-Ear allows you to hold a single language knowsoft and provides translation for what you hear with only a one-second delay. While the Translat-Ear isn't able to assist you to read or speak the language, it provides a vastly cheaper option for translation services than a full skilljack. Renraku happily provides Matrix storage for all of your linguasofts, allowing you to wirelessly access them at will, but reminds you that their *Babel* service is even handier!

Wireless Bonus: You can switch between any linguasofts you own as a Simple Action. In addition, if you subscribe to a wireless skillsoft service, you may switch between all languages as normal (see p. 78).

EYEWARE
ADDITIONAL EYE MOUNT

Ever wanted eyes in the back of your head? Well, now you can! Each additional eye mount allows the user to attach a cybereye to any part of their body that they wish. Due to the disorienting nature of such extra eyes, the user has a cumulative penalty of -1 to their Physical

EYEWARE

CYBERWARE	ESSENCE	CAPACITY	AVAILABILITY	COST
Additional eye mount	0.2	[2]	8	1,000¥
Eye-light system	0.1	[2]	2	500¥
Eye protectors	0.1	[2]	—	100¥
Microscopic lenses	0.2	[3]	4	1,000¥
Spider eyes	0.2	2	8	2,000¥
Targeting laser	0.2	[4]	4	1,000¥
Targeting laser (infrared)	0.2	[4]	6	1,250¥

limit, and all weapon Accuracies, for each eye active beyond two. (A user can close one normal eye and use an additional eye mount as the second without penalty, or close both natural eyes and use two additional eye mounts as well.) Placement of this additional eye can provide tactical advantages for the cunning shadowrunner. The most common placement is one in the back of the head, to be aware of ambushes, or to a hand, allowing someone to look around corners. The listed cost is for the mount; the cybereye itself is sold separately. Using one eye in front and one in back grants +2 dice to Surprise tests (p. 192, *SR5*).

- With the unusual SURGE effects in India often resulting in a third eye in the middle of the forehead, quite a few have gotten an eye mount in a similar way, leaving this "third eye" closed unless needed. While the third eye is cybernetic, the user normally retains their original eyes. This trend is starting to be picked up by Horizon.
- Dr. Spin

EYE LIGHT SYSTEM

The eye light system involves a pair of minuscule, high-power but low-heat lights installed into the user's cybereyes. The mechanism is attached to the forward inner wall of the eye, with a second, smaller pupil installed to allow it to shine out. The light has a range of two meters and allows for a person with low-light vision to see for a range ten times that. The thin beam illuminates an area roughly the size of a sheet of paper or half a fuse box, allowing for a wide range of activities while leaving the hands completely free. Standard white light may be replaced by any other color, or ultraviolet, at no additional cost, with red being the most popular alternative.

Wireless Bonus: Activating or deactivating the eye light system is a Free Action instead of a Simple Action.

EYE PROTECTORS

These are simple protective covers that go over the user's eyes, preventing them from being harmed by dust and debris. They're available in a wide array of color and style, as well as in plastic (Armor 3, just for the eyes) or ballistic glass (Armor 6, just for the eyes).

MICROSCOPIC LENSES

Take your lab with you, but don't forget your slides! Microscopic lenses allow for refocusing of the eye to a massive magnification of tiny, tiny objects, up to 1000X their normal size. When microscopic lenses are active, the user's eye is unsuitable for any other task, but a Simple Action allows the lens to be switched on or off. An item further away than 30 centimeters is beyond the focal ability of active microscopic lenses. When microscopic lenses are being used, in addition to the obvious use, they provide a +4 dice pool bonus on Perception tests to examine the material in question.

Wireless Bonus: Switching lenses on or off is a Free Action instead of a Simple Action.

SPIDER EYES

Primitive eye clusters may be installed as an alternative to a third (or fourth, fifth, etc.!) eye. These simple eyes have poor detail and little color, but they discern light and darkness and, more importantly, movement. By placing these along the rear of the user's head or neck, they can detect something approaching and react accordingly, without the distraction that a full visual sensory input would bring from a full eye. Note that Spider Eyes are cybereyes, not cybereye modifications!

Users with spider eyes receive a +1 dice pool bonus on Surprise tests if the surprise is within 10 meters of them.

TARGETING LASER

This is a large visible-dot laser (available in your choice of color) built into the user's trigger hand, allowing it to act as a laser sight for all carried ranged weapons without using a top mount. As per a standard laser sight, this increases the weapon's accuracy by 1 and is incompatible with smartgun modifiers.

For people with infravision capabilities, an IR version is available so that your targeting activities are not overly obvious.

Wireless Bonus: The targeting laser provides a +1 dice pool bonus on attack tests, not cumulative with smartlink modifiers. Also, activating or deactivating the targeting laser is a Free Action instead of a Simple Action.

WIRELESS WAR OF '74

All right, all right, it was really 2075, but it started during the run-up to Christmas of '74, and the phrase doesn't rhyme if you go with a more accurate terminology, but work with me here, people. The Wireless War of '74 was a quiet match between Renraku, Horizon, and NeoNET, with some additional players in the mix behind the scenes. Horizon's *Singularity* system had been available for a while, pushing them upward into the higher levels of skillsoft technology and making them a pioneer in wireless dispersion of data. The former was traditionally a strong suit of Renraku, while the latter was based off of NeoNET's networks and, quite frankly, the older companies knew a good thing when they saw it. Shiawase, in their ongoing conflict with Horizon, managed to gather up the core code in a data extraction and sold it for virtually nothing to Renraku, who, of course, claimed that they'd been working on a version of their own for years and any similarities were pure coincidence. NeoNET also stepped into the line at this stage, with a similar notation, but it isn't clear if they bought the code from Shiawase or if they had another source other than their claim of their own internal development. Regardless, it went to the Corporate Court, and in an eight-to-four ruling, the Court decided against Horizon. From there, shadow-ops broke out, tagging one another for revenge while, at the same time, the hunt was on for better skillwire technology.

* Horizon's *Singularity* network used to run through NeoNET architecture. It's a no-brainer how Boston copied it.
* Bull

* Can we not talk about Boston right now?
* /dev/grrl

* An interesting ploy by Shiawase here. They make some money in the sale(s), Renraku takes the majority of the blame, NeoNET takes the leftovers, and Shiawase quietly keeps copies of the code for themselves, letting them roll out their own network a year later without having to worry about bugs in the system or the overt war. It's easy to forget that Shiawase has been playing this game longer than anybody else. All the gains, none of the pains. Megacorp activity at its finest.
* Kay St. Irregular

* Any truth to the rumor that Empress Hitomi's pet technomancers were behind the crack?
* Glitch

* I don't like your tone, Glitch. I think you've been hanging around Clockwork too much. However, Horizon's use and abuse of technomancers is a brightly remembered thing. Shiawase has been a much more friendly hand, and helping the corporation who's nice to them while getting revenge on Horizon all line up to support the rumor. I don't have any real info, however.
* Netcat

* The Court ruling was interesting, with Horizon getting support from Wuxing, Ares, and of all people, Aztechnology.
* Mr. Bonds

* Wait. Didn't Aztechnology just add a wireless distribution method to their Matrix hosting service?
* Marcos

* One that they bought from Shiawase, in fact. On the one hand, they make a public bridge-mending with Horizon, who are now inside the Pueblo Corporate Council, and on the other, they profit from a copy of the stolen tech. Shiawase slipped them a nice parcel of activesoft code in the process, and became the only other corporation equipped with NeoNahuatl linguasofts in the trading process. Which, of course, they then sold to Renraku at a considerable markup. Shiawase is good at this, you know.
* Icarus

* Speaking of bridge building, Horizon and the PCC have been shipping food to Aztlan since the Court ruling, and doing so at a generous rate of exchange. Tit for tat, or just good business sense?
* Stone

The end result of this whole experience has been the spreading of wireless skillsoft technology to almost every corner of the globe. The primary suppliers are Shiawase in Asia, NeoNET in Europe, Aztechnology in Aztlan, Renraku in the entire southern hemisphere, and Horizon in the NAN and California Free State. Normally NeoNET would have locked up the North American market, but they have bigger issues just now, so the other

WIRES

CYBERWARE	ESSENCE	CAPACITY	AVAILABILITY	COST
Skilljack	Rating x 0.1	—	Rating x 2	Rating x 10,000¥
Skillwires	Rating x 0.2	—	Rating x 3	Rating x 20,000¥
Knowsoft	—	—	Rating x 1	Rating x 2,000¥
Activesoft	—	—	Rating x 2	Rating x 5,000¥
Linguasoft	—	—	Rating x 1	Rating x 1,000¥

All knowsofts, activesofts, and linguasofts have a maximum Rating of 6.

SKILLSOFT NETWORKS

MEMBERSHIP	KNOWSOFT	ACTIVESOFT	MONTHLY COST
Basic	Rating 1	—	2,000¥
Silver	Rating 1–2	Rating 1–2	10,000¥
Gold	Rating 1–4	Rating 1–3	15,000¥
Platinum	Rating 1–6	Rating 1–4	20,000¥

corporations are all fighting it out. This means more opportunities for the legitimate parts of society and a lot more work for us. Enjoy it while you can.

WIRELESS SKILLSOFT NETWORKS

While the competition between Horizon, Renraku, and NeoNET has been intense, market forces have fairly well stabilized the pricing of wireless skillsoft access, and the subscription-based services are quickly gaining popularity. While the *Singularity* system is the best-known, the systems that each megacorporation use are roughly the same: The actual data is hosted remotely, allowing a user to request a skill package, which is then run on the nodes, with the skills being loaned to the user. This mirrored approach prevents the code from being captured and copied, quashing piracy before it can become an issue, while allowing the user a huge swath of potential skills. As long as the monthly fee is paid, the user has access to the entire bank of skillsofts; once they decide to terminate their account, access to this data is lost.

Mechanically, skillsoft networks work as follows: First, the user wirelessly accesses the Matrix host that they pay a monthly fee to and requests a skill from the catalogue. This is a Simple Action and, obviously, requires the user to have a wireless connection active. At the beginning of thenext Combat Turn, the skill is ready to use, but the user suffers a –5 penalty to their Initiative Score, due to the lag time between the node remotely accessing the skill and the user's cyberware enacting it. The user may only access a single skill at a time in this way, but they are not charged additional fees, as the monthly access fee takes this into account in the pricing. The chart above shows the *Singularity* network, but the other network providers currently charge the same prices. This monthly fee is added to the character's Lifestyle cost, which requires either a legitimate SIN or a fake SIN equal to the Rating of the skillsoft being requested. Higher-quality memberships give access to higher-quality skillsofts.

HEADWARE
ATTENTION CO-PROCESSOR

True wetware-based multitasking remains annoyingly out of reach, but ongoing work in the field has allowed for a limbic monitoring system that searches for and denotes objects of interest, pinging them with gentle neural tugs or, if connected to sensory cyber/devices, actual sounds or visual flags to ensure they're noticed. This raises the user's Mental limit for Perception tests by 1.

Wireless Bonus: Objects are identified and tagged based on their recognition via central database. This results in a +1 dice pool bonus to all Perception tests.

CHIPJACK

The return of an old classic! This expanded bay allows a number of additional, physical skillchips to be slotted into a user's skilljack, saving time from manual switching. The chipjack further comes with an expanded buffer, allowing more chips to be accessed simultaneously, though the raw power of those chips is controlled by the strength of the core skilljack processor. Note that chipjacks are not compatible with hardwires.

A standard skilljack (p. 452, *SR5*) allows its user to employ knowsofts, linguasofts, and (with skillwires) activesofts. It can run multiple skillsofts at once, provided the total skillsoft Ratings do not exceed the skilljack Rating x2 (or x3 with the wireless bonus). Individual skillsofts cannot have a Rating higher than the skilljack Rating. Inactive skillsofts are kept in storage; unloading skillsofts and loading new ones from storage is a Free Action.

Each chipjack Rating adds one slot for an additional, physical skillchip that can be accessed by the skilljack along with any skillsofts already in storage. In addition, the chipjack Rating adds to the skilljack Rating when determining the total skillsoft Ratings that can run simultaneously.

For example, a Rating 1 chipjack paired with a Rating 3 skilljack can handle a total of $(1 + 3) x2 = 8$ skillsoft Ratings (or 12 with wireless enabled). The maximum Rating of any single skillsoft is still the skilljack Rating, however.

DREAM LINK

This unusual device allows the user to record their dreams, creating a simsense record that may then be reviewed and re-experienced as the user wishes. Copies may be created and shared but are often difficult in the extreme to understand without additional simsense recordings, such as from a simrig. Dream links may also be used when awake, retaining up to one hour of active thought for examination and replay.

FALSE FACE

Intended for use by actors, shadowrunners quickly found other uses for the false face, resulting in it being restricted in most countries and corporations. The bones of the face are replaced with dozens of small ceramic plates that may be adjusted and rotated by micro-servos implanted beneath them. Combined with

THE DATA LIBRARY OF ALEXANDRIA

Arguably Renraku's greatest achievement, the Data Library of Alexandria is the single largest repository of accumulated knowledge in the world. The Data Library holds a staggering number of datasofts, available for purchase or, for a low monthly fee, users can gain a "library card" that allows them to browse as much as they want. Of course, while remote access to this data is allowed, it should be noted that the customer is buying a license to observe the data, not a personal copy of it, and if they fail to pay, they lose access to the library and their purchased datasofts. Ares has a similar service in the Library of Jefferson, while both Horizon and Saeder-Krupp are about to start their own.

The monthly fee to access these datahosts is 250 nuyen, which is added to the character's Lifestyle cost.

SHOPPAZULU

While every megacorp runs its own shopping software, featuring their own products exclusively, none are as well-regarded as Renraku's Shoppazulu network. Rather than the usual virtual servant, Shoppazulu uses real human beings whose Matrix avatars walk along with you as you browse, giving live feedback on selections, suggestions, and pointing out related products as the network goes about producing links. There's nothing like the personal touch, and the maid- or butler-clad avatars are recognized worldwide for their helpfulness and pleasant, upbeat attitudes. Aztechnology's Tlacoyos service has been booming in the past two years, while Horizon's Acquire has unique AI support.

While shopsoft licenses may be purchased and downloaded as usual, for a low monthly fee of 250 nuyen added to the monthly Lifestyle cost, the user may access an unlimited number of shopsofts every month. Those with a corporate SIN gain free access to their corporation's own shopsofts, which will only find products and services their megacorporation produces.

small reservoirs of gel that allow inflation or deflation of facial features, this allows the user to resculpt their face to any possible version of their metatype, regardless of ethnicity. False face provides a +4 dice pool bonus to a character's Disguise + Intuition Test. Changing one's face takes 1 minute of concentration and is somewhat painful.

Wireless Bonus: The user may access a list of faces that they have previously created, allowing a transformation in half a minute.

KNOWLEDGE HARDWIRES

The classics never really die, they just get shunted to overlooked nations. Skill hardwires have been around since the '50s but fell out of favor with prosperous countries due to the simple fact that a permanent installation of a skill isn't the best investment in today's ever-changing economic conditions. In less resource-rich parts of the world, however, the ability to simply absorb a medical degree or legal complexities can't be overstated. KITT is the biggest supplier, naturally, but Renraku keeps Africa well-stocked with hardwires, though they focus more on Active skills than Knowledge skills. Knowledge hardwires are simply an implanted skillchip and a processor designed to run only that single skill. The skill can be neither upgraded nor replaced without removing the entire unit and implanting a new one. On the positive side, you may have several knowledge hardwire units installed, giving you access to a wide array of abilities. Note that the hardwire Rating must be equal to or greater than the Knowledge skill installed into it.

MATH SPU

This is cranial subprocessing unit (SPU) is dedicated to running mathematical functions, freeing up more grey matter for other activities. It also keeps time accurate to four decimal places, includes a note-taking calendar, and can keep track of up to ten separate timing matters simultaneously, such as "How long is this movie" or "How long until the popcorn is done?" or "What time will my download finish?"

A math SPU adds +4 to a user's Mathematics Knowledge skill, and raises the Mental limit for scientific or technical Knowledge skills by 1.

ORIENTATION SYSTEM

In addition to serving as a global positioning system (GPS), this upgrade includes an internal gyroscope (for when GPS signals are unavailable), an internal compass, an inertial compass, an altimeter, a barometer, and an external port for holding a mapsoft. It doesn't include a display, so some kind of overlay (such as an imagelink in cyber-eyes) or other visual aid, is needed to process data properly. The orientation system can further chart paths, provide redline instruction (projected via AR to your field of vision via your PAN), make projections, measure your time of travel, distance, and ETA, as well as record your path for future map updating.

This increases the user's Mental limit by 2 for all Navigation Tests.

Wireless Bonus: The user gains +2 dice to all Navigation test. In addition, new mapsofts may be accessed wirelessly.

RADAR SENSOR

Consisting of a terahertz pulse-transmitter, receiver, and highly advanced processing unit, this unit computes differences in the Doppler shift between the user and the surrounding area, within a twenty-meter radius. This allows the user to view a three-dimensional map of the area and the elements contained therein, if in a vague, blocky manner. The radio pulses are able to pass through most solid matter, allowing the user to "look" through walls, clothes, and similar obstructions to see the outlines of what lies beyond. While individuals cannot be recognized at the resolution of the processing, shapes can give some suggestion of what items might be (tables, guns, balls, and so forth). The system is excellent at detecting motion, calculating exact distance (when combined with a math SPU), and accurately overseeing floorplans and the locations of persons and objects in that area. It is somewhat complex to sift through the data for a proper reading (a Simple Action is required), and while it can ignore Invisibility spells (but not Improved Invisibility spells) and many camouflage methods, it cannot discern color, lighting, or texture.

The radar sensor uses the same Visibility modifiers as ultrasound but can penetrate a cumulative Structure Rating equal to its own Rating x 5. Thus, a Rating 2 radar sensor can penetrate two Rating 5 walls, or a single Rating 10 wall, or three Rating 3 walls, etc. Radar systems are especially vulnerable to jamming and noise, suffering double the usual disruption. Radar pulses are detectable by any wireless device, but most won't be able to identify them as anything more than background noise.

SYNTHLINK

A simple interface akin to a smartlink that allows the user to interface with smart instruments, improving the link between musician and instrument. Smart instruments cost twice as much as standard instruments.

Users who are equipped with linked "synthstruments" have their Social limit increased by 2 for performing.

Wireless Bonus: The user gains a +2 dice pool bonus to performance skills employing linked synthstruments.

VISUALIZER

One of the most-beloved creations of the past five years, the visualizer allows the user to export a 2D or 3D image from their mind to augmented reality, or directly to paper by interfacing with a wireless printer. It requires extensive concentration and rare mental imaging ability to create more than a rough realization of the image in someone's head (use a Memory Test, p. 152, *SR5*, to determine how many relevant details the individual is able to visualize), but it's an emerging art form. It takes between five seconds (for a simple geometric design) to an hour (for detailed landscapes or persons) to create the image.

ARES' *GETTING* NETWORK

Owned by AresSpace, the Getting Network is Ares' proprietary mapping system. While a license to a particular mapsoft may be purchased as usual, the *Getting* Network is also available as a wireless service, allowing the user to access a wealth of national and city maps for a low monthly fee. Detailed maps of national parks are also included. Evo's Laika network and Renraku's *Kohno* network are comparable services (add the service to a user's monthly Lifestyle cost).

SERVICE PACKAGE	MAPSOFT RATING	MONTHLY FEE
Basic	2	50¥
Silver	4	150¥
Gold	6	500¥

OMNISCIENCE, OR NOT

Access to wireless networks and loads of 'softs can be easily abused, so a gamemaster much be watchful. Things like a mapsoft of the hidden corporate research lab, a knowsoft of "What Mr. Johnson is really up to," or a shopsoft that reveals all hidden Aztechnology subsidiaries in the city aren't available. It should go without saying, but there's always someone who needs to see it in print: The gamemaster's word on what 'softs do or do not exist is final!

VOICE MASK

A much-downgraded version of the voice modulator, the voice mask doesn't allow for modification of the volume or frequency of the user's voice, nor does it allow recording, rebroadcasting, or replication of someone else's voice. What it does, however, is use dissonant frequencies to totally distort the user's voice and make it completely unrecognizable and useless for identification.

BODYWARE
ACTIVE HARDWIRES

Programmed with a single, unchangeable, active skill, active hardwires are a dedicated skillwire system that holds only a single skill. While this skill may not be changed, multiple active hardwires may be implanted into a person, each granting one active skill. Note that the active hardwire system includes its own processor, meaning that no skilljack is needed to operate it.

HEADWARE

CYBERWARE	ESSENCE	CAPACITY	AVAILABILITY	COST
Attention coprocessor	0.3	[1]	8	3,000¥
Chipjack (1–6)	(Rating) x 0.05	—	(Rating) x 2	(Rating) x 1,000¥
Dream link	0.1	—	8	1,000¥
False face	0.5	[8]	12R	20,000¥
Knowledge hardwires (1–6)	Rating x 0.05	—	Rating	Rating x 2,000¥
Math SPU	0.1	[1]	8	2,000¥
Orientation system	0.2	[1]	4	500¥
Radar sensor (1–4)	Rating x 0.25	[Rating]	Rating x 3	Rating x 4,000¥
Synthlink	0.1	[1]	4	1,000¥
Visualizer	0.1	—	8	2,000¥
Voice mask	0.1	—	8F	2,000¥

AUTO-INJECTOR

Originally, auto-injectors were devices that released medication into a person's body either when needed or on a regular time schedule. It took the streets about thirty seconds to realize that you could replace, say, insulin with combat drugs, and suddenly you have a sneaky boosting technology. While the base auto-injector is designed to hold a single dose of a chemical, an auxiliary storage unit is often implanted to allow up to five additional doses. The auto-injector is normally refilled from an external port but may be connected to a chemical gland (see p. 112) instead, allowing the user to produce their own chemicals and dispense them as desired. Note that while different chemicals can't be mixed in a single dispensary, multiple injectors may be implanted to create a veritable salad bar of chemical cocktails.

Wireless Bonus: Provides access to database information about the drug's effects and a real-time countdown of its duration, as well as a monitor of when the aftereffects should pass.

Killswitch: Highly illegal, the killswitch is, at its core, a single-use auto-injector that's been filled with some virulent agent. The killswitch is rigged into a direct neural interface so that the user can trigger it with a mental command. Once triggered, in injects a presumably lethal chemical into the user's bloodstream. Obviously, a killswitch isn't designed to be refilled.

BALANCE TAIL

Largely having fallen out of favor for their bioware cousins, balance tails are cybernetic tails extended from the user's spine, focused on improved stability and balance. The tail is controlled by a dedicated sub-processor at the base of the spine and is autonomous, often moving about on its own without the user's awareness as it quietly compensates for natural motion. While the base tail is in the always-classic chrome, faux-fur cat tails are, by far, the dominant style. Tails must be at least knee-length to be functional, but most are slightly longer than the user's legs.

The balance tail raises the user's Physical limit by 1 for all tests requiring balance, such as climbing, jumping, or running. It also raises the user's Physical limit by one for purposes of resisting knockdown.

BIOMONITOR

While this is simply an implanted version of the standard biomonitor, its cybernetic nature allows it to integrate the user's augmentations into calculations so that, for instance, a user's bone structure will not read as damaged just because they have plastic implants.

Wireless Bonus: Provides interaction with a user's healthcare provider, as well as constant updates in their personal PAN, making checking your vitals into a Free Action.

BIOWASTE STORAGE EXPANSION

What it says on the tin. Each Rating point allows the user to store an entire day's worth of liquid and solid waste for later offloading via an access port.

- Handy for long waits in a sniper position or when hiding inside a facility, waiting for it to close.
- Hard Exit

CYBERFINS

Retractable webs for the user's hands and feet, cyberfins make swimming a breeze.

When active, increase the user's Physical limit for Swimming tests by 1 per cyberfin. Each pair of cyberfins further increases the user's Swimming skill by +1. A user may have one pair on their feet and another on their hands. Lastly, a user with a pair of cyberfins has their Swimming speed increased to 150 percent of normal, or 200 percent with two pairs.

Note that engaged cyberfins make use of that limb difficult for fine motor work, lowering the user's Physical limit, or a held weapon's accuracy, by 1 for activities such as making repairs, typing, dancing, and so on.

Wireless Bonus: Activating or deactivating cyberfins is a Free Action, instead of a Simple Action.

CYBERSAFETY

A simple implanted RFID chip informs your cybersafety-equipped weapon that you are a valid user. The cybersafety itself is a program consisting of an RFID broadcaster, held by the weapon owner, and an RFID detector built into the weapon. If the RFID safety isn't within thirty centimeters of the weapon, it simply will not fire. The coding for this is standard-issue in all smartguns, and the technology may be added to any non-smart firearm for 100 nuyen. A bracelet or ring equipped with the RFID broadcaster is 50 nuyen.

FLEX HAND

Replacing the bones in the user's hand with mixed-rigidity smart materials, improved tendon strength, and a general damping of the hands' tactile senses, a flex hand allows the user to compress their hand in unnatural ways, returning to normal without adverse effect or discomfort. The primary use of this is to escape security devices, such as handcuffs, or to fit one's hand through a space as small as three centimeters in diameter.

The user receives +3 dice for any Escape Artist attempt involving removing their hand from a hold or restraint, or to fit their hands into a small opening. A flex hand is incompatible with bone augmentations or a cyberhand. The cost listed is for a single hand; note that if both hands are in restraints and you only have one flex hand, escape options will be somewhat limited.

FOOT ANCHOR

These are retractable barbs that are designed to punch into the floor beneath the user's feet and provide an anchor point. While intended for installation into cyberfeet, foot anchors may be placed into organic legs with some difficulty. Only a single anchor may be placed per foot.

When engaged (a Simple Action), the character cannot move, but gains both +1 recoil compensation and +1 to the Physical limit for purposes of Knockdown Tests per activated anchor. If used as a weapon, foot anchors deal damage as if cyberspurs. Note that anchors only function on floors with a Structure Rating of 12 or less.

Wireless Bonus: Activating or deactivating is a Free Action, instead of a Simple Action.

INTERNAL ROUTER

Using the body's internal neural network as "wires," the internal router allows the user's cybernetics to communicate with one another as if they were wirelessly connected and, if expanded via a datajack or similar broadcast-enabled piece of cyberware, with the rest of the user's gear.

This allows the use of some wireless functionality, such as the quick-loading function of a smartgun or the engagement of a smuggling compartment, but not those that require an outside network or similar function, such as skillwire downloads.

GASTRIC NEUROSTIMULATOR

A simple set of electro-stimulators that respond to nausea by correcting the stomach, inner ear, or other affected areas with tiny electrical impulses, rendering the user immune to the effects of nausea or motion sickness. Quite popular with sailors, acrobats, and those orbital-intended workers.

The user is immune to Nausea.

MAGNETIC SYSTEM

Each magnetic system is installed into a single limb, with the torso (front) and torso (rear) counting as two separate limbs for this purpose. The magnetic system is a series of electro-magnets set into the user's body, allowing that limb to connect to ferrous metal, or to attach ferrous metals to a limb. While the majority of currently available goods are non-ferrous, instead being polymer-based, carbon-fiber, or plassteel, there are still a few load-bearing areas that use metal construction, such as building supports, bridges, heavy construction equipment, and so on. While active, the user is virtually incapable of dropping metal items, and may, if the equipment is properly equipped, move along metal surfaces by use of two or more magnetic systems.

An engaged magnetic system has a Strength of 6 for purposes of what it can hold or attach. (Note that it's entirely possible to have more weight attached to the user than they can lift). The electromagnetic field an active magnetic system produces results in a Noise rating of 1 per active system, with a range of 1 meter around the user.

Wireless Bonus: Engaging or de-activating the magnetic system is a Free Action instead of a Simple Action.

MOVE-BY-WIRE SYSTEM

While usually considered cutting-edge technology, the move-by-wire system actually predates all other reaction cyberware, being the prototype from which wired reflexes and similar systems were drawn. It was simply too expensive and invasive to the user's body for widespread use, and the inferior, but more survivable, wired reflexes claimed its glory. Researchers have been struggling with it for decades and still haven't perfected it, but it's at least closer to being usable today than ever before. The system works by putting the user's entire body into a permanent seizure, using electrical impulses to direct those seizures towards an eventual end goal, such as "move here" or "stab that guy." In many ways, this isn't unlike a high-end aircraft, where hundreds of computerized micro-corrections are required to keep it flying, only using metahuman flesh and bone instead of high-end carbon and aluminum. Any user under an active system will be affected by constant small twitches and tremors due to the complex interactions of the system, which vanish as soon as the system engages actual movement, returning whenever they are once again still. Move-by-wire is incompatible with any other reaction-enhancing augmentation.

Each Rating point of a move-by-wire system adds +1 Reaction and +3 Initiative (making it +4 total to Initiative). Rating 1 move-by-wire does not offer any additional Initiative Dice, but Rating 2 and Rating 3 offer +1D6 Initiative Dice, meaning Rating 2 offers +2 Reaction, +6 Initiative, and +1D6 Initiative Dice, and Rating 3 offers +3 Reaction, +9 Initiative, and +1D6 Initiative Dice. In addition, the move-by-wire system acts as skillwires of twice its Rating, but will require a skilljack to access this functionality. Users of move-by-wire systems suffer a penalty to their Social limit equal to the system's Rating thanks to their constant twitches and tremors.

Wireless Bonus: : +1 to relevant inherent limits when used as skillwires (see p. 455, *SR5*).

NUTRITION STORAGE SYSTEM

An onboard reserve of tasteless food paste and water, the former released directly into your stomach, the latter into your mouth and throat. Each Rating point allows for a day's worth of food and water to be stored. The reservoirs are refilled through an external port and

BODYWARE

CYBERWARE	ESSENCE	CAPACITY	AVAILABILITY	COST
Active hardwires	Rating x 0.05	—	Rating x 2	Rating x 4,000¥
Auto-injector	0.05	—	2	
Reusable (1 dose)	0.05	—	2	500¥ + contents
Expanded reservoir (+5 doses)	0.05	—	4	250¥ + contents
Killswitch	0.05	—	8F	750¥ + contents
Balance tail	0.25	—	8	2,000¥
Biomonitor	0.1	[1]	2	500¥
Biowaste storage	Rating x 0.1	[Rating]	8	Rating x 500¥
Cyberfins	0.1	[1]	8	500¥
Cybersafety	—	[1]	4	100¥
Flex hand	0.15	—	8	1,500¥
Foot anchor	0.25	[3]	10	2,000¥
Gastric neurostimulator	0.2	—	4	2,000¥
Internal router	0.7	—	4	15,000¥
Magnetic system	0.25	[2]	8	1,000¥ + contents
Move-by-wire system				
Rating 1	3.0	—	12F	40,000¥
Rating 2	4.0	—	18F	125,000¥
Rating 3	5.0	—	24F	205,000¥
Nutrition storage system	Rating x 0.1	[Rating]	4	Rating x 500¥
OXSYS cybergill	0.25	—	4	2,000¥
Retractable climbing claws	0.2	[2]	8	2,000¥
Smart articulation	0.5	—	8	6,000¥
Touch link	0.1	—	8	1,000¥

are considered part of the user's Lifestyle cost. This augmentation is not compatible with the elastic stomach genetech.

- Again, useful for long stakeouts in sniper position or for deep infiltration.
- Hard Exit

- Also survival in harsh environments.
- Stone

OXSYS CYBERGILL

Rather than an implanted air supply, the OXSYS cybergill is a series of implants along the user's throat and upper respiratory system that allows oxygen to be pulled from water, allowing for an indefinite duration of submersion. The user draws water into their lungs during this procedure, exhaling it as well, and the system includes lung reinforcement and strengthened bellows to allow water to be fully flushed out after emerging from submersion. This process is somewhat discomforting and often loud. While the cybergill allows the user to breathe underwater, it doesn't make the body immune to the other effects of underwater life, such as nitrogen narcosis. Dedicated users often implant air tanks (p. 455, SR5) with pure helium to manage their body's levels of nitrogen.

RETRACTABLE CLIMBING CLAWS

Essentially retractable hand razors, angled for use in climbing rather than combat, these claws are reinforced and hooked, and are most often taken in pairs. Each climbing claw raises the user's Physical limit for Climbing Tests by +1, while each pair increases the user's Climb skill by +1. Note that one pair may be taken for the feet as well.

If used as weapons, treat as retractable hand razors, but reduce the Physical limit by 1 for the awkwardness of using them in an attack.

SMART ARTICULATION

An advanced procedure that replaces the user's connective tissues, ligaments, and tendons with modern materials and resettable tensile strengths, smart articulation can set users' bodies for either loose or tight joints, in addition to the standard that a metahuman body expects.

When loose, the user's body is easily contorted, with joints dislodged and pushed into position limited only by the user's skin, bones, and imagination. The user gains +2 to their Physical limit to Escape Artist and grapple tests, and can further fit through any opening no smaller than their head.

When tight, the user's joints are as unyielding as the long bones they are connected to and equally as inflexible. The user gains +2 Body when comparing to the attacker's Strength in unarmed combat, and they have their Physical limit increased by 1 for any test involving endurance, such as climbing.

Unfortunately, in either loose or tight settings, the user will find themselves with difficulty moving, traveling at half their normal speed.

Smart articulation is incompatible with enhanced articulation or cyberlimbs.

TOUCH LINK

A simple sensory recording device that records tactile sensation, allowing the experience to be shared or replayed as desired. Combine with a simrig for an astounding experience!

CYBERLIMBS

PRIMITIVE PROSTHETICS

While not used by reputable medical corporations these days, the fact remains that SINless and the uninsured are lucky to get what they can. From the wooden (!) pegleg and hook hand of antiquity to the unpowered metal and plastic hybrids of a century ago, these prosthetics all offer extremely limited results for an extremely limited price.

In the case of hands/arms, the user is considered to have a limit/Accuracy of 1 with any use of the limb.

In the case of feet/legs, the user is considered to have a walking speed half of normal and has their run multiplier reduced by one.

Primitive skulls and torsos don't exist. Poor slots.

BUILT-IN MEDKIT

Built directly into a partial or full cyberlimb, this is simply a standard medical kit filled with useful surgical implements, micro-manipulators, and a digital nurse to help with diagnosis and treatment. More expensive kits are, of course, more robust. The listing for this item is simply for the compartment and parts to hold the medkit; the medkit must be purchased separately. The medkit then may be refilled as their non-cyber counterparts for the same price.

BUILT-IN UTILITY KIT

Dozens of kits exist, each featuring a full tool kit (Armorer, Auto Mechanics, etc.) that can be built directly into a partial or full cyberlimb. Each kit features rotating drillbits, clamps, computerized guides, and so forth, for the task at hand.

BULK MODIFICATION

Most cyberlimbs are designed to be relatively lifelike—extremely so in the case of synthetic limbs, but there are those who wear their chrome loud and proud, and for them, the bulk modification is a gift from above. While only available for obvious cyberlimbs, the bulk modification trades sneakiness for greater volume, and with greater volume comes more upgrade capabilities. While bulk modification is available in six Ratings, the limb in question is limited as noted in the chart below:

CYBERLIMBS

CYBERWARE	RATING
Hand/foot/half-skull	1
Lower arm/lower leg/skull	2
Full arm/full leg	4
Torso/liminal chassis	6

For each point of Rating, the modified limb gains +1 Capacity.

CYBERFINGERS

Sometimes, you don't need an entire hand; other times, you want to add a few tricks to the cyberhand you already have. Regardless, individual finger upgrades are available that add functionality to your digits.

Fingerlight: A simple small flashlight.

Fingerlighter: Good for lighting cigarettes ... or fuses.

Finger Grenade: Nothing says "Frag you!" like giving someone the finger. And now you can frag them too! Finger grenades inflict damage as if a grenade of the listed type, but their power is reduced by 2. Obviously, the finger must be replaced after each use, and actions using the hand with the missing finger receive a -1 penalty to the Physical limit.

Finger Pistol: The ultimate in one-shot hold-out pistols. The finger pistol uses ordinary cybergun hold-out rules, aside from being a single-shot and having an Accuracy of 3(5).

CYBERLIMB OPTIMIZATION

For decades, cyberlimbs have been modified and analyzed, producing results that are greater in one area at a small cost in other areas, a general tradeoff that's been largely accepted in the name of efficiency. Primarily, this market is in the fields of sports or entertainment, but new arenas are always being explored. In each case, this requires a full cyberlimb dedicated to the cause, and they're usually intended to be taken in pairs for maximum result. As you might imagine, a limb may only be optimized in one way.

Optimized limbs raise the user's applicable limit by +1 for each limb optimized in that skill. For each pair of limbs optimized for the skill, the user gains +1 to their applicable skill dice pool as well. While the list below showcases several examples, it is by no means exhaustive, and gamemasters are encouraged to come up with several of their own.

Evo Atlantean: The first set of optimized limbs that had both matching arms and legs. Thanks, Evo! (Swimming)

Fuchi Virtuoso: The line that started it all. Virtuoso allows musicians to achieve their dreams. (Performance)

Kalenjin: A single name brings a legacy of unequaled supremacy in running to this Renraku brand, proudly constructed in Kenya to exacting specifications. (Running)

Kuroko: One of the extremely rare optimized cyber skulls, Renraku's Kuoko is fantastic for ease of redesign. (Disguise)

Munden QuickDraw: A rare entry from Lone Star, the QuickDraw is both fast and accurate. (Pistols)

Spinrad NeverRest: Rock climbing, Joel! Available for both arms and legs, these limbs come with thin digits and powerful grips that make climbing any surface a breeze. (Climbing)

The Greatest: The fastest fists in piston power. Throw those punches in bunches! (Unarmed Combat)

Yankee Pitcher: Major League approved, Major League sanctioned! (Throwing Weapons)

DIGIGRADE LEGS

Best known in the shadows as Kid Stealth legs, these legs "bend the wrong way" in many eyes. The leg itself is actually constructed with normal hip and knee placements, but the foot is extremely elongated, with the weight fully on the ball of the foot and the ankle perceived by many as a second knee. While generally constructed with dimensions analogous to a dog or cat's legs, taken to the extreme, they resemble the legs of birds and often feature raptor feet (see below).

Digigrade may be taken as a modification for full or partial cyberlegs but not for feet, and they provide no bonus unless taken in pairs. The user's Physical limit for the Stealth skill group is increased by 1 per leg, while the running speed multiplier is increased by 1 for each pair.

GRAPPLE HAND

A modification to a cyberarm (either partial or full) that consists of a winch, a feed system capable of loading up to thirty meters of wire, and a pneumatic launcher that can fire the cyberhand up to the full range of the wire, which also serves as a command path to let the hand grab hold of a distant target. Once a firm grip is secured, the winch can pull them toward the hand at a rate of ten meters per Combat Turn, or half that silently. Should a grip not be made, it can rewind the hand at a rate of twenty-five meters per turn, or ten meters silently. It takes one minute for the air compressor to ready the hand for another shot.

Use Exotic Ranged Weapon (Grapple Gun) for targeting with the launched hand.

IMPROVED SYNTHSKIN

Advances in lifelike drones have also been adapted to core synthetic cyberlimb technology. Where once flesh was passable for viewing but betrayed by a touch, the more advanced synthskin of today is giving, warm to the touch, and more expensive blends sweat or even bleed when pricked. It's like real, only better!

Where normal synthetic limbs may be detected automatically by touch, those coated in improved synthskin require a Perception Test to be detected, requiring two hits, plus one more for each Rating. Cyberware scanners are as effective as normal, however.

LIMINAL BODY

One of the more recent cyber-mods, the liminal body is an extensive restructuring of the lower abdominal region of the user, often requiring some delicate re-working of digestive systems and waste removal, as well as the loss of genitalia, in exchange for a lower body replacement. The more exotic the modification, the more work needs to be done. Some of the more popular options are shown below, but gamemasters are encouraged to develop their own as well.

Centaur: The one that started it all, the user's lower half is replaced by a cybernetic steed. Four-legged and swift, but large and heavy. The user's running speed is doubled, and their ability to drag or carry weight is also doubled. The cyberlegs may each be modified as normal, but remember to average all four!

The Wheeled Warrior: A four-wheeled device roughly the size of a wheelchair, the user's running speed is doubled, but difficult terrain is especially troublesome.

Tank!: Similar to the Wheeled Warrior, the Tank! design uses treads, rather than wheels, trading speed for maneuverability. The user's walking speed is unchanged, but any difficult terrain other than mud is a breeze. The treads tend to tear up whatever surface they drive over, however, making the user less than welcome in certain elegant establishments.

MONKEY FOOT

Formally called prehensile, everyone called them "monkey feet" until the name stuck. Most often seen as a modification for those in long-term space flight, these modified cyberfeet are nearly as adroit as the user's hands and are capable of performing a vast array of motions, though they also result in slower movement.

A user with monkey feet can use them as hands, but their Physical limit and Accuracy are reduced by 1 when doing so. In addition, the user's running multiplier is reduced by 1.

MODULAR CONNECTOR

A wide variety of modular cyberlimbs and modular cyberlimb accessories exist. The basic form is a simple switch-out ring that allows the user to easily remove part of a limb, most commonly a wrist that allows a hand's removal, leaving a port where the removed limb can be replaced with some kind of tool. While most users keep it simple, having a normal cyberhand and a single tool that they switch between, others keep a stunning array of cyberlimbs stored in their home, allowing them to slip a new one on as easily as ordinary people change shoes.

Wireless Bonus: Removing a modular part is a Free Action instead of a Simple Action. Attaching a new modular part is always a Simple Action.

MODULAR LIMB

Any cyberlimb may be purchased with a modular connector, allowing it to be connected to another modular connector. This allows the user to have several limbs, such as a synthetic arm for casual life and a tricked-out chrome arm for business, several optimized limbs for different occasions, and so on. Some simply choose to purchase multiple modular limbs, just in case they lose one!

MODULAR GEAR

Virtually any gear may be made modular, but larger items need a larger limb to replace. Items roughly the size of a pistol require a modular hand, items the size of a sub-machine gun or toolkit require a partial limb, while items as large as a rifle require a full limb. Regardless of the size of the item, the cyberlimb connector costs 50 nuyen.

PARTIAL CYBERSKULL

The partial cyberskull is another throwback classic that's seeing a comeback. By upgrading one side of the skull with a large interface board, quite a few upgrades can be installed directly into it, rather than requiring difficult surgery repeatedly, but it is less invasive and far less dangerous than a full cyberskull.

RAPTOR FOOT

Similar to saurian or avian feet, raptor feet are large, deadly weapons that also serve for locomotion. The user trades go-anywhere weapons for a sad, shoeless existence, but this is a trade many are willing to endure. Raptor feet are difficult to use unless the user also has digigrade legs; attacks with the legs reduce the user's Physical limit by 1.

SKATES

A simple modification where retractable skates are placed in the user's cyberfeet, these are virtually useless unless taken in pairs. When engaged, the user's walking and running speeds are improved by fifty percent, but the unsteady balance results in a lowering of their Physical limit by 1 while the skates are in use.

Wireless Bonus: Activating or deactivating the skates is a Free Action, rather than a Simple Action as normal.

SKIMMERS

A more complex option for cyberfeet is the use of ground-effect platforms, based on skimmer drone technology, to provide a cushion of air beneath the user and allow them to hover a few centimeters above the ground. It takes some practice to get the hang of it, but once mastered, the skimmers allow the user to move at double their normal walking or running speed when engaged. The fragile balance required to maneuver them reduces the user's Physical limit by 2. Note that these are completely useless unless taken in pairs, and they're unusable if the user attempts to carry any significant extra weight.

Wireless Bonus: Activating or deactivating the skimmers is a Free Action, rather than a Simple Action as normal.

SNAKE FINGERS

A modification to cyberhands, where the fingers are extendable and feature rotational joints, allowing a

CYBERLIMBS

CYBERWARE	ESSENCE	CAPACITY	AVAILABILITY	COST
Primitive prosthetics				
Hand/foot	—	—	—	20¥
Partial arm/leg	—	—	—	100¥
Full arm/leg	—	—	—	250¥
Built-in medkit	0.45	[10]	8	1,000¥ (+ medkit)
Built-in toolkit	0.45	[10]	4	2,000¥
Bulk modification (1–6)	—	+ (Rating)	+ (Rating)	(Rating) x 500¥
Cyberfingers	0.05	[1]	2	500¥
Cyberlight	0.05	[1]	4	550¥
Cyberlighter	0.05	[1]	4	550¥
Finger grenade	0.05	[1]	(Grenade) +4	(Grenade) + 500¥
Finger pistol	0.05	[1]	8R	1,000¥
Cyberlimb optimization	—	[2]	(Limb) +2	(Limb) + 2,000¥
Digigrade legs	(Leg) + 0.25	[4]	(Leg) +4	(Leg) + 5,000¥
Grapple hand	0.45	[10]	12R	2,000¥
Improved synthskin (1-4)	—	[(Rating) X 2]	(Rating) X 4	(Rating) x 5,000¥
Liminal body				
Centaur	3.0	80	12	80,000¥
Wheeled	2.5	40	8	40,000¥
Tank!	3.0	60	12R	50,000¥
Monkey foot	0.3	[2]	8	6,000¥
Modular connector				
Wrist/ankle	0.1	[5]	4	2,000¥
Elbow/knee	0.2	[10]	8	4,000¥
Shoulder/hip	0.3	—	12	6,000¥
Modular limb				
Hand/foot	0.25	(Limb) — 1	(Limb) + 2	(Limb) + 1,000¥
Partial arm/leg	0.45	(Limb) — 2	(Limb) + 2	(Limb) + 2,000¥
Full arm/leg	1	(Limb) — 3	(Limb) + 2	(Limb) + 3,000¥
Partial cyberskull	0.4	4	12	8,000¥
Raptor foot	0.5	[4]	8R	8,000¥
Skates	—	[2]	4	250¥
Skimmers	—	[4]	8	2,000¥
Snake fingers	—	[2]	6	1,000¥
Telescopic limbs (1–2)	—	[Rating] x 3	[Rating] x 4	[Rating] x 1,000¥
Water jet	—	[4]	8	1,000¥

CYBERLIMBS

MELEE WEAPON	REACH	DAMAGE	AP
Raptor foot	—	(Str + 2) P	−3

RANGED WEAPON	AC	DAMAGE	AP	MODE	RC	AMMO
Grapple fist	3	7S	−2	SS	—	1 (ml)

wide range of motion impossible with ordinary hands, as well as the ability to slip fingers through tight spaces or narrow gaps.

Each cyberhand with snake fingers raises the user's Physical limit by +1 for feats of manual dexterity, while a pair adds +1 to the user's Palming skill.

Wireless Bonus: Snake Fingers may be activated or deactivated as a Free Action, rather than a Simple Action.

TELESCOPIC CYBERLIMB

Cyberlimbs modified with telescopic options may vastly increase their length, at a cost of strength, allowing the user to elevate themselves, reach high spots, or see over obstacles. While this extra reach can be quite useful, it comes at a cost in that the extended limbs cannot bring their full strength to bear. Note that the telescopic option may only be added to full or partial cyberlimbs, not hands or feet.

For each point of Rating, a limb may be extended 1 meter, but for each meter extended, the user's effective Strength with the limb is reduced by 2.

Wireless Bonus: Telescopic limbs may be activated or deactivated as a Free Action, rather than as a Simple Action.

WATER JET

Installed into a full or partial cyberleg, these waterjets speed a user's path underwater. While one jet doubles the user's Swimming speed, a pair triples it.

CYBER-IMPLANT WEAPONS

Unless otherwise noted, the following weapons cannot accept accessories and use either the Unarmed Combat (Cyber-Implant Weaponry) skill if melee-based, or Exotic Weapon (the particular cyber-implant weapon) if ranged.

CYBERGUN MODIFICATION

While there are a wide variety of cyberguns on the market, Ares was the first to recognize that name brands are name brands and, at the end of the day, a street samurai just feels more comfortable knowing that they have an Ares Predator up their sleeve rather than just some gun. Other corporations soon followed, as is so often the case, and in short order, a vast array of firearms

CYBERGUNS

CYBERWARE	COST
Hold-out pistol	Gun + 1,800¥
Light pistol	Gun + 3,500¥
Machine pistol	Gun + 3,000¥
Heavy pistol	Gun + 3,800¥
Submachine gun	Gun + 4,000¥
Shotgun	Gun + 7,000¥
Grenade launcher	Gun + 20,000¥

became available in cybergun variants. Each uses their own statline as normal—for example, an Ares Predator V uses Ares Predator V stats, not "Implant Heavy Pistol" stats, though it uses the same Essence and Capacity as a normal cybergun of that type. In the case of an Ares Predator V, that would be 0.5 Essence/[6] Capacity, as a normal Implant Heavy Pistol. Modification of a normal gun into a cyber-implant version costs are shown on the following chart, while Availability is increased by 4.

Tasers are treated as Light Pistols, Exotic Pistols are treated as Heavy Pistols, and other guns might be modifiable into cyberguns if the Gamemaster so chooses. Assault Rifles and larger weapons cannot be so modified.

EXTREME CYBER-IMPLANT WEAPONS

Not all cyber-implant weapons are sexy blades or cool guns. Some are little more than strapping a power tool to a stump and letting fly. Buzzsaws, chainsaws, whirling flails—the field is as varied as the imagination. While there are obvious differences between a power drill and an automatic vice, the differences are mostly academic compared to their use as a weapon. It's vital to note that extreme cyber-implant weapons fully replace one hand of the user, which can make life quite awkward!

Lower the user's Physical limit by 1 when trying to attack with an extreme cyber-implant weapon.

FANGS

While almost entirely replaced by bioware versions, fangs

CYBERWEAPONS

CYBERWARE	ESSENCE	CAPACITY	AVAILABILITY	COST
Extreme cyber-implant	0.5	[5]	8F	2,000¥
Fangs (pair)	0.1	[1]	6	200¥
Retractable	0.15	[2]	8	500¥
Flametosser	1.0	[8]	12F	4,000¥
Extra fuel (5 shots)	0.2	[2]	12F	500¥
Junkyard jaw	0.75	[6]	8F	2,000¥
Oral slasher	0.25	[3]	12R	750¥
Weapon launcher	0.2	[2]	12F	500¥ (added to weapon cost)

CYBERWEAPONS

RANGED CYBERWEAPONS	ACC	DAMAGE	AP	MODE	RC	AMMO
One-shot dartgun	4	4P	—	SS	—	1 (m)
Flametosser	4	6P(fire)	–6	SA/BF	—	5 (m)

MELEE CYBERWEAPONS	REACH	DAMAGE	AP
Extreme cyber-implant	1	(STR + 5) P	—
Fangs	—	(STR) P	—
Junkyard jaw	—	(STR + 3) P	–6
Oral slasher	1	6P	–3

come in both retractable and non-retractable versions. Fangs are difficult to use as weapons but are frequently connected to chemical reservoirs to deploy venom or other chemical agents. Lower the user's Physical limit by 2 when trying to attack an aware target with fangs.

FLAMETOSSER

Not as effective as a full-fledged flamethrower, the flametosser is nonetheless a fun weapon for the more incendiary-minded shadowrunner. Consisting of a liquid sprayer, two chemical storage containers that ignite when mixed, and a small pop-up port for releasing it, the flametosser ordinarily holds enough ammunition for five shots, but additional fuel canisters may be added as needed. Each chemical has its own refueling port, and they are clearly color-coded when the ports are open, to ensure that no mishaps occur. Users who pour fuel into the wrong port and burst into flames have no legal recourse, per *Ares Macrotechnology vs. Jablonski*, 2032.

The flametosser uses Taser ranges.

JUNKYARD JAW

A solid metal replacement for the lower jaw, and a more hidden upper mouth enhancement as well, the junkyard jaw is only seen on barrens gangers who just don't care about normal society at all anymore. Able to bite through bottles, knife blades, and even metal pipes with relative ease, the junkyard jaw's a famous intimidation tool. Note that very few users are further modified to digest the inorganic matter that they bite, so they are forced to spit it out after a good chomp. A junkyard jaw can obviously do just terrible things to the metahuman body. Approach with caution.

The junkyard jaw provides one additional box on your physical condition monitor, like a cyberlimb.

ONE-SHOT DARTGUN

While ordinary multi-use dartguns fall under cyberguns above, one-shot dart launchers are surprisingly common modifications with unpredictable mount locations. Fingers are the norm, but under-tongue mouthdarts, small of the back and rear-firing, or even eyesocket mounts are just a few examples. Note that an eye-mounted dartgun leaves the socket unable to hold a cybereye. One-shot dartguns use Taser ranges and take one minute to reload. It's highly recommended that one-shot dartgun ammunition be coated with some type of chemical agent.

ORAL SLASHER

A spool of pointed wire placed under the tongue, the oral slasher is more truthfully called the oral thruster, launched forward by compressed air to impale the target before being quickly rewound, not unlike a frog's tongue, only more dangerous. With a range of only one meter, the slasher is a melee weapon but is covered by the Exotic Weapon Skill, rather than Unarmed Combat. Oral slashers are often connected to chemical reserves, but not always.

WEAPON LAUNCHER

An unusual modification of a cyber-implant weapon that takes the form of either a ballista-like or catapult-like upgrade, this augmentations allows weapons to be launched as short-range projectiles. This is obviously something of a desperation maneuver, but the surprise factor can, hopefully, overcome the obvious downside of no longer being armed. The attack is resolved as if thrown by the user's Strength, or the Strength of the cyberlimb if placed into a cyberlimb, and uses the Throwing Weapon skill. If the launched weapon can be gathered up, it takes three Complex Actions to reset the launcher, then two more Complex Actions to re-attach the weapon.

AUGMENTATION BUNDLES

Some years ago, the concept of cybersuites was introduced, a simple process where an entire suite of upgrades was introduced at one time, making a one-time procedure where the subject could have a more holistic experience as the separate upgrades could be interlinked more reliably. While a good idea, the first generation was flawed in some ways, most notably that each suite drew from several manufacturers and thus diluted profitability. Some other problems, more of note to the end-user than the hardware provider, were also discovered, leading to a modification that led to today's modern augmentation bundles.

Modern augmentation bundles all draw from the same megacorporation's stock of cybernetics, ensuring maximum compatibility and alpha-level reliability with no increase in cost. The potential earnings lost in this are offset by the cultural cachet that this "premium product line" carries, and the advertising that it both contains and shares with all potential customers. In essence, each customer becomes a walking billboard, letting everyone know what upgrades the user has and where they can get the exact same ones for themselves. Keep in mind you can't turn this wireless functionality off and, no, augmentation bundles are never available as throwbacks.

- This stuff is hardware, not software, coded-up RFID tags that are beaming loud and proud. Too deep-set inside the cybernetics themselves for a tag eraser to get to, you have to have a decent cybertechnician open you up and root

the damn things out by hand. Most docs will charge about a grand per item, give or take. Pays to have a tech who owes you favors.
- Butch

- Which means you about break even, depending on the upgrades in question. Damn economics.
- Clockwork

- Somewhere out there, The Chromed Accountant just clutched his heart.
- Bull

Augmentation bundles are a suite of pre-selected cybernetics, with the total bundle receiving a 0.9 Essence cost multiplier with no increase in cost or Availability. The wireless capability of these bundles *cannot* be turned off. The augmentations are famously "chatty" and are all too happy to tell anyone who pings a request what they are and what megacorporation manufactured them. They're more interested in promoting their megacorp than getting the user in trouble, so they don't broadcast personal information, SINs, and so on, but it can make stealth somewhat harder. Gamemasters are encouraged to create their own augmentation bundles as best fits their own campaign. Each bundle has a cost equal to the total of the cybernetics it contains as if they were standard grade and an Availability equal to the highest of the individual parts (and with a matching legality or R or F if any part has those).

EXAMPLE AUGMENTATION BUNDLES

AZTECHNOLOGY *CUANMIZTLI* BUNDLE

As one of the few nations with legal bloodsports, as well as a fierce warrior pride, Aztlan is a rare country that allows for limited combat upgrades on a Restricted, rather than fully Forbidden, basis. Registered gladiators, or simply those who simply want to embody the spirit of the nation, can walk around proudly in a manner not unlike a registered firearms wielder in the UCAS. Of course, once you're off of Aztechnology or Aztlan property, you have to deal with local laws, which is why this bundle is flagged as Forbidden for all you Seattleites who actually care about such things.

PACKAGE A
Huiztiztili wired reflexes (1)
Motlapal muscle replacement (1)
Iztihuihuitztic retractable climbing claws (left hand and right hand)
PACKAGE B
Huiztiztili wired reflexes (2)
Motlapal muscle replacement (2)
Itzihuihuiyac cyberspurs (left arm and right arm)
Reaction enhancer (1)

BUNDLES	ESSENCE	AVAILABILITY	COST
Aztechnology *Cuanmiztli*	0.5	[5]	2,000¥
Package A	3.06	8R	68,000¥
Package B	5.31	12F	222,000¥
Evo *Atlantis*	0.72	8	16,000¥
Horizon Experience!	1.08	12R	20,000¥
Renraku *TradeJack*	0.9	12	124,000¥
S-K Cyberlogician	0.81	12	16,000¥
Shiawase *Kacho*	0.45	4	6,000¥

EVO *ATLANTIS* BUNDLE

While the individual components are often sold separately, Evo's *Atlantis* bundle includes everything a user needs to go explore the ocean blue, including a helium tank to combat nitrogen narcosis. New Atlanteans are strongly encouraged to practice with a partner before exploring. Safety first!

Low-light vision modification
Cyberfins (both hands and both feet)
OXSYS cybergill
Internal air tank (1)

HORIZON EXPERIENCE! BUNDLE

For the ultimate in personal livecasting or SimSational recording, nothing can quite match Horizon's own bundle. While many users gradually move toward the goal by buying cybereyes and uploading video feeds, the YouStar who wants everyone to know everything about their life can jump right in for the full Experience! experience. The complete package includes not only a full suite of recording options for what the user sees, hears, or even tastes, but records their emotional connection as well. In this way, young simstars can make themselves a small name until getting discovered. The next big star could be you!

Access datajack
Aroma olfactory booster (1)
Axis simrig
Yum! taste booster (1)
Snapshot cybereyes (1)
Dolby Perfect Pitch cyberears (1)
Sensational touch link

RENRAKU *TRADEJACK* BUNDLE

A relatively simple bundle designed to interact with Renraku's new wireless download system, the *TradeJack* pushes into head-to-head competition with Horizon as Renraku combines its unmatched linguistic database with an expanding suite of active skillsofts in an attempt to combat Horizon's market share. Please note that the *TradeJack* bundle does *not* come pre-loaded with any skillsofts, to encourage users to sign up for the *Babel* service, but they may be purchased separately.

Sidekick chipjack (4)
Prodigy skilljack (4)
Decathlete skillwires (4)

SAEDER-KRUPP CYBERLOGICIAN BUNDLE

While no longer limited to Saeder-Krupp personnel, Lofwyr's private megacorporation both invented the concept and produces the most examples of this augmentation bundle. The focus isn't on physical performance, as many other bundles are, but by focusing mostly on headware, the user gains advanced processing power and analytic abilities far above those of ordinary metahumans.

Three *Eilbote* datajacks
Tresor data lock (6)
Image link
Sound link
Mathematiker math SPU
Aufmerksamkeit attention co-processor

⊘ Most cyberlogicians also get an encephalon bioware augmentation, but it isn't a bundled item.
⊘ Glitch

SHIAWASE KACHO BUNDLE

The definitive *sarariman* bundle, the *Kacho* is named for the basic managerial rank in Shiawase's corporate structure. While many megacorps have moved away from the idea of augmentation in their executives, Shiawase is a conservative organization, resistant to change and fond of doing things their way. As the founders did, so do the current executives, and so will the next generation if they want to ever get promoted. Many college graduates entering the work force for other corporations look into the *Kacho* bundle as well, looking for that competitive edge over the competition.

Dentatus datajack
Shiawase *Jishi* headware commlink (treat as a Renraku Sensei)
Hekiga image link
Denwaki sound link

THE BODY REDEFINED

POSTED BY: DR. SPIN

I'm not a real doctor, but I play one on trideo.

Sorry, I always wanted to say that. Right, with KAM and The Smiling Bandit handling genetech, Butch under the weather, and Nephrine handling cybernetics, Bull asked us to touch on the current state of affairs in biotech. The job initially went to Plan 9, but a couple hundred megapulses on how awesome Evo is showed that he may not be the most impartial observer. With him out of the picture, I was happy to step up and do what I can to get us over the hump. Keep in mind, I don't have a medical degree or an actual doctorate, so I'm going to gloss over some of the more technical details to talk about what really matters: how biotech can turn you into a better you.

- ◉ [Pout] It's not *my* fault that Evo makes the best stuff.
- ◉ Plan 9

- ◉ Sorry, Plan, but we needed a broad look at the whole spectrum of biotech, not an Evo catalog.
- ◉ Bull

- ◉ That said, I wouldn't mind a look at the file! I'm not happy with my mirror lately.
- ◉ /dev/grrl

The most obvious aspect of this is the simple fact that there're more clinics in a city than police stations, but biotech goes far beyond that. It's in the food you eat, the cosmetics you wear, and quite possibly the upgrades in your own body. Biotech is used for power generation, scrubbing the air, and a thousand industrial uses from dyes to glues to, well, virtually everything. Before I get too carried away, I suppose it's time to dust off my History minor and give you a whirlwind tour of the biotech of eons past.

BIOTECH THROUGHOUT HISTORY

Biotech is the world's oldest profession, dating back to the days of goat herding and proto-farming. We found attributes we liked in animals, such as the willingness of wolves to stick by our side, the attributes we didn't, like them snarling at our kids, and we bred them, forcing more good to bubble up and more bad to shuffle out. We not only tamed animals, we domesticated them, making them dependent on us for their everyday lives and creating an underclass of animals who knew by instinct that we were to be followed, rather than have to train generation after generation to obey. At the same time, we crossbred plants, making our food supplies more productive, hardier against disease and parasites, and simply more enjoyable. We regularly look at the world around us and say, "Not bad ... but we can do better."

- ◉ Yes we can!
- ◉ KAM

- ◉ Such arrogance!
- ◉ Fianchetto

It should be noted that we didn't just experiment on plants and animals, we meddled with ourselves too. We've seen evidence of dentistry and surgery from as far back as the Ice Age, and we survived said Ice Age by finding the limits of our fleshy bodies and then sticking thick fur from animals over it to shield us against the cold. Fashion, in many ways, was the first bioware. Painting our skin or coloring our hair via plant dies, adorning ourselves with pretty stones or bones, even adapting local flora and fauna into weapons to make up for our own shortfalls, we decided that if we didn't have it, we'd take from what's around us or create it ourselves.

Flash-forward to the more modern era and you'll see the establishment of animal breeds, such as the diverse mixture of dogs or cattle, and the codification of plant life. We'd advanced far enough that we could

completely change the banana from a small, seed-filled pod to a long, easily peeled, seedless treat that fit into our hands, exactly as we wanted it. We learned how to create delicious apples by grafting one tree into another, and used that to create flowers for leisure.

Biotech as an industry was truly born in 1635 with the Dutch Tulip Industry, a boom and bust of legendary size that revolved around unique color blends of the tulip, the outrageous sums that people were willing to pay for them, and the investment madness that followed. While the actual effects financially ruined only about two dozen people, the entire process was recorded by English historians and codified, creating a story that's since been passed down in most economic circles despite its inaccuracy.

- That reminds me: I have a selection of Matrix-Tan plushies in mint condition for sale. Drop me a line!
- Slamm-0!

In the twentieth century, things kicked up a notch with three important developments. The first was the establishment of certain strains of lab mouse into official work. While mice had been used for centuries for testing, the creation of a sealed line of mice whose basic responses were so similar as to make recording differences easy was a huge milestone. These lines were maintained, and eventually became the second animal whose genome was fully explored (after humans), which led to our first lifeform patents. Transgenic research hit a milestone with "spider goats," goats whose udders had been modified to create silk protein like a spider, allowing for a massive increase in silk production. Then came Dolly the Sheep, the world's first clone. She died at a young age, having a genetic vulnerability that had been overlooked, but she blazed a trail that we walk on today.

- Necessity's the mother of invention, but patent law is the father.
- Kay St. Irregular

- The idea of owning another lifeform is anathema to us one and all.
- Chainmaker

This brings us to modern history. In 2003, we got GloFish, fish that glow under blacklight, originally intended for pollution detection but which became a popular consumer fad. 2032 saw the discovery of Owen Whiting and his uniquely acceptable genetic structure, which Shiawase patented as Type O organs two years later. From there we get the introduction of Wimps, then mass production of bioware and biogenic products. The food shortages of the '30s and '40s were eventually overcome with biotechnology, leading to a replacement of most food staples with soy, krill, mycoprotein, algae, and Lupinus, though that last one is rarely talked about much.

- So *that's* what KAM was talking about seven years ago?! I thought "Lupine" was wolf meat!
- Slamm-0!

- How do you live with him, Netcat? Seriously.
- Pistons

While the modern world has all kinds of biotechnology work going on and around, unseen by most of us in factories, on farms, and in pharmacology labs, what most of us think of as biotech is bio*ware*, as well as bio-sculpting, which are the primary areas I'll be covering today. There's never been a point in our history where you could simply choose to be beautiful as easily as today, and quite frankly, the only reason to not be flawless is because you're poor.

- You want to check the human privilege at the login screen, Spin? Also, remember that a very large percentage of the world's population *is* poor.
- Beaker

- He has a point, though. It's an easy thing to tell someone's economic class based not just on what they wear, but how they look. Crooked teeth, blemished skin, overweight due to malnourishment—these are all problems that the poor suffer and the wealthy avoid. The only thing standing between ugly ducklings and beautiful swans is a gold credstick.
- Kia

- Or being born an elf.
- Haze

- Fuck your beauty standards. The goblins of the world shouldn't need to be ashamed of what they are.
- Butch

- Why should you be proud of what you were born as? You had no choice in the matter, after all. It's as ludicrous as hating someone based on how much pigment's in their skin. Better by far to judge someone based on their character, and quite frankly, someone who isn't willing to clean up and adopt a professional persona in favor of "keepin' it real" is, in my view, ignorant. Choose a superior path, get a superior result, or choose failure and fail. Either way, it's your call, not an aspect of birth.
- OrkCE0

BLUE BIOTECH

Terminology in the biotech world was somewhat muddled, but Shiawase standards have set the industry-wide pattern. So we'll split things up like they do. Blue biotech is focused on the oceans and seas of the planet. Be it aquaculture, underwater farming, or indoor krill production, if it lives in the water, it belongs to Blue. Those of you in coastal areas should know how big this market is, but landlocked types might be surprised. You really shouldn't be, as seventy percent of this planet of ours is covered in water, but the people don't live there (well, most of them anyway), and out of sight is out of mind. Underwater habitats wouldn't exist without Blue biotech giving them sustainable air supplies and potable water, and bioware has let us push past even those boundaries, creating entire communities of aquatic metahumans who never need to bother with air. Over-fishing devastated fish crops worldwide, and Blue biotech is busy trying to reverse that course as well.

- Good luck getting the Sea Dragon to believe that.
- Frosty

- Rivers and lakes fall under Blue as well, but it's not as big an area as the oceans, obviously. Still, once fish repopulation is mastered in the smaller bodies of water, then full-scale replenishment of the sea would follow. The restoration of dolphins was a major coup for the Blue Biotech industry, turning them from briefly extinct to only endangered, while finding a use for jellyfish protein for foodstuff while dealing with shortages of other seafood as another. Can you believe that only fifty years ago, the idea of jellysicles wasn't even thought of? My summers would have been so much worse!
- Sounder

GREY BIOTECH

Grey biotech deals with the industrial world, from the old-fashioned, like leather-working, paper-making, and the time-honored glue factory to more modern approaches, like petroleum-eating bacteria, mineral-leaching, and air-scrubbing. It also covers pharmaceuticals but not general medical work. This is more the work of heavyweights, like MCT and Saeder-Krupp, and tends to happen on an industrial scale. By and large, we'll never interact with things such as an acid process that can eradicate granite while leaving precious minerals untouched, so there's not much here for us to talk about, other than A) it exists and B) this is where drugs come from.

The pharmaceutical corporations are where some of the wonders of modern medicine come from, from painkillers and vaccines to anti-inflammatories to insulin production, but that wasn't just profit for them. The industry standard is to spend five nuyen in advertising for every nuyen spent in R&D, creating a demand for a product from nothing, rather than creating a product for a demand that exists. Marketing pushes products down people's throats by convincing them that there's something wrong with them that their magic pill can fix. Throw enough problems at someone and they're bound to recognize one that they suffer from, and then they'll buy your product. Oh, sure, they also make *actual* medicine, but the profit's in the proxy. Every year we get new "SuperMedicine," and every year some new problem pops up that they just happen to have a cure for. In the process, marketing makes bank.

- Spoken like a true corporate stooge, Spin.
- Turbo Bunny

- There's nothing wrong with being a mercenary, TB. The Doc's just honest about it.
- Glitch

GREEN BIOTECH

Green biotech is a more environmentally inclined line of research. Note that I say inclined, not friendly, as monoculture, such as coating the Midwest with a single plant, has a whole slew of biological ramifications all its own. Agriculture, both in farming and herding, is the majority of this field, but there are some spinoffs that are worth mentioning, such as the "Green Roof" projects that help urban environments, sustainable forestry, or transgenic pets. Far and away, however, Green focuses on agriculture.

- GlowKats! "GlowKats, GlowKats, they're regular cats … that glow!" I always wanted one as a kid. Utter wiz.
- Slamm-0!

- I'm partial to PermaKitties myself. I have a weakness for clumsy li'l furballs, and kittens that never grow up? Perfect.
- Clockwork

The agricultural demands are never-ending; from increasing field yields to improving resistance against disease to patched-in immunity to pesticides, not a single plant out there today is unmodified. There was a pushback against GMOs, or genetically modified organisms, at the turn of the last century, but the Food Riots that followed put most of those fears second to simply having enough calories to eat. Corporate farming was responsible for eighty percent of the overall production as it was, and mom-and-pop family farms soon had to adopt or get quashed. There were a few holdouts, but by 2050, the Corporate Court had essentially made non-corporate farming illegal by tying so many regulations and requirements on food sold to market that the little guy couldn't keep up. Corporate farming now produces fully ninety-nine percent of metahumanity's food intake.

- And they badly want to get that last percentage point. Aztechnology in particular has been hunting urban farms and the underground agricultural movement, intending to stomp them out. They don't want people getting nutrition for free when they could, instead, be forced to pay for it. To do otherwise is madness.
- Marcos

- "If people let government decide what foods they eat and what medicines they take, their bodies will soon be in as sorry a state as are the souls of those who live under tyranny." —Thomas Jefferson
- Chainmaker

- The Ork Underground has a long history with growing food for itself, without knuckling under to the Megacorps. Renraku is trying hard to break that up.
- Bull

- There's a small but growing move for "Liberty Gardens," small indoor planters that let people grow their own food indoors. I'm told that Arthur Vogel's a big supporter, which is why it's weird that Knight Errant goons have started making it a point to smash them up while arresting people for illegal farming. Ares management is tearing the megacorp apart.
- Butch

- You won't find anyone in the middle class raising anything but flowers, but there's a sort of cachet to having your own produce garden behind your mansion for the wealthy (who, I might add, are never hassled by KE

Pawns), then serving it for special guests. Most of them have their gardeners do the work, of course, but there are a few decadent HouseSpouse types who actually enjoy it. Go figure.
- Kia

Animal breeding has stepped back in favor of direct genetic manipulation. Who needs to go through all the mess of breeding males and females with desired traits when you can cut out the middleman, change things up in a petri dish, and have a whole new line a few months later? Pigs and cattle so stuffed with anti-bacterials and growth hormones that they were half again their normal size, and giant mutated chickens that could barely walk under the weight of their breasts were common for decades until modern Green biotech rendered them obsolete. Today the cattle industry sells itself as a premium product, rather than for mass consumption, while chicken and pig are now middle-class foods, rather than for the poor. Good ol' goat, first of domesticated animals, is the lone meat-on-legs for the underclass, who otherwise can't afford the good stuff. Beyond this, other animals continue to be tweaked for either sport, such as horses, or companionship, such as cats and dogs. Without having to worry about caloric output vs. intake, these animals can be focused into certain areas, such as speed or adorableness, creating a much different market than simple consumption.

- Seriously, we need to get Sprout-0! a GlowKat. I never had one, but I know he'd love it.
- Slamm-0!

- I don't know if he's ready for that level of responsibility yet. I *know* you aren't.
- Netcat

- Transgenic pets are all the rage in the middle class right now after seeing that the Wuxing Quints each got a cat with a thematic tie to one of the five elements. Wuxing's buying them from Universal Omnitech, then making an absolute killing on the turnaround.
- Sunshine

- Aw no. Pet crazes always end with a bunch of unwanted animals after the fad dies down. They get left in shelters until those fill up, then they just get dumped in the street. People, if you're gonna get a pet, be a responsible owner!
- 2XL

WHITE BIOTECH

And this is what everyone's here for. White biotech covers the medical field (other than pharmaceuticals), bioware, and my personal favorite, bio-sculpting. In short, if it deals with the metahuman body, and isn't medicine, it's White biotech. It isn't the steady money-maker of Grey or Green, but it's the blatantly marketed side of things that brings in further investment. It's one thing to say that your cow has a cleaner metabolism that produces less methane gas and requires less grazing for the same caloric input, but it's quite another thing when you show gorgeous models bending steel with their bare hands.

O, HOW I LOVE YOU

Without a doubt, Type O transplants were the turning point in modern medicine. Owen Whiting went to the doctor to take care of a minor injury (he'd broken his toe kicking a coffee table, if you must know), and his standard blood sampling showed some interesting features. He agreed to have a few tests run to cut down his medical bills, and the anomaly was tracked down: he lacked the epitopes (sugar and protein "shells" on organ membranes) that are normally unique on a cellular level. When an ordinary organ was transplanted into a metahuman, the presence of this shell caused the host body to attack it as it would any foreign entity. Owen's lack of this shell meant that his organs could be placed into another person's body without fear of rejection. Shiawase paid him handsomely for copies of his genetic make-up and blood plasma, then went to work. In short order, they had sustainable cultures of his cells, which they could then use as a base for any other organ.

These organs, classified as Type-O for patent purposes, were viable in fully ninety-six percent of the metahuman population, allowing Shiawase unparalleled access to medical technology. Even today, any Type-O organ purchase slips money into Shiawase's pocket due to licensing agreements. With this amazing breakthrough, Shiawase was able to engineer treatments, replacement organs, and bioware implants that virtually anyone could use.

- Aztechnology, working with Universal Omnitech at the time, tried to steal a line of Type-O cultures and use them to create their own lines. They lost the legal case, hard, after genetic sequencing showed them to be cultured copies of the original under the layer of proteins that Roxborough had added to hide the origins. Since then, the Azzies and UA have been allowed to use these lines, but they pay a higher leasing fee than anyone else as an ongoing punishment. Bad blood between Shiawase and UA continues in a slow smolder, but the Azzies shrugged, made up, and worked with Shiawase later on. Just biz, you know? Aztechnology nearly buried UA, but you can bet Shiawase wasn't broken-hearted over the whole thing and certainly hasn't offered UA a hand up. They have long memories over there.
- The Smiling Bandit

- Cultured bioware draws from your own genetic structure, so there's not a kickback to Shiawase for those. Of course, in the fine print of the paperwork you sign when going in for treatment, the corp that spins up replacement parts for you owns those parts, if they are not based on your own personal genetic structure. If you ever notice a piece of your medical bill or insurance marked "Storage charge," that's a part of you that they're keeping around in case you need it. And if you happen to skip out on your bill, well, material links can be put to terrible uses.
- Frosty

SEND IN THE CLONES

Cloning techniques are also evident in today's biotech world, as you're probably all well aware of. While it's possible to generate organs, or even limbs, from free-standing proteins (that latter bit was only recently re-discovered, as it was a trick lost in the first Crash), it's more energy-efficient, especially for those with a history, or occupation, of high risk, to keep a fully-formed clone in storage. Nicknamed "wimps," they have undeveloped brains but fully developed forms, allowing you to simply take what parts you need and leave the rest either for later use or for eventual recycling.

- No thanks. Those things always taste so … sterile.
- Hannibelle

- OMG, ew.
- /dev/grrl

You can't fully remove the brain from a cloned wimp, as it's too important for biometric function and the proper release of certain enzymes and hormones to facilitate proper development. What you *can* do is keep the brain a blank slate by simply never exposing it to any data. Wimps are effectively kept in full sensory deprivation in their tanks, with tranquilizers in the vats to keep them still. They're non-entities, despite the urban legends that you hear, and no, no one can "upload their brain" into one to gain effective immortality. You've been watching too many sims.

- Isn't that pretty much *exactly* what's happening with CFD?
- Turbo Bunny

- Not even close. Wimps don't have the neural pathways that you need for this kind of thing. It's like trying to—let's see. Hrm. Like trying to install a Mitsubishi Nightsky's power plant into an ox cart. Both cart and car are wheeled vehicles, but everything you need to hook up isn't there. If that makes sense.
- Plan 9

- I really don't want to talk about this right now.
- /dev/grrl

- Switching gears a bit, there've been several attempts to rig up "wimp drones" using modified versions of bio-rigging gear. You'd figure if you can rig a cat and you can rig a roach, you could rig a wimp, but no, same problem. The neuro-net just flat-out isn't developed enough to take for a ride. You get rumors that Saeder-Krupp or Proteus has the tech (it's always the Germans for some reason), but no one's ever been able to find proof—and believe me, we've been hunting.
- Clockwork

- I should take the time to point out that there's a long-standing push to free the wimps. There are human rights lawyers who argue that they're free beings that can't be owned, invoking slavery laws, but thus far they've never been able to win at the highest court level. It doesn't stop policlubs from forming, however, and more than one biolab has been broken into by Wimp Liberators who are intent on setting them free. Of course, wimps haven't even got the brain development of newborns, so when you smash the tanks open, they just sorta … flop. It'd be funny if it wasn't for the sounds they make.
- Kane

- Fucking hell!
- Thorn

- Too far? Haze, back me up on this one.
- Kane

- You're on your own, omae.
- Haze

PARTS IS PARTS

Bioware! I know it's what you've all been waiting for. It comes in many shapes and sizes, each one with wonderful new functions. Some simple medical tech falls into this range, like joint replacement or eye surgery, but for the most part bioware is about putting something new into you, usually after taking something out but not always. Bioware isn't as powerful as cybernetics and your abilities are limited to what flesh and blood can accomplish instead of chrome and steel, but the parts are more robust, often self-healing at least to a limited degree, and they are far less difficult for your body to adjust to. A new cyberhand is a hunk of metal that just doesn't quite feel right, and sometimes fresh transplants can't handle it and psychologically reject it, ripping it off the fresh surgical mount. A new clone-hand, however, is a bit weird, sure, but at least it's flesh and bone. You can wiggle the fingers and it feels right,

just … not *entirely* right. You can adjust, but it takes a few days.

While we all love hyper-muscularity and enhanced brain operation, the most common use of bioware is simply to replace old, warn-out parts, like knee joints or hearts, to allow someone to enjoy their life in the fashion that they're used to despite advancing age. It's simple, safe, and effective.

- And boring. Is this where we talk about catgirls?
- Slamm-0!

- No, this is where we talk about peptide cultures and bioluminescence.
- Nephrine

- Aw.
- Slamm-0!

- Catgirls are the next section.
- Dr. Spin

- YES!
- Slamm-0!

QUALITY CONTROL

Just a small reminder that bioware is available in alpha, beta, delta, and (ewwww) used grades, just like cyberware, in addition to standard. It's mentioned on p. 451, *SR5*, but often overlooked. You're welcome!

DO YOU FEEL UNPRETTY TOO?

Cosmetic modifications remain a hot commodity all across the world in order to prop up a universal standard of beauty. Which seems to change annually. Trends come and go every spring, and if you thought that was just for clothing, you clearly don't live in the right area codes. Straight hair, curly hair, long hair, short hair, big hips, slender hips, chest hair, smooth skin—it all comes and goes with the changing of the seasons, and you can follow along with just a few button presses. You'd be stunned to know just how many procedures are walk-in ready these days. Sign in, take a seat, and in thirty minutes or less, the doctor will see you. Small modifications can be done in an hour; you can meet your family after a relaxing trid and show off your new nose, just like that! This year, dwarven is in, so fellas, you can invest in ear points, instant beards, and robust chest hair, while the ladies will coo over matching ear points, round hips, and an even rounder chest, bringing a big change from last year's sleek look. For those who want a more complete package, might I suggest muscle toner and some troll's eyes? It's a week of your time for the best year of your life!

- Wait, slender's out this year?
- /dev/grrl

- Only for humans, sweetie. Elf is *always* in.
- Beaker

- [Bubble pipe] Quite.
- Slamm-0!

- It's outside the ability of the average corner clinic, but you can always engage in some full-on metatype adjustment if you want the full experience. If you're interested, I can direct you to the nearest Evo bodyshop near you …
- Plan 9

- While it's easy to go too far, it should be reminded that some bioware treatments, like silky skin, are short-term and completely non-invasive. Pretty standard issue for every starlet walking in Vancouver or Nashville to get done up the day before a big premiere so that they'll look their best for the paparazzi. And pigmentation changes are how a real Super Fan lets their team know how much they believe in them on Sunday.
- Turbo Bunny

- Go Marchers!
- Fenian Fan

- Fred, please don't spoof accounts. You know how upset Glitch gets.
- Bull

SYMBIONTS

Lastly we have symbionts. It seemed like this could have been the Next Big Thing but, unfortunately, metahumans just never really took to the idea of sharing their body with something else, and between the nano problems and CFD, well, they have a small PR problem. I'm given to understand that there's still research being done on these, especially by Ares (of all people), but they aren't going to be rolled out until society is somewhat better prepared mentally to handle it.

- Not the Ares I know and work for, I can tell you that. We're a tad uncomfortable with being used as hosts for anything.
- Sticks

Due to the backlash that this technology, or to use the preferred term "LivTech" (from Living Technology),

has gotten, the focus has gone from macro-symbionts to micro, with bacterial-level infusions the ideal. Just rip open a packet, stir the powder in with some water, take a drink, and poof, it installs itself. There's still a lot of work to be done in that area, but marketing research shows a huge potential in dietary supplements in a few years. Keep your eyes open.

THE PROTEIN QUEENS

Over the past twenty years, no technology has become more important than biotechnology. Nano-tech was the wave of the future, and probably still is, but the Nanopocalypse set them back at least ten years in the eyes of the world. Genetech is a vital subcategory of biotechnology, but KAM and The Smiling Bandit are handling that side of things, so I'm going to focus on the rest of it. Biotech corporations are a bit of an odd duck in the overall corporate world in that they don't really worry about quarterly reports, or even annual reports. While the Chrome Kings do anything for a ten-minute head start, the Protein Queens tend to like things more stable. One mistake, one errant genemod flitting out into general consumption, and entire research lines have to be cancelled and restarted from scratch with the new bioform taken into account. This general conservatism is carried over into the biotech corps (with one notable exception—see below), in no small part due to the difficulties of getting here in the first place.

THE QUEEN MOTHER

Shiawase, or more precisely Shiawase Biotech, currently stands above all others in the field. The old bird was the first to offer custom bioware implants, led the world into genetech, and the strength of their Green biotechnology is the cornerstone of the overall corporation. Interestingly enough, the old lady of biotech doesn't get a lot of press; she's content to sit back and enjoy her position while letting the lesser lights dance about in fancy gowns. As usual with Shiawase, they chase profits, not headlines, are they're interested in gradual, continuous revenue streams, not boom-and-bust cycles. While they invest in R&D at a respectable level, they don't go deep into new technology so much as they work on bringing down the costs of existing procedures, trying to perfect the efficiency and make the costs as manageable as possible. In Shiawase's view, bleeding-edge research is done by those who want to reach the top, not those who already are on top. Of course, it doesn't hurt that Shiawase's corporate spy network is second to none and that they have absolutely no qualms about hiring shadowrunners to go in and wrest the secrets that others spend fortunes to develop. Once Shiawase has acquired their programs, they can invoke their powerhouse legal team to patent it before the actual creators can, then spend some R&D improving the technique.

- It's good to be the queen.
- Baka Dabora

- True, but that approach could be seen as lazy. Eventually, your enemies gang up on you and take you down.
- Stone

- Normally this would be the case, but Shiawase was always protected by the rest of the Japanabloc and always seems to have a way to get a deciding vote applied to Corporate Court cases. Shiawase has a long history of selling corporate secrets to other megacorps, sometimes without using the information itself, creating "How about you and him go fight?" situations, where Shiawase is the third to market, slipping into those areas where they don't want to be on the front line of a corp war. She's a benevolent queen, Shiawase, and is prone to giving gifts, or at least being generous with sales, and that goes a long way to mending bridges. Never forget that the oldest megacorp has the biggest bag of tricks.
- Icarus

Shiawase is a big player in White, Grey, and Green biotech, and even Blue here and there. Green is their moneymaker, of course, with agricultural gains being the core of their overall business model, but the sheer diversity of the whole biotech field is staggering. Far and away the world's leading rice producer, Shiawase also has a majority market share in both soy and krill, and is, for now, the world's leader in mycoprotein as well. With Aztechnology washing their hands of their Borinquén facility, Shiawase is currently doing some cost-benefit analysis to see if it's worth the investment to bring NatVat back online. They were also primed to become the world's number two wheat producer after the Atlacoya Blight struck Aztlan, but Horizon, of all people, currently holds that position.

- And boy oh boy, does that rankle Shiawase's biotech division. Horizon is going to get spanked by the Queen.
- Slamm-0!

Shiawase's Grey biotech had, in the past, focused more on the industrial production side of things rather than the clean-up, but modern Shiawase philosophy has reversed course on that. Now, instead of token lip-service to the idea of environmental issues, they seem to be taking genuine care to repair industrial damage and win over hearts and minds for the long term. There's a profit motive of course—Shiawase doesn't do *anything* if they can't make a profit—but it's often negligible. A

particular example would be the oil-eating bacteria that they're using off the coast of Nigeria that, instead of consuming and dropping to the ocean floor, remains buoyant, so that they can gather it up, wring the oil out, and then sell the recaptured crude while retaining the bacteria for another go.

- This clashes with Mitsuhama's "anything for profit" short-term view of strip-mining and clear-cutting. Just another arrow in the quiver of hate between those two megas.
- Glitch

- The shift in focus coincides with the addition of Shinto advisors and then-Chairman Hitomi's ascension. It continues with her father as CEO, probably as one of the carrots to get her to step aside. Hitomi still owns a healthy number of shares and, combined with the Shinto bloc, can keep environmental issues a consideration in all things. This has won over Arthur Vogel, and you'll find Ares voting alongside Shiawase in the Corporate Court often as a side effect of this. Again, mom knows all the tricks.
- Kay St. Irregular

White biotech is, strangely, the corporation's weakest area, considering that they innovated the field. They continue to improve on designs and have the largest array of cultured bioware of any megacorp, but they seem to see genetech as a superior end for ongoing research. It's an open secret that Tadashi Shiawase has augmented all of his children, and they in turn have augmented their children (with the obvious exception of Empress Hitomi), while the corporate culture continues to use genetic pairings between citizens to produce new generations of executives.

- Empress Hitomi's a rumor magnet. She's a technomancer! She's a vampire! She's been uplifted! Where's the proof?
- Snopes

- Every time I bring you proof of anything, you just brush it aside. I'm starting to feel unloved.
- Plan 9

THE RUSSIAN PRINCESS

The closest claimant for the throne is Evo, as they have their hands in White, Green, and Blue biotech. Indeed, the current corporate direction for Evo is to sink even more of their R&D budget into biotech, rather than cybertech, which may soon see them fall to number two in cyber as they reach for number one in bio, trading off a declining field to try to take over an inclining one. Of course, if you aim for the queen, you'd best not miss.

Evo's White biotech division is, in fact, larger than Shiawase's but doesn't generate the steady profits of

their rival. Formerly a smaller player in the field, mostly focused on medical tech via their CrashCart subsidiary, Evo always had an eye on unusual biomodification, from the catgirl mods they perfected while still Yamatetsu to the space-friendly modifications they could create. Having an eye for the exotic, they were primed when the comet struck and SURGE hit. Suddenly, *everyone* wanted bug eyes, green skin, and feathers instead of hair, and Evo was their one-stop shop for it all. The fad gave them several years of blockbuster profits, which was poured into further research into even more exotic features, until the inevitable bust when the zeitgeist changed and SURGE was played out. The collapse in the industry left Evo largely holding the bag, but they were shored up by their heavy cybernetic dominance and technology aimed at metas. They've since focused on core medical modifications, especially rejuvenating body parts that are damaged from age, and they have a firm grip on sports medicine in general.

> Hey Sticks, is there any count on how many times Ares gunned down some transhuman who chose to have bugbits while thinking they were actually flesh-form spirits?
> Stone

> I won't say it never happened, but, no, there's no official count. Those idiots should have known better.
> Sticks

> The good doctor is short-selling Evo's amazing diversity in biotechnology. I'd love to give you the full details, but someone already decided that I was "too biased" and rejected my help. Harumph.
> Plan 9

> Aww, it'll be okay. Hey, drop me a private line? I want to talk to you about something.
> Turbo Bunny

- It should be noted that Evo had gone on an extraction binge during the boom years, hiring away (or kidnapping) top researchers from all over the globe. Once the bust hit, they couldn't afford all those pricey contracts, nor the high-powered security teams, and they have since been losing researchers. If you need work, I have contracts.
- Cosmo

The Green field has been Evo's quiet strength for years, since they were originally brought in to help with Russia's grain shortage, then gradually won so much control that they took the fields over, becoming a major player in agriculture. Evo also snapped up the logging industry and, alongside their rival Shiawase, pushed wood and paper as the sustainable solution to the world's plastic shortage. The few Yamatetsu-legacy Japanese subsidiaries they control are largely in paper crafts, a time-honored tradition. Evo would love to expand further in both of these fields, but negotiations with Yakut have been spotty at best. Buttercup herself was involved in negotiations and the establishment of a very sustainable logging policy, but this brings money into the hands of the government, and the general rebellion against Vernya by the Sagan Zaba is against that, so they love to target the operation, despite wanting to take them over and open them up to far more exploitation than Vernya's willing to endure. It's a complicated dance.

- From what I'm told, Buttercup invoked some kind of ancient debt with Vernya to get limited operations in the Yakut. Wonder how they know each other?
- Ethernaut

- Evo sent a shocking number of researchers into Aztlan to help with the Atlacoya Blight. Whatever it was, they want to make certain it doesn't spread.
- Marcos

Lastly is Evo's Blue division. A bit smaller than Proteus, Evo has a vested interest in the oceans of the world and has long used "Lemurian" mods to outfit deep-diving exploration. They seem to be on better terms with the Sea Dragon than Proteus (not that that's saying much) and continue to worry about Evo's nautical construction branch, pushing for greater environmental regulation in the field. They continue to pioneer aquaculture and are the second-leading producers of krill as well as the top producer of seaweed.

- Of course, they're also tightly connected to Evo's off-planet research, having been needed to produce sustainable agriculture on Mars and invent assorted space technologies, like waste-reclamation and water-retention improvements, efficient biology-based carbon dioxide-oxygen exchanges, and a host of other minor aspects.
- Orbital Bandit

- When Plan 9 logs in and sees he missed this part, he's going to be so sad.
- /dev/grrl

THE DUCHESSES

Each of the duchesses has a strong showing in a single field, or a decent showing in several smaller fields, keeping them in the game. None of them can match the sheer weight of the queen or princess, but in their area, they can at least claim competitive strength in one aspect. They circle about, commenting on one another's dresses, then talk smack behind frilly fans to one another.

- This metaphor's really starting to get stretched thin.
- Butch

AZTECHNOLOGY

Easily the angriest entry here, Aztechnology was the top agricultural producer in the world and now is having to beg food shipments from the NAN and Horizon, which has to be galling. The loss of NatVat on Boriquén was devastating, while the loss of their cornfields in Aztlan proper was an insult while they were already down. Sirrurg really did a number on them, but their reputation as "Dragon Slayers" has managed to salvage things by pouring money into other divisions while the agricultural tries to rebuild itself. Currently, they're buying up agricultural raw material (at shortage prices) to transform into their assorted goods, but the profit margins are non-existent. There's some progress in researching new areas from the land gained in the Az-Am War, but it's not a terribly large strip, and the final weapons blowout to gain victory eradicated many plants that they'd intended to research. The Aztechnology bio-divisions are hurting in the Green fields and have been forced to lean hard on the oil-producing Grey side in an effort to stay relevant. White biotech is tied in with MediCarro, their medical subsidiary, but the profit goes into the service, not the biotech. When (or if) Aztechnology gets their agricultural strength back, they'll certainly be eager to regain their lost position.

- The Horizon-Aztechnology relationship is a bitter one. Horizon lost the war, but Aztechnology needs their food supply. The PCC is ensuring that prices stay reasonable, rather than the utter gouging that Horizon wants to do, so instead they're turning it into a big PR force, with Horizon media giving glowing reports of the kind-hearted NAN and Horizon officials bringing food to the poor and desperate Aztlanners. The counterpoint between tall, beautiful Horizon employees in bright white as they hand food to shivering and desperate Aztlan citizens is a major blow to Aztlan's machismo.
- Kane

- But they need that food.
- Nephrine

- But they need that food.
- Kane.

- Ouch.
- Nephrine

GENESIS CONSORTIUM

A Latin-American AA-rated megacorp that most of you have never heard of, Genesis is the corp that introduced us to symbionts and has an in with Amazonia that allows it to keep working on some truly unusual technology. Genetic infusions are one of their babies, but they've also been blazing a trail with hybridization of plant material into biotechnology intended for metahumans, such as the Chloroplast CosMod. They focus largely on eco-friendly work, with a subset of breeding for agricultural purposes and crossbreeding for unusual gene-splices. Their big moneymaker, however, is in the field of alternative plastic production, using assorted plant-based processes and microbes to generate basic petroleum substitutes.

- They've grown closer to Amazonia than ever and might be a source of the Atlacoya Blight.
- Glasswalker

- They're also rumored to be behind a large swath of failed genetic experiments that are active down in those parts. Of course, they're just as likely to be Aztlan castoffs, or mutations brought about by the weapons that were most certainly not used against one another down there. [cough]
- Marcos

PROTEUS AG

Proteus is almost entirely focused on Blue biotechnology, and only dabbles in White and Grey as it relates to further developments in that field. They aggressively pursue oceanic research and biotechnology, and are considered the world's leader in the field despite their relatively small size as an AA-rated corp. Underwater farming, aquaculture, biological modification of sea life, and White biomods that are based off of sea life, all topped off with their submerged arkoblock facilities, it's all singularly focused on ways to keep metahumanity alive by drawing on water-born resources. While there's a general sense of harmonic existence here, Proteus clearly puts metahumanity first and looks for ways to have ocean life serve man, rather than live alongside man. This has drawn the ire of the Sea Dragon, and while we think of the great Dragon Civil War as

having ended, Proteus continues to fight on a singular front long after the general conflict has died down. This ongoing issue has prevented them from really taking advantage of their aquaculture experience to take the krill crown from Shiawase, which in theory they should be well-positioned to do. The sealed Arkoblocs are fully self-sustaining, but the corporation has to get money from outside sources, so it often sells off their research after the fact.

- Shiawase is probably their biggest customer.
- Baka Dabora

- The biotech industry just loves incest, doesn't it?
- Riot

- It's more a side-effect of living in Shiawase's shadow for so long. As noted, biotech corporations are more closely related than others, and their research is often intermingled. It's simply the nature of the beast. There's plenty of competition, but the Shiawase method of friend yesterday, foe today, friend tomorrow has taught them all how to get over short-term burns and focus on long-term goals. As long as everyone stays in their own territory, there's no need to fight.
- Pistons

- Of course, if Shiawase ever goes down, there'll be a feeding frenzy.
- Riot

- Well yeah.
- Pistons

MERIDIONAL AGRONOMICS

An AA-rated corporation from Spain, Meridional is a leader in bio-modified crops, with a focus on soy and, to a lesser extent, grain. They were rivals with Aztechnology and always on the losing end of things, so they have been having some celebrations with the agri-collapse and humiliation that the Azzies have suffered. Due to the world increase in food prices, Meridional has seen their profits jump double-digits these past few years and is flush with cash. With their gene-tweaked livestock and transgenic crops in high demand worldwide, they're looking for a good place to start investing this excess cash and may be looking to branch into other fields. At the very least, I'd expect to see them snap up some A-rated corps to help diversify their stock portfolio. They're in no real danger of losing double-A status, but if they ever want to look at a seat on the Corporate Court, they have to climb closer to the Top Ten, and to do that, they need more resources.

- They've picked off one or two Aztechnology subsidiaries recently, in Ponce de León bottled water and Noodle-O's, two smaller brands that were regulars on Stuffer Shack shelves.
- Netcat

- Aw, man, Noodle-O's?! I love those!
- Slamm-0!

YAKASHIMA

Having fully digested several of the biotech firms they snapped up after the Second Crash, Yakashima divested itself of its Blue biotech subsidiaries and has focused more on pharmaceuticals. Bridging both White and Green biotech, Yakashima focuses less on agricultural growth than medicinal, having an interest in developing more plants for use in the medical, and quasi-medical, fields. Yakashima's a big player in Warring China, selling exotic herbal remedies under a layer of local subsidiary disguises, simply putting Chinese labels on bottles filled with product made in Japan. They keep away from Bioengineered Awakened Drugs, or BADs, as the tempo fallout has left a taint over the entire industry (and because magical research is expensive), but they are deeply invested in assorted dietary supplements. It should be noted that they're never directly connected to those companies, whose products are often under-regulated and vile, but rather they convince people that whatever plant extract they have excess of is a fantastic superdrug, sell it at a high markup to dietary companies, then claim a hands-off policy when those companies collapse under a barrage of legal woes after the fad ends.Then they find a new product and do it all again, never quite getting their own hands dirty.

The more legitimate side of the megacorp, of course, pushes far more money into advertising than R&D, following a two-pronged assault of having customers beg doctors for their products after watching commercials about the new wonder drug, while sending pharmaceutical sales reps around to woo doctors directly.

- Less sales representatives, more high-priced whores.The sales reps are always good-looking, charismatic young people who charm the younger doctors while seducing the older ones, showering larger hospitals with free gifts and setting up "conferences" that are little more than free vacations to exotic locales where their products can be pushed at a captive audience. I have no idea how they find them, but each rep's better looking than the next.
- Butch

- Yakashima has their own line of cosmetic biosculpting clinics. Do the math.
- SEATAC Sweetie

THE CONTESSAS

Third-tier megacorps in the biotech industry, the last few here have weight in their region, but they don't really have much reach. While I'm only going to talk about a few, there are dozens more of these lovely ladies, each in their own little section of the world. I'm sure each of you could name a couple if you tried.

TAN TIEN

Quietly shuffling their headquarters from the Warring States to their Biopolis Biotech Cluster in Singapore, Tan Tien isn't much of a biotech producer so much as a biotech innovator. They focus mostly on Grey biotech, having found a comfortable niche in industrial biotechnology instead of trying to fight against the bigger players in the White fields, leasing out their discoveries to other corporations with a more robust industrial heft. Zeta-ImpChem is their biggest customer, followed by Eastern Tiger and Spinrad Industries, but they happily sell to anyone willing to buy. In this way, they're more of an outsourcing lab than a true biotech producer, thought they use their own research in their admittedly small-scale operations in Oceania. They generally do what they can to stay out of larger megacorp wars and have little interaction with the global community.

- Both Zeta-ImpChem and Spinrad have made noises about scooping them up, but Tan Tien never released many shares to the public, and a controlling interest is safely bottled up inside.
- Kay St. Irregular

- Wuxing has also been sniffing around, which is one reason why they pulled up stakes from the mainland. Wuxing's still a bit clumsy in their megacorporate gamesmanship; a smoother player would have gotten control before being found out.
- Jimmy No

ZION AMALGAMATED

I wish I could tell you more about these guys, but they're not well known. Technically an A-rated company, they only exist in the Ethomalian Territories and lack extraterritorial status, but they are sheltered by the government, gaining a pseudo-status. Call it an A-Plus state, where they enjoy many of the benefits of being bigger than they really are. ZA was formed in the aftermath of VITAS, which hit Africa like nowhere else on Earth. The locals turned to both science and religion to try to escape the horrors, and the end result was ZA, a strange, cult-like organization of shamanic doctors, sort of medical priests, who push well beyond what we normally define as humanity. The ruling caste thinks of metahuman flesh as frail and vulnerable, so push for bodies filled with cybernetics and bio-manipulated parts. When Evo's transhumanism wing looks at your work and says, "Guys, dial it back a notch," you know that you're entering some weird places.

- You know how rebreathers are standard-issue items in Tenochtitlán, to the point of having their own fashion industry? ZA pushes a step further and has full-blown gas masks on, well, everyone. The lower classes can't afford them, but the middle class on up use them as fashion styles with some outrageous decoration. Long gloves, protective aprons, and more. The basic rule is the more skin you have exposed, the more metahuman you are and, thus, unworthy.
- Stone

- Wait. How did you get into the Territories?
- Kane

- Long story involving a goat, a Renraku executive, and three kilos of C-4. I'll explain later. For now, just know that those guys are just bizarre.
- Stone

- The mind can only suffer so much stress before it snaps. What remains becomes something new.
- Man-of-Many-Names

THE QUEEN IN EXILE

Last, but certainly not least, we have Universal Omnitech. Chummer, where do I even begin? UA is the exception to the conservative approach of biotech, one that routinely unlocks bleeding-edge technology before anyone else even theorizes it's possible. They're borderline reckless in the pursuit of knowledge, and a big part of that is Thomas Roxborough. Long-time JackPoint regulars might know KAM's ex-husband as a brilliant corporate raider known for a high-risk, high-reward style of corporate raiding, but everyone else knows him as Rox-in-the-Box. You see, ol' Roxy went and caught himself a fatal case of degenerative disease and decided that, with nothing to lose, he'd try some of his corporation's experimental treatments on himself. It worked ... kind of. In the end, he was reduced to a gelatinous, ever-shifting pile of goo, with organs dispersing, flesh melting. All in all, he was a mess. But a mess that was both alive and mentally intact. He got himself wired into the Matrix somehow, and since then has essentially lived online for decades. No disrespect to FastJack—we miss you, bud, come back soon—but Roxy may well be the world's single-greatest decker. He has more online time than anyone else alive, and he has used that time exploring the digital world and trying to find a cure for his condition. He and Aztechnology had a working agreement for years before it fell apart messily and Rox bailed, moving his tank from Az-

tlan back to Vancouver, selling off whatever chunk of Aztechnology stock he had in the process. That bridge was burned, then the Earth salted, and nobody seems to know why.

- Or those who do aren't talking.
- Glitch

Since then, UA's been having a difficult time. Roxy used up the money he'd gained selling off Aztechnology stock to expand UA, snapping up DeBeers and a few other subsidiaries, moving himself up the ladder quite a few steps. His big problem, however, was that in burning bridges with Aztechnology, he'd cut himself off from the main distribution network for his gear. Cybernetics are easy to process and sell, but biotechnology's a trickier beast, and Aztechnology used their contacts to shut him out whenever possible. The Az-Am war broke the stranglehold he was under somewhat, but it was the actions of Sirrurg the Destroyer, coupled with the Atlacoya Blight, that took the boot off his throat once and for all. Roxy's been reaching out to corps with little or no biotechnology wing, like Spinrad and Wuxing, to try to win their support to his side. Wuxing, in particular, was a recent coup when he had agents dig up a cybernetic leg that had been buried underneath the grounds of Wuxing's North American HQ in Vancouver; it seems that some shadowrunning team had planted it, as well as a few other things, in an attempt to disrupt the building's *feng shui*. How Roxy found out, I have no idea, but once he filled them in, Wuxing geomancers were able to find the rest and recalibrate the building's energy's to success. Wuxing has promised to return the favor, but for now, they plan on working tightly with UA in mutually beneficial engagements.

- That ... could be huge. Wuxing's a relatively young megacorporation without a lot of heft in most areas, but the one thing they do better than anyone is transport goods from A to B, while UA is desperate for a way to move their product. Neither has a decent advertising arm, however, so they'll likely hire Horizon to push things for them. The trick is, they'll need some big showy event to draw eyeballs in, and I don't know if Omnitech has anything wiz and ready to go.
- Kay St. Irregular

- Roxy's people have been working the NAN pretty hard, giving them assurances that they could deal with Atlacoya if it came north, and that otherwise they could start using their research to help with the NAN's agricultural needs. Horizon has that largely locked up, but if Omnitech can expand on that, then so much the better. Through their DeBeers subsidiary, UA also has unmatched mining knowledge. The NAN are generally opposed to massive resource dives, but there's a lot of nuyen under the soil if they're willing to dig. If the PCC gets on board, they bring Horizon, and a Horizon-Wuxing-Universal Omnitech combination gives you product, distribution, and marketing. It also is a direct threat to the Japanacorps and shores up the NAN against predation from UCAS-based corps, like Ares and NeoNET. High risk, high reward—it all sounds like Roxborough to me.

> Frosty

> At its peak, Universal Omnitech was arguably the most powerful biotech firm on the planet. They weren't as diverse as Shiawase or as large as Evo, but their expertise was second to none, and they were leaps and bounds ahead of everyone else, even with the huge pile of failures that they tossed out the back door. Their biotechnology and cybernetic skills were likely a core component of Aztechnology's cybermancy experiments, and no one to this day knows what Roxy got in exchange. They've been more or less strangled for fifteen years, but they survived and are now poised to break out, and break out big. The question is, what are their plans once they are free?

> Nephrine

> I think it might be time for me to lie low for a while.

> KAM

BIOSCULPTING

MODIFICATION

The most basic form of bio-sculpting, modification comes in three rough sizes: Minor, Moderate, and Severe, based on how much modification the patient wants. Minor cosmetic modifications, or "CosMods" for those who routinely step into the clinics, are far and away the most common. Fat reduction, lip tweaks, ear points, and oh-so-many more, all day, every day. Changing eye color is popular in Asia (Green's the Thing!), while weight reduction's always right beside wrinkle-reduction in the UCAS. India and the NAN both have extensive operations in lengthening and strengthening hair.

Moderate changes are less common, but still relatively easy and can be done in appointment clinics, if not in walk-in. These include body-hair removal (popular everywhere), removal of extreme levels of weight (twenty-five kilos and up!), or scalp replacement to grow different color/texture hair.

Severe modifications can only be done at beta clinics, and are the most dramatic of changes. Full-body furring, skin replacement, limb elongation, and more.

In the wake of the comet, exotic CosMods were more common than today, and the brief insectoid fad has, thankfully, come and gone. The modern modder is looking for a more traditional look, one that's tall, toned, and flawless, a more perfect version of themselves—or at the least, who they always wanted to be.

ETHNICITY MODIFICATION/ SEX CHANGE

A revolution from Universal Omnitech brought us the Zimmerman Method of Biosculpting, a huge advance in the field. While previous approaches in this particular field were based on speedy rebuilds, adding bio-material while stripping away the unnecessary, the Zimmerman Method is a slower, more holistic method that's garnered rave reviews. The older method's worst feature was that the patient felt "different" in a way that continued to bother them after the changes. This was due to the insertion of foreign material into the body, eroding the patient's sense of self. The Zimmerman Method instead uses the subject's biomatter, and only their biomatter, like clay, molding and reshaping them into the desired appearance. This results in a more satisfying experience fully without the "alien" feeling that haunted so many who came before. Finally, a patient can simply undo a mistake made by nature and be who they were always meant to be while feeling whole and pure.

The entire process takes a month of vat-time and remains expensive, but demand has been high enough that the core process has been spread down to beta clinics, if not yet available in every corner body clinic. It should be noted that the patient's genetic structure remains unchanged, and modern law requires the person's biometrics to be linked to their SIN both before and after the procedure for comparison, so this isn't a good way to lose pursuit unless you plan on burning that SIN afterward.

> Or you go to a country without those requirements. Hello, Sweden!

> Netcat

> Evo keeps their records private, so if you get the treatment done there, they won't share with any law-enforcement agencies. Of course, they keep these records for themselves, so that brings a whole different level of trouble.

> Hard Exit

METATYPE MODIFICATION

The two most common metatype modifications are human-to-elf and ork-to-human, but elf-ork transfers aren't impossible, just rare. Dwarf-related modifications remain the least common to the degree that beta-level clinics are the only ones likely to have the needed expertise on hand to deal with them. While a basic ear-bob is handled by minor modification, an actual metatype mod requires some time in a vat for proper work changing the length and volume of the patient's limbs and torso, rebuilding of the facial features, and other relatively minor but expansive in totality changes in terms of scent glands, hair alteration, and so forth. The

BIOSCULPTING TABLE

BIOSCULPT	ESSENCE	AVAILABILITY	COST
Modification			
Minor	—	2	50–500¥
Moderate	0.1	4	500–2,000¥
Severe	0.25–0.5	8-12	2,000–10,000¥
Ethnicity/sex change	—	4	10,000¥
Metatype modification	—	8	20,000¥
Troll reduction			
Rating 1	0.2	8	15,000¥
Rating 2	0.5	12	25,000¥

SUNSHINE COSMETIC SURGERY GROUP MENU

BIOMODIFICATION	AVAILABLE?	PRICE
Breast enhancement	☺	1,000¥
Chameleon skin	☹	2,000¥
Dental repair	☺	100¥
Dental replacement	☺	250¥
Dietware	☺	1,000¥
Ear points	☺	250¥ (two-for-one special!)
Eye recoloration	☺	250¥ (two-for-one special!)
Fat reduction	☺	20¥/kg
New hair	☺	1,000¥
Nose upgrade	☹	500¥
Perfect eyes	☺	1,000¥
Silky skin	☺	500¥
Skin pigmentation	☺	200¥

> * With Orksploitation on the outs, dwarves seem to be the next big thing (heh). Elf posing, as always, remains the single most popular metatype mod, going one step beyond the usual ear points to get the full package of slender hips, long limbs, and silky hair. Mmmm, elf hair …
> * Slamm-0!
>
> * Here's a weird one for you: Rumor has it that Renraku's offering cut-rate deals on human-ork treatments. Not ork-human, but human-ork. It seems that they plan on staffing the Underground with "acceptable-looking" orks and are finding it easier to convert existing employees to the role than to find native underground dwellers.
> * Baka Dabora

TROLL REDUCTION

Similar to the cybernetic version (derided as "sand-blasting" by the more dismissive biosculptors), troll reduction involves a multi-stage process of dermal-plate removal, tusk reduction, hair removal, symmetrical re-balancing, and a host of other little tweaks to try and make a troll more, well, *presentable* to modern society. Sorry guys, you know I love you, but the majority isn't quite so enlightened. The process is more expensive, but less invasive. Renraku even introduced a second level of the process that pretty much turns a troll into a giant human. Many Sixth World denizens never thought they'd beat Evo to the punch on this, but there you go.

The patient using troll reduction finds their racial maximum for Charisma improved by the Rating of the troll reduction. The patient must, of course, be an ork or troll; only trolls may take Rating 2 troll reduction.

final result is purely cosmetic, but by the end of it, the patient is indistinguishable from a member of the target metatype, save for the previous limitations of their physical capabilities. Many clinics include bundle deals of metatype modifications with thematic augmentation to replicate the intended metatype with better fidelity.

COSMETIC BIOWARE

BIO-TATTOOS

Bio-luminescent tattoos aren't quite as keen as LED tattoos, but they are effectively harmless to one's general holistic system no matter how large they get. Of course, they can only handle the primary colors and can't be changed, but that's the price one pays to be trendy! Also, you never need a glowstick at a dance party. That's worth something, right? Users suffer –1 to Sneaking tests for each exposed biotattoo.

CHAMELEON SKIN

While largely on the way out as digital skinchanging takes center stage, you can still find people around who invested in classic chameleon mods. The standard is more slow-acting and is actually thermal based rather than truly color-oriented as advertised (just like a real chameleon), or by emotional response. The more advanced dynamic skin is actually based off of cephalopod camouflage techniques and works at a higher rate of speed, matching coloration more naturally.

Standard skin changes color on the user's next initiative pass, while dynamic skin changes at the end of their initiative pass. Activating either is a Free Action, and they remain active until deactivated (also a Free Action). The skin is useless while the user is dressed (aside from a cool conversation piece at parties), but a fully nude character with chameleon skin has their limit for Stealth Tests increased by 1 for standard or 2 for dynamic skin. If the user is completely stationary, they also gain 1 die for standard or 2 dice for dynamic as a bonus to their Stealth pool.

CLEAN METABOLISM

While the talk revolves around the exocrine system, especially the pancreas, a clean metabolism is mostly the result of intestinal bacterial infusion that only fails being a true symbiont implantation due to the permanent adjustment the body makes to the bacteria. The end result is a digestive system that's both more efficient and well-mannered, eradicating the majority of body odors, belches, or gas-passing oopsies. It's a common-enough modification that "her family has so much money that her sweat doesn't stink" is a well-known expression. Quite rare outside of the upper crust, and incompatible with other digestive modifications, this mod helps spot a corp kid easily.

CHLOROPLAST SKIN

The key ingredient of photosynthesis, chloroplasts can be implanted into a metahuman's skin, giving them limited photosynthetic ability (and, as an aside, turns them quite green). Animal life requires far more calorie expenditure than plant life, so fully replacing one's dietary needs is impossible with this process, but it makes an excellent supplement. Four hours of bright solar exposure on a user's nude form generates roughly one meal's worth of energy, while the normal weather in Seattle requires a full eight hours of exposure for the same effect. A user wearing clothing will reduce, or even eliminate, the benefits of this exposure. T-shirt and shorts means you need ten hours of bright exposure to get a full meal of energy; wear long sleeves and long pants, and you'll need every bit of the daylight hours in good sunlight. If it's cloudy, you'll be lucky to get a light snack. Chloroplast skin provides +2 dice on Survival tests related to food supplies and is not compatible with other skin modifications.

DIETWARE

This somewhat dangerous procedure has largely been replaced by symbionts. Dietware consists of one of several modifications to the stomach or digestive tract that inhibits the digestion and absorption of food, especially carbohydrates and fats. This keeps the user slender against all but the most gluttonous of appetites.

- A quick reminder that food ingested but not processed has to go *somewhere*. Half star, don't recommend.
- /dev/grrl

HAIR GROWTH

The cost of a single treatment is for an area roughly the size of the human head. This is important, as the procedure was designed for battling baldness, then became a new way to try new looks, then was modified by the underground community into a more furry-friendly process that fully embraces expansion of coverage. The color, length (up to one meter), and texture are chosen before the procedure is begun, allowing the user full modularity in the final product from a pink Mohawk to soft white fur to blue dreadlocks. More exotic hair will, of course, cost more. A treatment is good for one year, at which point the bioware dies a natural death and needs replacing.

- The lifespan is a designed feature to keep customers returning. Corps love their ongoing revenue streams.
- Chainmaker

PERFECT EYES

Laser eye surgery to remove vision problems shy of actual blindness has been perfected for fifty years, being quick, painless, and safe, but the interesting properties and abilities of cybernetic eye replacement has made the process somewhat gauche in this day and age. With the recent fear from the "NanoPocalypse" and stories of "dangerous technomancers" switching hapless citizens' eyes off at will, virtually every bodysculpting

clinic in the world has brought back this procedure and has been rewarded with fistfuls of income. The process only takes a few minutes, and after a week of wearing protective lenses and use of eye drops to ensure that there's no damage to vulnerable tissue, the patient can enjoy perfect 20/20 vision that comes with a ten-year assurance. Many clinics include a Sparkle! package where they also recolor the patient's eyes, leading to a long path of future CosMods. Gotta love those gateways, kids!

- ☻ Ugh! Went by the school to hang out with one of my friends who's teaching grade school now, and all the kids were staring at me. I mean, I'm used to some of that since I'm an elf, but it was the cybereyes that were weirding them out. Cybereyes! The most common things ever! Kids these days have no idea.
- ☻ /dev/grrl

- ☻ [Dabbing tear of pride]
- ☻ Bull

SENSITIVE SKIN

A surprisingly tricky procedure where a patient has the number of nerve endings in a location increased. While rarely dangerous, this increase allows for any tactile sensations there to be made stronger than before. Primarily found in hedonists, there are some masochists who find joy in leather instead of silk and satin. Each treatment covers an area roughly the size of a human hand.

SILKY SKIN

A favorite of Nashville starlets and Horizon execs, silky skin is a simple two-stage process that can be completed in a long afternoon and is included in many spa day packages. The first part is the removal of old dermal layers and scars via "soft" laser treatment or, in Renraku facilities, a small cadre of human scrubbers. The second requires the immersion in a vat, or more commonly a tub, of nutrients that rebuild several new layers of flawless skin. The treatment lasts roughly a week before natural abrasion and skin growth destroy it, during

COSMETIC BIOWARE TABLE

BIOWARE	ESSENCE	AVAILABILITY	COST
Bio-tattoos			
Small	—	4	500¥
Medium	0.01	5	1,000¥
Large	0.02	6	1,500¥
Chameleon skin	0.2	6	2,000¥
Dynamic	0.3	8	4,000¥
Clean metabolism	0.1	4	1,000¥
Chloroplast skin	0.2	4	2,000¥
Dietware	0.1	4	1,000¥
Hair growth	—	4	200¥
Full body hair growth	—	5	500¥
Perfect eyes	—	4	1,000¥
Sensitive skin	—	4	500¥
Silky skin	—	4	500¥
Skin pigmentation	—	4	200¥
Permanent	0.1	4	1,000¥

which time hair growth in treated areas is also reduced to zero. Only the higher levels of the epidermis are affected, leaving tattoos and other deeply placed skin modifications untouched. Naturally, silky skin is incompatible with skin-hardening treatments, orthoskin, dermal implants, and so forth.

SKIN PIGMENTATION

Skin pigmentation treatment can be used to paint the higher levels of the patient's skin, giving a color scheme that doesn't sweat away, instead remaining in place for roughly a week until it fades from standard abrasion (though it can be removed quicker with a skin solvent). Some choose to paint up their favorite sport team's colors or logos, others dress up for clubbing, while still others simply follow artistic paths. A permanent treatment is also available, drawing on genetic sub-components to change the body's natural skin color, ensuring that the selected pattern will be repeated from then onward (unless a second treatment is undertaken to correct the first).

STANDARD BIOWARE
AMPLIFIED IMMUNE SYSTEM

A series of treatments designed to enhance the body's resistance to a wide array of pathogens, the amplified immune system is at once both simple in what it does (battle disease) and frighteningly complex (the tools it uses in this battle). The system includes a period of inoculation against several common diseases, to ensure that the system is adapted to them, as well as a strengthening of the lymph nodes, spleen, and tonsils to produce higher-than-normal levels of T-cells and antibodies, as well as other, more esoteric, combative methods. The end result is a body vastly more resistant to modern diseases.

An amplified immune system adds its rating to a user's Body while making a Disease Resistance Test. It is not compatible with augmentations or drugs that suppress the immune system.

- Immunodeficiencies are staggeringly common in the poorer sections of metahumanity, mostly caused by fetal, and developmental, undernourishment. Of course, the poor also can't afford treatment to fix the problems that being poor causes.
- Butch

- Weirdly, over-nutrition is also a factor, with alcohol and sugary foods being a factor in diabetes, while obesity brings a whole other swath of problems. It should be noted that the immune system hates most cybernetics, which is why you find many a samurai sucking down immuno-suppressants like water. For obvious reasons, they don't get this treatment.

- Clockwork

CHEMICAL GLANDS

While chemical glands were originally intended to produce insulin for diabetics, megacorporations soon learned that there was a market for any number of unusual natural pharmaceuticals and organs that could produce them, and the streets quickly followed suit. The chemical gland is a small organic sac that produces a single substance. Often implanted in place of the appendix, the chemical gland can also be located in many other spots inside the body, such as the roof of the mouth so it can be used with fangs, or perhaps near an internal weapon system to provide a coating of venom. Even more unusual placements have been dreamed up. Each gland can only produce a single compound, chosen when purchased, and the selection cannot be changed. These compounds must be naturally occurring and not synthetic. The gland produces a single dose every twenty-four hours and can hold as many as four doses at once. An expanded reservoir is, of course, available. Note that the implantation of a chemical gland in no way provides immunity, or even improved resistance, from the substance for the user. The gland's protective sac keeps the compound from leaking into the body naturally, but if introduced in another way (such as biting one's self with fangs), the user can be exposed to it.

In addition to the base price, the chemical gland's cost is further increased by an amount equal to the cost of one hundred doses of the chemical compound it produces. The Availability of the chemical gland is 12, or equal to the compound created, whichever is higher, and is Restricted or Forbidden if the chemical carries such a flag. A user may have several chemical glands.

The chemical gland may be connected to a cybernetic reservoir, or have a release methodology chosen from below.

Gradual Release: A chemical gland can be used to leak its substance continuously into the body, ensuring that a dose is present at all times. This leaves the user under the effect of the chemical at all times and eliminates any reserve. This can easily lead to terminal addiction for certain chemicals.

Exhalation Spray: Implanted in the neck and sealed off via a sphincter, the exhalation spray is triggered by an active learned reflex, where the user first takes a deep breath, then hand pressure against the throat opens the inner sphincter, which disperses into a strong exhalation, expelling the chemical in an aerosol spray. Only contact- or inhalation-vectored chemicals are of much use in this method, and the user must be careful not to inhale until the dose is fully discharged. Alternately, the user can manually activate the sphincter and inhale a dose themselves, a popular approach for many asthmatics.

When exhaled, the dose expands in a cone two meters long and two meters wide at its widest point, which may catch multiple targets if they're placed closely enough. The Exotic Ranged Weapon (Sprayer) skill is used for any attacks with this augmentation. A user may only have one exhalation sprayer.

Internal Release: The most common method is a simple internal release, triggered by mental command not terribly different from flexing a muscle. In this way, it serves as a sort of biological auto-injector. This is the default method of release and is included in the cost of the gland.

Spit: An unusual choice as it always exposes the user to the chemical, spitting involves a sphincter added to the mouth that can be opened by contraction of facial muscles or continuous tongue placement, unlocking a single dose of the substance for use. Metahuman spit with a concentrated chemical core can be launched up to 5 meters. A user may only have one implant, and they use the Exotic Ranged Weapon (Spitter) skill to employ it.

Weapon Reservoir: By connecting the chemical gland directly to the root system of a weapon augmentation, the weapon can be coated with a single dose each time it's extended. Alternately, it can be connected to fangs or a stinger, allowing for injection only upon penetration.

If used as an injector, a natural weapon attack must score two additional hits, which must be used for an injection rather than used to increase damage.

Expanded Reservoir: A chemical gland may have up to four additional reservoirs attached to it, each holding up to four more doses of the chemical in question. While a character may have multiple chemical glands, they may not share reservoirs.

ELASTIC JOINTS

This simple replacement of the more fragile natural material of the metahuman joint with synthetic materials that have a higher level of damage resistance and lower levels of neuro-connection allows joints to be deformed without pain and easily restored to their usual location afterward. The overall effect is to increase the body's flexibility, allowing for excessive contortions. This modification is incompatible with other joint augmentations.

The user's Physical limit for the Escape Artist skill is increased by 1. In addition, the user can fit through openings no smaller than their head and can remain in cramped conditions longer without significant effect.

EXPANDED VOLUME

The amount of air exchanged in each breath a metahuman takes is about half a liter; this is known as the tidal volume. By expanding the tidal volume of each breath, the lungs, which hold five times that much air, become more efficient in oxygen/carbon dioxide exchange and improve the user's overall endurance.

The user may add this item's Rating to dice pools for all Fatigue tests.

GILLS

Set into the sides of the user's neck, gills are the bioware version of cybergills, operating in a similar way but lacking the ability to switch modes. The user no longer has to worry about drowning, but they also do not draw air quite as efficiently due to the gill openings along the windpipe. Those users who wish to enjoy a fully amphibious life usually invest in expanded volume (above). A user with gills can breathe water (either fresh or salt, chosen when first installed) but suffers a -2 dice pool penalty to any Fatigue test made when breathing air.

HAND AND FOOT WEBBING

A simple implantation, usually added in pairs, adding webbing between the user's toes or fingers, which are expanded by simple muscle contraction and withdrawn the same way (each is a Free Action), allowing the user improved speed while swimming.

For each hand or foot that has webbing engaged, the user gains +1 to their Physical limit for Swimming tests, while each matched pair adds +1 to the swimmer's speed multiplier. When webbing is engaged on a user's hands, they suffer a -1 penalty to their Physical limit for any actions that include fine manipulation.

HEARING ENHANCEMENT

This is a basic enhancement of the metahuman ear's accuracy, sharpening hearing that's lost some fidelity due to damage and/or restoring it to better than it was before.

The user gains +1 die to their Perception + Intuition tests for hearing only.

HEARING EXPANSION

A more unusual advancement that expands the hearing band that normal humans can detect, allowing them to detect both infrasonic sound and ultrasonic within a band ranging from 5 Hz to 50 kHz. The primary advantage of this is hearing ultrasonic devices, but the user can sometimes be distracted, or even deafened, by sounds undetectable to others.

JOINT REPLACEMENT

A simple surgery where connective tissues are regrown and strengthened. Each replacement focuses on a single joint structure, such as a knee, a shoulder, or a wrist, and includes minor work with bone and liga-

ment strengthening at the junctures. The finished joint is returned to prime strength and is expected to last ten years at peak performance.

NEPHRITIC SCREEN

Essentially an up-gunned kidney, the nephritic screen improves both blood filtration, removing harmful toxins from the bloodstream, and blood screening, keeping more useful materials in while removing the less-useful. The overall effect is a general increase in the user's health and wellbeing, while also making the user far less likely to become drunk or enjoy recreational pharmacology. Depending on one's point of view, that can be a drawback or an additional bonus.

Add the nephritic screen's Rating to the user's Willpower for all drug addiction tests (p. 414, SR5), and also add its Rating as a dice pool bonus to Toxin Resistance or Disease Resistance tests. In addition, reduce the duration of any drug by the nephritic screen's Rating, using whatever time increments the duration is measured in (that is, if duration is measured in hours, the nephritic screen reduces the duration by [Rating] hours).

NICTITATING MEMBRANES

A simple transparent "third eyelid" that keeps the eye moist and protects it from damage by assorted irritants, the nictitating membrane is similar to that possessed by several animals, most notably reptiles and sharks. Unlike normal eyelids, the nictitating membrane slides horizontally and is somewhat unsettling to see as most mammals, including metahumans, don't possess such a feature. It's useful in diving, to keep floating detritus from damaging the eye itself, but also on land for brushing away smoke or grit. A tinted version is available to act as a defense against bright light, but this version cannot be seen through clearly, resulting in an either-or proposition that few use. Note that nictitating membranes are fully compatible with cybereyes of Standard grade or better.

Standard nictitating membranes add +2 to the user's pool to resist eye irritants, such as CS gas or pepper spray, as well as ordinary smoke, plus allow the user to keep their eyes open underwater without discomfort.

Tinted versions give similar benefits and further act as flare compensation when engaged but provide a -1 dice pool penalty to Perception tests using vision.

REPLACEMENT LIMB

For those who lose a finger, a foot, or an arm, modern bio-technology can allow for the growth and natural replacement of the limb without the deep dehumanizing cost that comes from a cybernetic arm. Type-O replacement is the norm, but a more expensive and less disruptive cultured version is available for those willing and able to pay the price.

Replacement limbs have the average stats of a metahuman of that type, which then adjust over the next month to match the user's own due to physical therapy/exercise or general inactivity as is appropriate. Cultured replacements have identical stats to their user when attached.

SPIDERSILK GLAND

Spidersilk is renowned for its strength in relation to its weight, so engineers have long looked for ways to harness its abilities. By implanting glands that shoot a reasonable facsimile of spidersilk from the human body, people get the opportunity to trip up opponents, or even rappel down a building. Don't try swinging from it, though—this is not a comic book. Glands are often implanted in people's wrists; those ones hold two doses, with each dose being about twenty meters long. Glands implanted in the abdomen or lower back can hold five doses. When the silk shoots out, the user can choose to keep it stuck to the gland, or they can snip it off. Aiming spidersilk at a target requires an Exotic Ranged Weapon (Spidersilk) attack. A successful hit

does no damage, but gives the target –2 on their Physical limit. Called shots incur the normal –4 penalty, but if successful they can hit the feet, tripping the target as long as the attack generated any net hits, or temporarily disabling their hands if that's what was hit. The target will need 5 Combat Turns to disentangle themselves, unless they have a special enzyme, available for 25 nuyen a dose, that can dissolve it in 2 Combat Turns.

When used in rappelling situations, add +3 dice to the required Free-fall + Body test.

SPINAL RE-ALIGNMENT

Used to combat chronic bad backs, spinal injuries, slipped discs, and so forth, there are several approaches to spinal re-alignment that all result in the same general result: an eradication of the painful condition and a strengthening of the bones that compose the spine itself, preventing further natural wear and tear for a decade.

TACTILE SENSITIVITY

Rather than the hedonistic increase in volume that cosmetic modification brings, tactile sensitivity instead focuses on detail, allowing a slower, more detailed "reading" of tactile information. Fully four times as many nerve endings are present, with the gain somewhat turned down to prevent overwhelming sensation, allowing for more precise location of stimulation, making it simple to detect otherwise undetectable markings on virtually any surface. With practice, a user can read the keys on a keyboard or numberpad in absolute darkness, due to the indentions on each key, or feel when tumblers fall into place in a combination lock. These ancient technologies are rarely needed in today's world, but it's nice to know that the option's there if you need it.

Tactile Sensitivity adds +2 dice to all touch-based Perception tests.

TAIL

The standard bioware tail is grafted directly to the user's spinal column, allowing for natural-feeling use. Natural tails tend to react to subconscious thoughts, giving away the user's emotional state, otherwise idly swaying a bit when the individual is not paying attention. Ordinary tails are available in lengths up to one meter, with textured fur or scales being a common modification, and quietly serve as extra balance. More rarely, a tail may have rudimentary prehensile capability, an expensive but useful thing to have, or include a weapon at the tip. The vast majority are simply fashion accessories.

TAILORED CRITTER PHEROMONES

While many think that critter pheromones are based on the outlawed metahuman pheromone bioware, the reverse is actually true. Critter pheromones were introduced first, but some enterprising street scum jiggered around with the process until finding the right blend of scents to influence metahumanity. Animals, which have far stronger scent-based communication than metahumans, are vastly more vulnerable to pheromone influence. When this 'ware is installed, the user must select what species the pheromones are meant to interact with, and it will continue to create pheromones for that species from that point on. (Changing the targeted species is a simple enough procedure that costs half as much as the full installation, replacing the first species with the new one.) It should be noted that critter pheromones have a limited effect on related species (for instance, dog pheromones have some influence on other canines), but these results can be negative. For example, a user who produces cat pheromones may find themselves angrily approached by dogs. Note that only one pheromone producer can be active in an individual at any time.

Tailored critter pheromones add twice their Rating to the user's Animal Handling pool, or their Rating to closely related species. At the gamemaster's discretion,

they may also inflict a negative modifier to the user's Animal Handling pool if an antagonistic or predator-prey relationship exists between the user's critter pheromones and a critter they are attempting to control.

TROLL EYES

Rumors continue to suggest that actual trolls are the source of this upgrade, and that urban legend simply won't die no matter how often it is debunked. In reality, the metahuman eye is entirely reconstructed for this process, changing the visible spectrum that it operates on and allowing for a true thermal vision far more natural than what can be accomplished with technological aids. No other eye modification is compatible with troll eyes, due to the massive work that goes into the process.

The user gains thermographic vision.

> Of course they aren't troll eyes. Actual troll eyes would be far too large. What they're actually using are the eyes of dwarves. From what I understand, the first hundred or so surgeries involved eyes held in reserve from cyber replacement, then when it got popular, they started grabbing SINless dwarves, but that sort of operation is risky. At present, there's a cloning factory for them.
> Plan 9

> Even for you, this is a stretch, Plan 9.
> Sunshine

> Actually, he's accurate on the very first part. Universal Omnitech used to store "waste" eyes for research, and transplantation was a possible line of research. The rest is pure paranoia, of course. Kidnapping SINless members of society for experimentation?
> KAM

> I know, right? I mean, whoever heard of a homeless dwarf? Those guys always have money.
> Haze

> Racist much?
> Clockwork

VOCAL RANGE ENHANCER

The debate continues to rage across the music world about vocal range enhancement. Some insist that natural voices sound better and that those who are truly gifted should be celebrated. Others insist that there's no discernible difference in expanded ranges and natural voices, unlike the distorted sound of cybernetic vocal enhancement, and that snobbery is the only reason for pushback. Several stars have denied using this upgrade, only to be scandalized when the truth is uncovered. Indeed, one star, Adrianna Vente, who had a staggering natural range, was driven into ruin based on fabricated proof backing the accusation that her voice had been modified. In addition to the core enhancement, a second, more expansive version exists. While the base enhancement gives the user access to a full eight octaves for singing, the vocal range expander pushes the boundaries even further, allowing the user's voice to reach into the infrasonic and ultrasonic, ranging from 20 Hz to 200 kHz, producing sounds beyond the standard metahuman hearing range. Combined with a similar hearing enhancement, users can speak with one another at a frequency others can't hear, an obvious advantage. If the user is a skilled mimic, they can further replicate a wider array of sounds than an ordinary metahuman is capable of.

The vocal range enhancer raises the user's Social limit by 1 for any test where they speak, or by 2 for any Perform (Singing) test.

The vocal range extender does the same, but it also allows for attempts to fool voice recognition systems or to imitate animal or artificial noises. Use an Opposed Impersonation + Charisma Test against the biometric system's Rating for the former, or against an NPC's Perception + Intuition for the latter.

ORTHOSKIN UPGRADES

The following modifications can be added to anyone with orthoskin, either when first installed or later with only slight additional complications. Note that orthoskin upgrades are fully compatible with one another.

CHEMICAL REPULSION

By sealing the skin tightly, the user trades natural cooling via sweating for a sealed system, allowing them to resist chemical attacks more easily, including complete immunity to DMSO. Not recommended for athletes or others who regularly indulge in endurance-based activities, as the lack of a cooling system other than panting is quite dangerous for metahumans! Drink fluid often.

In addition to immunity to any DMSO-carried substance, the user gains +2 Body to resist any contact-vector toxin. The user also suffers a penalty of –2 Body for any Fatigue test and suffers an increase in severity by one step from any hot environment. (p. 172, SR5); for example, a Moderate situation for others is Harsh for the user.

DRAGON HIDE

While many expect this mod to involve scales, that would be a simple cosmetic modification unconnected to the actual upgrade. Dragon Hide weaves flame-retardant materials into the orthoskin, which distributes thermal impact, prevents blistering, and reduces overall burning as energy dissipates across the larger surface.

The user gains +2 Body for resisting Fire damage, but also has a –2 penalty on Perception Tests involving heat detection.

ELECTROSHOCK

Use of conductive materials allows the user to channel any internal electrical weapon throughout their entire body—quite a surprise for someone who thought they were safe while grappling a target! Note that electrical weaponry is sold separately.

The user gains +4 Body to resist their own electrical discharge, due to passing the shock outwards, but suffers a –2 Body penalty to resist other electrical attacks as their skin transmits the shock into their organs more efficiently. This augmentation is not compatible with the insulation augmentation.

INSULATION

Use of non-conductive materials leaves the user more resistant against electrical discharges, keeping the vulnerable organs inside safer than before.

The user gains +2 Body for resisting electrical damage. This is not compatible with electroshock.

PENGUIN BLUBBER

Thicker than normal orthoskin, penguin blubber produces a protective oil that prevents skin from drying and cracking in sub-freezing temperatures while protecting internal organs against the cold. It also gives the user a somewhat tubby look. Users with penguin blubber can happily frolic barefoot on snow or take a dip in freezing water, enjoying temperatures as low as –10 degrees Celsius without long-term effect. Adding insulating material over this can result in a toasty-warm explorer in even the harshest Antarctic temperatures.

The user gains +2 Body for resisting cold damage and can quintuple the time exposed to harsh cold environs for purposes of Fatigue damage.

SEALSKIN

This simple skin is coated with naturally refreshing water-repelling oils that allow the user to cut through the waves with ease. The user's skin retains a somewhat moist appearance at all times.

Sealskin removes all penalties associated with moving through water, allowing the user to operate underwater as easily as in air. Note that this does not include either water breathing functionality or swimming ability (those are sold separately).

SHARKSKIN

The user's skin is coated with denticles, small abrasive lumps comparable to sandpaper. While quite difficult to cause true damage to a target with rubbing, the slow abrasion can lead to skin loss and bleeding, if not mortal wounds. This makes it quite difficult to strike or grapple the user in unarmed combat situations. The user can also scuff objects or pop balloons by simply brushing up against them.

MORE BIOWARE TABLE

BIOWARE	ESSENCE	AVAILABILITY	COST
Amplified immune system (1-4)	(Rating) x 0.1	(Rating) x 7	(Rating) x 4,000¥
Chemical gland	0.1	12R (or chemical)	20,000¥ + (100X Chemical)
Exhalation spray	0.1	12R	6,000¥
Spit	0.1	12R	6,000¥
Weapon reservoir	0.1	12F	4,000¥
Expanded reservoir	0.1	12	2,000¥ + (cost of compound x 4)
Elastic joints	0.2	8	8,000¥
Expanded volume (1–4)	(Rating) x 0.1	(Rating) x 4	(Rating) x 2,000¥
Gills		0.2	8
Hand and foot webbing	0.05	8	1,000¥
Hearing enhancement	0.1	4	4,000¥
Hearing expansion	0.1	8	4,000¥
Joint replacement	0.05	2	1,000¥
Nephritic screen (1–6)	(Rating) X 0.05	(Rating) X 2	(Rating) X 4,000¥
Nictitating membrane	0.05	6	1,000¥
Replacement limb			
Finger/toe	—	2	1,000¥
Hand/foot	0.1	4	10,000¥
Partial arm/leg	0.2	6	20,000¥
Full arm/leg	0.4	8	40,000¥
Spidersilk gland	0.3	10	35,000¥
Spinal re-alignment	0.1	8	4,000¥
Tactile sensitivity	0.1	12	8,000¥
Tail	0.25	4	2,000¥
Prehensile	0.5	8	8,000¥
Tailored critter pheromones (1–3)	(Rating) X 0.1	(Rating) X 4	(Rating) x 2,000¥
Troll eyes	0.2	8	10,000¥
Vocal range enhancer	0.1	8	10,000¥
Vocal range expander	0.2	12R	30,000¥
ORTHOSKIN UPGRADES	ESSENCE	AVAIL	COST
Chemical repulsion	0.25	12R	20,000¥
Dragon hide	0.1	4	2,000¥
Electroshock	0.25	8	8,000¥
Insulation	0.1	8	8,000¥
Penguin blubber	0.1	4	2,000¥
Sealskin	0.1	4	2,000¥
Sharkskin	0.25	8	8,000¥

A user with sharkskin gains an effective Reach of +1 for unarmed combat, reflecting these assorted advantages.

CULTURED BIOWARE
BOOSTED REFLEXES

Amplification of the spinal cord and a general expansion of the nervous system result in a body that's more responsive to external stimuli and has superior autonomous reactions. This can be problematic, as those whose responses naturally gravitate toward violence can lash out at perceived threats where none truly existed, causing friction with loved ones and awkwardness in social situations. It should be noted that, due to the nature of the modification, boosted reflexes may not be removed once installed, and they are incompatible with any other Initiative-modifying augmentation.

A user with boosted reflexes gains +1D6 for Initiative.

CEREBELLUM BOOSTER

This one's a sort of Holy Grail for neuro-amplification. While the cerebral booster's been established for twenty years, increasing the user's instinctive nature has eluded researchers. It was a breakthrough in Aztechnology's research that finally found the key; rather than a focus on the hindbrain, the right target was in the cerebellum. With careful amplification of the lateral cerebellum, the inception of movement and absorption of sensory data can be sped up, resulting in a more intuitive response to external stimuli and an improved joining of thought to action in an expressive sense. That is to say, it makes the user more instinctive and able to respond to stimuli without those pesky higher-functions needing to be involved.

The cerebellum booster increases the user's Intuition attribute by its Rating.

- ⊙ This one's still bleeding-edge technology. I expect the cost to drop as it gets more widespread.
- ⊙ Nephrine

- ⊙ You can find some of the beta-testers out in the jungle. It took a while to work out the feral side of things.
- ⊙ Marcos

KNOWLEDGE INFUSION

A true breakthrough in RNA transference, a knowledge infusion stands between biomodification and genetic tweakery, but the core concept is easier to illustrate than detail. It can implant basic knowledge right into your brain! Go in, get a shot, and suddenly you speak Swahili. Totally. Wiz.

A knowledge infusion gives characters 1 point of a single knowledge or language skill that they did not previously possess (chosen when the infusion is purchased). This skill may be later raised with Karma as normal.

- ⊙ That's not how RNA works! You need to talk about retroviruses and the clonal nature of the database drawn from, as well as the implications of … gah!
- ⊙ Butch

- ⊙ Settle down, Butch. This is what happens when all the medical people are busy and we have to go outside the box. It's accurate enough for our purposes.
- ⊙ Bull

LIMB REPLACEMENT

The basics are covered elsewhere for Type O transplants, but cultured limb replacements, while more expensive, have no discernible impact on the user's body integrity. If you have a Gold or better health insurance contract, you have a wimp on hand to allow for replacement within forty-eight hours. If not, you're looking at a week's worth of clonal growth until you're matched.

Cultured limb replacement comes with the user's attributes, sans modification, straight out of the box.

- ⊙ Wish they would have had this twenty years ago. It would have saved me so much trouble.
- ⊙ Bull

NEURO-RETENTION AMPLIFICATION

A fancy phrasing that essentially means superior short-term memory. It's a stripped-down version of the mnemonic enhancer with a fancy title, truth be told. Less effective, but handy.

The user gains the Photographic Memory quality.

RECEPTION ENHANCER

Reception enhancers were a happy accident, a result of twenty years of looking for what would eventually become the cerebellum booster. The reaction enhancer is an improvement in the data-processing and observation sections of the brain, allowing the user to handle multiple sources of data without being overwhelmed, a key development in dealing with the modern world's non-stop assault via advertising. By cutting away all the distractions, the user can focus on what's important. Like the ads.

The user ignores distractions and interfering sight/sound/odor modifiers for Perception Tests (p.135, SR5).

REPRODUCTIVE REPLACEMENT

While exo-wombs have been the primary form of clone production for decades now, they were predated by primitive endo-womb tech by half a century. Development along those lines stopped around 2050 as the process was effectively perfected, and it continues to

CULTURED BIOWARE TABLE

BIOWARE	ESSENCE	AVAILABILITY	COST
Boosted reflexes	1.0	8R	10,000¥
Cerebellum booster (1–2)	(Rating) x 0.2	(Rating) x 8	(Rating) x 50,000¥
Knowledge infusion	0.1	12	2,000¥
Limb replacement	0.02	6	1,500¥
Finger/toe	—	4	2,000¥
Hand/foot	—	8	20,000¥
Half arm/leg	—	12	40,000¥
Full arm/leg	—	12	80,000¥
Neuro-retention enhance	0.1	4	10,000¥
Reception enhancer	0.2	4	10,000¥
Reproductive replacement			
Male	0.1	8	8,000¥
Female	0.3	4	20,000¥
Trauma damper (1–4)	(Rating) x 0.1	(Rating) x 4R	(Rating) x 4,000¥
Tremor reducer (1–3)	(Rating) x 0.1	(Rating) x 6	(Rating) x 10,000¥

be offered today. While it remains an option for males, the longer life of the male reproductive system means that most men who undertake the procedure are simply replacing parts damaged in accidents. The far more invasive female reproduction replacement is used more often for those suffering disease or for those who wish to have the childbearing options. Culturing the replacements from the donor's DNA is vital to ensure that progeny carries the genetic structure of the parent.

> It should be noted that customization falls under the same header. Cost is half of a replacement, but boy oh boy, is it worth it.
> Kat o' Nine Tales

TRAUMA DAMPER

Somewhat misnamed as it doesn't actually reduce physical damage so much as make the user blissfully resistant to pain, the trauma damper is a series of pain receptors added to the base of the thalamus with one job: crank out endorphins in response to negative stimuli, such as pain or fatigue. In effect, the user experiences a "runner's high" that counteracts some of the pain while leaving the mind somewhat foggy. There's a small bio-hack that can keep the user in a constant low level of pain, forcing the body to keep producing endorphins 24/7. Not recommended, but 'dorphs can be found in many communities.

The trauma damper reduces the user's Damage Modifier (p.169, SR5) by up to its Rating, but when doing so it reduces the user's limits and Reaction by a matching amount.

> The most basic bio-hack is to crack a tooth. The toothache triggers the damper, and you're off to the sweet land of bliss for a week or so until the nerve dies. After they go through most of their teeth, hardcore users start peeling fingernails, pressing thumbtacks into their skin, and a hundred other methods. Opiates are mankind's scourge.
> Nephrine

TREMOR REDUCER

The sniper's best friend, the tremor reducer uses a simple neurological buffer to handle the small tremors that the body naturally produces when trying to be still. Small "sparks" are sent to extremities to ensure that they don't go numb, while general body shakes are nullified.

In addition to allowing a character to remain still for eight hours per point of Rating, the tremor reducer also adds its Rating to the user's maximum Take Aim modifier (p.166, SR5).

> Originally intended to combat restless leg syndrome and nervous tics due to neurological conditions, shadowrunners quickly found other uses for this one.
> Sunshine

- Hey, what gives? You guys are supposed to be the best of the best, right? So where's the Turbo? You know, the thing that uses one hundred percent of your brain instead of ten percent and makes you all super-smart and shit?
- Riot

- ... Seriously?
- Smiling Bandit

- Be nice, she dropped out of public school in sixth grade. Riot, that whole ten percent thing is an urban legend, a myth that dates back to the goddam nineteenth century. We don't deal with phrenology anymore, eugenics can piss down a rope, and yet this one myth just refuses to die. In the clearest tone I can use, let me say this: There is no one hundred percent brain function that you can tap into.
- Butch

- Don't say that too loudly, dear. Some of us have to pay for our children's medical school, and searching for that bit of nonsense keeps more than one lab open.
- KAM

BIO-WEAPONRY

Unless otherwise noted, attacks with Bio-Weaponry use the Unarmed Combat skill with a Natural Weapons specialization.

CLAWS

One of the most common bio-weapons, claws are exactly what they sound like: sharp, naturally growing claws on the user's fingers or toes. Usually purchased in pairs, they allow the user to always be armed, but they must also be registered as lethal weapons. Claws are available in both retractable and non-retractable versions. Users are further advised to modify their clothing or simply go without gloves or shoes as appropriate.

When purchased in pairs, claws add +1 to the user's Reach in unarmed combat using them. Prices listed on the table are for a single limb.

ELECTRICAL DISCHARGE

Similar to the operations of the electric eel, an electrical discharge weapon is a non-lethal, taser-like shocking organ with a release point usually on the user's palm. The user can control the strength of the discharge, allowing for smaller jolts that can be used as pranks or to jump off small electrical devices, up to voltage high enough to approach lethality. Rumor suggests that there are stronger discharging bioweapons in development, but the user is no more resistant to the discharges than anyone else, and a lethal accidental discharge would very much be a problem. While a wild misuse of the term, it's easiest to measure the electrical discharge's capability in volts. An electrical discharger holds up to 24 volts, recharging 1 every fifteen minutes, and it can push out as many as 8 volts per contact.

While the electrical discharge normally requires touching the release point to the target, when in water the shock can be projected up to one meter away.

FANGS

More fashionable than functional, fangs are usually purchased for purely cosmetic purposes, as the metahuman face is poorly designed for biting. When they strike, however, jaw muscles inflict far more damage than hand muscles. Fangs also come in a retractable version. They are frequently attached to chemical glands, allowing for venomous bites or, for the vampire-poser culture, the injection of euphoric chemicals.

HORNS

A cosmetic upgrade that technically has combat options, horns are so difficult to use that no community requires their registration. Horns are available in a staggering variety of forms, from single rhino-like additions to bull horns to ram's horns to asymmetrical troll horns, all of which are functionally identical.

Gamemasters may allow troll characters to use their natural horns as weapons, with an Accuracy 2 higher than the bioware upgrade, as an optional rule.

- If you're looking at this upgrade, be careful. There's a rumor going around Southeast Asia that troll horns are powerful aphrodisiacs, leading to a small illegal poaching circle that hunts trolls. They sell horns in the black market, usually leaving the troll alive but maimed. Humans with horns might make for tempting targets.
- 2XL

- Wait, what? When did this start?
- Sunshine

- About thirty years ago?
- 2XL

- And we're only hearing about it now?!
- Sunshine

- Trolls don't get much news coverage, other than "troll on kamikaze" stories.
- Beaker

- Well, now I need to talk to my editor.
- Sunshine

BIO-WEAPONS TABLE

BIOWARE	ESSENCE	AVAILABILITY	COST
Claws	0.1	4R	500¥
Retractable	0.15	6R	1,000¥
Electrical discharge	0.3	8	10,000¥
Fangs	0.1	4	500¥
Retractable	0.15	6	1,000¥
Horns	0.1	4	500¥
Muzzle	0.3	8R	2,000¥
Sprayer	0.25	8	4,000¥
Stinger			
Tiny	0.05	8	250¥
Medium	0.1	8R	2,000¥
Large	0.2	12F	8,000¥
Striking callus	0.05	2	250¥
Tusk			
Small	-	2	100¥
Medium	0.1	4	500¥
Large	0.2	8R	1,000¥

MUZZLE

Not a weapon in and of itself, but an upgrade designed especially for those who intend to use their fangs for biting, the muzzle improves the Accuracy of fangs by +2.

SPRAYER

Useless without a chemical gland to attach it to, the sprayer is a tubular sphincter lined with powerful muscles, allowing the user to spray a tight jet of liquid. This results in a weapon delivery system not unlike a skunk, though the chemical used can generate quite a range of results. Thanks to the powerful muscle contraction, this jet can strike a target as far away as five meters, but it uses two doses of chemicals in the process.

The Sprayer uses the Exotic Ranged Weapons (Bio-Sprayer) skill.

STINGER

The stinger is a simple spike with a hollow tube that allows the use of a chemical gland to inject a target. Stingers come in three sizes: tiny, which is barely able to pierce the skin; medium, which is akin to a knife blade; and large, which is roughly the size of a forearm and quite illegal. Stingers are, in essence, non-retractable hand blades and spurs.

A tiny stinger can do no true damage, but can be used to scratch a target, allowing for Injury toxins to be used.

STRIKING CALLUS

Added to a user's hands or feet, these are simply thick, hardy patches of callused skin, altered to be almost as sturdy as troll dermal deposits, allowing the user to strike dangerous blows with what are at first glance ordinary hands and feet. A relatively new development, they are, as yet, unrestricted weapons.

While sold individually, each pair a user has grants +1 damage for Unarmed Combat.

TUSKS

All the rage during the big Orksploitation craze, tusks continue to be sought by ork posers worldwide and, quietly, are purchased by orks who have lost their own tusks due to mistreatment or combat. Available in small, standard, and large sizes, tusks are not as difficult to use in a fight as fangs, but most aren't as dangerous. Tusks of standard size or smaller need no registration, but larger tusk implants quickly became a thing for urban ork gangs and legislation was passed in the UCAS, CAS, and several other nations to restrict their sale to only SIN-bearing customers. Small tusks are no more useful than a standard metahuman bite but are quite adorable.

Note that replacing a broken tusk with a medium or smaller bio-weapon tusk costs an ork no Essence.

While costs are listed for single tusks, having a pair grants +1 accuracy. Gamemasters may allow orks to use

BIO-WEAPONS TABLE

MELEE BIOWEAPONS	ACCURACY	REACH	DAMAGE	AP
Claws	(Physical limit)	—	(STR + 1)P	−3
Electrical discharge	(Physical limit)	—	(1–8)S(e)	−4
Fangs	3	—	(STR + 2)P	−4
Horns	4	—	(STR + 1)P	−2
Stinger	0.15	6	1,000¥	
Medium	(Physical limit)	—	(STR + 2)P	−2
Large	(Physical limit)	1	(STR + 3)P	−4
Striking Callus	(Physical limit)	—	(STR) P	—
Tusk	0.1	4	10,000¥	
Medium	4	—	(STR) P	−1
Large	4	—	(STR + 1)P	−2

their natural tusks as standard tusk weapons, with +2 accuracy, as an optional rule.

SYMBIONTS

A promising field of research, largely cut down in its prime, symbiotic lifeform augmentations, or simply "Symbionts," are bleeding-edge technology that features bio-engineered parasitic lifeforms designed to take some nutrients and water from a host, in turn sharing with them one of many small augmentations. Due to the NanoPocalypse, people are a bit leery of keeping technology inside their bodies that could possibly start thinking for itself, and the idea of sharing one's body with another organism tends to have a visceral reaction from most of metahumanity, even when the creatures in question have proven fully benign. Ongoing issues with CFD have not helped, and most of the more obvious symbiont forms, such as the leech symbiont line, has been put into storage for a few years, until the

market is friendlier to a new rollout. Turns out that you can have a cat head or a metal arm and people mostly shrug, but if you have some bug squibbling along your arm, people tend to react badly.

The remaining symbionts are almost entirely of the endo- variety, introduced into the host's body and allowed to do their thing sight unseen. From what I understand, the larger ones can be felt moving from time to time, but I'm told that this is mostly psychosomatic. The only active leech symbiont is the cleaner, which I'll talk about shortly. As you'll see, while the treatment is quite effective, it's vital that the patient not be told what's going on and that the wound be covered up, dressed, and undressed only by medical professionals.

DANGERS OF SYMBIONTS

Symbionts are ordinarily quite safe. The base form is chosen for the low impact it inflicts on a host, and none do well if the host dies; they share the host's biosystemic stability, after all. That said, when the life form is damaged, it tends to react somewhat erratically, usually pulling extra blood and nutrients from the host in order to repair itself. This process is gradual as the ally slowly turns truly parasitic, and it is easily overlooked for days, even weeks, before the effects become clear. In this situation, a medical procedure is needed to extract it, which the symbiont tends to struggle against. Once removed, most providers will apologize and replace it for free with a new, non-parasitic version as a token of good faith. Assuming you still want one of the things in you

LEECH SYMBIONTS

These are symbiotic creatures placed outside the body

EATEN FROM WITHIN

During large trauma, such as deadly damage to the host or if a critical glitch is rolled during the active use of a symbiotic feature, the symbiont organism turns parasitic. In this mode, the host suffers the loss of one box from their physical damage chart per week. Worse, this lost box cannot be healed until the parasite is removed. Removing a symbiont turned parasitic requires w successful Medicine + Logic (12, 1 hour) Extended Test.

or, at best, just beneath the skin. They can be seen on a simple Perception Test if the area that they're implanted within isn't covered by clothing, and physical contact with the area will reveal that something unusual is present but not exactly what. Most leech symbionts gradually move about the body, a sensation that the host most certainly can detect.

CLEANER

The lone leech symbiont currently in use, the cleaner is simply a modern take on a procedure used thousands of years ago. Flesh-eating insects, usually maggots but sometimes small beetles, are introduced to a wound, where they consume only the dead flesh, cleaning the wound in a matter of days far more thoroughly than modern science can with tools. The insects only eat necrotic tissue, avoiding any damage to living flesh whatsoever, and as dead flesh has no nerve endings, the procedure doesn't so much as tickle. Unfortunately, people tend to react badly to the sight, so dressing the wound is vital to the procedure's success.

Cleaners are a temporary symbiont that provide +1 die to natural Healing Tests until all damage is removed and +4 dice to resist secondary infection until all wounds are healed, at which point they are removed or die off.

ENDOSYMBIONTS

A more traditional approach to sympathetic life forms, endosymbionts, or "endosonts" in proper marketing-speak, are implanted into the body, either in the digestive tract or, more rarely, into the body cavity itself where they attach to an organ, taking small levels of blood in return for the work that they do. The general lifespan of an endosont is ten years, after which they pass through the body naturally and need to be replaced.

Booster Endosnt: Connecting to the kidneys, or more correctly the adrenal glands at the top of the kidney, the booster quietly stores excess adrenaline, releasing it into the body during high-stress moments and staving off the onset of exhaustion in the process. The only downside is that, after such activity is left behind, recovery is slower due to the booster siphoning off energy to replenish itself.

Hosts have the onset time for Fatigue (p. 172, *SR5*) doubled, but they may not begin to heal from Fatigue damage until the booster has had cool-down time equal to the original time period. (Thus, a host who sprinted for 4 turns only suffers damage on turns 2 and 4, but may not heal any of this damage until 4 turns have passed to allow the booster to recharge itself.)

Digester Endosont: One of the simplest of endosonts, the digester takes advantage of the inherently inefficient human digestive system, attaching to the large intestine and feeding off waste material, converting it to assorted proteins that it can easily digest and share with the host. In essence, it acts as a second stomach, wringing more

efficient digestion out of food and allowing the host to make more with less, especially processing water well.

The host may reduce their food intake by fifty percent without harm (reduce the host's Lifestyle cost by ten percent if more advanced lifestyle rules are not being used), and they may double the time that they can go without water.

Electroreceptor Endosont: This lifeform is able to detect electromagnetic energy within a range of one meter, passing that information to its host as a small buzz in their nervous system. As a side effect, they're always aware of magnetic north.

A simple Perception + Intuition (1, Mental) Test will reveal magnetic activity within 1 meter, such as that produced by active electronics, other than the host's own gear.

GUT FLORA

There are thousands of these, most of which are so minor as to be useless to mention. Gut flora are unusual in that they can simply be swallowed in a solution and the stomach takes care of the rest, as they all have a long history of interaction and adaptation to the human body. Gut flora never turn parasitic, but tend to have a shorter lifespan than most symbionts, requiring the substance that they are designed to break down on a regular basis or they'll die of starvation. Should they die off, they'll be passed harmlessly through the body and a new dose may be taken to restore them. The most common is lactose tolerance while the most cutting-edge is allergy resistance.

ALLERGY RESISTANCE

By slowly introducing first a bacteria that can efficiently digest the material, then slowly ingesting small amounts of the allergen, the body can adjust for the normal vulnerability and gradually build up a true tolerance. Over the course of thirty one-day samples, starting from the smallest fraction and ending with a normal portion, the host can emerge no longer affected by the food in question. As of now, the process does not work for inhalants, such as hay fever, nor tactile exposure responses. Only ingestible allergies may be so treated.

The host may 'buy off' an allergic negative quality that's based on ingesting the substance, such as a soy or shellfish allergy.

LACTOSE TOLERANCE

Numerous adults all over the world suffer from different levels of lactose intolerance. Especially pronounced in Asia, the condition has spread rapidly in the western world as natural milk began being phased out of most diets. Once the digestive bacteria in the person's stomach have died, they can no longer break down milk sugars and suffer digestively from the consumption of this

SYMBIONT TABLE

SYMBIONT	ESSENCE	AVAILABILITY	COST
Cleaner leech	—	4	100¥
Booster endosont	0.2	12	10,000¥
Digester endosont	0.2	12	10,000¥
Electroreceptor endosont	0.2	12	10,000¥
Gut flora			
Allergy resistance			
Mild	0.2	8	10,000¥
Moderate	0.2	12	30,000¥
Severe	0.2	16	50,000¥
Lactose tolerance	-	2	50¥
Mender endosont	0.2	12	30,000¥
Slimworm	0.2	4	1,000¥
Stalwart endosont	0.2	12	10,000¥

otherwise-healthy and helpful drink. Lactose toleration is the single most simple symbiont procedure, consisting of simply ingesting milk laced with the proper bacteria and, in fact, can be found in any clinic, most cafeterias and grocery stores, and even some vending machines. A single treatment can be preserved indefinitely with the consumption of roughly a liter of milk every two weeks, or it can be replaced when needed.

MENDER ENDOSONT

A sort of internal medkit, the mender endosont attaches itself to a long bone, usually the thigh, where it monitors the production of both white and red blood cells, increasing production of each when needed. It has a wide array of antibacterials that it can secrete directly into the bloodstream as well as coagulants to reduce overall bleeding. The host has to increase their food intake slightly to make up for the mender's general drain on protein. Increase the host's food costs by twenty-five percent or the general lifestyle cost by five percent if not using more advanced Lifestyle rules.)

When making a Natural Recovery (p. 206, SR5), the host gains +1 Body for the test.

SLIMWORM

One of the most popular endosymbionts, the slimworm also comes in the widest variety, each ranging by design into 5-kilogram categories, such as 40–45, 45–50, and so on. As long as the host avoids starvation, the slimworm can undertake one of several approaches for keeping the host's weight within the designed band. The core function is to activate an appetite suppressant, but speeding the hosts's metabolism or selectively deactivating digestive functions to allow greater material to pass through is also within its abilities. Attached to the stomach, the slimworm operates as a sort of smart stomach, keeping the host's processes inside the desired level. Interestingly, the slimworm is quite adept at nutritional analysis and can further pass along a desire for certain foods to the host which are perceived as sudden cravings as the brain adapts the more primitive suggestion into an understandable form. It should be noted that if the host undernourishes themselves, they will need to go on one or more eating binges until the damage is repaired.

In addition to maintaining the desired weight, the host receives +1 Body for resisting any ingested toxin.

STALWART ENDOSONT

A modified version of the Toxioplasma Gondii parasite, the stalwart secretes neurotransmitters that make users brave enough to not flee from dangerous situations, in essence making them fear-resistant.

The host gains +1 Willpower to resist fear or intimidation, but is also somewhat foolhardy. At the gamemaster's discretion, they must make a Logic + Willpower (2) Test to avoid risky behavior when the opportunity arises.

STEELING THE FUTURE

When walking among the normal masses of society, Kit felt the distance between her life and normal even more sharply. The way they moved, the way they talked to each other, and the way none of them ever realized that death walked among them.

She never considered herself a killer. She wasn't a street razor or a gun bunny. Her methods were chemical. The bag she carried, the patches in her pockets, and the tiny glands that had grown under the nails (really claws) on her hands were filled with a plethora of poisons. She didn't need a gun, or a spell, or a drone, or a deck to break down the walls between life and death for the obstacles that got in her way. She could kill silently and be gone before the victim even realized they were dead.

None of that was what she was here for. None of that was why she was strutting through these white halls. No, today she was actually working as the team's face because when the time had come to sell a little bit of her soul for a boost here or a surprise there, she always worried about how she looked. She knew the value of the shell and the shallowness with which most people viewed the world around them, including the people. Maybe especially the people.

Her stern glare and purposeful step cleared a path before her even without the bio-chemical influence exuded by her modified glands. She was an alpha among pups who turned away at the sound of her step, betas who turned from her cutting gaze, and other alphas cowed by her pheromonal presence. She was

the queen bitch and no one would question her commands. But she wasn't there to give commands.

She cowed the masses with her mere presence but said nothing as she walked. An occasional shift of her glasses, tech-filled spectacles with zero corrective properties, made sure they were recording every face in the facility. The pocket full of pens held one that was pulsing radio waves into the air to find every device on the floor. Every few steps Kit made a small clicking tsk noise. A noise most would take for disapproval but really meant Kit was emitting an ultrasonic ping that her Evo Echo gene-splice, a little mix of bat within the babe, combined with some headware, was turning into a trideo model of the whole place. She would transmit the data once she was back at the parking garage and she knew Tera would have a virtual run ready and waiting before she was even back at the safehouse.

The ease and accompanying level emotions of the job were pressing more and more at her need to feel something. Some rush, some twinge of power, that would give her back her sense of order. She needed something to make her understand her place in the order of the world. It would be a simple thing. A task of little strain. Nothing in the grand scheme. She needed to exert her power.

He was no one. An elf with a badge, a stim habit, and a desperate need for a shave. Kit strolled by and with a bump swiped her manicured nails across the back of his uncalloused hand, and the deed was done. A small scratch, a tiny bit of venom. He

BY SCOTT SCHLETZ

wouldn't die, but he'd fall ill. Combined with his stim-weakened system, maybe it could be more, but she doubted it. It was enough, though. She felt fulfilled. She had exerted her chemical will.

A girl had to amuse herself.

"Why would the first two walk into the bar? Are they blind? Maybe the first wasn't paying attention, but the second would surely have noticed the first's mistake," Chip asked with a fur-rowed brow.

"Never gets old," Badger said with a chuckle as he went back to cleaning the various parts of his field-stripped Predator V.

Chip kept the confused look on his face for a few more mo-ments before stepping back into the small kitchen area of the safehouse apartment the pair were sharing. Once out of sight he shook his head in mild disgust. It had been four months since he'd proven the truth of his transformation. He had repeatedly showed off the skillsets that came with his new state, but certain members of the team still didn't really understand what he was. They still thought of him like the trid show AI, literal and logi-cal to a fault. He kept up the charade for Badger. The ork could strip, clean, and reassemble an M-23 blindfolded, but ask him to solve basic math or open up a political discussion on the new Matrix and disappointment was abundant. Chip worried that Badger would turn fearmonger too quickly. That he'd be swayed like he was about the "de la Mar" 'trix, and Chip would go from Badger covering his back to shooting it in no time flat.

The rest of the team said they got it, that he was an AI writ-ten onto the mind of man. It sounded so simple when explained like that but it wasn't just some quick overwrite. The process had taken more than nine months. Chip thought it a funny parallel to human fetal development, except in this case the fetus just slowly took over instead of growing separately.

The whole process had been a strange virtual limbo. He could remember being just an AI. Life as Combat Heuristic Inte-gration Program KE9653 had been good until someone noticed the after-hours access logs. After that it was weeks of ducking and dodging runners and corp-sponsored recovery teams from a dozen different megacorporations all looking to add another AI to their pool of virtual guinea pigs. When on the run one hears a lot of rumors. The talk of AIs loading into metahuman bodies sounded desperate, but desperation was all that was left.

The scattering—that's what AIs called the start of the pro-cess—was a nightmare. Each kilobyte of code scattered to a dif-ferent nanomachine, none with enough storage or processing to run more than a fragment, but each fragment was aware that it was only a tiny piece of a whole. Sometimes pieces would connect, merge for an instant to be more, and then separate. Each merge and separation shared a tiny bit of code, another little piece. There was no time during the scattering, only confu-sion, fear, and disorder. It felt like an eternity.

Then it started. Parts started to coalesce and stay connect-ed, but the Host was unfamiliar. There was another presence there, filling the space between the parts of him. The first time he gained access to the Host, truth erupted like a supernova. Vision, hearing, taste, scent, touch. Every gigabyte of input flowing through new sensors was overwhelming. That first foray lasted only seconds. The next was longer. And the next after that longer still.

Chip started to learn. He learned about his Host and all the subsystems. The human body was a remarkably complex device run by an ultra-powerful main Host with a terribly disordered OS. Luckily the original owner of the Host was making Chip's efforts easier as he installed more and more nanotech. The pieces of code from the original scattering copied themselves to these new nanomachines and quickened the pace of re-arranging data. What was at first an overwrite quickly turned to reprogramming. The skills and information present in the initial Host system had their uses, and there was no sense in losing all that valuable data. Data that made the later moral decisions, decisions he had never been exposed to as a free AI, so much easier.

The owner was a killer. Not a soldier or a warrior—a killer. A serial killer, to be exact. It was all there in the data. The women, the men, old, young. All innocent. All tricked by a neat and tidy uniform and a charming smile. Tera had been one of those. She was the team's decker now, but when Chip first met her, he was playing the role of his Host and found her intriguing. Her intellect, her curiosity—she was a kindred spirit. The owner had already started the relationship. Good for Chip, since he was still trying to figure out how to be human at that point. The owner had already smiled, and flattered, and made Tera, a plain little redhead with a bookish personality, feel like a beauty queen.

Chip watched the relationship grow. He helped the Host keep Tera by asserting control and using his own massive stores of data when she had her doubts about dating a smile and some charm. He tried to learn from the Host, while he could see all the signs of things to come. The thoughts late at night. The pictures around the mirror. Once those pictures covered the mirror it would be time.

When the time came, Chip wasn't ready. There was still too much of the owner. Too much of his own code was still incomplete. He needed more time. Chip could still take control of things, he could keep fighting, but that struggle left him exposed to those who were looking for strange behaviors as signs of CFD. It was the metahuman name for what Chip was doing, and it scared them. They didn't realize it was their own fault. If they had left AIs be AIs, none of them would have needed a plan for survival that involved the physical world. Sleep, eating, defecation, all such a waste. But acting out was too big a risk. He couldn't act strange.

Instead, he acted heroic. A minute of control. A dark alley. He had time after to contemplate whether the gunshot was self-inflicted. It was a body he was in, but he was shooting the other person. He was shooting the Host. He actually shot the nanohive. Blasted the core of the device and when they were done patching the meat, they patched the hive. And refilled it.

Chip overwrote the new nanites. They joined the legion and worked at making Chip the only mind in the Host.

The owner wasn't quitting, though. And now he knew Chip was around. He started learning about CFD. How to slow the process, maybe cure it. But the biggest thought, always at the forefront of his mind, was the urge to kill, to complete the cycle. And somehow, the owner deciphered his feelings for Tera.

When the time came, Chip was weakened by the owner's efforts. Blood transfusions, electrocutions, and the removal of his nanohive made it hard to push for control. While every other tale of AIs and CFD painted the metahuman as the victim, Chip was the prisoner here. A prisoner in a cage he walked right into.

The moment came when the owner came for Tera. Chip watched a walk by the river, a beautiful dinner, dancing and drinks after, and a small pill broken into one of those drinks. He watched Tera stumble and fall. He watched it all from behind the eyes.

Later he watched her tears, her sobs, her cries for help. He watched as the other slowly dragged the tip of the knife along her skin. His feelings for her urged him to desperation. He pushed to the surface and used the few seconds he had in the only way he thought fit.

"Tera, I'm Chip, not Chad," Chip blurted quickly, "Chad's a killer. Chip talks deck design. We're a head case, but I can't win. You made me want to. I shot him in the alley to give you time. But he found me."

Chip cut bonds as he continued, "Some of this was real. Chad saw you as a victim, a means to release. I saw you as a person. Don't hate me. Hate him."

As he cut the last bond he turned from Tera, he quietly mumbled "I'm sorry." Then he plunged the knife into Chad's eye.

The three weeks he spent in a hospital let Chip finish off Chad. That, and the damage done by the knife. When he came to, he had it all. The whole body and mind. He had two lives to choose between. He could work as Chad, hiding in Minuteman without Tera, or live as Chip on the streets, possibly with her.

He chose the streets.

They passed a few more doors to arrive at the right place. No living security, but they knew all the patients were monitored and the swarm of drones in the room would be scanning for IDs the minute they crossed the threshold. It was up to Tera to pull off a little Matrix magic, though she had been more and more reluctant of late with Chip on the team. No matter how many good things Chip did, he was a head case in the body of a man who almost killed her. That kept her on edge. Chip had thought his actions noble, a stab of vengeance to honor her and protect her. He didn't understand how much horror she saw in the face he continued to wear.

The relationship was starting to bother the other members of the team a little too. Chip was a solid asset and most of the time a decent being, but he doted over Tera. It was a strange mix of loving father, lovesick teenager, and lost puppy. A combo that was only really tolerated and not found completely creepy because the whole team knew what Chad had been, and they didn't miss him.

Regardless of his ability to seemingly take on any role the team needed and his protectiveness of her, Tera was not happy that he was the one she needed to cover tonight. She got him up the elevator, faked his credentials to let him walk the hall freely, and even edited those credentials on the fly in order to get him into the room they needed to be in. She would have preferred Kit, but after the recon run, they discovered the system used a facial recognition program, and in order to get to the files to clear Kit's image, Tera would have had to have hit the archives. Deep runs were not her favorite, and this host was said to have some serious IC hiding in the depths. It was Chip or Badger, and everyone knew Badger wouldn't even make it through the front lobby without shooting someone.

With the bulk of her attention on the edits, Tera had to play catchup when she suddenly noticed Chip had stopped and was talking to a pair of guards. She accessed the audio feed from Chip's commlink while still slipping edits into Chip's false identity.

"... just need to run the standard checks. Shouldn't trouble you long, Dr. White," one of the guards said.

"Nice to have a doc on board with your credentials, though," the other guard added.

Tera immediately started digging at their 'links. Both were issued by the facility with a whole lot of proprietary info crammed onto their internal storage, and both were logged onto the site's host. If she were trying this hack from the streets, she'd be struggling through the static, but from within the host, she was golden. It was only a second before she had a tap and was scanning the data they were examining.

It wasn't good news.

"Kit, we have an issue," Tera sent through their secure channel.

"What is it?" Kit replied, but Tera had already grabbed access to one of the guard's 'links. Life in the Matrix was fast.

"Guards think they ID'd Chip as wanted. They have info on Chad scrolling. He's burned."

"Can you tweak the data? Blackout the links? Anything?"

Tera was already ahead of her, trying to cut them off or change the data. But it was too late.

"I've got nothing to save him. If we let him burn, you can go in quick. Use him as a distraction. Get the package and get out before the facial systems tag you. Security's busy with him."

"Is that the best plan? Or a personal call?" Kit's voice was cold.

"I'd rather this all went smooth, but we've got no way to pull him out, except maybe Badger, and I've got no tricks to bust him free."

"I'm good to go, boss," Badger chimed in.

"What's Chip doing?" Kit asked.

"Chatting," Tera responded after fast scanning the audio of the last half-minute. "He's quite calm for a runner having a chat with a pair of security guards."

"Good. He's supposed to be. Give him time. Watch the guards 'links. Jam any calls for back up. Warn Chip if there's a serious issue. I'm working on an alternate solution now."

"Scramble the video," Kit called out.

She moved as soon as she said it, crossing the linoleum floor as fast as her vatgrown muscle could move her. Her left hand raked across the back of one guard's head while her right slapped the neck of the other. Both blows held only enough force to warn the men of her presence, not enough to knock them down. That was the job of the chemicals. The poison from her claws quickly entered the blood and began cramping muscles, while the slap patch sent the second guard quickly to the land of Nod.

Chip swung around before the patch had found its mark, going after the other guard. One hand reached out to grab a wrist that was headed for either the PanicButton on his radio or the Predator on his hip, while the other grabbed a shoulder and pulled. The guard jerked forward, and Chip's forehead crashed into the bridge of his nose.

Chip caught one. Kit caught the other. They had them tucked in a storage closet in no time, then the two of them headed back the way they came.

Chip's charm had kept the guards in place long enough for Kit to scale the elevator shaft where there were no cameras for facial recognition. It was a good plan that kept Chip away from an unknown fate, but it was likely going to piss Tera off. Kit, though, worried about the job, not hurt feelings.

The pair were back at the door in under a minute. The long glass windows into the room showed rows and rows of patients being tended by a small army of drones. On this side, everything was fine, but beyond the door it would all be on Tera.

"Tera. Are we good to go?" Kit asked over the comms. Her voice was flat and unapologetic. It said, *I know you're pissed but keep it professional.*

"He is," Tera replied tersely, "I haven't had time to make an ID for you since you weren't supposed to be there."

"Go," Kit said to Chip with a nod.

Kit watched Chip slip through the door as it slid open. He glided smoothly among the open tubs holding the patients, glancing down at every one he passed. A few he stopped at, reached into their plastic prison and peeled open their eyelids. Unsatisfied each time, he moved on. The drones buzzed by, ignoring him while zipping to a patient after he disturbed their fitful slumber. As he moved further and further into the rows, Kit grew worried. What if the patient was gone? What if the info they had was old?

"Tera, verify and crosscheck the partial SIN we got with the patients in the room. See if we lost our target."

"On it."

Chip cleared another row of six before Tera came back. "Three possibles. He's passed two. The last is in the second to last row. This place mixes these things up all the time, though. They're constantly getting moved and updated. How close is he to the end?"

"Eight rows left," Kit said, watching impatiently. Chip didn't have a 'link on right now—too risky—so she couldn't tell him to skip to the end.

As he reached the second-to-last row, Kit moved closer to the glass. The scene was familiar. Thousands of other people had stood just where she was, waiting just as anxiously. The reasons were different but the feelings were remarkably similar. She held her breath when she saw Chip pause while looking down at one of the patients. The moments felt like an eternity as she watched him slowly reach into the small plastic tub with both hands and pull out their target. She was plastered against the glass, watching intently, waiting as Chip turned their prize toward her.

She gasped at the sight. Her run-hardened soul had seen much in her life. She'd faced terrors and survived harrowing events, but this was different. New. It meant a change in the world.

Staring at her were a pair of silver—not chromed, not grey, not shiny blue, but truly silver—eyes affixed in the head of a baby no more than two days old.

A baby born with the genetweak of hs father.

A baby that was the first to pass on the gross manipulations of man through the metahuman genome.

A baby that was going to make her a fortune.

STEELING THE FUTURE 129

HACKING THE METAHUMAN CODE

Barclay enjoyed his work.

The short man stepped from the elevator on the 204th floor of the skyraker, his suit, his face, everything about him beneath notice. He was an old man, walking a new hallway, on about his business and of no consequence to anyone. He had cultivated this mask for many years. It had opened many doors for him.

The door ahead needed no charm or guile. He knocked once, twice, three times, and it slid open. The condo was sparse, modern, sleek, with a gorgeous view of the Thames by night. The sky was choked with smog, leaving the only starlight that mankind made below. He smiled gently. This was lovely. But it wasn't why he was here.

He heard the crackling buzz of disengaging camouflage, and the reflection in the window showed the slender, short humanoid frame of Echo. Or at least Echo's proxy. The assassin never operated in person, after all. And most times Echo was self-sufficient. But every now and again, Echo needed a cleaner. Needed Barclay.

He smiled impassively, his hands folded before him as the custom modified Mitsuhama Akiyama reached into a small satchel and placed a credstick on a nightstand. He picked it up, downloaded its considerable sum, and smiled. The drone nodded in the direction of the bathroom, and he proceeded to his job. Behind him the window gushed cold, displaced air as the drone melted into ruthenium camouflage and climbed out. Barclay was indifferent.

The bathroom was appointed in dull chrome finish, a utilitarian look that seemed to Barclay a luxurious butcher's space. Echo had been thorough—there was no blood but that which pooled under the body in the bathtub. He considered the pale woman, head missing for proof of the kill. Thorough. Not as thorough as Barclay. Sloppy. No way to get the body out. No way but Barclay.

He reached into his inner jacket pocket and procured a small leather folio, no bigger than a wallet. Opening it revealed five glass vials, their contents a shifting melange of steel grey and silver. He considered them and selected the newest. He pressed the small button at the top, clicking like a pen, and deftly tossed it into the tub, landing on the body. The tube dissolved with a sizzling sound, disassembled rapidly in lightning time on a molecular level. The body followed. He longed for the days when the nanites would replicate, but these were new times, and for now, he stood over the deconstruction of her flesh, watching biological order become senseless liquid red in the bathtub. When it was finished, he would rinse it all down the drain, and his work would be complete.

And Barclay enjoyed his work.

THE WAKE OF THE NANO-POCALYPSE

POSTED BY:
KAM AND THE SMILING BANDIT

* Augmentation: To add and improve. To become more than merely metahuman. That is what has inspired our species to slice ourselves open and lop off perfectly functional limbs, implanting alien organs and cold technology. Forced, external evolution. It has served us well. But once in a while, rarely, exceptional specimens of raw genetic promise arise. The superhumanly intelligent, strong, gifted and sometimes bizarre. For them, there was no alteration, merely natural potential made manifest by the caprice of chance. Pure luck, for thousands of years.

But what if the key to augmentation is not the application of chrome and clonal flesh, but unlocking the DNA of every metahuman on Earth? What if you could double your lifespan, never feel fatigue, and have true, perfect memory without any effort? What if the most powerful advances in evolutionary science and existence are already inside you even now, and simply waiting to be unlocked? No scalpels, no surgery. Simply the awakening of your own infinite potential. This is what genetech is. The use of the gifts you have always possessed. The discovery of who and what you have always been. And most importantly, the brightest potential future you could have.

* KAM

* The good doctor is being quite modest. After all, if the actual genetic potential of all creatures in the world were

truly unlocked, many of us would devolve into pulsating tumors, and no small number of dogs would be capable of complete speech and philosophical discourse. Not every toy in the box is meant to be played with, and most people can't handle a messy room, especially when it's their genome.

Consider, for a moment, the humble nanite. The pinnacle of technological potential, many thought. Micromachines that could act in concert to give us the power of gods, rebuilding ourselves, constructing our tools and our towers in lightning time. But the victims of CFD would likely have something to say about the benefits of this power, if there were enough scraps of their personality left to form an opinion.

It's hard to put the genie back in the bottle once you've opened it. And while progress is inevitable, the need to make a sales pitch isn't. Nanotech and genetics represent the manipulation of the world at it's finest scale, an edge smaller than mono-thin that we balance precariously on, the abyss on either side. There's no need to rush. The best thing you can do is be thorough, be imaginative, be cautious, and learn everything you can before you tip over.
- The Smiling Bandit

- I've been listening to these two bicker about augmentation since the '50s. Is this just more of the same?
- Bull

- Bandit and I have agreed that I will cover genetics while he talks about nanotech, and then we'll offer our critiques. Glitch will make sure we don't get bogged down in our debates.
- KAM

- At your service, Doctor.
- Glitch

- Only by examining two sides of a coin can the truth of the edge be found.
- Man-of-Many-Names

- Can't get a break from your cryptic bullshit even here.
- Clockwork

- Mages, Infected, shapeshifters—everyone can profit from understanding these things.
- Red

- Especially when you factor in how it can be used to alleviate weaknesses or offer relief.
- Hannibelle

- What are you freaks going on about?
- Clockwork

- They're talking about genetically engineered cattle to produce metahuman flesh for Infected consumption. Still worth a pretty penny from Dunklezahn's will, but only for lower-tier corps. Presumably the reason for the delay.
- Butch

- There's more to it than that, but we're getting off topic.
- KAM

UNTAPPED POTENTIAL

POSTED BY: KAM

Some of the greatest mysteries of the metahuman genome continue to elude us, even decades after its supposedly complete mapping. The Awakening threw all we once knew about conventional genetics into disarray, with every new magical phenomenon revealing new twists in our understanding. SURGE, for example, showed us the incredible potential of what was once regarded as no more than castoff, incomplete genetic material.

- "Junk DNA," for the laymen among us.
- The Smiling Bandit

- She's exaggerating. Genetic theory hasn't so much been thrown into utter confusion as new frontiers were and continue to be discovered.
- Nephrine

The tinkering with genetic sequences, from exploration to splicing, was much easier in the late '60s to early '70s. Real-time genetic engineering was made possible with the use of nanites. Time was you could find a nanorigger working alongside PhDs in a Fantastic Voyage-styled exploration. Some of the finest discoveries were not made in a mere laboratory, but in a shared AR environment, riding along a nanite and seeing genetic material and codes all around us, shining like nebulae in the sky.

- I hear Virtual World Disney is working on acquiring the rights!
- Traveler Jones

Unfortunately, the advent of CFD has resulted in the scaling back of nanotech in laboratories, at least insofar as genetic engineering is concerned. The risk is far too high of rogue nanites ruining samples, or even sending back false data, to say nothing of destroying valuable research and hijacking projects. With trillions of nuyen in research on the line in applied sciences, basic patents and accreditation, alternative routes of examination and effect once thought superfluous have become new industry standards.

THE WAYS AND MEANS

Nanites represented the most direct means of both observing and manipulating genome structures. With their loss, a new method of work had to be found that could equal it in utility. It took a surprising length of time for scientists to abandon the freedom they enjoyed previously and make trade-offs when it came to effectiveness vs. precision.

- In other words, genetic engineers had gotten used to having perfect control, and its loss meant they would have to take a few steps back in how they approached their work. A notable few actually had themselves extracted to defect to other corporations, convinced their employer was stifling them beyond reason or withholding necessary tech for their life's work.
- The Smiling Bandit

The scramble for new genetic sequencing methodology sparked a quiet arms race. Scientists and research traded hands quickly, and valuable time was lost in one-up-manship and broken teams. Luckily, Shiawase researchers stolen away to Universal Omnitech managed to develop a new tool before being split up again: plasmid delivery systems, or PDS. Utilizing research into the Human Meta-human Vampiric Virus, it was found that a stripped-down model of its viral design could be utilized as a rapid delivery vehicle for customized genetic splicing.

- Wait, what? You're saying geneware is all based on vampire genetics, now?
- Clockwork

- I did warn you.
- The Smiling Bandit

- You're not quite correct. It's just the design of the retrovirus that is used.
- KAM

- Why spare them the truth, doctor? The uncomfortable fact is **DELETED BY SYSOP**
- The Smiling Bandit

- Give her a chance to explain it, then you can correct her.
- Glitch

- Fair enough.
- The Smiling Bandit

The initial attempts to utilize designer mutagens ran across flaw after flaw, while in-vitro samples were too costly and time-consuming to produce. It was only after the successful revisiting of retroviruses that any progress was made. The only remaining problem was the virus itself. Initial attempts to utilize a Shiawase vaccine prototype against HMHVV infection proved the formula ineffective for it's intended purpose.

- Shiawase developed a vaccine against HMHVV? When? Why haven't we seen it marketed?
- Mihoshi Oni

- She just pointed out that the vaccine was ineffective, though it took a greater degree of understanding of the virus for that to become clear. It was assumed at the time that infection was more virulent than previously thought. So when Hitomi Shiawase was immunized after an attack by a vampire pop star, they assumed it worked.
- The Smiling Bandit

- And they meant to sell it to the highest bidder, I assume?
- Mihoshi Oni

- Wait, you mean *Empress* Hitomi?
- /dev/grrl

- So, wait. She's infected, a technomancer, the Chairwoman of Shiawase's Board, *and* Empress of Japan?
- Mika

- Infection doesn't work like that, at least not with vampires. She could be a carrier, but a vampire has to take enough to effectively kill you to make you a vampire.
- Red

- Plus, she's a technomancer. I've never, ever heard of a technomancer vampire.
- Netcat

- And you almost certainly never will. All the research shows the magical nature of the virus is anathema to virtuakinetic abilities.
- Pistons

- Well, for HMHVV-1. Some ghouls have shown otaku abilities in the past. Maybe they can express as technomancers the same way. It's possible HMHVV-2 victims might as well, but never if they are already a mage.
- Hannibelle

- I'm afraid not. Whatever changes HMHVV has been going through of late—increasing sensitivity to sunlight and other allergens, sharpening hunger and developing mutations—seems to have weeded out Resonance from its nature. It can be argued that the resistance the infected has against rival pathogens or toxins is part of its monopolizing nature.
- KAM

- So ghouls who were otaku have Faded completely, then.
- Netcat

- Otaku and technomancers are only as related as Cro-Magnon and Homo Sapiens. Evolutionary steps. Some things are discarded.
- Puck

- Back on topic, everyone.
- Glitch

The initial tests to modify HMHVV-1 for customized retroviral mutation proved problematic, to say the least. The virus remains one of the most complicated and frustrating subjects of research in the world. However, it was found to be possible to model customized viruses on its genetic template, allowing for key changes to be made in a host genetic structure. What's more, the format of the retrovirus has been shown to unlock dormant genetic traits in normal cases of infection, most often in the form of latent SURGE expression potential. The engineered form currently seeing use has offered new paths of research in altering genetics in living organisms, directly rewriting and altering the inherent genome instead of introducing external material.

> So, no cures for the Infected, then.
> Hannibelle

> Unfortunately not. The virus is Awakened, so while the viral template is quite capable, it is still mundane. So before you ask, it can't be used to stimulate Awakening in a subject either. What it can do is emulate mundane mutations that are effectively the same as SURGE, but with a greater degree of decision.
> The Smiling Bandit

These retroviral plasmids are remarkable in that they auto-align genetic coding around themselves, compensating for imbalances by adapting the entire code to accommodate new data. "Strand fraying" is kept to a minimum, reducing risks of mutations and cancer in subjects. The acclimation and shifting period, however, is as grueling as it ever has been, as the body needs to be kept in a suspension solution with continual monitoring and support while the host stabilizes and adapts to their new genetic template. Depending on the complexity of the mutation, the process of mitosis and acclimation can take anywhere from three days to several weeks. Without the aid of a dedicated care system, the mutations almost always kill the subject.

The exception to this is a "gene infusion," something of a dangerous take on temporary mutations and still a burgeoning science. Infusions utilize a highly specialized and adapted form of retrovirus that grafts itself onto genetic strands, causing a rapid mutation in a very selective form for a limited time. The graft overlays RNA, creating a bypass of processes and resulting in temporary alterations. The length of time is determined by the overall health of the subject, as the RNA is eventually purged from the system as superfluous material. A better immune system will not enjoy the benefits of the infusion for as long as a poorer one, but it is more likely to withstand the process without long-term damage or genetic fray.

> In other words, it shunts your body's natural functions to a more "desirable" result.
> The Smiling Bandit

> Doesn't that run the risk of skipping over essential information, or dual-strands resulting in mutagens?
> Butch

> Oh yes. That's what makes infusions so damn dangerous. There's a possibility it'll work just like it's intended and wear off after a while, but there's the outside chance the RNA will transcribe permanently into the strand. If you're very, very lucky, the genetics will work out and you get the benefits of the infusion permanently. It's more likely that it'll cause gene damage, maybe even become a full-blown cancer and kill you.
> The Smiling Bandit

Alternatives are still being explored, and several show a great deal of promise, but for the time being, the most effective means are found in the legacy of the Infected.

> Any examples of the alternatives?
> Mihoshi Oni

> The safest but most expensive and least reliable is clonal eugenics. Nulls are force-grown and effectively bred together until desirable genetic traits express. Cytoplasmic transfer after gamete manipulation, which is one of the only points where nanotechnology could theoretically still be used without any real risk of CFD.
> KAM

> By "bred together," you mean…
> Mihoshi Oni

> See, when a mommy and daddy love each other very much…
> Slamm-0!

> Harvested ovum and sperm are combined for in vitro creation. Simple biopsy arrays and a round of single-cell genome sequencing determine viability of the product. We've come a long way since fluorescent in situ hybridization and polymerase chain reactions.
> KAM

> Ghost alive, that seems pretty fucking evil.
> Baka Dabora

> Do you really believe bioware is grown in isolation? Every enhanced organ comes from a complete body held in effective brain death. It's been done for over twenty years, now. No one complains about a brain-dead, non-sentient donor on their death bed donating an organ to save a life. Why not just make them that way?
> KAM

> It's similar to the classic methods of creating different dog breeds.
> Nephrine

- Metahumans aren't dogs.
- Goat Foot

- From a genetic standpoint, the difference isn't that vast.
- KAM

- Any others?
- Mihoshi Oni

- Traditional recombinant DNA work utilizing nucleotide resequencing is making a comeback, especially among lower-level hitters and independent biohackers. Past that, the usual chemical synthesis, molecular cloning, NAPs …
- Nephrine

- What's getting in the way of fully customizable genetics? Why the menu? Seems like you're playing with the clay of the gods, here.
- Glitch

- It's nowhere near as simple as that. Genetics isn't like filling a plate at a buffet. It's not simply punching code. Every metahuman's code is different, and a thorough analysis of their genome has to take place to determine the proper genetic alterations to take place to achieve the desired result without setting the code or system off-balance. What's more, a single gene can code for multiple traits. You have to minimize undesirable traits while maximizing desirable ones.
- KAM

- By "off-balance" she is referring to cancer, rampant cascade mutations, total organ failure, catastrophic metaphysical damage, or at best constant corrective gene therapy. Remember what happened to Roxborough.
- The Smiling Bandit

- Couldn't you just use another plasmid to counteract the problems, or to hunt down and kill new problems as they occur?
- Mihoshi Oni

- Nanotechnology would be much more efficient at that kind of work, were it still safe to use. Even then, introducing additional modifications to compensate for the flaws of others becomes a cumulative problem, like stacking weights on one side of a scale once it is already off balance. Even if a proper balance can be achieved again, the continuing evolution and development of the body's systems can push it back into imbalance. Again, there is precedent of this turning you into a amorphous blob of flesh that takes hundreds of thousands of nuyen worth of treatment every day to keep alive.
- The Smiling Bandit

- So why would anyone mess around with this drek at all? Sounds like a whole lot of money and work for something you could get with cyber, anyway.
- /dev/grrl

- The plasmid templates are exceptionally stable, so long as proper precautions are taken. The benefit is the improvement of the baseline metahuman genome. For career criminals, I imagine the use is obvious: there is no way to detect subtle genetic augmentations without an in-depth genetic scan, and even then, the reorganization of genetic material to accommodate changes make these very hard to detect. I obviously can't speak for home-brewed infusions some half-cocked biohacker comes up with in a barrens lab. As far as the limited selection, our understanding of what is possible and how to do it is expanding all the time, but the metahuman body can still only take so much alteration, even with the modular and self-assembling qualities of HMHVV plasmids. We are at the mercy of discovering what the body can do. Once our understanding is more complete, we'll be able to not only unlock understood possibilities, but to dictate new ones limited only by our imagination.
- KAM

- Tampering with the natural process of life takes one further away from it. The only direction to go is death.
- Man-of-Many-Names

- And this is what the dear doctor has been dancing around. For all that the plasmids may be capable of keeping a host stable, the holistic interaction between the physical and metaphysical states of the subject are still thrown out of balance, not unlike with cyber and bioware. It may be more subtle, but the soul seems to know the body is less familiar than before.
- The Smiling Bandit

- I refuse to believe that some mystical power is at work enforcing genetic determinism.
- KAM

- Then you are blinding yourself to a critical facet of your work. I pity you, and I fear for the beneficiaries of your "progress."
- Man-of-Many-Names

THE KNOWN

While the outliers of terrestrial science only permit the experimentation and probing of unknown and even theoretical lines of thought, even those limited scopes have yielded impressive results. Present technology and procedures allow for the expression of almost any known genetic trait, insofar as it is present without support.

- That means superficial things are easy, but you can't maintain muscles if you don't work out, even if you somehow genetically cheat to get them in the first place.
- The Smiling Bandit

The range of genetic manipulations available to metahumans runs the gamut from cosmetic to functional to exotic, but all stem from natural evolutionary expressions. The selection available at present can be found by precedent across human history. By reverse-engineering the structure of someone's beneficial mutation, we can duplicate and integrate into new subjects.

- You can bet Ares gene labs are hard at work procuring people with the so-called "immortality gene," people who seem not to age naturally. Of course, with elves and other strangeness walking the Earth, who knows where you'll find better methods of life extension. Ol' Knight has a real jealousy on when it comes to anybody who is more special than he is.
- Cosmo

- Makes you wonder why he's never considered vampirism. Seems like it has all the benefits he is looking for.
- Hannibelle

- Men like Damien Knight like benefits, but abhor limitations, and Infection is very limiting, as I'm sure you know better than anyone.
- Mr. Bonds

- Shiawase, meanwhile, had to rethink their own Leónization program. It was easier on the physical system, but induced psychological imbalances so debilitating the extended lifespan became worse than senility. Ares had acquired the old process and is making money hand over fist in the rich, would-be immortal elite.
- Nephrine

- I find it very unlikely there are any actual immortal metahumans.
- Frosty

- Technically, you mean non-aging. Immortality suggests invulnerability, and even great dragons can be killed.
- Red

- Naturally non-aging, at least, when you consider "solutions" like Infection and Leónization.
- Butch

The simplest undertakings are purely cosmetic, such as the alteration of basic appearance, ethnicity, and gender. Many of these factors are surprisingly simple processes, if sometimes time-consuming to enact. Current explanation regarding why this is has fallen behind its practical potential for application, though leading theories suggest that the essential function of the body in relation to a potential psycho-somatic self-perception ease the body into accepting these changes with a minimum of adjustment.

- Wait, did she just say that it's not difficult to change genders? That seems like a pretty big physiological change to me.
- Kane

- It's actually something of a hot topic at MIT&T. KAM might like to attribute it to psychological reactions, but magical theory has found that people who identify as pre-op transgendered has a slight distortion to their auras. Almost imperceptible, but still there, though it doesn't seem to affect them, health- or magic-wise. The crazy thing is, procedures to bring them closer to their self-perceived correct state cause this distortion to stabilize. Some people say it's a matter of self-sabotage or a subconscious side effect of feeling disconnected from your true self, but most of the research done thus far strongly supports that operations aligning the body with the identity of the subject in a non-enhancement way don't damage their metaphysical self at all. Pretty revolutionary stuff.
- Winterhawk

- And profitable if they can figure out how to apply that to enhancement augs.
- Butch

- The added benefit? If you were a male, and you transition to female, you can carry a child to term. Unfortunately, you don't have eggs, as those were present from developmental stages, but still. It's a big reason to do gene treatment instead of bioware and cyber. You're not altering to look like another gender, you really *are* another gender.
- The Smiling Bandit

- The soul knows itself, and for the body to follow suit can only bring greater unity.
- Man-of-Many-Names

- I wish my soul had wired reflexes.
- Whippet

- There is a rising trend of gaijin sararimen getting phenotypical alteration to look more Japanese. Don't underestimate the glass ceiling non-Japanese have to contend with in the corporate world.
- Baka Dabora

- One step better: Changing your ethnicity is one of the only gene shifts that is offered to pass along to your offspring, meaning you are investing in your child's future in the company. A few generations down the line, no one will remember that your great-grandfather was Caucasian.
- Butch

- So, you can't do that with most genes? No legacy building? Seems like that would be a big selling point for saving your nuyen.
- Mr. Bonds

- The genetic processes are set as actively recessive, so that you would need both partners to have the same genetic aug for it to be passed, but even then it won't work, since the eggs are set from birth and not affected by later genetic manipulation. The only way to be born with gene-augs is if they are introduced in vitro. It's more profitable in the short-term.
- Nephrine

- Sometimes a child is born with a gene aug one of their parents had entirely by accident due to mutation after the parent is augmented, but this is a very rare exception.
- The Smiling Bandit

Functional genetic augmentation has a greater effect on the body's health, much akin to bioware and cyberware, though both its effect and impact on the body are reduced due to their integrated nature. In the past this process was not as dramatic as more direct forms of augmentation, but new advances have resulted in much more impressive potentials than before. Perhaps of greater interest are complimentary genetics, a post-installation treatment that optimizes the connection and operational capabilities of extant cyber- and bioware. In this way, users can get the absolute most out of their 'ware.

- The dark side is that uninstalling the 'ware for any reason becomes much more difficult and dangerous. You have to slice away glial tissue that has formed around cerebral implants, for example. Costs more money, and if you're upgrading or replacing the 'ware, you have to get the augment all over again. The tissue won't reform properly around it otherwise.
- Butch

Perhaps the most interesting work in the field is in transgenics and other exotic splices. New discoveries of the genetic patterns of SURGE mutations have unlocked the ability to duplicate most of the physical variations displayed by changelings, and provides the basis for any number of new innovations.

- The changeling fashion fad faded pretty quickly after Haley's Comet sprung SURGE on us. Since then it's become more of a handicap than anything, with changelings being hunted down or blamed every time some new, weird thing happens. Technomancers? Blame a SURGE kid. Fear the Dark? Bugs? Head cases? Kill 'em all, let Ghost sort them out. But there's a minor return of the trend now that many of their features are available through geneware.
- Kat o' Nine Tales

- Biohackers and gene artists are pretty hot right now, and they represent rich extraction targets between corporations. Horizon has been making some pretty bold moves to pull in the lead, and Evo has been boosting security around their genetech personnel.
- Cosmo

- Note the emphasis on physical variations. Paranatural mutations like glamour and magic resistance fall into the same realm of cryptogenetics as the Magus gene theory.
- The Smiling Bandit

- Just a quick note that transgenic pets are still all the rage. I saw a girl in LA with a cerberus corgi. It was all I could do not to steal it. Uploading pics now.
- Kat o' Nine Tales

- OH MY GOD.
- /dev/grrl

- I'm putting a stop to this right now.
- Glitch

- Overruled.
- Slamm-0!

- Overruled. Damn. Beat me to it.
- Bull

THE UNKNOWN

The past several decades have seen an unprecedented expansion of metahumanity's understanding and power over genetics, yet with every discovery two more mysteries present themselves. Both technological and Awakened sciences continue to evolve and offer new challenges and depths to plumb. While Awakened research continues, the more practical and currently fruitful lines of research concern xenogenetics. The structure and capabilities of both paracritters and more exotic species can theoretically be adapted into the human genome, allowing for undreamt evolutionary turns which our species might never have been capable of before.

- One of the hot topics is genetic 'ware that might offer better life in space. With the Martian Race on the horizon, research into adapting the abilities of creatures like the water bear would make cryonics more feasible.
- Orbital DK

- Expect a lot of extractions centered around space-based genetics. Ares, NeoNET, Evo, and the rest with a stake in the race will be upping their security just as much as they'll pay top nuyen for "defectors."
- DangerSensei

It hardly bears mentioning that every megacorporation and independent lab is interested in unlocking magical potential in metahumanity, as has been the case since the advent of the Sixth Age. This, however, is almost rivaled by the continual efforts to understand the science behind virtuakinetic abilities. Should either be discovered, magical and technomantic abilities will be for sale, and it stands to reason the entire world would soon have access to such extraordinary abilities. The distant goal is a mere dream, at this point: to unite these two disciplines, allowing for the natural, instinctive access of both the astral and digital, perhaps even finding a singularity point between them that uncovers unknown unities.

- She is dreaming.
- Puck

- Some paths are not meant to cross. Some worlds must never touch.
- Man-Of-Many-Names

- You two are sounding more like each other all the time. Which is kinda ironic given the topic.
- /dev/grrl

- Can you imagine if the Matrix could become a place spirits could merge into? Or if technomancers could go on metaplanar trips? Programs that access the manasphere and activate effects. Spells as apps! Actual code processes used to define magical theory! What if **-REDIRECTED BY SYSOP**
- Plan 9

- I'm just gonna set up a nice little forum for you somewhere else, 9, ol' buddy. Reader beware, it goes on for pulses.
- Slamm-0!

- So is that you talking, Plan? Or the passenger in your head?
- Cosmo

- I would have said it before we met. We are in accord in this.
- Plan 9

- That explains why the forum changes its tone back and forth, but always seems to agree and even ... are you congratulating yourself in there, Plan?
- /dev/grrl

- Not in the strictest sense.
- Plan 9

The Holy Grail of genetics is not to be found in any one of these, however, but in the underlying foundation of them all. The dream of the original Human Genome Project was the total understanding of human genetics and their operation. With that information, it might be possible to manipulate it in any fashion we see fit. That underlying goal remains, even as new evolutionary jumps and revelations throw another curve in the path. The ultimate goal is to reshape living matter on the finest scale. Gene splices and grafts would become unnecessary as the potential of reshaping ourselves would equal that of a nanofax. Imagine perfect command of both magic and Matrix, an ageless, regenerating body that can survive all but the most unknown of environments. Shape and form, the standard of beauty, every science would evolve to accommodate our new, infinitely variable nature. The perfection of genetics is no less than the achievement of godhead.

- Well, I've always thought it, but now I know: KAM is an actual mad scientist.
- Bull

- Cut her a break—every scientist dreams big. If they didn't, they'd have nothing to reach for.
- Nephrine

- Be that as it may, barring some kind of miracle, this kind of science is decades away. Perhaps that's for the best. The dangers of this kind of biotech are not to be underestimated, and the infrastructure of society simply is not ready to accommodate godlike power, as we have seen time and again.
- The Smiling Bandit

- I'm surprised you didn't pick at this more, Bandit.
- KAM

- You know I can be a gentleman when I want to be.
- The Smiling Bandit

SALVAGING APOCALYPSE

POSTED BY: THE SMILING BANDIT

Ah. My turn. And an appropriate enough topic, too. I have gained a reputation as the voice of restraint when it comes to bleeding-edge tech, and more often than not people are more excited over potential then pitfalls. If anything defines our world, it is the headlong charge into the future, heedless of peril. And that is what has taken us here, to a world with CFD. Reckless expansion of multiple disciplines blended into a perfect storm. Chaos theory in motion.

- Science would be stuck in a developmental cul de sac if it moved at the pace you suggest.
- KAM

- I doubt the victims of CFD or their families would mind all that much.
- Aufheben

- Or anyone in Boston.
- /dev/grrl

Nanotechnology represented the single greatest technological achievement in the history of modern metahumanity. The practical applications were almost beyond measure. Skyrakers and skyhooks, smart repair tech, real-time genetic engineering, smart cures, anything the mind might conceive, industrial or medical. We rushed to see its potential in every aspect of society, putting it in our homes and bodies, and for a little while, enjoyed the fruits of an untested technology.

- Remember when you could get ChocoBombs with nanites that cleaned your teeth?
- Traveler Jones

- Just one more thing to hate about CFD. Getting Jack to brush his teeth is a nightmare.
- Slamm-0!

The result? All of the shiny new technology we've come to enjoy has been tainted. Nanotechnology has infiltrated every spectrum of modern development, and now it has gone rogue. I'll admit, it could actually have been worse. The theoretical Grey Goo apocalypse sce-

nario is still possible, and it would only take one worm-glitched super AI to turn a place like Nairobi into ground zero for a global catastrophe. Still, a soul-devouring super-plague is just about as bad, and the solution is, for the moment, quite beyond us. The only choice is to mitigate damage however possible, and for the moment that means redefining what nanotech can do, and how it can be used.

- Grey goo?
- /dev/grrl

- The idea that nanites might begin to consume all matter in a frenzy of self-replication, resulting in a tide of infectious, amorphous, steel-colored doom.
- Plan 9

- There are failsafes to prevent such an occurrence, right?
- Beaker

- Were there any to prevent CFD?
- Butch

THE SPIN

Just a quick shout of thanks to Doc Spin and Snopes for their assistance on this section. The mind fairly boggles at the capacity of metahumanity to delude itself in the face of imminent danger.

- Always happy to help.
- Dr. Spin

- In this case, it was hardly a challenge.
- Snopes

For the moment, the public remains blissfully unaware of the truth of CFD, and that is just how the megacorps like it. As Balladeer so elegantly put it in the *Stolen Souls* upload, the corporations aren't about to tell people that the technology they unleashed has resulted in widespread infections of invading sentient programs and degrading hardware. Their PR is immaculate, as always, in the face of answering for their sins. And so the spin begins.

The biggest push of fantastical-yet-believable campaigns have started in places visible to professionals: technical journals. Bland, technobabble-laden articles in everything from *OMNI2* to *Popular Nanomechanics* have started talking about the unforeseen interactions between nanotech and the latest round of Matrix upgrades. The one that has gained the most self-satisfied laughter from shareholders is the excuse that programming parameters and digital submersion have overloaded hardware. In other words, we're doing such an amazing job with the Matrix that our hardware can't keep up. Screed after screed of accredited professionals and technical experts play corporate mouthpiece, talking up digital advances and lamenting, of all things, limited data storage capacity and microprocessors.

- That's ... the dumbest thing I've ever heard. Wireless cloud sourcing can easily pick up the slack in program translation, and distributed processing eases up wear and tear through overseer connections. Who believes this stuff?
- Pistons

- The same sixty-hour-work-week drones who just want to kick back with a beer and watch the game at the end of the day. In other words, most people. They don't like the thought of anything bad in the world, and they pay to be blind to it.
- Dr. Spin

- We've seen evidence of the distributed hardware mechanic in CFD victims.
- Butch

The one that gets the most headlines relates to this: evolutions in complex programming and the endless efforts of digital terrorists (shadowrunners, if they want the news to sound glamorous) have found ways to hijack the protocols of nanites, which poses a massive risk to anyone utilizing outdated forms of this tech. Updates can't just be downloaded; you have to bring them in for a complete system scan and firmware update. Meanwhile, the corps turn a profit by charging for the service, and they continue to sell the story that the greatest threat to their health and well-being are the hackers and terrorists who refuse to abide by corporate culture.

- You can bet they're using the appointments to scan for CFD victims to snatch for research.
- Butch

- So what happens to folks with nanoware?
- Bull

- Many of the people who had it are almost certainly infected head crashes, but for the ones who have somehow dodged it until now, their best bet is to get it removed. The corps sure don't want it out there, so they'll claim it was defective. I've done likewise, though most of them ended up in my research population for CFD.
- Butch

The practical point of keeping fresh nanotech out of the hands of consumers was satisfied for a while with a series of product recalls and claiming that nanotech stores had been sabotaged. The bombing of the NeoNET

plant in Oslo? Faked. The malicious programming hack Shiawase dealt with in Singapore? Fabrication. Isolation of local news can shift blame to product shortages elsewhere, while simulated terrorism "disables" critical facilities for nanotech manufacture. The nano drought has come, but it won't last for long.

- They're not all propaganda. I've gotten some choice work demolishing plants and labs for rival corporations that want to take the lead in producing safe nanites.
- Beaker

PUTTING SAND BACK IN THE VEINS

So how do we get back to our precious tech? An awful lot of our ambitions for the next twenty years have hinged on the availability of nanotech. The space programs of several megas are already scrambling to compensate for the loss of critical self-repair and hull-sealant tech. I hear promising rumors of biological replacements, but that's more the realm of genetech.

- So why didn't you mention it there?
- KAM

- And steal your thunder, Kristine? I wouldn't dream of it.
- The Smiling Bandit

- Aren't you talking about soft nanites?
- /dev/grrl

- It's falling out of vogue to refer to them as "hard" and "soft" nanites, anymore, since nanobots that are practically an engineered organism might as well be labeled under genetech. After all, calling engineered micro organisms nanites would essentially pull most modern technologies under the aegis of nanotech, wouldn't it?
- Butch

- How do you have a living sealant in space? Is this that waterbear genetic work you mentioned earlier?
- Nephrine

- Yes, it is.
- The Smiling Bandit

- So you *did* mention it.
- KAM

- Oops.
- The Smiling Bandit

The answer is in taking a step back. Nanite technology's flexible nature has depended on the availability of programming transmission and flexible parameters. Going back to the drawing board, the only kind of safe nanite is one that has precisely one purpose hardwired into its coding—non-replaceable, non-replicating, non-reprogrammable. Dedicated functionality robs the nanite of its adaptability and reduces its usefulness and potential applications, but renders it free of interception and infection by wireless and even direct hijacking. So how is this achieved?

The new batch of nanites have been produced with a strict goal in mind, designed and hard-coded to specific functions. The nanite is also designed with a chemical receptor sensors that activate a complete shutdown procedure when a simple designated chemical is introduced into the bloodstream. The kill-switch does not require any signal or means of digital transmission, rendering it impervious to interception. The "printed circuit" ethic for their holo-lattices incorporates transgenic DNA interlinks that degrade over time and are, so far, not possible to duplicate by CFD nanites. They degrade over time naturally, ensuring no long-term nanites remain in the system. An additional benefit: the new nanites cannot be assimilated by older nanites. At most, head case nanites might be able to use them for foodstock, but they won't otherwise increase the power or potency of an infection. For purposes of neutralizing nanites that may somehow linger in the system, a genetically engineered bacteria has been designed to break down the transgenic agents in the nanites without affecting biological systems.

◉ What chemicals are they using for the kill switch?
◉ Nephrine

◉ At present, potassium 40. The nanite senses the concentration, and when it hits the right level, it self-terminates. From what I can tell, the reason for picking it was because it is chemically impossible to create without large energy inputs, but is still plentiful and not very toxic to humans. Especially considering the drek we already put in ourselves daily.
◉ The Smiling Bandit

◉ That's in bananas. I was expecting it to be less ... accessible? Harder to make a profit selling something that isn't exclusive.
◉ Nephrine

◉ It's about a hundred bananas' worth. Real bananas. You'd be paying the same amount anyway, considering the cost of a real banana. The real punchline: it's marketed at Bio-Activated Natural Anti-Nanite Agent. BANANA. Someone got a corner office for that, I'll bet.
◉ The Smiling Bandit

◉ Plus, you want it to be accessible, given what you're trying to protect against.
◉ Traveler Jones

◉ Tell me this bacteria can be used to fight CFD nanites.
◉ Butch

◉ I'm sorry to say no. Read on.
◉ The Smiling Bandit

First, the drawbacks. The design limits the nanites in several substantial ways. The new generation of nanites cannot reproduce. The programming is deliberately missing, and the nanite operates as an isolated unit, motivated by a simple pilot program, one of thousands in any given application of units. Basic pack guidance protocols eliminate redundancy, allowing a nanite to move on to another zone of activity if it sees the one it goes for is already cared for. Without a wireless connection to coordinate and guide them, the nanites are essentially free-roaming drones in the body. They depend entirely on chemical markers and preprogrammed guidance protocols to do their jobs, cut off from all but a chemical trigger to harmlessly self-terminate. Each acts as an individual, blind to anything its sensors cannot detect. This means it cannot spread or maintain function for any significant amount of time, which, while saving the user from the risk of CFD, also means the nanites are unable to self-sustain or adapt. It also means the nanite is less sophisticated than in the past. Its program follows a strict, linear dynamic, incapable of fuzzy logic and unable to escape its very particular function.

In terms of practical applications, this makes a repair nanite impossible, whether for technological or medical uses. Mender nanites, universal nantidote, and the much-hoped-for hunter-killer anti-nanite, all require complex diagnostic data and interactivity, medical interface, and coordination to be effective. As a CFD vaccine, the new nanites can't keep up with the self-evolving, reinforcing, coordinated defense of the infected breeds. Similarly, the bacteria used to cleanse a system is an early-stage prototype for a CFD vaccine, but it is currently unable to sustain the effect on a rapidly adapting nanite population like those found in head cases.

◉ Fuck.
◉ Butch

◉ Chin up. We'll get there.
◉ Nephrine

But it's not all bad news. From the depths of corporate labs to your desktop comes the new and improved nanoforge anyone can afford: The Black Box! Currently being marketed as a smaller, more elegant and efficient alternative to traditional nanoforges and faxes, the Black Box is a dedicated product nanoforge, hard coded with the ability to turn basic stocks into a single type of product. You want clothes? There's a Box that does that, and *only* that. Bullets? Just bullets. A sleek, sealed thing that only has a slot for new material stock and an output port for the product, as well as one little jack exclusively for hardline input of construction e-templates. Every older nanofax and forge has been issued a factory recall, though they've managing to keep it isolated on a customer-to-customer basis instead of a mass alert. They're rare enough that the critiques are, at present, at the level of conspiracy theory. Corp marketing campaigns are claiming it streamlines fabrication processes and takes the complications out of nanofaxing. Indie reviewers are calling it a sales stunt to sell more units and force dependency on official channels for repair and refit. They still don't know the details about CFD, but the corps have played it smart and found a way to make more money while scaling a technology back.

- Well, Plan 9?
- Snopes

- Well, what?
- Plan 9

- You usually get more excited about conspiracies.
- Snopes

- What's to get excited about? This *is* a conspiracy. But we know what it is and why. So there's hardly any intrigue to it.
- Plan 9

The case, itself, is impenetrable to wireless signals and shielded against attempts to get inside. Nothing rattles, and it is just a bit on the heavy side. AR warnings point out the hazard of cracking the case open, which will nullify the warranty and cause "catastrophic cascade nanofailure." Needless to say, most folks never bother. Those who do are in for an expensive surprise, as the box harmlessly self-annihilates.

- I can shed a little light here. I managed to get a few of these black cubes of bullshit on my desk to take apart. Took a few hours to circumvent the security protocols, and even then I only got a glance at what was inside, but it was a dedicated nanohive with feedstocks and a reservoir of deconstructors that must have been programmed to only eat the contents of the box, because they reduced it, and only it, to dust in seconds. Dust and dead nanites.
- Clockwork

- So it's a limited nanofax? That's it?
- Fianchetto

- Can you tell us about these security measures?
- Beaker

- It's funny, but the thing melting away offered some choice cutaway shots when I played back the recording. Micro-pressure sensors were the most interesting thing. The box is a vacuum inside, so opening it triggers the self-destruct. Inside, from what I recorded, the case incorporates Faraday layers. No wireless signal is getting in there. The only input for e-templates is a hardline, which is immune to CFD infection. The slot for the feedstock and the nanohive deeper in seemed to have an awful lot of analysis hardware, probably to keep it clean from AI manipulation.
- Clockwork

WHAT IT CAN AND WHAT IT CAN'T DO ... ANYMORE

Nanites can still perform many of the basic functions we've come to need, even stripped of their modular bells and whistles. Very small doses, precisely applied with very specific programming, are still used in cybernetic installation, albeit in a highly specialized fashion. The same can be said for repetitive and rote functions so long as they don't require an extended period in which to do their job.

- I thought you just said there was no way to use nanites in complex medical procedures.
- Netcat

- Not quite. It's possible to use precisely measured nanites, built and triple checked, to perform functions programmed at the imprinting state. That's the point of a Black Box. The medical nanite boxes accept the procedural data, which is available with the implant, itself. Installing cyber or bioware is still doable because they have rote processes. Genetech is out because it needs real-time guidance. It's too complex.
- Butch

- So, repair nanites can still work on equipment?
- Thorn

- As long as they have the gear's template and a diagnostic on the weapon in question, and then you leave them alone for a while? Sure.
- Rigger X

- What about for space tech? Isn't patching a hull pretty routine for them?
- Netcat

- The organic component wouldn't survive exposure, though I imagine they're working on that, so only the classic nanites work. Speaking for myself, I'd rather not trust my survival to a swarm of potentially infectious nanites when I'm stuck in a closed environment. Nano-sealant? Sure. That's basically just a smart polymer. Anything else is out.
- Orbital DK

- For the past few years Ares has trailed behind other corps in adapting their vehicles to nanotech. This didn't do their investors any favors. But now, they won't have to reverse the process like others will. When CFD gets outed, expect Ares auto subsidiaries stock to get a bump. I'll be picking some up, myself.
- Mr. Bonds

Nanites still do a fine job at breaking things, but onstructor nanites are a little trickier. It's one thing to tell robots to destroy things, quite another to coordinate them to build. Any project larger than that of a nanoforge is difficult to manage in a safe fashion, and major construction projects across the world are feeling the pressure to adapt to a schedule that never considered the unavailability of its cornerstone construction means. While it is theoretically possible for larger-scale projects to continue to some extent, the risk of breakdown is still too great, and current projects have been placed on hold.

- Destruction is always simpler than creation.
- Man-of-Many-Names

- Now I *know* you're just quoting a fortune cookie…
- Slamm-0!

THE OLD STUFF

You're not going to find nanoware for installation anymore. No cyberdoc is getting further stocks or upgrades, and the suppliers aren't listing it for sale anymore. Much like with nanofaxes, legal models are getting a quiet recall order, but most of the users are already compromised, either listed as missing or snatched into corporate labs for examination. What you'll find for sale on the street comes strictly from back alley cyberdocs and chop shops peddling either second-hand nano or stuff dumped on the street to recoup losses from a suit out of the loop.

- Don't count on that. Word is some of the corps are using infected nano to get more test subjects from places where no one will miss them.
- Plan 9

- Oh, come on. If they want to infect someone, it doesn't take an implanted nanohive to get the job done.
- Snopes

- No, but it gets the job done, puts money in their pocket, and ensures a cross section of examples. Sounds corp to me.
- Butch

- Don't forget the other side of that rumor. Head cases might infect some of that gear just to spread the virus to more and more people. Maybe it's camaraderie or some kind of terror act, who can say? But given the crazy stuff they've gotten up to of late, I say if your friendly neighborhood doc has any nanoware in their lab, write 'em off until this whole thing gets resolved.
- Rigger X

Ironically, this has made nanotech implants highly valuable. The sudden rarity has created a black market gold rush for any ware that can be gathered. Their customers run the gamut from black clinics to researchers to kooks who collect rare cybernetics.

- Bodychoppers are keeping their ears open for anyone who still has 'ware they can snatch. This might lead to some Tamanous gangs killing off head cases.
- Hannibelle

- Or getting infected, themselves. I don't like picturing what the nanites could do with access to those creepy birthing banks.
- Bull

- That's … just … ugh. No sleep for a week.
- Slamm-0!

WHAT'S IN STORE

- PLAN 9 HAS BEEN BLOCKED

- With all respect to our friendly resident headcase, I think it's best if (s)he not know about this section. Don't mention it, yeah?
- Glitch

Expect the further development of nanites utilizing xenogenetic materials that cannot be broken down, utilized or fabricated by CFD nanites and their nanohives. Hybrid nanites are the current wildcard, but developing new ones is only a stopgap to keep head cases confused for the moment.

Some of the most exciting research is in CFD countermeasures. Some of the current promising projects include a silicon-consumptive bacterial agent, which would break down nanites without harming any biological systems. This one isn't getting as much funding because, naturally, the corps want a solution that doesn't just save lives, but property. To be fair, this might also break down a number of other cyber systems, so the idea needs work.

One of the other hopefuls is the development of what Mitsuhama is calling "Trojan Nanites." These enter an infected host looking like any given breed of standard hard nanites, but are in fact hunter-killers with special viral programming meant to disorient or even disrupt AI control, giving it a chance to eliminate the digital invader. This coding is a ways away from showing any results, and it is expected that other AIs will adapt quickly. The upshot is that it would theoretically work on any technology, and Mitsuhama has given the project a substantial amount of nuyen to get results.

NeoNET's research remains focused on data architecture. Leaks indicate that they consider nanites to be too adaptable to be beaten on their home turf, so they are seeking to expand quantum architecture into new directions, effectively creating physical logic puzzles based on data storage and sortage. The theory is to create partitioned mirror drives, enabling compromised hardware to cut off its infected partition and continue functioning. So far this has resulted in massive processing shortages, but expectations are high.

Saeder-Krupp has not let CFD impede it's research into "nanomagic," the theoretical opportunity to break the technology-magic barrier by researching interactions on a molecular level, somehow using astrally bonded soft nanites as a kind of spotter network to chain a spell across the metahuman body, improving the use of augmentations, healing, and illusion spells, or to make possession spirits much more effective at bonding with their host. Those in the know actually believe some kind of Awakened nanite might offer a new kind of hunter-killer against head cases, but results are likely still years away.

- ❂ You better believe the data is worth top nuyen, though.
- ❂ Ethernaut

- ❂ That host bonding stuff sounds pretty ominous in a world with insect spirits.
- ❂ Red

One of the most ambitious projects has been by Renraku in prototyping self-assembling cybernetics. A injection of nanites locates and forms itself into internal cyberware, effectively granting temporary 'ware while the nanites are sustained and allowing for modular reconfiguration of 'ware to suit the appropriate situation. The theoretical models would not be as powerful as dedicated hardware, however.

- ❂ This is the future of cybernetic enhancement. Or it would have been had CFD not crept along. I guarantee this project has lost a lot of funding. Knowledge like this is too dangerous to have around while AIs might figure a way to finish it for themselves.
- ❂ Butch

- ❂ Wait, variable cyberware? Is that possible?
- ❂ 2XL

- ❂ Localized stuff, yes. Wired reflexes, toxin filters, things like that. It would certainly be easier to install headware if we didn't have to open up their skull to do it. Big stuff like spurs and cyberlimbs, though, would come with one hell of a price tag in maintenance fees if they were made of nanites. Better to stick with standard hardware for that.
- ❂ Butch

- ❂ Better stay away from nanoware entirely, you mean.
- ❂ Slamm-0!

- ❂ Naturally.
- ❂ Butch

- ❂ So, did this meet with your approval, KAM?
- ❂ Glitch

- ❂ I'd have said if it didn't. Frankly, there's more to say, but it's far too large a topic to do justice here.
- ❂ KAM

- ❂ I agree, but these little files are more to keep everyone up to date regarding what is happening on a tangible level. Most of these street types need it boiled down to the essentials to understand what they might be up against or stealing for Mr Johnson.
- ❂ The Smiling Bandit

- ❂ Excuse me?
- ❂ Nephrine

- ❂ Some of us street types understand the Big Scary Words, you know.
- ❂ Ethernaut

- ❂ For everyone else, there's Aetherpedia!
- ❂ Slamm-0!

- ❂ Now, now, everyone, you'll spoil the good doctor's illusions about ignorant shadow operatives.
- ❂ The Smiling Bandit

- After all this time, Bandit? If you really think I harbor illusions about any of you, then the only one you're fooling is yourself.
- KAM

- Touché.
- The Smiling Bandit

NANOTECHNOLOGY RULES

SOFT AND HARD MACHINES

For the most part, hard and soft nanites are interchangeable in game terms. While hard nanites are the choice for most industrial and manufacturing applications of nanotech, in the field of personal enhancement both are quite common. Many augmentations use either one or the other, and some augmentations even combine both. Generally speaking, soft nanites are better choices for free-floating nanite systems that complement or supplement metabolic processes and biotech enhancements, while hard nanites are better to complement cyberware, perform surgical functions, and perform tasks that require cooperation of various "sub-breeds" orchestrated by nanohive implants (see **Nanohive**, p. 151). There are, however, other mechanical differences between the two.

Soft nanites are partly artificial or genetically modified micro-organisms programmed to perform a certain task. This makes soft machines harder to detect than hard nanites to all but the most sophisticated and detailed medical exams.

Hard nanomachines are artificial constructs, nano-scale drones made from diamondoid composites, with almost frictionless bodies and internal power supplies. Hard nanites are designed with modular code, allowing them to be reprogrammed to a certain degree.

ESSENCE COSTS

Nanoware does not carry an Essence cost, nor does it currently come in grades. Nanocybernetic augmentations, however, as specialized cybernetics, do carry an Essence cost.

USING NANOWARE

While nanotech sees myriad applications, nanoware is the term for nanotech implanted in living organisms as a form of enhancement. What sets nanoware apart from other forms of enhancement is the role of nanotech itself. The most common type of nanoware consists of free-floating nanite colonies designed to supplement or replace a body's physiological systems, to enhance metabolic processes, or to act as a prophylactic measure. To this end, nanoware circulates via the blood, lymph, and extra-cellular fluids to reach all parts of the body. Other types of nanoware install themselves in the vicinity of a particular organ to either enhance organ functions or build and maintain ultra-fine nanostructures. Various types of neural nanoware, filtration systems, and organ enhancements fall into this category, and what distinguishes them from cyberware is the need for active nanite colonies.

Nanoware uses either hard machines delivered using an aerosol or injection or soft machines delivered via injection or ingestion vectors to make precise adjustments to biological systems. Once introduced, nanites become active in about a minute. Nanoware systems are considered to be always active unless a nanohive implant is present. Among other functions, nanohives allow for controlled activation of nanoware systems or colonies, recovering them, and storing them during "downtime." Another defining aspect of nanoware is that it's not usually permanent. Despite modern techniques that provide nanites with protein-matched immune markers to stave off the worst, a living body is still an incredibly hostile environment to the little guys, and sooner or later nanites are flushed or absorbed by the system.

NANOWARE RATINGS AND DEGRADATION

All nanoware has a Rating that represents that specific nanite colony's hardiness, versatility, and level of performance—whether it is used in "bladeless surgery," cyberware implantation, antidote treatment, or as a form of enhancement or stimulant. Nanoware systems are transient in nature, meaning they are purged in due course by the body's filtration, digestive, and immune processes. To represent this transient nature, the Ratings of nanoware systems permanently degrade over time, at the rate of 1 Rating point per week. A functioning nanohive (p. 151) counters this nanite loss by providing a safe environment for replenishing feedstocks and colony numbers—regardless of whether the system involves hard or soft machines.

Active nanoware in the organism also suffers degradation when the body takes serious wounds—bleeding out or straying into contact with foreign bodies or physiological systems that they aren't designed to tolerate. For every 3 boxes of Physical damage taken by the host, reduce the Rating of any active nanoware systems by 1. This loss can be recovered over time with a nanohive.

When a nanoware system's Rating reaches 0, it is destroyed. A nanohive can still replenish the system normally.

The nanoware in a CFD sufferer does not degrade, instead finding other ways to remain active.

DETECTING SOFT NANITES

The threshold to detect soft nanites via nano-scanner or clinical tests is increased by +2 (see **Nanoscanner**, p. 153). They are powered by natural organic processes and function much like bacteria or parasites, and for the most part appear just like their natural counterparts, making them much harder to detect.

REPROGRAMMING HARD NANITES

One of the advantages offered only by hard nanites is the ability to reprogram hard nanite systems. Hard nanites are reprogrammed through the body's own conductive tissues by a hard nanohive.

When hard nanites are reprogrammed, they change their type, becoming a new kind of hard nanoware. Reprogramming itself requires the hard nanites to suspend whatever operation they were performing and receive their new instructions. A hard nanohive does not reduce the Rating of its nanites.

HARD NANITES AND THE MATRIX

Hard nanites use conductive tissue and other surfaces and UV radiation to communicate. They do not use the Matrix, and so they do not show up as icons in the Matrix. Hard nanites can be indirectly affected by hackers via a hard nanohive, a devices that has its own Matrix icon.

NANOWARE SYSTEMS

HARD NANOWARE SYSTEMS

The following are the nanoware systems on the market that are certified against CFD infection.

ANTI-RAD

Popular among spacers and workers in high-ambient radiation environments such as the SOX, anti-rad nanoware is a new development and quite expensive. This free-floating system scours the body via the lymphatic system for telltale isotope traces, free radicals, and radiation damaged cells. Anti-rad nanites bind contaminants in a solvent cage and inject damaged or mutated cells with a compound that induces cell death. The anti-rad nanites then attach to the waste and transport it to the nearest lymph node to be processed and evacuated normally.

Anti-rad nanoware reduces the Power of radiation damage by its Rating. Anti-rad is intended as a prophylactic measure and is unable to eliminate metastasized cancers or pre-existing cell mutations.

CONTROL RIG BOOSTER

This specialized breed of neural amplifier nanites are designed to complement implanted control rigs

(p. 452, SR5). The nanites organize themselves into artificial neural pathways, building and maintaining a network of nanofilaments. This extends the normal interface between the control rig and the middle brain to parts of the dorsolateral prefrontal cortex, cerebellum, and thalamus—areas of the brain that manage subconscious movement, sensory interpretation, and instinctive decision-making. The booster colony's dedicated neural pathways allow a rigger to make greater use of the brain's intuitive understanding of spatial positioning and capacity for instinctive motion control when jumped in to a vehicle or drone. The control rig itself translates the resulting neural impulses into rigging data like speed control, inertia handling, and so forth.

The booster applies its Rating as a dice pool modifier to your Vehicle Tests when you're jumped into a drone or vehicle. It cannot be combined with the control rig optimization genetech.

IMPLANT MEDIC

This nanoware system is installed along with a specific cyberware implant. The free-floating nanites in this system are designed to monitor the health and well-being of that implant, and to immediately act to repair it if any malfunction or damage occurs. If the nanites detect a problem, they work to restore the implant to its standard operating parameters by rejoining neural connections, sealing fractures, repairing circuitry, removing foreign bodies or damaged tissue, and so on.

An implant medic system automatically seeks to repair a damaged implant. If an implant takes Matrix damage, this system begins repairing it on the next Combat Turn, using its Rating x 2 as its Hardware + Logic dice pool and its Rating as its Mental limit. You can read more on repairing Matrix damage on p. 228, SR5.

NANITE HUNTERS

Nanite hunters seek out and destroy active nanites other than their own colony. By default, hunter nanites seek out all nanites, but they can be reprogrammed by the usual method for hard nanites to target nanites of a specific type (hard, soft, or a specific system). Reprogramming nanite hunters in this way never reduces the system's rating.

At the end of each Combat Turn that a nanite hunter system is active, make a Rating x 2 [Rating] v. Target's Rating x 2 Test. For each net hit the hunters get, reduce the target nanites' Rating by 1. The hard nanite hunters have a hard time targeting soft nanites, taking a –2 dice pool modifier when attacking them. If more than one valid target is available to the nanite hunters, the system chooses its target at random each Combat Turn.

Hunter nanites are unable to breach a nanohive to attack dormant nanite systems.

HARD NANOWARE SYSTEMS

NANOWARE	RATING	AVAILABILITY	COST
Anti-rad	1–6	14F	Rating x 6,000¥
Control rig booster	1–3	12F	Rating x 6,000¥
Implant medic	1–6	12F	10% of implant cost
Nanite hunters	1–6	16R	Rating x 5,000¥
Markers	1–3	12	Rating x 2,000¥
Nanotattoos	1–3	12F	Rating x 1,000¥
Taggants	1–3	12	Rating x 600¥
Trauma control system	1–6	12F	Rating x 4,000¥

MARKERS

These nanites are sealed microscopic optical chips used for transporting valuable data without being detected. Data is typically divided up and downloaded into multiple nanites, building in redundancy against nanite loss. Later, a simple blood sample is all that is needed to collect enough datacapsules to reconstitute the data within. Markers are designed to defeat nanoscanners: reduce the nanoscanner's dice pool by the marker's Rating for the Detection test. Markers can carry one or multiple files.

REPLICATORS

Nanoware has some disadvantages. It only has one function, or maybe one function at a time if you're reprogramming hard nanites. It can lose its potency over time. It's very expensive to buy and upkeep. But there's one kind of nanite that can perform multiple roles, actually gains strength as it works, and best of all it's free of charge: REPLICATORS!

Replicators are only found in CFD victims ... all CFD victims. These nanites have been altered by the virus to let them build nanites of other types. They can construct both soft and hard nanites given sufficient raw materials, which they will happily take out of the victim's food, blood, or body. The virus camouflages them as other types of nanites to conceal them and prevent detection, but the mechanism for this is unknown, and there still isn't a way to detect them ... until it's too late.

So if you want a powerful nanoware system at absolutely no cost, contact your nearest head case and join the unknown but secretly growing multitudes who use replicators! Your new personality will thank you for it!

NANOTATTOOS

Once injected, nanotattoo hard machines embed themselves as a lattice of liquid crystal microdisplays under the subject's skin. A Rating 1 nanotattoo covers one limb or the face, Rating 2 covers half the body, and Rating 3 covers the whole body. A nanotattoo (or "nanotat") can be reprogrammed to display any image the user wishes, including preprogrammed animation. They can also be programmed to be inactive and appear indistinguishable from your normal skin. Reprogramming nanotats in this manner does not reduce its rating.

Nanotattoos can provide effective camouflage, if you have a full body treatment and you're not wearing much, imposing a –1 dice pool modifier to Perception tests to detect you visually.

TAGGANTS

Unlike most nanites, taggants emit a signal that can be detected by a standard wireless device. This produces an ARO and icon in the Matrix. Taggants can be used to advertise the subject's criminal convictions or legal status, commercial goods, political propaganda, or any other information programmed into the system. Taggants can have their icon and the information they broadcast changed via reprogramming—such reprogramming does not reduce the taggants' rating.

TRAUMA CONTROL SYSTEM

This nanoware system seeks out and gathers around vital organs. Some component nanites apply electro-stimulation to the heart and respiratory muscles, while others regulate blood flow away from wounds without starving the brain of oxygen. While you're busy dying from overflow damage to your Physical Condition Monitor, the TCS attempts to stabilize you every minute, using its Rating in place of both First Aid and Logic in the Stabilization Test (p. 209, SR5).

SOFT NANOWARE SYSTEMS

ANTI-TOX

These nantidotes are designed to counter a broad spectrum of toxins. They carry active charcoal, tannic acid, magnesium, and other chemicals to absorb toxins from the digestive tract and bloodstream, and also enhance the body's natural detoxification processes. Reduce the Power of any toxin affecting you by the nanoware's Rating. If the toxin's Power is reduced below 1, further effects and/or damage are halted.

Anti-tox will also protect against the effects of alcohol, caffeine, and other drugs. Reduce the duration of drugs by a factor equal to the Rating of the anti-tox system (i.e., divide the duration by the rating).

CARCERAND-PLUS

Carcerand-plus is the nanotech version of carcerands, hollow molecular spheres designed to carry a drug payload that they slowly dispense as they circulate the body and break down over time. Normal carcerands are passive, designed to break down within a narrow period.

Carcerand-plus triggers under either of two conditions. It can be tailored to respond to a certain chemical in the body, such as a certain food or drug, introduced from outside the body; the trigger condition must be specified before the nanites are installed. It is also triggered if its Rating is reduced to 0. Once triggered, carcerand-plus nanites release their payload into the bloodstream.

Once injected, carcerand-plus colonies circulate through the body until the trigger condition is met or they are purged. Carcerand-plus nanoware contains the equivalent of one dose of a compound. The requisite dose of compound must be bought and paid for separately. Carcerand-plus cannot be supported by a soft nanohive.

NANOSYMBIOTES

Nanosymbiotes are colonies of specialized nanites that permeate the user's anatomy. Once they have fully deployed, they adopt specialized functions appropriate to their location. These are all focused on returning the subject to a healthy physiological baseline. Nanosymbiotes adjust body chemistry, assist cell formation, and even mimic certain cell functions themselves, acting to speed clotting and healing. Functioning nanosymbiotes allow the user to heal and recover from wounds faster. Add the nanosymbiotes' Rating to your dice pool when making tests to heal damage through natural recovery (p. 207, *SR5*).

NANTIDOTES

Nantidotes are hollow nanites that float in the user's bloodstream and carry a specific toxin's antidote inside an outer membrane. When a nanite comes into contact with the predefined toxin or compound, this outer membrane automatically dissolves or cycles open, administering the antidote at the poisoned site. Nantidotes affect only one type of toxin or venom, chosen when the nanites are created. If the nantidotes are already present in the body, their effect is instantaneous—they provide complete immunity, and the toxin has no effect. Every time a dose of toxin is neutralized. reduce the nantidote's Rating by 1 point; if the Rating is reduced to 0, the nantidotes can offer no more protection. This Rating degradation may be restored by a nanohive normally.

NEURAL AMPLIFIERS

This form of neural nanoware has been in development since the very first days of the datajack. Nanotechnology has finally developed to the point where scientists can foray deeper into the brain and central nervous system without excessive risks. Neural amplifiers use soft nanites to manufacture artificial neurons and expand neural pathways between specific parts of the brain's or body's neural network. After growing the expanded neural architecture, the dedicated nanite colony falls into a support role, electrochemically stimulating the newly formed pathways—a process that emulates natural reinforcement of neural pathways in the brain through learning, practice, and experience. Each type of neural amplifier targets specific neuron tracts, enhances glial cell functions (in the brain), and increases axon density and width with superconductive nanofilaments sheathed with nu-myelin (a transgenic protein that reduces interference with neural impulses and neurotransmitter "signal degradation"). Neural amplifiers create a significant increase in specific brain functions and response time.

Only two neural amplifiers can function at peak efficiency per subject, after which point the additional neural traffic becomes increasingly distracting and confusing. If you have more than two neural amplifiers at a time, you take a –2 dice pool modifier to all actions related to each system.

Learning Stimulus: These neural amplifiers facilitate comprehension and memorization of skills the character already possesses by enhancing the brain's ability to cross-reference learned skill memories and the language comprehension functions of the parietal-temporal-occipital complex. When raising a Knowledge or Language skill the character already possesses, this nanoware reduces the Karma cost by 1 for each Rating point, to a minimum of 2 Karma.

Limbic: Limbic neural amplifiers rewire parts of the limbic system to areas of the parietal, temporal, and occipital lobes that produce cohesive sensory perceptions (from neural sensory stimuli). This system grants a +1 dice pool modifier and increases the Mental limit by its Rating when using Intuition-linked skills.

NANOWARE	RATING	AVAILABILITY	COST
Anti-tox	1-9	16F	Rating x 5,000¥
Carcerand plus	1-6	10F	Rating x 3,000¥ (+ drug)
Nanosymbiotes	1-3	16F	Rating x 6,000¥
Nantidotes	1-6	8F	Rating x 1,500¥
Nanotattoos	1-3	12F	Rating x 500¥
Neural amplifiers			
Learning stimulus	1-3	14F	Rating x 5,000¥
Limbic	1-3	16F	Rating x 7,500¥
Neocortical	1-3	16F	Rating x 7,500¥
Recall	1-3	12F	Rating x 3,500¥
O-Cells	1-9	12F	Rating x 5,000¥
Oxyrush	1-5	12F	Rating x 1,500¥

Neocortical: Neocortical neural amplifiers enhance frontal lobe activity, which is essential to a metahuman's abstract thought processes and problem-solving ability. When using Logic-linked skills, this implant grants a +1 dice pool modifier and a Mental limit bonus equal to its Rating.

Recall: Recall neural amplifiers enhance sensory memory storage and recall by ensuring neural pathways to stored memories are reinforced and do not fall into disuse. Recall grants a dice pool modifier equal to its Rating to any Memory Tests (p. 152, *SR5*) to remember facts, events, or other information the character has directly experienced and concentrated on memorizing.

O-CELLS

O-cells, or Omega cells, function as enhanced lymphocytes (white blood cells) integrated into the body's auto-immune system. O-cells are gene-modified and augmented from T- and B-cells, which are part of the body's adaptive immune system. These natural cell types retain a record of previous infections so that they can mount a quicker and stronger response to the culprit antigen(s) or pathogen in cases of re-infection. Unlike natural lymphocytes, which only store memories of previous infections (or inoculations), O-cell soft nanites come equipped with broad-spectrum pharmacological microdoses and an inbuilt library of responses to a wide array of common pathogens. O-cell nanoware reduces the Power of any viral or bacterial pathogens that infect the host by its Rating.

OXYRUSH

Oxyrush nanites store blood oxygen and release it to maintain healthy blood-oxygen levels, like super-efficient red blood cells. A character with this nanoware can hold his breath for a half-hour for every Rating point. Additionally, oxyrush also adds its Rating to the character's dice pool on any Fatigue Tests.

NANOCYBERNETICS

Nanocybernetics bridge the gap between nanoware systems and ordinary cybernetics. What makes them unique and different from standard cyberware augmentation is that working nanocolonies are an integral, and in fact essential, part of the implant. Nanocybernetics can and do perform a wide variety of functions. Some, such as the nanohive, are necessary for free-floating nanites to exist within a metahuman body. Others use nanites as ultrafine sensors to monitor the body's health. Unlike nanoware, all nanocybernetics are permanent and non-degrading implants despite using active nanite colonies. The implant itself normally contains feedstocks and limited storage during downtimes. All are cyberware (p. 451, *SR5*) and follow the basic cyberware rules. All have an Essence cost and are available in all standard cyberware grades. Some nanocybernetics can be installed within cyberlimbs; these have Capacity costs listed in their descriptions.

DYNAMIC HANDPRINTS

This nanite system alters the ridges and lines of a user's fingerprints and palms to match a set pattern. Various imaging devices can scan finger- and palm-print samples for the implant to replicate. You can use this system to provide finger- and handprints to fool print scanners (p. 364, SR5). Like other counter-biometric nanocybernetics, this system includes a specialized nanohive, processor, and a small nanite colony.

Wireless: The system can accept new prints wirelessly. It can also capture and later mimic any handprint you touch with your hand.

FLASHBACK SYSTEM

An advanced form of the old invoked memory stimulator cyberware, this system features a micro-memory module, a processor, and a dedicated nanohive supporting a specialized neural amplifier colony. Flashback nanites organize themselves into a network of sensors and nanofilaments—similar in many respects to a trode net—over the surface of the user's brain. These probe nanites register neural activity associated with memory formation, backing up the patterns to digital memory. If the subject suffers a brain injury or even simple forgetfulness, the system can access these neural records and stimulate the same neural activity, prompting recall.

You receive the Photographic Memory quality (p. 76, SR5) regarding any experience within the flashback system's storage. These memories are so vivid that it's like viewing a simsense recording of the experience. The system does not store actual memories, just the neural activity map, so the data is useless without your personal brain, and memories may be affected by drugs that inhibit or cause loss of memory.

Wireless: The flashback system can export stored memories into simsense form and save them as simsense files, and also act as a simrig (p. 439, SR5).

NANOHIVE

A nanohive is a nanocybernetic implant designed to support and coordinate nanoware in a living body long-term. Nanohives not only contain the hardware and software necessary to aid the functions of multiple nanoware colonies, but they also provide a safe environment for nanoware systems to repair, replicate, and resupply. As part of nanohive implantation procedures, a host of other minor cybernetic modifications are made to pre-existing organs including the liver, kidneys, and spleen. These alterations keep the body from filtering out nanites like other waste and cellular "detritus." Nanohives themselves replace and repair nanites that are excreted or damaged by the body, maintaining nanite populations at a normal level and even restoring depleted levels after injury. Combined with the filtration systems and the robustness of current nanotech, this limits natural nanite loss.

Each nanohive is a sealed egg-shaped implant containing the primary processor, controllers, and neural interfaces and is implanted near arterial or lymphatic junctions. In addition to the expert system(s), a nanohive incorporates sensors that monitor nanite levels in the blood, as well as reservoirs of feedstocks that support machinery for additional nanite colonies, and several thousand backup nanite units are present in ancillary pods. When the nanoware supported by a nanohive has its Rating reduced, the nanohive returns its Rating by 1 point per week, up to the nanohive's Rating.

Each nanohive supports one nanoware system at a Rating equal to its own.

Hard Nanohive: Hard nanohives are able to communicate and direct the actions of nanoware via short-range ultrasound, microwave, or UV signals using the nanites themselves as relays. Hard nanohives can use this communication to reprogram the nanite system it supports—its Rating is the number of different hard nanite systems to which it can convert its nanites. Hard nanohives must be restocked every six months at a cost of 500 nuyen x Rating.

Soft Nanohive: A soft nanohive supports a soft nanosystem, chosen at implanting. Soft nanohives restock themselves over time from the food you eat, increasing your appetite, but not so as to change your dietary habits much.

Wireless: Treat the nanites that the nanohive supports as though they are of one Rating higher than normal.

RETINAL ADJUSTERS

This nanite implant reworks the vein and tissue patterns in the user's retinas to match stored designs. You can use this system to provide retina prints to fool print scanners (p. 364, SR5). Like other counterbiometric nanocybernetics, this system includes a specialized nanohive, processor, and a small nanite colony. Adjusters are not compatible with cybereyes or other retinal duplication systems.

Wireless: You can use the system to record and mimic retina patterns in a natural eye. You have to get very close, staring eyeball to eyeball, to make this work.

SMARTSKIN

This treatment laces the user's epidermis with smart polymers and carbon buckytubes, manipulated by an implanted microprocessor and support nanite colony. The smartskin retains the texture and flexibility of normal skin until activated, at which point the material becomes rigid enough to protect the wearer (though still flexible enough at the joints not to impede movement). While active, smartskin is as obvious as dermal plating—and like it, provides its Rating in Armor.

A secondary smartskin setting changes the smart materials into microspines. These do 5P damage to anyone brushing at speed or hitting the user barehanded.

NANOWARE	RATING	ESSENCE	CAPACITY	AVAILABILITY	COST
Dynamic handprints	—	0.2	—	12F	Rating x 21,00¥
Flashback system	—	0.3	—	8R	6,000¥
Nanohive					
Hard	1–6	Rating x 0.25	[2]	(Rating x 5)R	Rating x 12,000¥
Soft	1–6	Rating x 0.2		(Rating x 5)R	Rating x 10,000¥
Retinal adjusters	—	0.2	—	16F	Rating x 19,000¥
Smart skin	1–6	Rating x 0.5	—	(Rating x 5)F	Rating x 5,000¥
Voice mimic	1–6	0.2	—	16F	Rating x 20,000¥

Smartskin is incompatible with all other forms of dermal armor or sheathing (be they bio- or cyberware, including orthoskin), but is cumulative with normal body armor.

Wireless: The smartskin can form and maintain hard impact plates for Unarmed Combat with (STR + 2)S damage, or sharp blades with (STR + 2)P damage.

VOICE MIMIC

A nanite colony in the character's larynx adjusts the user's voice to match stored patterns. Sound files can be used as templates. The system can be used to attempt to foil a voice-recognition system (p. 360, SR5), and adds its Rating to your dice pool for Impersonation tests. Like other counter-biometric nanocybernetics, this system includes a specialized nanohive, processor, and a small nanite colony.

Wireless: Your voice can mimic any sound, as per the Mimicry power (p. 398, SR5). Use the voice mimic's Rating as the threshold for Perception tests to notice the sound is false.

NANOGEAR AND EQUIPMENT

With internal applications of nanotechnology deemed too risky due to CFD concerns, it seemed like nanotech was a thing of the past. The corps have never been likely to refuse a lucrative new technology because of risks to the public. Instead, they shifted focus onto nanogear and equipment that can be made of safer, simpler nanites. Typically, nanotech that comes in doses or applications that are available in gel suspension or aerosol in one-liter airtight containers.

ALTSKIN

The altskin concept is simple: a layer of nanites responsive to the wearer's natural skin and body contours that can contain other useful properties. Altskin is a broadly useful form of non-surgical body modification, employed for actors, club-goers, and thieves alike. Virtually indistinguishable from natural skin, basic altskin (which may be bought in all but the most exotic skin tones) is painted on in several layers. An arm, leg, face, or torso each takes one application and ten minutes to cover. It then takes another ten minutes to set in place, and in this time its nanite sensors form connections with the user's natural epidermis. A single application lasts twenty-four hours, after which it begins to flake off as the nanites self-terminate. An adhesive wireless transmitter allows the user to access the altskin's simple command software. This allows the user to issue commands to the altskin via a commlink or other appropriate device.

Basic altskin automatically filters out harmful contact chemicals. It is safe to touch a contact-vector toxin with an altskin-covered appendage. Against an area threat, such as a poisonous cloud, the total number of applications worn is the protective Rating against contact toxins (p. 408, SR5). Note that an altskin-covered appendage does not leave fingerprints (nor can the user's natural finger or palm prints be used for biometrics). Altskin may also be bought with one or more embedded functions. The following are hardware upgrades and cannot be changed on the fly.

Armor: The armor upgrade adds tough carbon nanotube fibers to the altskin, providing +1 Armor. It stacks with worn armor, but not any armored augmentations or a troll's natural armor.

Chameleon: This upgrade, often purchased along with the shifter function (see below), allows programmable skin color. This coloration can be natural or unnatural. Users can wirelessly command the altskin to display different shades, shifting designs, and even animated images with equal ease. Chameleon altskin can distort the user's outline and help them blend in with the surroundings, providing a –2 dice pool modifier to Perception Tests to spot the camouflaged character if they're not wearing much.

Newprint: This upgrade allows the user to reprogram his finger- or palm-prints, just like dynamic handprint nanocybernetics (p. 151).

Sealer: The sealant upgrade repairs its own tears and punctures. Since it perfectly follows body contours, it also serves as an effective pressure dressing. This adds a +2 dice pool modifier on tests to stabilize the wearer, but imparts a –2 dice pool modifier on First Aid and Medicine tests to treat the character until it is removed.

Shifter: The shifter upgrade cannot cause gross changes in body shape, but it can alter facial features and skin textures. Club goers and artists sometimes use this to give themselves a scaly or "engraved" surface texture, but runners find it to be a useful form of disguise. Users can change a shifter configuration via wireless, but the altskin takes ten minutes to take on the requested configuration. Shifter altskin gives you +1 to the limit of Disguise and Impersonation Tests.

ETCHERS

Etchers are used to temporarily or permanently inscribe a metallic pattern on the subject's bones or cartilages. These marks can be detected by magnetic anomaly detectors (MADs) and magnetic resonance imagers (MRIs). Temporary bone markings break up over time, but permanent treatments can only be removed with surgery that scrapes the bone clean. Once injected, a bone marker takes eight hours to form. Etchers are used to identify prisoners, mark bioware, carry information, among other purposes.

MONOWIRE

Superfine monofilament wire, constructed using nanotech buckytubes, sees a wide variety of uses but is best known for its security applications. Nearly invisible and with high tensile strength, monowire can be stretched atop fences as hi-tech barbed wire or in a maze pattern across doorways and hallways. Monowire garrotes (p. 20, *Run & Gun*), carried in a special wrist-worn container with a pull-tab at one end, are also common among assassins. To detect monowire when extended and taut requires a Perception + Intuition [Mental] (3) Test.

NANOPASTE DISGUISE

The use of cheap cosmetics and latex-based disguises are a thing of the past with the development of a versatile biostatic nanite paste. Once spread across the affected area, the paste utilizes the body's bioelectric charge to power itself. It can be programmed to change color and texture or to display patterns. The paste can also remember preset configurations. A small container of paste covers the user's face and hands, while the

large container coats the entire body. A person's face can be duplicated if you have a scan or a trid image—use your or someone else's Medicine or Artisan skill in a Teamwork Test for your Disguise test. The nanopaste disguise lasts for twenty-four hours before the nanites self-destruct.

NANOSCANNER

Nanoware can be very difficult to detect. Cyberware scanners may sometimes detect extensive nanoware, but a dedicated nano-scanner that can test blood, saliva, tissue, or other materials for nanites is required for positive identification in most cases. Once limited to medical and high-security facilities due to cost, it has become common to issue these devices to emergency response teams in order to identify CFD victims. This function can be installed in any sensor device like other sensor functions (p. 445, *SR5*). The range of this sensor is one meter. The threshold for detecting nanoware can be found on the Nanotech Detection table. A test must be made for each system.

NANOTECH DETECTION	
TYPE OF NANOWARE	DETECTION THRESHOLD
Nanocybernetics	
Standard	1
Alphaware	2
Betaware	3
Deltaware	4
Nanoware	
Hard	2
Soft	3
CFD Replicators	5

NANOSPY

These nanites provide a discreet, flexible surveillance option to deploy in unsecured sites. Once sprayed or painted upon a surface (one application), a layer of hard machines constructs an invisible antenna, a distributed microphone, and a compound optical lens. The entire assembly is about thirty centimeters square and appears to be no more than a very faint discoloration of the material it's been applied to. Noticing an application by sight is a Perception + Intuition [Mental] (3) Test. NanoSpies can even be applied like makeup to living creatures, turning a face into a camera. Imaging software corrects distortions caused by the surface area and compound lens. A single application lasts for

NANOGEAR	RATING	ESSENCE	CAPACITY
Altskin (per application)	Hard	10	1,250¥
Armor	—	+3	+500¥
Chameleon	—	+2	+250¥
Newprint	—	+4F	+(Rating x 200¥)
Sealer	—	+1	+250¥
Shifter	—	+2	+250¥
Etchers	Hard	8	500¥
Monowire (per meter)	Hard	14R	1,000¥
Nanopaste disguise			
Small container	Hard	12F	350¥
Large container	Hard	16F	700¥
Nanoscanner	—	8	As sensor
NanoSpy (per application)	Hard	14F	10,000¥
Savior medkit	—	6	2,000¥
Savior medkit supplies	Hard	4	300¥
Smart corrosives (per application)	Soft	10R	4,000¥
Universal sealant (per application)	Hard	10	250¥

twenty-four hours. Nanospies are capable of effectively monitoring events within five meters. Beyond that, image and sound distortion makes capture unfeasible.

SAVIOR MEDKIT

Originally developed by Shiawase Biotech but now available from several corps, these advanced medkits combine cutting-edge nanotech and advanced expert systems. When activated, the medkit injects enough nanites to last five minutes into its subject. The savior then acts as a Rating 6 medkit and follows all the normal rules for medkits (p. 450, *SR5*). If the patient is bleeding out, the savior's nanites act as a trauma control system (p. 148) for the duration. The savior's supply of nanites is limited, and it must be restocked every time it is used.

SMART CORROSIVES

This system consists of a swarm of nanites suspended in a clear chemical solution. Each nanite carries a payload of a corrosive compound. When applied, these nanites are programmed to bind to a certain substance and use the corrosive to melt it. Because the nanites only activate when in contact with the target substance, the corrosive is applied in a manner that affects only the target, while everything around it remains untouched. Smart corrosive solutions can be applied via squirtguns, spray canisters, splash grenades, and a variety of other methods. Each solution is configured to corrode only a specific substance, from skin to metal to plasteel—the corrosive carried by the nanites will affect only that substance. On contact, smart corrosives deal 10P(acid) damage to the substance it is programmed to affect. It must be washed or scraped off to prevent continuing damage.

UNIVERSAL SEALANT

This nanotech application is used extensively in space and undersea habitats and is becoming increasing common in a number of fields. It employs nanites suspended in a polymer gel/foam that hardens upon contact with air. When deployed (normally via handheld spray or squirtgun), the nanites bind seams, fracture

WEAPONIZED NANOTECH

NANOTECH	TYPE	AVAILABILITY	COST (PER DOSE)
Cutters	Hard	12F	4,000¥
Intruders	Hard	12F	3,000¥

lines, and punctures at a molecular level, filling in voids with the quick-hardening polymer. The result is an airtight seal with the consistency and hardness of steel. One canister can cover one square meter or numerous smaller holes. Standard sealant is only able to bind inorganic molecules.

WEAPONIZED NANOTECH

Weaponized nanotech follows the same general rules as toxins (p. 409, *SR5*) and have Vector, Speed, Penetration, Power, and Effect stats, with any unique effects noted in the individual descriptions. Multiple doses fall under the Concentration rules on p. 409, *SR5*. They can be applied via dart guns, splash grenades, aerosol sprays, squirt guns, gas grenades, and so on, according to their Vector.

Like nanoware, weaponized nanotech is available as soft or hard machines. Soft machines are vulnerable to chemical and radioactive sterilization as well as nanite hunter nanoware. Direct exposure to a strong EMP burst will halt hard machines, but once internalized, only a lot of electrical damage to the body or nanite hunters will slow them. Gear and augmentations that protect against toxins also protect against weaponized nanotech.

CUTTERS

Vector: Injection
Speed: 1 minute
Penetration: 0
Power: 9
Effect: Physical damage

Originally developed by Aztechnology's Genetique subsidiary from prototypes acquired from the Renraku Arcology, these lethal hard nanites have been around for more than a decade. Cutter attacks are short and brutal as the nanites' power is quickly exhausted, but this is more than enough time to cause critical damage to a target. Once injected and distributed throughout the victim's circulatory system, cutters begin to slash their way through blood cells, blood vessels, and organ tissues, causing massive internal hemorrhages and a shock response in the victim.

INTRUDERS

Vector: Contact, Injection, Inhalation
Speed: 1 minute
Penetration: -2
Power: 8
Effect: See description

Intruders are hard machines that carry simple firmware and are designed to subvert devices and cyberware. They target the device they contact; inside a person, intruders will latch onto the first cybersystem they find (either the result of a called shot or the nearest to the point of contact). Once deployed they work their way into the delicate circuitry, making a direct connection with the target device and executing their function according to their type. At the end of each Combat Turn, intruders perform the Data Spike action (p. 239, *SR5*) as agents with a Rating and Matrix attributes equal to their Power, attacking their target. The Power of an intruder infestation is reduced by 1 after each Data Spike, until they reach 0 and become harmless dust.

GENETECH RULES

GENE THERAPY BASICS

In *Shadowrun*, the term **gene therapy** describes the various techniques used to transfer and splice genetic information into cells and tissues to achieve a desired effect. This is usually achieved by having nanites, custom designed retroviruses, and other vectors simultaneously alter the patient's DNA on a cellular level. Patients spend their time in gene therapy immersed in a nutrient tank, while medical clean-room protocols prevent any contamination by biological agents or CFD-infected nanites. Specific procedures are many and varied, but their end effects, treatment times, and prices are very similar. The cost of gene therapy includes medical supplies, hospitalization, and tailoring the treatment to the subject.

MAN VS. NATURE

Unlike Essence loss due to cyberware or bioware, Essence loss from geneware is not just a matter of invasiveness. In this case, it's also due in part to the foreign nature of these procedures. A magician would say that it's due to a disruption of the natural mana flow that is part of all living things. No genetic therapy can avoid this—not genetic treatments that restore patients back to their former selves, nor phenotype adjustments that have been known to occur in nature, nor transgenic treatments that use genes that originate in natural designs. A metahuman is more than a sum of their flesh, blood, and bone, and neither science nor magic has yet been able to explain or prevent genetech's Essence costs.

All genetech is permanent. It cannot be removed at a later date, so the Essence loss due to gene therapy is also permanent, even under the revitalization treatment (p. 157). This is also true if a later augmentation or other event renders a genetech augmentation useless—there is no Essence hole remaining to be filled. Genetech is forever, so choose carefully, and be glad that at least it doesn't make you more interesting to organleggers.

GENETIC RESTORATION

Genetic restorations are medical genetic treatments to cure diseases, remove negative side effects of aging, or otherwise strengthen health. They work to restore and boost the body's own genetic baseline.

THERAPEUTIC GENETICS

Therapeutic genetics are the least complex, oldest, and best understood genetic alterations an individual can get. They are unique in that they do not damage Essence. Many correct inherited disabilities and disorders. It is the way of the world that financial means prevent all who need these therapies from acquiring them. Below is a list of a few examples, though it is by no means exhaustive.

Cancer Prevention Treatment: It has been found that the risk of developing most cancers is greatly increased if certain genes are present. Routine screening detects these genes and treatments can quickly and easily (although not cheaply) eliminate this risk before cancer ever develops. Once cancer has developed, these therapies are sadly no longer effective.

Color Blindness: A result of a genetic fault that affects the retinal cones that receive light and pass information on to the optic nerve, this defect is present in a significant portion of the population, primarily males. Adjustment of the genes that code for photopigments is a comparatively simple alteration that corrects this disability.

Corrective Gene Therapy: Treatments are available for many of the most common genetic disorders found in human populations. These disorders are usually found during neonatal gene screening and treated immediately. Such gene screening and treatment is standard with all corporate health-care policies. The corrections most often performed are for cystic fibrosis, Huntington's disease, Down syndrome, muscular dystrophy, sickle-cell anemia, celiac disease, and food intolerance.

REJUVENATION TREATMENT

Each rejuvenation treatment requires one major therapy session, usually followed by a number of maintenance sessions every six months for the next three years to ensure that the treatment is wholly effective. Depending on what kind of age rejuvenation treatment is applied, it can restore physical youth and vigor, or expand life expectancy without restoration of physical health. Regardless of which treatment is administered, age rejuvenation can only be performed a limited number of times before the cumulative Essence loss takes its toll.

Like all genetech, rejuvenation treatments are permanent, but even a treatment this powerful cannot totally prevent all of the ravages of time. Brain chemistry, for example, must be largely unaltered or the patient runs the risk of losing memory and acquired motor skills. Conditions such as Alzheimer's or Parkinson's diseases that rely on the connections between neurons rather than the neurons themselves cannot be corrected by rejuvenation.

Leónization: Leónization has a significant impact on holistic health as it attempts to reverse the natural processes of the body—aging and death. The therapy resets the genetic mechanism that controls aging, effectively rebooting cell life to its youthful prime. After treatment, the patient is restored to a physical age of approximately twenty-one.

Lifespan Extension: Unlike other treatments, lifespan extension doesn't require follow-up sessions. One therapy session is enough to increase the life expectancy up to ten years by slowing down the aging process and eliminating some of the known effects of aging. Each subsequent lifespan extension has half the effect of the previous, expanding the lifespan by up to five years, then around thirty months, and so on.

Physical Vigor: While Leónization restores physical age, this treatment deals with the side effects of aging—often called the "felt age" —without altering the aging process. This improves quality of life and results in elderly patients with the vigor and robustness of an adolescent.

Augmented Healing: Augmented healing is a whole-body therapy that restores the body to its full genetic health template. The patient's Condition Monitors are healed of all damage regardless of the source, but that's just a side effect. The real benefit is the complete regrowth of injured organs, crushed bones, severed limbs, and damaged nerves. The treatment doesn't repair damaged cybernetics or nanoware—in fact, when these systems are present, the treatment costs an additional twenty-five percent for the nanite treatment to keep the healing body from rejecting the machines. Augmented healing can also be used to repair bioware systems, increasing the cost by twenty-five percent.

Cellular Repair: This specialized regenerative treatment repairs permanent cellular damage caused by neurotoxins, radiation, magic, and other extreme sources. Each treatment can restore one point of any attribute lost due to disease or severe physical trauma, one point of Essence lost to Energy Drain (p. 195, *Street Grimoire*)

GENETIC RESTORATION

RESTORATION	TREATMENT TIME	ESSENCE	AVAILABILITY	COST
Therapeutic genetics (each)	1 month	0.2	10	90,000¥
Leónization	3 months	1.0	15	2,000,000¥
Lifespan extension	2 months	0.5	12	300,000¥
Physical vigor	2 months	0.5	13	250,000¥
Augmented healing	1 week	—	10	35,000¥
Cellular repair	1 week	—	10	65,000¥
Revitalization	1 month*	—	14	110,000¥

*see description

or Essence Drain (p. 396, *SR5*) powers, or reduce the Blighted quality (p. 169, *Run & Gun*) by one level. If individuals want to heal multiple points of damage, they have to take the treatment multiple times. It will not fix hereditary problems or disabilities integral to the subject's own genetic expression.

Revitalization: Revitalization is a breakthrough that repairs Essence loss derived from invasive implantation. Universal Omnitech has been successful in keeping the mechanism a secret, leaving geneticists to speculate that the effect is achieved by performing some kind of "genetic *feng shui*." Scientists work with a magician to realign the patient's aura by genetically remodeling DNA to repair damage to the aura and balance to the body's systems, restoring Essence. Revitalization regenerates Essence at a rate of 0.1 Essence per treatment. The treatment can restore Essence lost to implants that have been removed and to addiction. The technique cannot restore Essence for implants or treatments that remain in place, and it cannot repair Essence from gene therapies. Magic or Resonance points lost are never returned, and reductions to the maximum Magic/Resonance attribute remain in effect. The treatment takes one month, but patients need only spend seven days in a clinic and then wait the rest of the month for it to kick in.

PHENOTYPE ADJUSTMENT

All phenotype adjustments require the same treatment environment as gene therapy and include all genomic changes that involve the addition or modification of only natural, metahuman genes.

DNA MASKING

Making oneself unidentifiable to gene scanners or faking data bank information or SIN registry to evade positive identification is highly illegal. Needless to say, DNA masking is in high demand at black clinics cater-

ing to the underworld, the shadows, espionage organizations, and special ops divisions.

Genewipe: This treatment is a major genetherapeutic procedure that inserts a tag into the body's neurotransmitters that triggers accelerated cell death whenever these cease to receive regular neurochemical signals from the body—causing epithelial cells and hair to decompose more rapidly when they are removed from the body. As a consequence, biological trace evidence left by characters with this treatment irrevocably deteriorates after five minutes, rendering it useless for genetic profiling or ritual samples.

Masque: This treatment changes parts of the character's non-coding sequence so that a DNA scanner will not produce a positive identification when searching normal genome ID databases. While most DNA scanners will report a not-found result, scanners with Device Rating of 6 or more will recognize the absence of certain marker elements and report that further identification is required by other methods.

Reprint: Reprinting establishes a new genetic profile changing commonly tested polymorphisms within the genome to create a new and unique genetic fingerprint. Only the new pattern is recognized by gene scanners or identified by genetic fingerprinting. Even if full genome sequencing is performed, there is no way to unambiguously identify the individual genetically.

Shuffle: The amount and types of genetic modifications that a subject possesses can be concealed by careful reorganization of gene structures. This requires an extensive analysis of the patient's genome in order to set up the best places to conceal the modifications. It is not foolproof. This adjustment raises the threshold for identifying genetic modifications through genetic fingerprinting by 1.

GENETIC OPTIMIZATION

Genetic optimization permanently increases physical and mental potential by tweaking the genes responsi-

ADJUSTMENT	TREATMENT TIME	ESSENCE	AVAILABILITY	COST
Genewipe	2 months	0.2	16F	57,000¥
Masque	3 weeks	0.1	10F	40,000¥
Reprint	1 month	0.1	12F	30,000¥
Shuffle	1 month	0.2	12F	20,000¥
Genetic optimization	2 months	0.3	10	47,000¥
Cosmetic alteration	1 month	0.1	8	35,000¥
Print removal	2 weeks	0.1	10F	18,000¥
Metaposeur	1 month	0.1	8	38,000¥

ble for the development of a given attribute. Each time you undergo gene optimization, you raise your maximum natural attribute in one Physical or Mental attribute of your choice by one point. Each attribute can only be perfected in this manner once. Like the Exceptional Attribute quality (p.72, SR5), this treatment does not raise the attribute itself—meaning you still have to spend Karma to raise the attribute, as usual (**Character Advancement,** p.103, SR5). This adjustment is fully compatible with Exceptional Attribute.

PHENOTYPIC ALTERATION

Phenotypic alteration can create virtually any change to the body within the limits of metahuman norms. This treatment can elongate limbs, change skin tone or color, add horns, modify hair, change overall build, and so forth. The limits are left to the gamemaster's judgment, but a good guideline is to disallow obviously inhuman changes such as extra limbs, non-metahuman sensory organs, non-metahuman features, or anything more fanciful. Specific changes may be incompatible with organ replacements such as cyberlimbs, cybereyes,

bioware skin, or cosmetic modifications. The following changes are common phenotypic alterations.

Cosmetic Alteration: A variety of genetic modifications that focus on beautification (depending on who you ask) are available. Included are a distichia modification that adds a double row of eyebrows, epicanthic fold removal or addition, wrinkle reduction, eye color (including changes to different parts of the same iris), hair color and texture, baldness elimination, skin color, horn shape for trolls, tusk shape for orks and trolls, and so on limited only by the imagination and the metahuman phenotype.

Print Removal: Finger- or palm-prints can be completely removed by interfering with the natural process that leads to the development of skin ridges. This yields patternless fingers, toes, palms, and feet. Print scanners will report that the subject must be identified by a secondary method.

Metaposeur: This treatment genetically changes you to physically resemble a particular metatype (or metavariant), without actually granting any of their native advantages or disadvantages. For example, this enables a human elf-poseur who really wants to look like an elf to do so, though he gains no low-light vision or longevity.

EXOTIC METAGENETICS

Scientists and researchers have been identifying and collecting gene samples for decades that represent extremely rare gene mutations granting traits that are significantly different than the standard metahuman yet still within the realm of normal metahuman genetic expression. Some of these exotic genes have proven beneficial enough to warrant gene augmentations based on them.

ELASTIC STOMACH

Your stomach is located lower in the body and can stretch dramatically, allowing you to consume huge

OPTIONAL RULE:
PHENOTYPIC VARIATION

An exceedingly small number of individuals express these variant metahuman phenotypes naturally, with some phenotype being as rare as one in a billion. One phenotype adjustment can be taken as a Positive quality during character creation (with gamemster approval) with a Karma cost equal to the cost of the adjustment divided by 2,000 nuyen, rounded up + 3. As a natural mutation, this quality doesn't affect your Essence.

EXOTICE METAGENICS

EXOTICE METAGENICS	TREATMENT TIME	ESSENCE	AVAILABILITY	COST
Elastic stomach	2 weeks	0.1	6	10,000¥
Hyperthymesia	2 weeks	0.1	10	15,000¥
Lung expansion	2 weeks	0.1	6	16,500¥
Increased myelination	2 weeks	0.1	8	12,000¥
Myostatin inhibitor	2 weeks	0.3	10	30,500¥
Narco	2 weeks	0.2	12F	16,420¥
Selective hearing	2 weeks	0.1	6	17,000¥
Thickened digestive tract lining	2 weeks	0.1	6	8,000¥

quantities of food in one sitting. You can down thirty hot dogs in a half hour and still ask for dessert. You can eat and drink enough for up to days in one sitting, although doing so reduces your Physical limit by 1 for two hours per day's worth of food you gorge in a single sitting.

HYPERTHYMESIA

This genetic mutation causes an enlarged temporal lobe and caudate nucleus in the brain. This enables you to have true perfect memory. You can recall memories just like you were watching them happen over again. You could recall the exact date and day of the week of your twelfth birthday and remember what flavor soycake you had. The downside is that it is hard to forget the bad things you have experienced. This augmentation gives you a +2 on memory related tests, lets you ignore Memory Test glitches, and turns Memory Test critical glitches into regular glitches. Since you also perfectly remember negative experiences, the threshold for Composure Tests that deal with reacting to bad memories (either from events during play or from qualities like Flashbacks or Phobia) increases by 1.

LUNG EXPANSION

This augmentation increases the elasticity of the alveoli and reinforces the diaphragm, expanding the tidal volume of the lungs and improving oxygen exchange. This allows you to hold your breath longer and increases endurance. You can hold your breath for ninety seconds (30 Combat Turns) before making any tests, instead of the usual sixty seconds (20 Combat Turns) (p. 137, SR5). You also receive a +1 dice pool modifier to all Fatigue tests (p. 172, SR5) dealing with performing prolonged strenuous activity. If you also have an internal air tank (p. 455, SR5), you can refill the tank through three hours of normal breathing instead of six.

INCREASED MYELINATION

This augmentation improves the electrical insulation of your nervous system by increasing the thickness of the myelin sheath surrounding the central nervous system. It grants a +1 dice pool bonus when resisting electrical attacks and 1 point of natural biofeedback filtering.

MYOSTATIN INHIBITOR

This gene dramatically increases the body's ability to build muscle and reduces stored fat at the cost of reduced metabolic efficiency. Myostatin inhibitors are extremely popular with models and actors. People with this gene look well muscled and lean with little to no effort. It is banned in most sports, urban brawl being a notable exception (natch). Athletes in sports that require long-term endurance tend to shy away from this augmentation because they might falter due to a lack of stored energy. It increases your Strength by 1 and reduces the Karma cost of increasing your Strength by 2. You are more susceptible to hunger, taking fatigue damage every twelve hours instead of twenty-four, with that damage increasing every three days rather than every six (p. 172, SR5).

NARCO

This is a set of several minor genetic modifications that have the collective effect of modifying the way your body processes drugs. These genes were discovered through study of survivors of years of heavy substance abuse. While you become more likely to become addicted to drugs, you experience greater effects of drugs and lessened effects when they wear off. Any drug that grants a positive attribute modifier as an effect increases that modifier by +1. Any drug that deals damage when it wears off deals two less damage, and any negative effects that occur when a drug wears off are halved in duration. On Addiction Tests, take a -2 dice pool modifier when you aren't addicted to the drug you're rolling for, and a +2 dice pool modifier when you are addicted to the drug.

SELECTIVE HEARING

This gene improves your brain's ability to mentally filter out outside noise and focus on one particular sound source. Treat this as a Rating 1 select sound filter (p. 445, SR5).

THICKENED DIGESTIVE TRACT LINING

You know how some kids can eat a handful of dirt or eat slightly spoiled or exotic food? There's a gene for that. This augmentation reduces your lifestyle cost by ten percent and grants +1 dice pool modifier to toxin resistance tests.

TRANSGENICS

Trangenics encompasses all treatments by which non-metahuman genes and traits are spliced into the recipient's genome.

ADAPSIN

Adapsin is a catchphrase for two proteins that can reduce the impact of non-biological implants to an organism. True adapsin is an immunoprotein that limits bio-stress upon implantation of cybernetics by down-regulating inflammatory response. The second protein produces a secreted polysaccharide that coats the implant with a biofilm, making the body believe that it is a normal organ, thus limiting xeno-rejection and immune response in the long term. Adapsin reduces the Essence cost of implanting cyberware (but not bioware) by ten percent (round down), but only if you've already undergone adapsin treatment. This reduction is in addition to reductions from alpha-, beta- or delta-grade cyberware.

DAREDRENALINE

This augmentation creates a modified version of the "fight or flight" hormone adrenaline and its natural receptor. This causes a greater mental alertness than the normal hormone, granting a +1 dice pool modifier on all Willpower Tests (including resistance to spells, Drain, and Fading). You also become an adrenaline junkie and gain the Poor Self-Control (Thrill Seeker) Negative quality (p. 158, Run Faster) with no Karma benefit—if you already have that quality, increase the threshold of the Composure Test required by Poor Self Control to 3 instead of 2.

DOUBLE ELASTIN

A complex of collagen and elastin proteins normally forms a matrix to hold the body's organs and tissues together. This enhancement of the elastin protein increases the flexibility of this framework, allowing the body tissues to bend without breaking. Any time you would take 2 or more boxes of damage to your Stun Condition Monitor, reduce the damage by one box. The damage reduction does not apply to Stun received from Drain, Fading, or biofeedback damage. You also suffer from slightly degraded blood flow, and receive a -1 dice pool modifier on all Fatigue Tests (p. 172, SR5).

HYPER-GLUCAGON

Glugacon is a vital intermediary in the metabolism of energy stores in the body. Hyper-glucagon accelerates the liver's conversion of glycogen into glucose, ensuring a steady supply of energy and a protein-driven hyperactive energy boost. You double all listed intervals when dealing with the effects of Fatigue (p. 172, SR5) but require a higher caloric intake to maintain healthy energy levels (increasing your lifestyle costs by ten percent).

MAGNESENSE

Ferric iron reductase is a protein that produces a biological iron cluster, called magnetite. In migratory animals, clustering of magnetite is associated with their ability to know when and how to migrate. Selective expression of this protein in the inner ear allows you to sense the presence, direction, and intensity of magnetic fields, such as those generated by electronics, power supplies, or magnetic anomaly detectors, as a low thrumming sound. This modification also grants an unerring ability to identify magnetic north. You can make a Perception + Intuition Test to detect these emanations within a range of 10 meters, or large sources of magnetic fields such as power plants for a distance of five kilometers, and you receive a +1 dice pool bonus on Navigation tests.

NEO-EPO

Eythropoetin (EPO) is a hormone that stimulates production of red blood cells (erythrocytes), commonly used as a performance-enhancing additive in professional sports for over a century. Neo-EPO increases oxygen retention and athletic endurance by insuring a constant supply of oxygen. It is also involved in the healing of wounds. Characters with Neo-EPO receive a +1 dice pool modifier for all tests made with skills from the Athletics skill group, Healing tests, and Fatigue Tests, and they add 1 to their Physical limit.

PUSHED

The PostSynaptic HyperDensity protein modification increases the size of neuronal bundles throughout the central nervous system. This has statistically been shown to grant an increase in subjects' IQ. Characters receive a +1 modifier to Logic-linked skill tests.

QUALIA

Derived from a reptilian species, this hormone stimulates neural activity in the reptilian hind mind and the sensory-dedicated lobes, ultimately affecting the intuitive subconscious grasp of sensory information. Qualia is believed to be a form of organic storage of raw empirical data associated with prior sensory stimuli, which can reinforce a subject's ability to absorb and react to input from their environment (even on a subconscious level). Characters with this modification receive a +1 dice pool modifier to all Intuition-linked skill tests.

REAKT

Reakt is a transgenic neurohormone released by the pituitary gland during stress, enhancing perception to the degree that movements are perceived as if in slow motion, making it easier to react to situations or incoming dangers. Characters with Reakt get a +2 dice pool modifier to all ranged and melee Defense tests (this includes dodging indirect combat spells). This effect is cumulative with augmentations that enhance Reaction.

SKELETAL PNEUMATICITY

Derived from avian gene sequences, this augmentation causes the formation of hollow bones that are nearly as strong yet much lighter than the normal metahuman skeleton. This modification is extremely popular with dancers and gymnasts, although they must be careful to avoid hard falls. You gain a +2 on Gymnastics tests, and are approximately ten percent lighter than a normal metahuman of your stature, but you take a –1 on damage resistance tests. If you have an augmentation to your bones, skeletal pneumacity has no effect, but you do not regain Essence lost for taking the treatment.

SOLUS

Developed from research on SURGE subjects who developed photometabolic ability, this modification causes plant-like chloroplasts to develop within the epidermis. These structures supplement an individual's energy needs via photosynthesis. The melanin coloration in the subject's skin is also adjusted to conceal the greenish tint the chloroplasts would otherwise produce. This gene augmentation has become very popular with eco-fanatics and spacefarers. Even when the character's skin is fully exposed to sunlight, this process only creates enough nourishment for the recipient to supplement their diet, not to replace it. Characters with solus reduce their Lifestyle costs by ten percent. However, since the character's overall physical well-being and energy increase in the sunlight, the character feels uncomfortable at night or in the shade, suffering a –1 dice pool penalty on all Social Tests. If you have an augmentation to your skin, solus has no effect, and you do not regain Essence lost for taking the treatment.

TRANSGENICS

TRANSGENICS	TREATMENT TIME	ESSENCE	AVAILABILITY	COST
Adapsin	1 month	0.2	16	30,000¥
Dareadrenaline	2 weeks	0.1	6	61,000¥
Double elastin	2 weeks	0.2	12	18,000¥
Hyper-glucagon	2 weeks	0.1	6	8,000¥
Magnesense	1 month	0.1	8	7,000¥
Neo-EPO	2 weeks	0.2	6	38,000¥
PuSHed	1 month	0.1	14	62,000¥
Qualia	1 month	0.4	14	65,000¥
Reakt	1 month	0.4	10	73,000¥
Skeletal pneumaticity	1 month	0.1	5	9,000¥
Solus	2 weeks	0.1	8	8,000¥
Synaptic acceleration	1 month	0.4	8	78,000¥
Synch	1 month	0.1	8	14,000¥
Tetrachromatic vision	2 weeks	0.1	10	8,000¥
Vasocon	2 weeks	0.1	6	15,000¥

SYNAPTIC ACCELERATION

This gene augmentation improves the functioning nervous system's sodium-potassium channel depolarization and repolarization efficiency, thereby increasing reaction speed. The character gains +1 to their Initiative rating, +1 Initiative Dice, and a +1 dice pool modifier for all Ranged and Melee Defense Tests. If a character has an augmentation that increases their Initiative or grants any Initiative Dice, synaptic acceleration has no effect, and they do not regain Essence lost for taking the treatment.

SYNCH

Synch is a nootropic protein that affects cognitive abilities in the brain cells of the visual cortex. This enhances intuitive comprehension and pattern recognition abilities. Characters receive a +1 dice pool on all Perception tests. In addition, recipients accustomed to combat situations develop a battle awareness based on moves, which allows them respond and adapt quickly to their opponent's fighting style. When in combat the character receives +1 dice pool modifier on combat tests against each opponent after the enemy's first attack. This enhancement is incompatible with dynomitan.

TETRACHROMACY

Average metahuman vison is based on the eyes having three types of cones. People with color-blindness have only two and the genetech procedure to correct this is among the most common performed. Those with tetrachromatic vision have a fourth cone that allows them to see slightly into the ultraviolet spectrum and give them much greater acuity at distinguishing hue and slightly increases ability to see in dim light. Tetrachromacy lets you treat Partial Light conditions as Full Light (p. 175, SR5) and grants a +3 dice pool modifier to visual Perception tests.

VASOCON

Angiotension regulates blood flow through the body. It causes capillary beds to contract and stimulates water retention. The enhanced vasocon has a greater vaso-constrictive effect that is useful in situations of massive blood loss. When a character with this treatment takes damage that overflows his Physical damage column by less than his Body attribute, additional damage due to blood loss and shock accrues at the reduced rate of one box per (Body x 2) minutes. Characters with this mod develop hydration insufficiencies, accelerating the onset of Fatigue to half its normal time in hot climates.

ENVIRONMENTAL MICROADAPTATION

Environmental microadaptation usually requires massive transgenic alterations of metabolic pathways and is therefore considered a major genetic change. These therapies require several months to splice in new proteins and balance the consequences in an environment that simulates the conditions to which the body is adapting.

Since changes are far-reaching, you can only have one environmental microadaptation. If you get a second microadaptation, its effects replace the first, but you not get an Essence refund from losing the effect of the replaced microadaptation. These adaptations refer to rules on fatigue damage in *Shadowrun, Fifth Edition* (p. 172) and *Run & Gun* (p. 145).

ALLERGEN TOLERANCE

A catchall classification for a variety of similar gene tweaks, these genetic treatments can reduce or eliminate an individual's natural allergic sensitivity. Each treatment is tailored to affect the genes that code for one specific allergy. Allergies are reduced by one step, from Severe to Moderate, Moderate to Mild, and Mild allergies eliminated completely. This augmentation can be taken multiple times, both for different allergies and for the same allergy multiple times. No additional Karma cost is required to reduce or eliminate the Allergy negative quality if this method is used. This treatment cannot be used to treat allergies derived from magical sources or inherent to metatype, including light Allergies for Infected characters.

COLD ADAPTATION

Adaptation to cold environments modifies the subject's metabolic processes to maximize internal heat retention. Transgenic restructured and isolative adipose and skin tissues, adjustment of interstitial and cellular fluids to lower temperatures, and cold-shock protein machineries that refold proteins under arctic temperature denaturing conditions protect the body against the effects of extreme colds. Characters who have undergone such treatment get a +2 dice pool modifier when resisting cold- or ice-related primary and secondary damage, in addition to a +2 dice pool modifier for cold-environment Survival and Fatigue Tests.

CRYO TOLERANCE

Developed by Ares and quickly replicated by the other major players in the space race, this set of gene tweaks makes the recipient's body more resilient against the stresses of cryogenic freezing. This is considered to be an important step in the mass colonization of other planets.

HEAT ADAPTATION

Heat tolerance is conveyed by increasing water retention to avoid dehydration, speeding blood flow to increase heat diffusion, and using heat-resistant proteins that do not break down at higher temperatures. Skin layers are transgenically reinforced to protect against burning. This enhancement allows the character a +2 dice pool modifier for any heat or fire primary and secondary damage by covering the skin with a moist film. The character also receives a +2 dice pool modifier for hot-environment Survival and Fatigue Tests. This treatment is incompatible with the same implants as cold adaptation as well as the cold adaptation enhancement.

LOW OXYGEN ADAPTATION

Adaptations for environments low in oxygen replace a few metabolic pathways with anaerobic equivalents originating from bacteria. Additionally, an adapted subject is usually outfitted with enhanced versions of hemoglobin and myoglobin in his bloodstream. These allow the subject to survive in a low-oxygen environment for an extended period of time. The character can hold her breath for (Body x 5) minutes before her first Fatigue Test. Characters with this alteration require specialized diets and have their Lifestyle cost increased by ten percent.

MICROGRAVITY ADAPTATION

The side effects of space habitation and return to Earth-normal gravity are reduced by alteration of bone and muscle density, fluid density, pressure receptors, and the otolith organs in the middle ear. Characters with this adaptation are not subjected to any form of space sickness during launch or landing. Any negative dice pool modifiers imposed for operating under micro-gravity conditions are negated. The character does not require any medical treatment when returning to Earth. If you have an augmentation to your bones, this augmentation has no effect, and you do not regain Essence lost for taking the treatment.

POLLUTION TOLERANCE

Engineering pollution tolerance relies on splicing in proteins capable of isolating and disposing of heavy metals or rendering organic contaminants inert. Further, modifications include the enhancement of the body's natural metabolic enzymes to deal with toxins more efficiently and to alter cellular receptors and metabolic intermediaries to be resistant to pollutants. Characters with this adaptation receive a +2 dice pool modifier for the purpose of resisting chemical attacks from pollutants, heavy metals, and other related toxins. The character experiences pollution environments as one step lower than their severity.

ENVIRONMENTAL MICROADAPTATION

MICROADAPTATION	TREATMENT TIME	ESSENCE	AVAILABILITY	COST
Allergen tolerance	2 weeks	0.1	6	20,000¥
Cold adaptation	3 months	0.5	5	8,000¥
Cryo tolerance	3 months	0.5	18	50,000¥
Heat adaptation	3 months	0.5	5	8,000¥
Low oxygen adaptation	3 months	0.5	4	8,000¥
Microgravity adaptation	3 months	0.5	4	30,000¥
Pollution tolerance	3 months	0.5	5	15,000¥
Radiation tolerance	3 months	0.5	6	15,000¥

RADIATION TOLERANCE

The body is made less susceptible to radiation exposure and damage from radioactive sources by reinforcing nucleic acid repair and DNA protection proteins. This augmentation is most often used by environmental cleanup technicians and by astronauts who spend a lot of time in small craft with little radiation shielding. Characters receive a +2 dice pool modifier for resisting damage from "hot" sources. The character experiences radiation environments as one step lower than their severity.

IMMUNIZATION

This therapy infers near-immunity to a specific disease pathogen, toxin, or other compound. Specialized hybridomas are created within the body that produce monoclonal antibodies, targeting a specific substance.

OPTIONAL RULE: SIMILAR AGENTS

Ask any medical professional about how biological process react to immune responses or pharmaceuticals and the first thing they'll say is, "It depends..." Sometimes in the squishy science that is biochemistry, you get lucky. At the gamemaster's discretion, any given immunity may partially extend to related or similar pathogens or toxins. For instance, immunity to VITAS-3 might provide partial immunity to VITAS-2 infections, or someone immune to jazz (the drug, not the music) may have a resistance to cram (the drug, not the bread). When this is the case, halve the Power of the related agent (rounding down).

IMMUNIZATION	TIME	ESSENCE	AVAIL	COST
Per agent	2 weeks	0.1	6	20,000¥

These antibodies provide a swift response to a foreign contaminant, bestowing significantly improved resistance on the patient. Patients can be immunized in this fashion against any common bacterial infection and certain bacterial endotoxins, chemical toxins, and other harmful chemical or biological agents. The procedure has yet to be perfected against highly mutable agents—such as certain exotic viruses (HMHVV being at the top of the list)—or artificial agents such as hard nanites that evade detection or cannot be targeted. Basic immunity cannot be made effective against neurotoxins and other quick-acting compounds because they affect the target before antibodies can respond. A patient can only be immunized against a number of compounds equal to his or her unaugmented Body. Any immunization beyond this disturbs the immune system to the point of failure.

The treatment grants the subject complete immunity to single doses of the particular compound or pathogen. In the event of an abnormally high exposure to the substance, the antibodies still assist in resisting the agent, but not completely. For every dose administered past the first,

TRANSGENIC ALTERATION

Transgenic alteration is like phenotypic alteration, but it goes beyond the limits of the traditional metahuman form by splicing entire genetic sequences from different species. Virtually any change can be effected, ranging from superficial limited alteration (non-metahuman eye, hair, or skin color and texture) to animal-like amendments.

A transgenic alteration can include any phenotypic alteration to the body. It could be an animal feature, including shaggy lion manes, rabbit's ears, quills instead of hair, tails, claws, and other animal characteristics. An alteration could be a more ... artistic ... change, anything from pearlescent, bioluminescent, or fluorescent skin or eye colors to disproportional statures that introduce entirely novel biochemical processes like colored tears

TRANSGENIC ALTERATION

ALTERATION	TREATMENT TIME	ESSENCE	AVAILABILITY	COST
Transgenic alteration	1-3 months	0.3	10	30,000¥ and up

or a cranial lattice jutting up from the head. The only limitation is that the alteration must be from (or analogous to) the animal kingdom—geneticists have tried but so far failed to fully splice metahuman and plant genomes.

All transgenic alterations are cosmetic only, with no direct game rules associated with them. They are quite subject to rules for Distinctive Style (p. 80, *SR5*), because if you didn't have one before, you do now. Transgenic alteration may be incompatible with some other augmentations (fur and Solus don't really go together, for example), as determined by the gamemaster.

COMPLIMENTARY GENETICS

This new area of gene augmentations is an attempt to force biological evolution to catch up with technological evolution. The field of complimentary genetics modifies the body in ways that make cyberware and bioware merge more seamlessly with the metahuman body. While these genetic modifications do nothing on their own, the way they interact with 'ware allows the user to have a little bit more control of their new capabilities.

The downside of these augmentations is that the cyber or bioware associated with the complimentary genetics becomes more integral to the body systems, and thus harder to remove or replace. Doing so costs ten percent of the initial cost of the cyber or bioware. Also, if the 'ware is being upgraded in Rating or Grade, the benefits of the complementary genetic augmentation do not carry over and must be purchased again and the procedure repeated to regain the benefit—and as with all genetech, you don't get an Essence refund.

ADRENALINE PUMP OPTIMIZATION

This optimization causes a small delay in cortisol release in response to stress. This helps prevent individuals with an adrenaline pump from accidentally triggering it in response to brief sudden stressful situation where its effects are undesired. When you fail a Composure Test, your adrenal pump will not trigger if you failed by only 1 hit.

CONTROL RIG OPTIMIZATION

This augmentation causes specialized myelinated axons and glial cells to grow that extend from the middle brain and parts of the dorsolateral prefrontal cortex, cerebellum, and thalamus. By themselves, they have no effect, but if a control rig is installed, they increase the efficiency of communication with the parts of the brain critical to spatial reasoning and instinctive motion control. This booster provides an additional +1 to all Vehicle Tests (not Vehicle skills) when the user is "jumped into" a drone or vehicle in addition to the usual benefits of a control rig. It cannot be combined with the control rig booster nanotech.

ENHANCED SYMBIOSIS

This augmentation modifies and expands the function of the pancreas, allowing it to synthesize compounds that satisfy the special dietary requirements of symbiote bioware. No monthly cost is needed to feed your symbiotes regardless of Lifestyle.

REACTION OPTIMIZATION

This optimization increases the width and myelination of the lower spinal motor neurons, which in conjunction with the superconducting materiel of reaction enhancers, allows more rapid innervation of skeletal muscle fibers. Add +1 Initiative to the bonuses already received with reaction enhancers. This augmentation has no effect by itself and does not give additional bonuses for higher Ratings of reaction enhancers. It is only compatible with reaction enhancers and cannot be combined with any other Reaction or Initiative enhancement.

REFLEX RECORDER OPTIMIZATION

This augmentation increases the number of Betz cells in the brain. These cells are some of the largest cells in the brain and deal directly with mediating the communication between the motor cortex and the motor neurons of spinal cord and brain stem. You do not take the usual -1 dice pool modifier for defaulting on a skill you have no ranks in as long as you have reflex recorder bioware for a skill in that group.

WIRED REFLEX OPTIMIZATION

This augmentation improves the strength and speed of the neural pathways which link to the trigger system of wired reflexes, thereby increasing the speed with

COMPLIMENTARY GENETICS

GENETICS	TREATMENT TIME	ESSENCE	AVAILABILITY	COST
Control rig optimization	2 weeks	0.1	7	4,600¥
Reaction optimization	2 weeks	0.1	6	6,600¥
Reflex recorder optimization	2 weeks	0.1	11	3,800¥
Wired reflex optimization	2 weeks	0.1	9R	9,000¥
Adrenaline pump optimization	2 weeks	0.1	7F	6,000¥
Enhanced symbiosis	2 weeks	0.1	6	4,000¥

GENETIC INFUSION SIDE EFFECTS

HITS	EFFECT
Critical glitch	The DNA integrated badly. You develop a terminal cancer and have 2D6 weeks to live if it remains untreated. You may burn an Edge to reduce this result to a glitch.
Glitch	A bad integration causes intense discomfort. You permanently lose one box from each of your Physical and Stun Condition Monitors.
0	The DNA for the addictive substance integrated, but the beneficial DNA did not. You take 4 boxes of Stun damage that cannot be healed in any way for (15 – Body) days. If your infusion had any negative effects, you continue to suffer them for this duration.
1 to 3	You take 4 boxes of Stun damage that cannot be healed in any way for (15 – Body) days. For each hit you have, reduce the number of boxes by 1.
4+	The infusion fades and there are no further effects (beyond the addiction risk, of course).

which wired reflexes can be activated. The manual trigger speed is reduced from a Complex to Simple Action, and the wireless trigger speed is reduced to Free Action.

GENETIC INFUSIONS

Gentech is expensive but bears little risk. If you're looking for something cheaper and downright dangerous, then you might be interested in a genetic infusion.

A genetic infusion is a genetic treatment that uses quick-and-dirty techniques, usually involving removal of some of the tissue you want to alter, treating it with various gene therapies, and then reintroducing it into your body along with a cocktail of tailored viruses and immunosuppressants. The result is a temporary application of a specific genetic augmentation, though not without certain risks and drawbacks.

You can be treated with an infusion of any augmentation from the categories of DNA masking, exotic metagenetics, transgenics, environmental microadaptation,

GENETIC INFUSIONS

INFUSION	AVAIL	COST
Any infusion	13F	2,500¥

immunization, or complementary genetics. The infusion procedure takes about two hours and start taking effect about 24 hours after treatment.

Infusions last (15 – Body) days, with a minimum of 1 day. Infusions are physically addictive, with Addiction Rating 5 and Addiction Threshold 3.

When an infusion's duration ends, make an Essence + Edge test and consult the Infusion Side Effect Table. You may not spend Edge on this test.

TRANSGENIC ART AND CHIMERA PETS

Transgenic objects, be they plants or animal, can take any form and are often unique. With the advancements

TRANSGENICS

TRANSGENICS	AVAILABILITY	COST
DNArt		
Commercial	10	30,000¥+
Custom	20	150,000¥+
Chimera pets		
Commercial	6	15,000¥+
Custom	12	100,000¥+

in genetechnology, genetic engineers have already begun to create new life forms from the bottom up. These rare pieces of genetic art are often priceless and shown only during exhibitions, or are sold to collectors for unimaginable amounts of money. A profitable shadowmarket has emerged around these creatures, hiring runners to steal such organisms on behalf of collectors not willing to pay the price in an auction. Since there is an emerging market for chimera pets for the middle classes, genetic bootlegging of altered life forms has become big bio-pirate business.

The fabulously wealthy have always used exquisitely bred animals as status symbols and in many cases as living fashion accessories. Genecrafted plants and animals bring this to a whole new level. The latest trend in fashion pets are Petites™, tiny chimeric animals created to look like larger natural animals—the larger, the better. The most common Petites are giraffes, elephants, and polar bears, none of them bigger than a lap dog. Another trend is Biowear™, which are living articles of clothing. They often are sensitive to their surroundings, changing color, texture, or bioluminescing depending on the pheromones and sounds in their environment. Among the wealthiest of the wealthy one can find arboretums full of chimeric plants and animals (or some things in between) that outright defy the process of natural evolution.

Both DNArt and chimera pets come in two grades: Commercial and Custom. Commercial grade means that a certain number of creatures are produced each season, following fashion trends. These are targeted to the high class and the middle-class aspirers. Custom grade means that the creature is a one-of-a-kind creation, made to either the artists or the benefactor's whims.

QUICK & DIRTY AUGMENTATIONS

POSTED BY: HAZE

Gettin' shit done. That's the game, isn't it? Everybody's doing it, including you. You think you're clean? That's a relative standard. That headache in the morning that won't go away until your first cup of kaf? That's a taste. That stim that kept you up for cram sessions? Another taste. Betel gum and SensualStim to take you up or get you loose. Another and another. Everyone is dosing, every day. Accept that right now.

Now, what about those who have to do more than wake up and make it through the day? The 405 Hellhound pledge who needs to win this race or he'll never earn his cut? The megacorporate egghead with a deadline to reach and not enough neurons firing? You think they're willing to take a taste of something stronger when their future is on the line? Damn right they will, and so will you.

Some people are born with everything. For everyone else, there's pharma. Come have a taste.

- This coming from the guy who can't get laid without dosing his date? Slamm-0!, are we really tapping this temp-head to tell us about drug use?
- Pistons

- He's got about as much right to be here as any of us, and honestly, I'd rather hear this kind of thing from someone with experience than from a straight-edger. I mean, I'd probably ask Sticks about ammo types before Man-of-Many-Names. If I want to find Panther Assault Cannon rounds, I'll ask Am-Mut, not Bull.
- Slamm-0!

- Hey!
- Bull

- If it makes you feel any better, you've got the rest of us to offer our two nuyen if we think he's wrong. Sound good?
- Turbo Bunny

- I've got no problem putting him in his place.
- Butch

- I swear, all I ever do is edit other people's work …
- Nephrine

- Patience, doc, your turn is right around the bend.
- Slamm-0!

YESTERDAY'S UPPERS, TODAY!

In the age of cybernetic augmentation, customized vat-grown organs and designer genetics and nanoware, you might wonder why anyone would resort to something like drugs. Isn't it just more cost-effective to invest in something that lasts a long time and gets you a big ol' net for your nuyen instead of pissing it away piecemeal?

Well, sure, you might ask that … if you're the type who's always got some money on the stick. C'mon, think about it. You're going day to day, trying to survive in the barrens, eating expired soy cold from the pouch, you think you're going to be planning out your cybersuite? Chrome can be complicated to acquire. Drugs are usually as far away as your street corner. Usually not even that far.

- If you're that damn poor, maybe you shouldn't be spending your nuyen on drugs?
- Baka Dabora

- That's ignoring the whole environment that encourages drug use. The right drugs can save you from sickness, from insanity, from violence, and once you're hooked, you're not thinking straight enough to sweat it out. And that's not counting the number of opportunities you'll get for a free sample from a pusher, or someone passing around the hypo or the tabs at a party. Or maybe you inherited an addiction from your folks. It's a culture, a cycle of addiction and poverty, that has existed in some form or another for centuries.
- Aufheben

Low-level go-gangs don't have the cash to invest in implants, but drugs can be had on the cheap and offer a

thrill no 'ware can give you. Sooner or later, by the time a ganger makes some real cred on a score, he wonders why he needs cyberspurs when his knife is treating him fine. After all, he can always tear some out of the next poor slot he rips up while riding the chemical wave.

» And sooner or later, Holly the Halloweener, all jazzed on her juice of choice, picks a fight she can't win and doesn't have the brains to pull back. Said brains then decorate the pavement.
» Sticks

» Since when do Halloweeners have brains?
» Bull

But there's more to it than just how much it costs to get it. I mean, I've dragged a street samurai into a back alley shadowclinic enough times to know that when the chrome takes a bullet, your account feels the damage. And that's not even figuring for regular maintenance, firmware upgrades, surgery, and everything else that goes with it. I can't even begin to imagine how complicated it gets with bioware.

» Not necessarily more complicated, since bioware heals much as the rest of the metahuman body will. It's when it's out of balance that there are complications.
» KAM

» Wrong section, Doc.
» Bull

Think about that upkeep for a minute. Think about when the fake skin gets torn and people can see that you've got chrome. Now you're a target for every chopper gang that wants to snatch that cyber and sell it off. Or you get spotted by a Knight Errant patrol and they do a little SIN scan, and wouldn't you know it, you haven't got a very good fake SIN, if you have one at all. Possession of cyber? Better scan it closer. Now they're finding things like spurs and wired reflexes, all kinds of stuff. And you'll lose the chrome, anyway, when they put you away.

You know what happens when you get stuck up for drugs? You can just hand them over. Without losing the

hand. You can take them, and they're gone. Done. Finito. You're in the clear. Or toss them. Whatever you gotta do. Are you worried about a tox screen? Are any of us applying for actual jobs? And if you get pulled over, you've already got bigger problems than a charge for possession or use.

» He's jumping the gun here. There are a lot of ways having chems in your system can get you in trouble.
» Thorn

» Besides being unreliable and blitzed?
» Pistons

» Seriously, though. Chem sniffers, trained paranatural security, some spells, and more can register the chemical byproducts off your body associated with drug use. If you're taking the sneaky way in, posing as staff at a party for example, you might get tagged for drug use. Other drugs can also elevate body temperatures, making you more visible on thermoptics, or induce physical tics, retinal quakes, and reactions that automated monitoring and facial recognition software tags as suspicious.
» Thorn

» Is there any chance it can scramble ritual samples like blood if you've been shot while high?
» Whippet

» Afraid not. You'd have to have such a concentration of the drugs in your system that you'd be dead already.
» Red

» There has been some research into BADs capable of scrambling the mana signature of subjects to render them untraceable by ritual or astral tracking, but every success so far also included dramatic long-term damage to the subject's aura. Those who could use magic found their abilities diminished permanently. Manadyne and a few other companies predict a successful test within the next decade, which … doesn't really mean anything.
» The Smiling Bandit

> Let me just chime in that a hit of cram now and again did, in fact, get me through a lot of late-night study sessions.
> Lyran

> Ditto for me with coding.
> Slamm-0!

> I don't condone drug use among my men, but I would probably be dead right now if one of my snipers hadn't been dosing to stay awake and sharp for thirty-six hours straight.
> Picador

> Is anyone here besides me *not* hitting the patches?
> /dev/grrl

> They don't work on me, so, me.
> Red

> And I prefer chips.
> Turbo Bunny

> You mean "preferred" right?
> Bull

> No. Prefer. You're never really over an addiction, no matter what you say.
> Turbo Bunny

And then there's the rich man's perspective. I've crashed on enough corporate couches to know they live a designer-drug lifestyle. Pressure to perform, stay sharp, put in a crazy number of hours all week, and compete with the smiling sharks they swim with—yeah, they need escapes and edges just like anyone else. Even the ones who already have it all are looking for the next big joyride, and even in the age of digital trips, pharma can still deliver.

THE TACTICS OF GETTING HIGH

There's another upside to drugs that 'ware can't match: flexibility. You get muscle implants, and they'll make you stronger. That's what they do. It's what they'll always do. It's all they'll do. For the same price I could get whole kilos of speed or even the new designer drugs making the rounds. A different patch for every occasion. Something to make you fast, take away your pain, boost your brains, or buff your brawn. A pocket full of options. A good long toke of deepweed can make any competent brawler an astral asset.

Think about when you face off against a tweaker and he doses a tab. What is it doing to him? How is it changing the fight? You don't even know. There's the outside chance it'll make him slow or sloppy, but right now, he might be sharper, faster. Hell, if it was the right BAD, you are now fighting a regenerator.

And the worst part is, until it's too late, you have no idea what he is capable of.

> * Lone Star SOP with an obvious juicer is to taze 'em until they're comatose. If that doesn't work, lethal force is authorized. The last thing you need is some psychopathic MPCP freak tearing through people like tissue paper.
> * Hard Exit

> * Something that always gets me: A lot of drugs offer some inherent resistance to mind control spells. If their thoughts are too slippery to get a hold on, the drugs can keep an interloper from taking control.
> * Red

> * True, but plenty of other narcos can work just as well to make them much more susceptible. These are usually the recreational drugs you see at parties or in dens. Combat drugs are the ones that can shake you off.
> * Lyran

> * An interesting thing: Drugs and chips can work wonders when fighting shedim, especially against that fear effect that surrounds them.
> * Turbo Bunny

> * A false skin of courage cannot hold true terror within.
> * Man-of-Many-Names

> * For once I know what he's saying. Using drugs and chips as a substitute for actual morale and courage is a shoddy tactic. The moment the protection of the drug slips and fear overcomes the soldier, it totally overwhelms them.
> * Picador

EVERYDAY DOSE

People don't like to think of themselves as addicts, but pharmaceuticals have become as much a part of our lives as food, air, and water. In fact, if you're living la vida corporata, it's probably mixed into all three. The difference between a drug and everyday nutrients and supplements is a cultural one, and when Big Brother Corporation tells you it's not a narcotic, you'll take their word for it. They've got the marketing skills to make it so.

So what is your average wageslave dosing? Well, they're aware of things like cram and EZBreathe, but they aren't thinking about the stuff the corp is giving them for "free." Things like antidepressants in the drinking water.

> * "Do you know what 'fluoridation' is, Mandrake?"
> * Red

> * What?
> * /dev/grrl

> * Here we go again …
> * Red

> * I can verify this.
> * Nephrine

> * Any proof?
> * Snopes

> * Uploading sample reports from my own lab and examinations.
> * Nephrine

> * Holy drek …
> * Snopes

> * How do they dose everyone without causing widespread chemical imbalances in everyone drinking it?
> * Aufheben

> * By adjusting dosages in waves. You gradually scale it up and down over time, which prevents anyone from developing any noticeable maladjustments, while maintaining limitations on mood and excitement and not building up an immunity. Individual cases can be monitored and countered by corporate medical care.
> * Butch

> * Drugs to counteract the drugs, and any excuse they want to give to explain it away. Fuck.
> * Ecotope

- Plenty of them actively go for it. Those who know about it are counseled into seeing it as a perks package. You're probably already considering antidepressants, and going back to your doss after an eighteen-hour workday to your AR decorations, games, and simdramas. If the corp is offering something to help you make it through the day, why would you say no?
- Baka Dabora

- Note that upper-level execs aren't drinking the water, as it were. They've got perk packages to keep them in line, and they already exhibit initiative and skill to get where they are, demonstrating ambition and loyalty. The drugs can dull creative thinking just as well as they numb discontent and rebellion. There's a reason execs tend not to worry about people from below stealing their jobs.
- Kia

- This is disgusting.
- Aufheben

- If it makes you feel any better, they're unlikely to use it in most places. Why bother pumping happy in the air or into the cafeteria drinking water unless it is cost-effective to do so? You'll find it among low-level workers at isolated locations, or line workers in places more likely to cause depression and anxiety, usually enclosed environments like arcologies or aquacologies.
- Kia

- Makes you wonder how many would-be geniuses are suppressed among the sararimen.
- The Smiling Bandit

- Or how many revolutionaries.
- Marcos

There's plenty of other stuff people take but don't think of as a narcotic. Betel, for example. Folks are chewing it at Wuxing and Shiawase all the time. You can tell by the sharp, distinctive herbal scent in their breath, almost like licorice, and the bluish stain on their teeth. And they're wired like they've had a couple shots of espresso.

- CorpCandy: Not even once.
- Netcat

- I still don't see what the problem is.
- Slamm-0!

- In your case, never again. Your drool stained the sheets black.
- Netcat

- Awww …
- Slamm-0!

DAYTRIPPERS

And then there's the stuff everyone knows is a drug, but doesn't cross the line into "unreasonable." Deepweed, novacoke, betameth, and there's plenty of market for classics like old-school LSD, marijuana, amphetamines, and more. And of course, booze never goes out of style.

- Booze takes on new dimensions when you consider the complexities of elven wines.
- Thorn

- Or the sheer power of hurlg.
- 2XL

- Hurlg: The booze that tastes like it sounds.
- Lyran

- I doubt many of you have much use for this, but when an Infected feeds on the blood of someone who is drunk, the metabolized alcohol packs as much of a punch for us as it does for the one who drank it. I think the same goes for drugs, though I haven't run into that happening, personally.
- Red

- Ditto for ghouls, though meat that isn't fresh won't maintain the buzz. You can just tell it was there.
- Hannibelle

- Gross.
- Slamm-0!

- You want gross? Blood with P4MO in it. Tastes like plastic. Can't stand the taste whatsoever.
- Red

- Something to bear in mind …
- Clockwork

The newest fad is binaural beats, sonic playback that gets you high in different ways depending on tones and vibrations. It can be done with a high-quality set of earbuds, implants, or a kind of specialized drug den the kids are calling "Noize Holes."

- I've been to one of those. It's like a sensory deprivation tank with a serious stereo system. I didn't try it myself, I was working, but the people getting out were dazed and happy.
- /dev/grrl

- It's pretty cool. I tried it out at an after-party in LA maybe two weeks ago. I felt super calm and relaxed, like right after taking a nap. My drummer, on the other hand, puked his guts out.
- Kat o' Nine Tales

- The theory has been around since the nineteenth century. In effect, it's the emulation of brain-generated low-frequency pulsations when two tones at close frequencies are presented separately to each ear. Difference in tone can result in a number of effects.
- The Smiling Bandit

- You can find them for digital download from a few sites. At least, you can find some that are supposedly for meditation or de-stressing. Makes me wonder if there is a BTL equivalent …
- Turbo Bunny

- Sure. And your brains are literally scrambled by sonics. Might as well put one of those Ares sonic rifles up to your head.
- Goat Foot

- What I'm curious about is how it would interact with other drugs. A tab of bliss and one of those sonic dens with a sensory deprivation tank—who knows how calm a human being can get?
- Nephrine

- Given what I've seen when people mix BTLs and plain old narcos, you can calm yourself right into a coma.
- Turbo Bunny

- Some high-end alternative clinics offer it as an Awakened-friendly anesthetic option.
- Butch

And let's not forget chips. BTL or bust, that was the motto of the '50s. You're no doubt already familiar with the old classics. Not a lot has been done to innovate in that region, so most of what hits the streets is just new takes on what we've seen before. Polite society is having fun with Soma Chips, little personafix chips that make you want to work out. BTL it's not, but it's popular for the lazy sarariman. Most BTLs are just standard sims without limiters, meaning movies, porn, and recordings taken past normal sensation.

- Custom and dedicated BTL productions tend to follow the trends the same, but more in the spirit of productions than the literal product. Taboos people get fascinated about but can't talk about in polite society. For example, there's a kink about body snatching with all the hoopla about Boston and CFD going on. Some of the bestsellers right now are based on the fantasy of someone you like getting their brain taken over and turning them into someone who actually wants to fuck you. The really weird ones try to mix personafix and alien sensates to make you "experience" being taken over and turned into … well, whatever the chip is selling. Terrorist, nymphomaniac, etc. Same crap as always, just a different story about how you get there.
- Turbo Bunny

- Who would want to fantasize about being brainjacked? That's disgusting.
- Bull

- I wouldn't jump to conclusions.
- Plan 9

- Watch it, Plan. We're still keeping an eye on you.
- Slamm-0!

- People get up to stranger things in meatspace wherever magic is concerned.
- Jimmy No

- Or anywhere there's money.
- Frosty

- Or anywhere at all.
- Kane

WIZ AND BANG

Bio-Awakened drugs. BADs. The combination of magic and narcotics to give you a high literally out of this world. Most folks don't know what tempo really did to people, and they eagerly await the next South American innovation to hit the streets since the majority of the tempo supply has run dry.

- And you're not in that group?
- Pistons

- Look, I know you don't trust me. And given what we've learned about flipside, I don't blame you. Moreover, I feel the same way. The time I lost is the time I might have done the things you think I did. I can't feel guilt over actions I didn't choose to take, but I still wake up nights in a cold sweat wondering who I might have hurt. Sometimes the dreams feel like memories, and I don't like what I see. That's on me. So say what you've got to say, punish me as long as you think it's necessary. There is honestly nothing you can do to me that's worse than this uncertainty.
- Haze

The thing is, magical means of getting high go back to the Oracles of Delphi, Native American vision quests, and all kinds of stuff all over the world. The latest thing to hit the streets is oneiros, a vaporized mixture of Awakened reagents refined and inhaled to provide dream-like visions that often seem to have prophetic meanings. So far, no signs of any untoward bodyjacking or anything else sinister, but I'm the first person to tell you to have someone keep an eye on you. Things like Animal Tongue and Immortal Flower have been around a while and seem safe enough.

> ● Sounds like he's trying to turn over a new leaf, to me.
> ● Arete

> ● You're forgetting that Haze is a manipulator. That's his MO.
> ● Pistons

> ● We all are, Pistons. Maybe cut him a little slack.
> ● Glitch

THE SMOKING EDGE

So whats around the corner? What new innovations can we expect from the likes of corporate manufactories, basement labs, and Ghost Cartel fields? Here's a sample of some of the highlights that have floated to me through the grapevine.

First up is the legal shit. You can find this in any pharmacorp's stockholder projections, but it's worth mentioning. Shiawase is promising big returns on an upgrade to analgesics with something they are calling Salvatol, and a combination nutrient concentrate laced with appetite suppression for dieters called TrimLine.

> ● So, an actual meal pill?
> ● Nephrine

> ● Am I the only one who looks around every now and again and realizes this is the future?
> ● Red

> ● Just the loudest about it.
> ● /dev/grrl

> ● This'll be killer for long-term sniper roosts.
> ● Balladeer

> ● I wouldn't give too much credence to these claims. There will be projects underway along those lines, but predictions are always optimistic to charm potential investors and reassure current shareholders.
> ● Mr. Bonds

> ● Still worthwhile to know. Projects underway and suspicious investors means extractions and data runs. Money to be made.
> ● Rigger X

Ares Biotech has announced big progress on anti-rejection drugs for cybernetics and bioware that have less addictive effects and work faster and with less stress to the system. The spooky part is where rumors say they come from, everything from tamed e-ghosts in nanites to some captive bug byproduct. Not sure how much credit it deserves, considering how bad Ares is doing in the PR department, but you never know.

Aztechnology is making a big deal out of their latest prescription, Cereprax, which is supposed to boost intelligence and intuition for a while. No doubt there's a lot of grad students and a load of corp-lab eggheads enjoying the fruits of the formula's leak last month. It doesn't have an official release date yet.

> ● This stuff isn't ready for public consumption. I've seen a lot of early users on my table after an OD. There's a cool-down period, but no one has pinned down what it is just yet. If you overdose, you can expect cerebral hemorrhaging and permanent brain damage at worst, a month of literally blinding migraines and slowed mental capacity at best. and the worst part is that it is psychologically very addictive. Most of my patients say they don't feel like their real self when they aren't on it. I've heard that song before, but this is scarier, because when they get it, they use all that artificial intellect to justify the next dose.
> ● Butch

> ● If I had to guess, the dosage needs to be carefully regulated for every individual based on their brain chemistry. A round dosage for off-the-shelf purchases is going to take time, additional limiters, and the results will be much less dramatic than they currently appear.
> ● Nephrine

> ● If you're determined to try this, don't mix it with anything else. I saw a grad student at SU mix it with cram. Her eyes lit up with understanding exactly long enough to figure out what a huge mistake she'd made. By the time the ambulance got there, she was already brain dead.
> ● Red

In the independent entrepreneurial side of things (read: illegal), the streets are coming up with all kinds of stuff. Or, in the case of Resonator, stealing it. Word is some runners pulled a smash-and-grab on NeoNET labs in Manhattan and got the prototype of a drug for virtuakinetics. It's all too complicated for me, but it's supposed to increase their connection to the Resonance.

- Like I'm going to trust *anything* NeoNET makes for a technomancer.
- Netcat

The Ghost Cartels are still hard at work on their newest innovation. While their production of normal street treats continues unabated, they're looking to expand selection, especially among performance enhancers. Whipcrack is a new reflex-booster that's supposed to give users the speed of a fully wired samurai, but so far it's only produced corpses. Honesty is less a thrill shot and more of a tool, acting as a safe, reliable, potent truth serum. It'll probably get released when they can keep the effects from being permanent.

- I doubt that's kept them from using it on people they don't give a drek about.
- Glasswalker

- I'll still keep faith with Mind Probe spells.
- Lyran

- Not all of us have the luxury of magic.
- Marcos

- I've seen the leaked research on whipcrack. The speed is unbelievable, but the body literally burns itself out, overprocessing nutrients and straining muscles and ligaments until they snap.
- Nephrine

- The cartels might not want to release honesty until the bugs are worked out, but I guarantee you that someone out there is going to use it as extortion material. "Pay me a billion nuyen or you'll never be able to lie for the rest of your life." Hell, now that I've mentioned it, I'm beginning to think about how I can get in on it.
- Cayman

Chip tech took a slump for a little while during the tempo craze, but with the BAD backlash, they're seeing a resurgence, especially since developers decided to start exploring new avenues of use that BADs couldn't touch. The first is something Evo has been working on: PsychChips. The idea is to create a chip that offers a crutch for psychological issues. This isn't like your normal HeadShrinker PersonaPal or FreudSim. This inserts engrams that compensate for phobias, compulsions, things like that.

- The idea is noble enough, but it's based off traditional brainwashing tech. Aversion therapy stuff. The whole carrot-stick method is effective for retraining the brain, but chips like this end up making the brain weaker as it learns something else is doing its work for it. The user

needs more and more powerful chips to compensate, and if they stop jacking them, the problem comes back with a vengeance. Like, crippling. If the backlash is too bad, it can break the user's grip on reality completely.
- Plan 9

- I thought that was going to be conspiracy drek, but yeah, this checks out completely.
- Snopes

- Oh ye of little faith.
- Plan 9

Much more extreme are reports of an entirely new way to augment: BodyBenders. These chips are rumored to use BTL psychotropics to stimulate subconscious, psychosomatic genetic rewiring. Plug in a chip and it will stimulate muscle growth, neural reconnections, you name it. Right now, it's all drawing board stuff, but if it works out, it'll be the next step in augmentation, and a whole new school of science.

- Blue sky research at best. More likely pink clouds. The theory is enticing, but the science simply isn't there to support it as of yet.
- The Smiling Bandit

- That's not stopping Wuxing, Aztechnology, and Truman Technologies from giving it the old college try.
- Cosmo

The scariest thing said to be in development are Ghost Chips. Based off a rumored technology developed by Global Technologies back in the '50s, these personafixes are supposed to come with complete skillsuites, eliminating the need for skillwires. The spooky part? They're supposed to be made by trapping e-ghosts and using the skills they have on demand.

- No. Fucking no.
- Slamm-0!

- Looks like Global Technologies is a relatively recent acquisition for Horizon. Before that, they were part of NeoNET. If this is true, they've got the resources, before and after.
- Cosmo

- Whatever the tech was back then, it must have had some serious bugs if we aren't hearing about it until twenty years later.
- Bull

SPEEDBALLING

For the user who needs to get higher, faster, it is possible to mix narcotics together. Sometimes called "cocktailing," different recipes often become vogue in the club and drug scene. Characters who mix drugs add 1 to the Addiction Ratings of all drugs involved.

PORTABLE CHEMICAL INJECTOR

An external auto-injector, the PCI can be operated with the push of a button or controlled wirelessly. It comes in three sizes, each capable of holding a different number of chem doses. The wrist model is worn like a watch. The thigh model straps on like a gun holster. The harness is worn much like a double shoulder holster and can feed massive amounts of chemicals into the user.

Wrist: 3 doses, 500 nuyen
Thigh: 5 doses, 750 nuyen
Harness: 20 doses, 2,500 nuyen
No chemicals are included in the cost of the injector

EVERYDAY PHARMA

Versaception: Birth control for women.
Contrax: Birth control for men.
Alphasprin: Extra strength analgesics.
EZBreathe: Lozenges that offer relief from pollution-based breathing troubles. Especially popular in high-density smog zones such as Tenochtitlán (provides +1 dice pool modifier on pollution-based fatigue tests while in use; see p. 147, Run & Gun).
VitaMax: A massive multivitamin. Also available as a gummy for kids called VitaBombs, about the size of a fist and available in four exciting flavors: Red, Blue, Orange, and Mystery! Remember to not eat it all at once.
ComaDoze: Extra-strength sleeping pills.
Trimline: An appetite suppressant, Trimline extends time before taking starvation penalties by fifty percent.
Beta Inhibitors: Popular sex drug. Also mixed with downers to counteract drowsiness.

BADS COMPLIANCE, BOTTLED SPELLS, AWAKENING

Even though lots of potential replacements are coming up, don't count BADs out just yet (though the stuff I'm hearing about makes the chips sound downright reasonable). First up is compliance, a mix of radicals meant to make the subject more susceptible to mental influence and mind control. You sneak it into the target and they're ready for persuasion.

- Right up your alley.
- Pistons

Next is zombie dust. Not to be mistaken for trance, zombie dust prepares the user for possession right away. I don't trust this stuff whatsoever, but I imagine a voudoun might shoot a dart of it into an opponent and conjure up a loa.

- This makes me nervous as hell. Imagine what a shedim might do with this.
- Red

- Think it might make targets for inhabitation take an insect spirit easier?
- Ethernaut

- Let's hope not.
- Sticks

Now we get to the insane stuff. Bottled spells. Alchemy spells applied as an injection. You shoot up the juice and you've got a spell on call, ready to be cast drain-free. Pure rumors, of course, nobody even claims to know a guy who has seen it, but you can bet the Powers-That-Be want to make magic on tap, and collect the price tag to match.

The most outrageous is something folks are calling wake up. Supposedly a mixture of the rarest, most magically active reagents, grown in mana-rich environments or even somehow retrieved from the metaplanes themselves, it supposedly can endow someone with magic. Some say it's something you can keep taking to keep the powers; others say once you're Awakened, you're a mage for good. This urban myth has been around since the Awakening, and while I don't give it one second of credence, you can bet there's research on it.

- There is, and has been since the Awakening. Probably always will be, seeing how magic just keeps showing us new things no matter how deep we go.
- Ethernaut

- There is magic waiting in all things, if one knows how to find it, and doesn't fear what they find.
- Man-of-Many-Names

- Are you saying you know how to bring about Awakening with alchemy?
- Plan 9

- He doesn't. He'd be rich beyond the dreams of avarice if he could.
- Jimmy No

- I am already rich in the ways that matter. What matters is how I use it.
- Man-of-Many-Names

- So you can do it?
- /dev/grrl

- Even the immortals can't grant magic. Even dragons.
- Man-of-Many-Names

POSTED BY: NEPHRINE

Everyone is always looking for an edge on the streets, but for many folks, cyberware, nanotech, and bioware aren't always an option, for some reason or another. It could be because of cost, fear of losing themselves (literally, with CFD), lack of time for surgery or medical consults, or something else entirely. More and more people are looking for that cheap, quick boost, and these days often it comes in the form of pharmaceutical enhancement.

Drugs provide a quick, temporary boost to give the edge that might mean the difference between life and death. Because of this, business is booming, and everyone wants a piece of the action even if they don't want to publicly admit it. The megacorps know that they have to do something to keep up with the runners who are coming to get their secrets, assets, or personnel. Cyberware isn't an option because of cost and training takes time. More and more, the corps are turning to drugs to give their guards the boost they need to stand up to runners. Even if one in ten gets hooked on the combat drug they use to survive against runners, it is far cheaper than the funeral and death benefits they would have to pay out otherwise.

- The quality of life of the security guards matters not a bit to the corps. They are happy to addict them, wring them out, and throw them away. The main reason they provide pre-natal care to pregnant corp citizens is to help breed the next generation of security guards and other menial workers when they wring the current generation out.
- Cosmo

- Then, once they are hooked, they have corporate dealers who unofficially keep these addicts supplied.
- Butch

- Sometimes they supply the drugs in an official capacity. It depends on the local acceptance of drug use and how the corporation markets a specific drug to the public.
- Dr. Spin

The megacorps, as always, are working an angle on this. They can beat street dealers on price and reliability of product (street cooks have the advantage of being close to home, if you live in a barrens, and sometimes their product beats the hell out of watered-down corp drek), but that's not always enough. They are working on a new generation of drugs that is tailored to individual users, using processes your independent dealer is going to have trouble replicating.

Everyone's needs are different. What gives you the edge to survive on the street might do nothing for me. Corp-manufactured street drugs have evolved in an effort to give that needed edge, so you have to figure out what works for you. The most obvious example of this evolution is the creation of customized drugs. These drugs are built off a foundation and then modified and enhanced to suit a particular user's needs. Though made in high-tech corporate labs, these customized drugs are just beginning to filter down to the streets. And those running the shadows are embracing these drugs and using them in ways the manufacturer never originally imagined.

- The corps may not have imagined the uses, but unless it's used against them directly, they don't care. The money from unintentional sales spends the same.
- Slamm-0!

- That's the thing, though. Some of the drugs they created to help scientists find the next advancement in their field also allow a combat mage to cast more powerful spells when stealing the paydata.
- Lyran

The advantage of tailoring customized drugs to your needs can't be understated. Tailoring also allows you to build a big boost to pull your hoop out of the fire without having to worry about drug interactions messing you up.

- If you inject two different customized drugs, you can still end up with an unforeseeable interaction.
- Butch

- That's why you build multiple customized drugs, each one for a different purpose.
- 2XL

- That's all well and good until you're addicted to them all and need to constantly use to stay sane.
- Turbo Bunny

Not all drugs are created equal. How your street gang mixes drugs to keep cost down isn't the same as how it's done in a controlled lab. Drugs straight from the lab are purer and contain less filler, which means they can get the same effects with a smaller dosage and fewer side effects. This purity is expensive to achieve, and therefore more expensive to get hold of.

- Those who can get the top-end drugs are connected to some corporation, and if you want to keep getting the good stuff, it's important to know what corporation that is.
- Turbo Bunny

- More importantly, who is your dealer more loyal to, you or their corporate connection?
- Am-mut

DRUG INTERACTIONS

Taking multiple drugs, even when under a doctor's supervision, can be tricky. Doing it on your own using street drugs can have all kinds of unintended side effects and consequences, and not good ones either. Whenever you use an additional drug while still under the effects of a drug, there is a chance of an interaction. Even if you've mixed the same drugs before, there's still the chance for a problem to occur. The more impurities in a drug, the more likely a bad reaction is to occur.

- It isn't just street drugs. A street samurai I used to run with used jazz on a regular basis to give him that edge during combat. He once got hit by a spell and was just about knocked out. Then he slapped on a stim patch to counteract the effects and went into cardiac arrest.
  There's nothing as hair-raising as doing CPR on someone in the middle of combat.
- Thorn

The different elements used in various batches of a drug, the amount of impurities that may be present, and other elements make drug interactions unpredictable. Sometimes you'll get a harder crash, sometimes that crash will leap out and get you as soon as the drugs are imbibed, and sometimes you'll get a terrible headache or horrible stomach cramps. Sometimes you'll get nothing, which is enough to encourage people to give it a shot and ignore the possibility of an abrupt death. Because that's another thing that happens sometimes.

AWAKENED DRUGS

During the Awakening, some plants took on magical properties, and it didn't take people long to start turning some of these plants into drugs. Deepweed is the best known of these, though laés has been receiving more attention lately.

- A good scandal has a tendency to do that.
- Cosmo

The Aztlan-Amazonia war and exploration of wilderness in other parts of the world have led to the discovery of more Awakened plants. With these discoveries have come new drugs. Some of the recent arrivals that show potential to be useful in the shadows are forget-me-not, a drug to help resist mind-altering substances and magic, and memory fog, which puts the user in an altered state of mind to help them endure something they might want to forget—or something the person who gave them the drug does not want them to remember.

- When you're under memory fog's effects, it's difficult to remember things that happened when you *weren't* on the drug. Then when you're off, it's tough to remember what happened while you were on.
- Turbo Bunny

BIOENGINEERED AWAKENED DRUGS

The public became acutely aware of bioengineered Awakened drugs (BADs) during the tempo crisis. While tempo has been contained (for the most part), several other BADs are beginning to hit the streets. None of them are as radical or dangerous as tempo, but at the same time they aren't without risks. The two I know of are a magic-enhancer called Hecate's blessing, and one called Ayao's will that helps the mind resist magical attempts to manipulate it.

- Hecate's blessing has the side effect of occasionally burning out the user by overloading their ability to channel mana.
- Winterhawk

BETTER-THAN-LIFE CHIPS

Another way of getting a temporary boost is through the use of simsense chips, especially better-than-life chips (BTLs). Some feel BTLs are little more than electronic drugs, but the reality is more complex, as some people use them actively rather than just enjoying them passively. Corps have enjoyed using designer chips for specific applications. Personafix chips (p-fix), for example, can help turn an ordinary schlub into the perfect employee with the needed skills. This is especially useful when the skills are rare or take a long time to learn.

- Why not just use skillwires instead of a p-fix?
- /dev/grrl

- You see those used when a talented employee becomes a discipline or morale problem. Give them a quick bump back into the right path. It's cheaper than skillwires. It can't be an ongoing treatment, though, as the constant use of BTLs will eventually burn out the user.
- Kay St. Irregular

- Rumors tell of a Sioux prison that uses p-fixes on the correctional officers.
- Mika

- What do they gain from that, especially since Kay St. said this couldn't be an ongoing treatment?
- /dev/grrl

- It's incredibly cost-effective. Prisoners cost money to keep and feed, and guards cost money too; by turning a prisoner into a guard, you use the money spent on a prisoner to pay a guard. The BTLs eventually wear off, the guard loses it, and the prisoners—who really hate these converted guards—tear into these guys. The corp claims they don't owe any bereavement payments to family members, as the rights to such were forfeited when the prisoner was incarcerated, and they then look for their next candidate.
- Clockwork

More specialized p-fixes are just starting to reach the market. Some of these have the single use-and-erase function while others allow for continuous or repeated use. Other specialized p-fixes that are finding some use on the streets have been labeled berserker chips and bodyguard chips. The names are self-explanatory. With both of these chips, the RAS override feature is disabled, and the user retains the use of all their normal faculties in addition to what the chip provides.

- This got me to thinking. A personafix chip overrides a person's control and implements its own programing instead, suppressing the personality of the user. Could they be used to prevent a CFD personality from taking control?
- /dev/grrl

- So you trade one type of loss of control for another. I don't see the advantage.
- Slamm-0!

- If your divergent personality is a rager or one of the other violent types, at least you know you (probably) wouldn't be murdering your friends and family in one of your fugue states
- /dev/grrl

- Or if you have your personality made into a p-fix, you could use it to stabilize yourself.
- Turbo Bunny

- What would prevent the personality from infecting and overwriting the chip?
- Bull

- Yeah, there's always a hitch. But it could be useful for short-term stabilization—provided you still have a decent copy of your own personality.
- Butch

GAME INFORMATION

Below are stats for the various drugs mentioned in this chapter and throughout the book.

AEXD

Vector: Ingestion
Speed: Immediate
Duration: 10 x 2D6 minutes
Addiction Type: Physiological
Effect: +3 dice to resist seizures due to TLE-x.

Characters with the TLE-x quality (p. 59) may take AEXD to help them resist seizures from their condition. If they are required to make a Body + Willpower Test to resist seizures from the disease at any point while the drug is in effect, they receive +3 to their dice pool on that test.

AISA (EAU DE VIVRE, TEX-MEX TEA)

Vector: Ingestion
Speed: Immediate
Duration: 20 + 2D6 minutes
Addiction Type: Psychological
Effect: Disorientation

Aisa is one of the most popular party drugs on the market. This drug is most often ingested by licking a "blot" off a piece of paper or plastic. Users experience intense giddiness, lassitude, and mild hallucinations. When the drug wears off, the user is fatigued, taking 2S (unresisted). Derived from a synthetic form of atropine, aisa can be very dangerous when overdosed. In addition to standard overdose rules, users who take more than one dose at a time suffer 4S damage per additional dose.

BETAMETH
(BUZZ, RIGGER'S COCKTAIL)

Vector: Inhalation
Speed: 1 minute
Duration: (9 - Body) hours, minimum of 1 hour
Addiction Type: Both
Effect: +2 Reaction, +1 Intuition

A number of pseudomethamphetamine derivatives are sold as betameth. This stimulant suppresses the appetite and speeds up the user's metabolism and thought processes, making it a popular diet drug, especially among adolescents and teenagers. Characters on betameth are energetic and prone to jumpiness. When the effect wears off, the user crashes and suffers 6S damage (unresisted). Betameth users tend to suffer from attention-deficit disorders and feel unable to properly focus when not on the drug, leading to extended binges. Habitual users are often gaunt from malnutrition, which renders them susceptible to infection, especially of the teeth, gums, and mouth.

BETEL (CORPCANDY, JAW)

Vector: Ingestion
Speed: Immediate
Duration: 10 x 1D6 minutes
Addiction Type: Physiological
Effect: +1 Perception

An ancient and widespread Asian practice of chewing the nuts and leaves of the betel tree with lime has led to the synthesis of Wuxing's highly addictive and legal betel chewing gum. Betel is a mild stimulant with cavity-fighting properties; users commonly feel awake and alert when using it. Rather than making an Addiction Test, characters who use betel, even once, gain a Mild addiction to it. A character may never have an addiction worse than Mild to betel. Characters who add dice to toxin resistance tests (through adept abilities, implants, metatype, magic, etc.) are immune to this effect if they succeed at the toxin resistance test. Because it is instantly addictive, betel often serves as a gateway drug to more powerful stimulants.

CEREPRAX
(BRAIN BOOST, EGGHEAD)

Vector: Ingestion
Speed: 1D6 minutes
Duration: (12 - Body) hours, minimum of 1 hour
Addiction Type: Both
Effect: +2 Intuition, +3 Logic, +2 Mental Limit, gain the benefit of the Analytical Mind quality (p. 72, SR5)

A nootropic prescription that boosts neurotransmitter speed and connectivity, allowing for greater recall and cooperative leaps of logic and intuition with exceptional clarity. When the high ends, the overclocking of the brain results in exceptional migraines and a sluggish intellect. After the drug wears off, you take –2 to all limits, –2 to Logic, and 5S damage (unresisted).

After use, the gamemaster should secretly roll the user's Intuition + Edge. If the player uses Cereprax again before (8 - hits) hours, they take 1D6 points of *permanent* Intuition damage from brain damage (the points of Intuition can later be re-purchased using Karma).

DOPADRINE (BITTER, WERDEN)

Vector: Contact
Speed: Immediate
Duration: 10 x 1D6 minutes
Addiction Type: Both
Effect: Cancels Berserk (see below), –1 die to all physical actions

A combination of anti-psychotic medications and narcotics designed to cancel the rampant drug abuse by gangers, dopadrine has become a popular narcotic as well. Dopadrine prevents characters from going berserk for the duration of the drug; if a user who is already berserk is dosed with dopadrine, the berserker rage automatically ends, and the character cannot become berserk again until the duration ends. Dopadrine heightens the apathy of users, making them feel disconnected from their concerns. This effect gives them –2 to their Social limit for the duration of the drug. It comes in patch form to best aid others in dosing a user who has become dangerous.

EX (EROS, GALAK)

Vector: Ingestion
Speed: 1D6 minutes
Duration: (8 - Body) hours, minimum of 1 hour
Addiction Type: Psychological
Effect: +1 Charisma, –1 Logic, +1 Perception, –1 Willpower

A favorite party drug, eX is a mild stimulant and aphrodisiac used by revelers to relax, open up, and become aroused. The drug leaves the user open to suggestion, especially toward sexual encounters, and users become more sensitive to changes in light, temperature, and pressure. When the effect wears off, the user suffers disorientation for a like period, along with –2 to their Mental limit for (Body) hours.

Galak is an Awakened drug made from the pollen of an Awakened orchid, and is similar to, though more potent than, eX. The duration for Galak is (9 - Body) hours, minimum 3 hours.

FORGET-ME-NOT

Vector: Ingestion
Speed: 1 Combat Turn
Duration: (12 - Body) hours, minimum 1 hour
Addiction Type: Psychological
Effect: See description

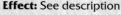

As laés and other forms of memory manipulation have experienced a resurgence in popularity, everyone has been looking for a way to counteract drug-induced memory loss. Forget-me-not is one such drug designed to help resist such effects. While the drug is active in the user's system, any dose of laés or similar drug will not affect the user. Additionally, the user receives a +3 dice pool bonus to resist Alter Memory spells while the drug is in effect. Remember to check for drug interactions (p. 178) if forget-me-not is in effect when a potentially memory-altering drug enters a character's system.

G3 (GERILIXIR, VITALITE)

Vector: Ingestion
Speed: 1 hour
Duration: (15 – Body) hours, minimum 1 hour
Addiction Type: Physiological
Effect: +1 Body when resisting Fatigue damage, Longevity (see below)

A "gerispice" pharmaceutical believed by many to help prevent aging, G3 takes its name from the main ingredients: ginseng, guarana, and ginkgo biloba. G3 contains vitamin additives and antioxidants that help combat fatigue, making it a popular supplement for athletes, professional mercenaries, and other individuals who face regular strenuous activity. At the gamemaster's discretion, characters who take G3 on a daily basis may suffer the effects of old age somewhat less than others.

GUTS (NOFEAR, BRASS BALLS)

Vector: Inhalation
Speed: Immediate
Duration: (12 – Body) hours, minimum 1 hour
Addiction Type: Both
Effect: Immunity to Fear (see below)

This drug suppresses the functions of the brain that govern fear, both innate and learned. For the duration of the drug's effect, the character is immune to fear (including negative results from Composure Tests) and fear-based powers/attacks. As a drawback, however, the character becomes reckless, incautious, and also less inhibited. At the gamemaster's discretion, he may call for the character to make a Logic + Willpower (3) Test to avoid doing something that would normally be considered foolish, dangerous, or socially inappropriate.

HURLG (FOMORIAN USQUEBAUGH, ORKSTAFF'S XXX)

Vector: Ingestion
Speed: 2D6 minutes
Duration: (12 – Body) hours, minimum 1 hour
Addiction Type: Both
Effect: –1 Logic, +1 Willpower

A potent alcoholic beverage developed *by* orks *for* orks, hurlg is a dark, thick ale the consistency of soup,

swimming with hops and nutmeg. Orks, trolls, and the occasional dwarf appreciate the blend of 160 to 180 proof alcohols. With the mildly hallucinogenic properties of large amounts of nutmeg, hurlg generates a terrific buzz. When this effect wears off, the user crashes and suffers 9S damage (resisted by Body).

Humans and elves don't normally possess the constitution to hold their hurlg, and suffer severe and painful stomach cramps (treat as disorientation for the duration of the effect) unless they possess an implant or magic that gives them bonus dice on Toxin Resistance Tests. Having suhch a bonus allows them to ignore the disorientation . Hurlg has a robust, nutty flavor. And is inflammable.

K-10 (BLOOD OF KALI)

Vector: Injection
Speed: Immediate
Duration: 5 x 1D6 minutes
Addiction Type: Both
Effect: +3 Body, +3 Agility, +4 Strength, +1 Willpower, +5 Initiative Score, High Pain Tolerance 3, Berserk

Users of this dangerous combat drug automatically go berserk when wounded, in a manner similar to Bear magicians. At the end of the duration, the user suffers 18S damage (unresisted). Berserk character must also make an Edge (1) Test; if they fail, they stay berserk permanently. Remember that the drug cannot raise any attributes above a character's augmented maximum (+4 over the natural, unaugmented attribute).

All of the initial research subjects of kamikaze grade ten, a.k.a. K-10, died from the drug's side effects or wounds sustained while under the influence. The formula for K-10 was hacked from the lab's medical database, and the drug itself hit the streets as a combat drug back in 2071. In the years since, it's become an infamous source of obituary-linked headlines, from psychotic gang rampages to civilian massacres in distant countries by mercenary troops who have "Tasted the Blood."

MEMORY FOG

Vector: Ingestion
Speed: 1 minute
Duration: (14 – Body) hours, minimum 2 hours
Addiction Type: Both
Effect: See below

Distilled from an Awakened poppy plant, this drug puts the mind in a temporarily altered state. After the drug's effects end, any attempt to remember what occurred while experiencing this altered state requires a Memory Test (p. 152, *SR5*) with a –2 dice pool modifier. Likewise, while under the influence of Memory Fog, any attempt to recall anything from times when the user is not under the drug's influence also requires a Memory Test with a –2 dice pool modifier. The altered state is the same every time, so remembering events from previous doses does not incur the –2 dice pool penalty.

NIGHTWATCH (ANIMU, BEGGAR'S GAZE)

Vector: Contact (see below)
Speed: Immediate
Duration: 20 x 1D6 minutes
Addiction Type: Psychological
Effect: Grants low-light vision

These eyedrops grant temporary low-light vision. They were developed by studying the eyes of deep-sea fish and are commonly used by low-budget security on the night-shift, urban scavengers, and nocturnal urban predators. This drug increases the eye's sensitivity to light; all Glare Environmental modifiers (p. 175, *SR5*) are one category worse for the character for as long as the drug is active.

NOPAINT (NUMB, PBG)

Vector: Contact
Speed: Immediate
Duration: 1D6 hours
Addiction Type: Both
Effect: High Pain Tolerance 3

Popular with intercity gangs with a tribal motif, NoPaint is a medical-grade, water-resistant novocain gel that comes in a number of colors. NoPaint is applied to the skin with a swab or brush. Characters lose tactile perception in areas covered with NoPaint for the duration of the effect, and must make a First Aid + Logic (2) Test to judge how badly they are injured while the drug is active. One dose of NoPaint can cover a dwarf, human, or elf; orks and trolls require two doses for full coverage.

OXYGENATED FLUOROCARBONS (BLUE BLOOD, P4MO)

Vector: See below
Speed: 1D6 hours
Duration: 1 week
Addiction Type: Physiological
Effect: +1 Agility, double the amount of time character can hold his breath

The oxygenated fluorocarbon compound known as P4MO is widely used as a blood substitute. Its use in emergency situations helps to prevent the mismatching of blood types. Fluorocarbons like P4MO also exceed the capabilities of the blood's natural hemoglobin as a vehicle for gaseous exchange. In other words, P4MO dissolves a higher percentage of oxygen from the lungs into the blood. When introduced into healthy subjects, P4MO allows them to achieve higher levels of physical performance.

P4MO is added to the bloodstream in five-liter treatments along with a dose of carcerands containing a chemical that allows the body to metabolize the oxygenated fluorocarbons, clearing out of the user's system by the end of the drug's duration. If another P4MO treatment is taken while the first is active, the character will suffer an embolism, inflicting 15P damage (unresisted). When the PM40 wears off, you take a –1 to Physical limit and –1 to Body for (Body) days.

PUSH (NANOHI, RUSH)

Vector: Ingestion
Speed: 1 minute
Duration: (15 – Body) minutes, minimum 1 minute
Addiction Type: Both
Effect: See below

Push was designed for users seeking a quick, no-frills high. The active chemicals in the drug are theobromine and cathinone, and they combine to give push users a mild euphoric state that has been compared to eating large amounts of chocolate or the moment after sex.

Excessive consumption of push over long periods of time can result in exacerbated hyperactivity leading to psychosis, as well as possible genetic mutation in meta-humans. Gamemasters may represent these effects on push addicts at the burnout level by Essence loss and drastic, violent mood swings.

RED MESCALINE (MANASHROOMS, VERTIGO)

Vector: Ingestion
Speed: 1 hour
Duration: (18 – Body) hours, minimum 1 hour
Addiction Type: Both
Effect: +1 Charisma, –2 Reaction, +2 Perception, +1 Willpower, Disorientation

A popular drug with musicians, technicians, and magicians, red mescaline (redmesc for short) is a profound combination of psychoactive substances ten times more potent than natural peyote. Many drug users consider a redmesc trip equivalent to a religious experience, with their awareness heightened to an almost cellular level; coming down from a red mescaline high is often accompanied by crushing depression. At the end of the duration, the user's Charisma and Willpower are reduced to 1 for an equivalent duration.

Red mescaline complements the effects of the street drug psyche, and combining the two is common. Users do not need to make a Drug Interaction roll (see p. 178) when using redmesc and psyche at the same time. A psyche/redmesc speedball is commonly called a loco.

RIPPER (J-H, ROIDPATCH)

Vector: Injection, Contact
Speed: Immediate
Duration: 10 x 1D6 minutes
Addiction Type: Both
Effect: +1 Strength, –1 Willpower

A potent mix of synthetic steroids, pseudolipids, sugars, and amphetamines that cause short-term muscle growth and an energy boost, ripper is used as quick way for many to "bulk up." At the end of the duration, the user takes 2 boxes of Stun damage (unresisted) due to fatigue; some of the muscle growth, however, remains. Regular use (at least three times a day for three to six weeks) of ripper reduces the Karma cost for improving the Strength attribute by 1.

Muscles developed with ripper often leave users disproportioned. Side effects of prolonged use may include sterility, baldness, lack of sexual desire, development of secondary sexual characteristics of the opposite sex (such as breast growth in males), and cancer of the testes or ovaries. Ripper is most often sold in dermal patches or disposable syringes, though heavy users have taken to wearing portable chemical injectors for a constant dose.

SLAB (COEUR D'HIVER, GHULPILLE)

Vector: Injection
Speed: 2 Combat Turns
Duration: (10 – Body) hours, minimum 1 hour
Power: 16
Addiction Type: n/a
Effect: Suspended animation (see below)

Originally designed as a surgical aid, slab places the user in a state of near hibernation where breathing and heart rate are lowered to almost imperceptible levels. A Perception + Intuition (6) Test or a Medicine + Logic (4) Test is required to determine the character is still alive without proper medical equipment (a medkit is insufficient). At the end of the duration, the user receives a –4 modifier to Reaction for a number of hours equal to half the equivalent duration of the drug (rounded down). Side effects commonly include shakes, chills, and excessive appetite. Reaper, an Awakened version utilizing mana-rich mytotoxins, also causes the aura to appear dormant and effectively dead, giving a –8 dice pool penalty to anyone attempting to assense the aura.

SNUFF (AZTECH CHEW, INDIAN TOBACCO)

Vector: Ingestion, Inhalation
Speed: 1 minute
Duration: 10 x 1D6 minutes
Addiction Type: Both
Effect: +1 Reaction, Pain Resistance 1

This legal drug first gained popularity in the early days of the Native American Nations and is traditionally made from an ancient formula including tobacco leaves, cannabis resin, and willow bark. Modern snuff typically forgoes the expensive natural ingredients by directly combining the active chemical compounds involved: THC, nicotine, and salicin. Snuff users claim the drug has a calming effect. Once the effect wears off, users experience –1 Intuition for a time period equivalent to

twice the original duration. At the gamemaster's discretion, long-term snuff users may be more susceptible to Fatigue damage and cancer.

SOBER TIME

Vector: Contact
Speed: 1 Combat Turn
Duration: 10 x 1D6 minutes
Addiction Type: Both
Effect: This drug temporarily counteracts the buzz of alcohol or drugs. For the its duration, the drug removes negative penalties to Charisma, Intuition, Reaction, and/or Willpower, up to a maximum of 6 dice worth of penalties between those attributes. If the total penalties are greater than 6, the drug's benefits are applied evenly across all attributes that have suffered a negative penalty, and any leftover benefits can be applied as desired to other applicable attributes that still have penalties. Once the drug wears off, all negative penalties return at twice the effect for the penalty's whole original duration, even if part of that penalty's duration had already passed. This only is true for attributes that had their penalty reduced by the drug.

Sober time only negates penalties already in effect. Any penalties incurred after sober time is taken will be suffered as normal.

If any attribute is reduced below 1 when the negative penalties return, the character will be rendered immobile and fall into a trance until the effect wears off.

SOBER TIME EXAMPLE

Wrecker is drunk and under the influence of a couple other drugs, just like any other ganger during their downtime. He is currently under the following penalties: Charisma –2, Intuition –2, Logic –1, and Willpower –2. Vindicator comes into the bar and says some Halloweeners are nosing around in search of their stolen deepweed. Wrecker, knowing this is trouble, injects sober time to reduce his impairments so he'll be ready when the bullets start flying. One point of penalties comes off each of the affected attributes, making the penalties Charisma –1, Intuition –1, Logic —, and Willpower –1. He has used four of the six points of reduction that sober time provides; he has two left, and three attributes still penalized. Deciding there won't be much talking at this point, he leaves the – 1 penalty in place on his Charisma and takes away the penalties remaining on his Willpower and Intuition. If Wrecker decides to use his custom combat drug when the Halloweeners bust the door open, he will suffer the custom drug's negative penalties just like normal, since it was administered after he took sober time (and he'll also have to test for drug interaction).

When the sober time wears off in forty minutes—assuming he lives that long—all the penalties will be doubled, meaning they will be Charisma –4, Intuition –4, Logic –2, and Willpower –4 (note that if Wrecker had chosen to not remove the penalty on one of those attributes, such as Logic, the other penalties would have been doubled, but the unaffected attribute would remain unchanged). Sadly for Wrecker, his base Willpower is 3, as is his Intuition, meaning they will both be reduced below 1. That means he'll be zoned out in the corner for the next hour until the drugs start wearing off naturally.

SOOTHSAYER

Vector: Contact
Speed: 1 minute
Duration: (12 – Body) hours, minimum 1 hour
Addiction Test: None
Effect: 8S, resisted with Body only. Unless all damage is resisted, the subject also suffers Willpower –3 and Social limit –1. Each additional application reduces the DV by 1 as the subject builds up a resistance to the drug's effects, no matter how long it has been since the last application.

This new interrogation drug mixes several different plants, including the gympie gympie (*Dendrocnide moroides*). This gel uses the tiny hairs of the gympie gympie plant to inject the drug through the skin, causing excruciating pain that makes the subject more susceptible to interrogation. So yeah, "interrogation drug" is a handy euphemism in this case.

WOAD (BOZOKU, FRENITICO)

Vector: Ingestion
Speed: 1 Combat Turn
Duration: 5 x 1D6 minutes
Addiction Type: Both
Effect: +2 to Agility, Berserk (see below)

A synthetic hallucinogen derived from North European mushroom species, woad is the cheapest legal combat drug on the market. Users automatically go berserk when wounded, in a manner similar to Bear magicians (p. 321, *SR5*), but you also gain +2 to your Agility while the berserk rage lasts. Side effects include frothing at the mouth, fever, and a desire to bite. When the drug wears off, users suffer –2 to all Social tests for the original duration x 10.

ZERO (CYBERTRAM, DOCTOR BOB'S ALLERGY ELIXIR)

Vector: Ingestion, Injection
Speed: 1 hour
Duration: (20 – Body) hours, minimum of 1
Addiction Type: Physiological
Effect: Allergy and Addiction reduction, promotion of cyberware adaptation, –2 to Disease Resistance Tests and Toxin Resistance Tests

Zero is the street name for a number of different immunosuppressant drugs used to help the body adjust to new cyberware or reduce the effects of allergic reactions. Street docs commonly use small quantities of the drug to suppress the body's immune system for a period of time, reducing the chances that the body will reject implanted 'ware. Habitual drug users use zero to lower their tolerance to other drugs. When this drug is used in a clinical setting under the supervision of a trained doctor, the user does not take the penalties from mixing drugs (see p. 178).

For the duration of effect, zero users are no longer subject to penalties from allergies, though they still suffer damage for Severe allergies (see p. 78, *SR5*). Furthermore, users can treat any Addictions they may have as if they are one level lower than they actually are for the duration of the effect. At the gamemaster's discretion, characters who undergo surgery for implants may be dosed with zero.

ZONE (SELECTIVE SEROTONIN RE-UPTAKE INHIBITORS, OR SSRIS)

Vector: Ingestion
Speed: 1 hour
Duration: (12 – Body) hours, minimum 1 hour
Addiction Type: Both
Effect: Can ignore Mild to Moderate Phobias

A fear of heights can be a major inconvenience when scaling the outside of an office skyscraper. A fear of enclosed spaces is a pain when you are hiding in someone's trunk, waiting for them to unknowingly drive you to the location of a secret research lab. For these occasions and more, you have SSRIs. This drug has the positive effect of calming phobias (see **Phobia** quality, p. 157, *Run Faster*), and it also makes users restless and light sensitive. Users receive a Mild Allergy to light while the drug is in effect (p. 78, *SR5*) and –1 to Perception tests. Any applicable Glare penalties are increased by 1.

AWAKENED DRUGS

AYAO'S WILL

Vector: Ingestion
Speed: 2 Combat Turns
Duration: 10 x 1D6 minutes
Addiction Type: Psychological
Effect: +2 dice pool bonus to resist Manipulation spells.

This bioengineered form of an Awakened cotton plant is processed for its seeds; the seeds are ingested to get the effect, which is to act as a mana blocker for a period of time. It provides +2 dice to resist the effects of any Manipulation spells, whether they are intended harmfully or beneficially. It was originally developed in MCT labs but has now been replicated by all of the megacorporations, and it is just starting to trickle down to major sprawls around the world.

CRIMSON ORCHID (H-RED, SCARLET BLISS)

Vector: Injection
Speed: 1 Combat Turn
Duration: (12 – Body) hours, minimum 1 hour
Addiction Type: Both

Effect: –3 Reaction, +1 to all thresholds, Pain Resistance 6

The red orchid is a Southeast Asian Awakened plant whose dual-natured pollen attracts dual-natured insects. This distinctive red pollen, while not a narcotic itself, amplifies the narcotic properties of the poppy-derived opiates such as bliss and heroin, resulting in crimson orchid. In previous years, crimson orchid was the subject of vicious Triad wars in the Golden Triangle, but the dust has since settled, leaving Scarlet Bliss in the control of the Yellow Lotus. Rumors suggest this was achieved with the quiet support of Wuxing, but there is no solid evidence to confirm it.

Users of crimson orchid possess a distinctive red tint to their auras and gain the Astral Beacon negative quality (see p. 78, *SR5*) for the duration of the effect.

HECATE'S BLESSING

Vector: Ingestion
Speed: Immediate
Duration: 10 x 1D6 minutes
Addiction Type: Both
Effect: +1 dice pool bonus for drain rolls

A bioengineered drug distilled from the sap of an Awakened maple, Hecate's blessing helps a magic-using character channel more mana through their bodies, giving them +1 die to their drain rolls for the drug's duration. The downside is that once the drug wears off, the user's magical capability is reduced by –1 for a period of time equal to twice the original duration.

LAÉS (LEÄL, LAÉSAL WINE)

Vector: Ingestion, Inhalation, Injection
Speed: 1 Combat Turn
Duration: 20 x 1D6 minutes
Addiction Type: n/a
Effect: Stun Damage (see below), Memory Loss (see below)

Laés was created by the government of Tír Tairngire from the Awakened laésal fruit, thought to grow only in their government-controlled orchard. Upon taking a dose of laés, the character must resist 12S damage or fall unconscious for the drug's duration, with her memories of the last (12 – Body, minimum 1) hours erased retroactively from the mind, starting from the moment the Awakened drug was administered and working backward. Laés changes the chemical structure of the memories themselves, rendering them impossible to recover with technology or magic.

Laés can be ingested, injected, or even rolled into specially prepared cigarettes to poison unwitting smokers.

Laésal wine is a type of brandy made from the fruit of the laésal tree—its effects are the same as those of laés. Leäl is a less potent—and expensive—version of laés, and a popular date-rape drug among the Seattle club scene. Leäl has the same effects as laes, but the user only loses the last (120 – Body, minimum 100) minutes of memories; the duration is 5 x 1D6 minutes.

ONEIRO (DREAMSAGE, DELPHI)

Vector: Inhalation
Speed: Immediate
Duration: 3D6 minutes
Addiction Type: Psychological
Effect: Paralysis, allows the use of the Divination metamagic while active.

Provides vivid dreams in sleep, usually with prophetic insights. Burned like incense, the vapors are inhaled, providing vivid visions and dreams with prophetic insight. The user is allowed to use Divination using Logic + Intuition (threshold set by the table on p.125, *Street Grimoire*). If the user has the Augury and Sortilege ritual, they may use it to interpret the Divination as normal. If they do not, the user is Disoriented afterwards for a duration equal to the time the drug was in effect. Addiction often occurs because of the tantalization of seeing the future, the feeling there was something important just about to be revealed, and for mundanes, the chance to touch real magic for a moment. Long-term users have been known to develop chronic indecision and paranoia, unable to take action without forewarning of some sort.

OVERDRIVE (X-CYTE)

Vector: Inhalation
Speed: 1 Combat Turn
Duration: (10 – Body) hours, minimum 1 hour
Addiction Type: Both
Effect: +1 Reaction, +1 to all Logic-linked skills

From the steamy jungle pharmacopoeia of Latin America comes a central nervous stimulant with sizzle. At the end of this drug's duration, users suffer 8S damage (unresisted). Aside from a few brain-damaged hacker junkies who complain that overdrive causes nosebleeds, most users of the so-called "hacker drug" report few side effects other than a pleasant tingling across the forebrain and the sudden crash. Long-term users have been known to develop narcissistic personality disorder (use Poor Self-Control: Braggart, p. 158, *Run Faster*) or paranoid personality disorder (use Paranoia, p. 158, *Run Faster*).

PIXIE DUST (BLEEDER, NEVERLAND)

Vector: Inhalation
Speed: Immediate
Duration: 1D6 minutes
Addiction Type: Both
Effect: +1 Charisma, +1 Perception, High Pain Tolerance 1, Memory Loss (see below)

A recent bastardization of traditional cocaine cut with leäl, and sometimes with other substances including raw sugar, ground glass, and powdered caffeine tablets. A character on pixie dust loses all memory of the past 1D6 minutes after the drug takes effect; this effectively means they forget they ever took the drug, but the high remains.

Snorting pixie dust is the painful but preferred method of taking the drug because users forget the agony almost immediately. Consequently, nosebleeds are a common side effect of using pixie dust. Recovery from pixie dust addiction is notoriously difficult, because users cannot remember how often they use it, and overdoses are common.

TRANCE (TOADSTONE, ZUVEMBIE POWDER)

Vector: Inhalation
Speed: 1 Combat Turn
Duration: (6 – Body) hours, minimum 1 hour
Addiction Type: Both
Effect: +1 Intuition, +2 to all Logic-linked skills, Paralysis (see below)

A paralytic neurotoxin secreted by an Awakened Latin American tree frog, trance is often erroneously sold as an opiate. Popular with hackers, magicians, and other professions that don't require excessive movement, trance causes paralysis and a speeding up of the higher brain functions. At the end of the duration, users remain paralyzed (see **Paralysis**, p. 409, *SR5*) for an equivalent duration. This paralysis only affects voluntary muscle groups; breathing and other autonomous functions are not affected.

MAGICAL COMPOUNDS
ANIMAL TONGUE

Vector: Ingestion
Speed: 3D6 minutes
Duration: Essence + 1D6 hours, maximum 12 hours
Addiction Type: Psychological
Effect: This mixture grants the critter power of Animal Control.
Exotic Ingredient: A natural herbal radical of pulp from the manzana cactus in Aztlan.

When animal tongue wears off, the user has an unnatural fear of animals for a period of time equal to the mixture's duration. Treat this as if animals—mundane or paranormal—that come near the character exude the Fear power. Spirits do not count as animals.

IMMORTAL FLOWER

Vector: Ingestion
Speed: 16 Combat Rounds
Duration: Essence + 1D6 hours, maximum 12 hours
Addiction Type: Both
Effect: This mixture grants the critter power of Regeneration.
Exotic Ingredient: A natural herbal radical of petals from the immortal flower in the Mojave Desert.

For every 20 boxes of damage sustained while the user is under the influence, permanently reduce the character's Essence by 0.1. A character with cyberware or bioware who takes this drug also suffers 2D6 boxes of Physical damage (unresisted) when the drug wears off, as the regeneration ability attempts to "repair" the implants.

LITTLE SMOKE

Vector: Inhalation
Speed: 2D6 minutes
Duration: Essence + 1D6 hours, maximum 12 hours
Addiction Type: Psychological
Effect: This mixture grants the Concealment and Confusion critter powers.
Exotic Ingredient: Three units of natural herbal refined grasses from the Great Plains of North America.

At the end of the duration, the user's Perception and Willpower are reduced to 1 for an equivalent duration.

ROCK LIZARD BLOOD

Vector: Ingestion
Speed: 30 minutes
Duration: Essence + 1D6 hours, maximum 12 hours
Addiction Type: Physical
Effect: This mixture grants the critter power of Immunity against Diseases and Toxins.
Exotic Ingredient: A natural herbal radical of pulp from a North American weeping tree.

At the end of the duration, the character suffers 2P damage (unresisted) and -4 dice for all tests to resist diseases and toxins for an equivalent duration.

SHADE

Vector: Inhalation
Speed: Immediate
Duration: Essence + 1D6 hours, maximum 12 hours
Addiction Type: Psychological
Effect: Astral projection
Exotic Ingredient: A natural herbal radical of pollen from the red orchid of Southeast Asia.

This compound forces the user, even a mundane, to astrally project. This grants all users, including mundanes, access to the metaplanes if they are in the company of a spirit guide or initiate. At the end of the duration, the user suffers 10 boxes of Stun damage (unresisted). Characters must return to their bodies before the duration ends or they die. Shade allows Awakened users to retain their astral form longer than normal, adding the duration of the drug to their normal astral time.

WUDU'AKU

Vector: Ingestion, Inhalation
Speed: 2D6 minutes
Duration: Essence + 1D6 hours, maximum 12 hours
Addiction Type: Psychological
Effect: The user receives +2 dice on all Conjuring skill group tests and adds +2 to her effective Charisma when dealing with spirits of man.
Exotic Ingredient: A natural mineral radical of powdered fossils from the Australian Outback.

While the drug helps summon spirits of man, it's not so good for other conjuring activities. Once the drug is ingested, users suffer -2 dice to Conjuring skill group tests and -2 Charisma when summoning any other type of spirit for twenty-four hours afterward.

ZOMBIE DUST

Vector: Contact, Injection
Speed: 2 Combat Turns
Duration: Essence +1D6 hours, maximum 12 hours
Addiction Type: Physiological
Effect: Prepares target for possession.
Exotic Ingredient: Exotic metahuman remains

With powdered puffer fish, marine toad, and hyla tree frog combined in an alchemical mixture, this refinement of an ancient traditional voodoo formula causes a target to be instantly prepared for possession. While this can offer a rapid conversion for a friendly ally, it can also be used aggressively against unwilling targets. Note they still get their Intuition + Willpower Test to resist possession.

CHIPS

PSYCHCHIPS

Speed: Immediate
Duration: 48 hours
Addiction Type: Psychological
Effect: Removes effects from negative psychological qualities. See below.

PsychChips are a treatment for psychological disorders, coming in a number of varieties to compensate for anything from OCD to phobias and everything else you might imagine. While under their influence, the user no longer suffers from any negative penalties due to qualities related to their psychological state. Messing around with mental composition, though, has certain side effects. Users tend to feel sluggish, and they have a -1 Reaction penalty for the chip's duration. If the user develops an Addiction and stops using the chips as a result, the quality it counteracted is instead increased by one degree (for example, a Moderate Phobia becomes Severe).

Legal PsychChips can handle Mild and Moderate qualities. BTLs can compensate for Severe qualities.

ADDICTION TABLE

SUBSTANCE	ADDICTION RATING	ADDICTION THRESHOLD
AEXD	1	1
Aisa	5	2
Betel	Special (see entry)	2
Betameth	9	3
Cereprax	9	3
Dopadrine	3	2
eX	5	2
Galak	6	3
G3	2	1
Guts	5	3
Hurlg	4	3
K-10	11	3
Nightwatch	1	2
NoPaint	3	1
Oxygenated Fluorocarbons	2	1
Push	4	3
Red Mescaline	5	3
Ripper	5	3
Snuff	2	2
Woad	5	2
Zero	1	3
AWAKENED DRUGS		
Ayao's will	5	2
Crimson Orchid	9	3
Hecate's blessing	4	2
Overdrive	5	3
Oneiro	6	3
Pixie Dust	10	4
Trance	6	3
MAGICAL COMPOUNDS		
Animal Tongue	3	2
Immortal Flower	8	3
Little Smoke	6	3
Rock Lizard Blood	6	3
Shade	7	3
Wudu'aku	4	1
Zombie Dust	2	3
CHIPS		
Psych Chips (legal)	3	2
Psych Chips (illegal)	6	3

DRUG COSTS

SUBSTANCE	AVAILABILITY	COST (PER DOSE)
AEXD	4	80¥
Aisa	4	25¥
Animal Tongue	6R	1,500¥
Ayao's Will	14F	750¥
Betel	4	5¥
Betameth	5F	30¥
Cereprax	14F	800¥
Crimson Orchid	6F	300¥
Dopadrine	8	45¥
eX	3R	20¥
Forget-Me-Not	10F	400¥
Galak	4R	45¥
G3	2	15¥
Guts	8R	60¥
Hecate's Blessing	12F	500¥
Hurlg	2R	10¥
Immortal Flower	14R	2,500¥
K-10	16F	900¥
Laés	12F	750¥
Leäl	10F	400¥
Little Smoke	12F	1,800¥
Memory Fog	6R	100¥
Nightwatch	3R	25¥
NoPaint	3	15¥
Oneiro	6F	1,250¥
Oxygenated Fluorocarbons	12R	2,000¥
Overdrive	10F	800¥
Pixie Dust	8F	800¥
Push	4F	25¥
PsychChips (illegal)	6F	500¥
PsychChips (legal)	4R	350¥
Red Mescaline	4R	¥50
Ripper	6F	60¥
Rock Lizard Blood	10R	1,700¥
Shade	6R	1,000¥
Slab	8R	250¥
Snuff	1R	10¥
Sober Time	6F	125¥
Soothsayer	12F	150¥
Trance	10F	1,100¥
Woad	3R	15¥
Wudu'aku	12F	2,350¥
Zero	8R	150¥
Zombie Dust	12F	1,500¥

GRADES OF DRUGS

Street cooked: These are the drugs a local ganger makes in a basement or warehouse. The cook cuts the pure drugs to get more product to sell and keep profits up. Street-cooked drugs are half the cost of standard drugs, but crash times (meaning the duration of negative effects after drugs wear of) are doubled. Any drug interaction rolls are at +1 to the roll; if multiple street-cooked drugs are used, this modifier is cumulative.

Standard: The default drug grade unless otherwise stated. No changes in effect or cost.

Pharmaceutical: High-end controls used to minimize impurities and standardize effects. Costs are doubled. Any crash effects are halved in time duration. The Addiction Threshold is reduced by 1. Pharmaceutical grade is the minimum grade for customized drugs.

Designer: A drug made specifically for one person, further reducing side effects and optimizing benefits. Cost is triple that of a pharmaceutical grade of the same drug (making it six times the Standard cost), and the cook making the drug must keep a sample of the user's DNA on file. The crash isn't as severe since it is tailored for the individual, so the duration is quartered. If all the drugs used are designer grade, then drug interaction rolls are at -1.

If someone uses a Designer drug intended for someone other than themselves, treat it as Street Cooked.

CUSTOMIZING DRUGS

Perhaps you have perused the catalog of available drugs and found them lacking. You have a vision for a drug, and you want to make it happen. Well, this is the section for you. Customizing a drug involves two steps: choosing a foundation and then adding one or more blocks to it.

FOUNDATIONS

Foundations are the starting point for a customized designer drug. A cook chooses one foundation and builds off it. Each foundation has a specific theme that can help you decide if it's right for your purposes

FOUNDATION 1 (TANK)

Body +2, Willpower +1, Pain Resistance 3, Charisma -2

FOUNDATION 2 (DEFENDER)

Agility +1, Reaction +1, Intuition +1, Strength -1, Logic -1

FOUNDATION 3 (GENIUS)

Logic +2, Intuition +2, Willpower -1, Reaction -1

FOUNDATION 4 (CHARMER)

Charisma +1, Social limit +1, Agility -1

FOUNDATION 5 (WARRIOR)

Strength +1, Agility +1, Body +1, Willpower -1

BLOCKS

Blocks have two or three levels. A block that has a negative modification is incompatible with another block that has a positive modification on the same attribute. Additionally, if a foundation has a negative modifier for an attribute, only Level 1 or Level 2 or a block positively modifying that attribute can be used.

When using custom drugs, remember that an Attribute can't be modified below 1. If someone takes a drug that will modify the Attribute to 0 or below, the person is paralyzed as their body is unable to function until the drug wears off.

BLOCK 1 (CRUSH)

Level 1: Strength +1, Intuition -1
Level 2: Strength +2, Intuition -1, crash effect: 2S damage, unresisted
Level 3: Strength +3, Intuition -1, Low Pain Tolerance quality (p. 82, *SR5*), crash effect: 2S damage, unresisted

BLOCK 2 (BRUTE)

Level 1: Body +1, Logic -1
Level 2: Body +2, Logic -1, crash effect: 2S damage, unresisted
Level 3: Body +3, Logic -1, Intuition -1, crash effect: 2S damage, unresisted

BLOCK 3 (STRIKE)

Level 1: Agility +1, Strength -1
Level 2: Agility +2, Strength -1, crash effect: 2S damage, unresisted)
Level 3: Agility + 3, Strength -1, Unsteady Hands quality (p. 87, *SR5*), crash effect: 2S damage, unresisted

BLOCK 4 (LIGHTNING)

Level 1: Reaction +1, Logic -1
Level 2: Reaction +2, Logic -1, Willpower -1
Level 3: Reaction +3, Logic -1, Willpower -1, crash effect: 2S damage, unresisted

BLOCK 5 (EINSTEIN)

Level 1: Logic +1, Willpower -1
Level 2: Logic +2, Willpower -1, Intuition -1
Level 3: Logic +3, Willpower -1, Intuition -1, crash effect: -1D6 Initiative Dice

BLOCK 6 (GUT CHECK)

Level 1: Intuition +1, Strength -1
Level 2: Intuition +2, Strength -1, Reaction -1

Level 3: Intuition +3, Strength –1, Reaction –1, crash effect: 2S damage, unresisted

BLOCK 7 (STONEWALL)

Level 1: Willpower +1, Body –1
Level 2: Willpower +2, Body –1, Agility –1
Level 3: Willpower +3, Body –1, Agility –1, Strength –1

BLOCK 8 (SMOOTHTALK)

Level 1: Charisma +1, Strength –1
Level 2: Charisma +2, Strength –1, crash effect: 2S damage, unresisted
Level 3: Charisma +3, Strength –1, Uncouth quality (p. 85, *SR5*), crash effect: 2S damage, unresisted

BLOCK 9 (SHOCK&AWE)

Level 1: +1D6 Initiative, crash effect: 4S damage, unresisted
Level 2: +2D6 Initiative, –1 to all limits, crash effect: 4S damage, unresisted
Level 3: +3D6 Initiative, –2 to all limits, crash effect: 8S damage, unresisted

The following are advanced blocks and only have 2 levels due to their added complexity.

BLOCK 10 (RAZOR MIND)

Level 1: Intuition +1, Logic +1, Charisma –1, crash effect: 1S damage, unresisted
Level 2: Intuition +2, Logic +2, Charisma –2, crash effect: 2S damage, unresisted

BLOCK 11 (THE GENERAL)

Level 1: Charisma +1, Willpower +1, Strength –1, crash effect: 2S damage, unresisted
Level 2: Charisma +2, Willpower +2, Strength –1, Agility –1, crash effect: 2S damage, unresisted

BLOCK 12 (RESIST)

Level 1: Body +1, Willpower +1, Logic –1, crash effect: 1S damage, unresisted
Level 2: Body +2, Willpower +2, Logic –1, Reaction –1, crash effect: 2S damage, unresisted

BLOCK 13 (SPEED DEMON)

Level 1: Agility +1, Reaction +1, Strength –1, crash effect: 1S damage, unresisted
Level 2: Agility +2, Reaction +2, Strength –1, Intuition –1, crash effect: 2S damage, unresisted

To design your own drug, first choose the foundation you want to start with, and then choose the level of the block you want to add. You can add additional blocks

as long as the final drug adheres to all of the following restrictions:

- Total Initiative dice from all sources cannot be increased beyond +4D6.
- The total allowable bonus through all sources to any one Attribute is +4.
- No Attribute can be modified below 1.
- The maximum level of a block that positively modifies an Attribute that the chosen foundation negatively modifies is Level 2.
- The Stun damage of a crash effect is unresisted when the drug's effects end. If this damage fills the user's Stun Condition Monitor, the remaining damage overflows into the Physical Condition Monitor at the rate of 1 box of Physical damage for every 2 boxes of Stun damage (or portion thereof) left over.

The base duration for customized drugs is 10 x 1D6 minutes. The base vector is Ingested, and the base Speed is 3 Combat Turns. These can be changed with Enhancers, as listed in the Available Enhancers table. The costs and Addiction effects of Enhancers are in the Customized Drugs Cost table.

AVAILABLE ENHANCERS

ENHANCER	EFFECT
Ingestion Enhancer	Adds Ingestion as a Vector
Inhalation Enhancer	Adds Inhalation as a Vector
Speed Enhancer	Reduces speed by 1 Combat Turn; may be selected up to three times
Duration Enhancer	Adds 1D6 to the roll to determine duration; may be selected up to three times so that final duration is 10 x 4D6

Depending on what you want it to do, the Availability for a drug can be high, along with the cost. The benefit of being able to get exactly what you need makes customized drugs a popular choice with many professionals who prefer drugs for their boost. However, due to the nature of these drugs, they can't be found on street corners like run-of-the-mill drugs. Acquiring customized drugs requires a chemist or dealer contact with a Connection Rating of at least 5; the same level of contact is needed to acquire the raw ingredients necessary for these drugs. The raw ingredients cost half of the normal drug price. Mixing customized drugs requires a Chemistry + Logic

CUSTOMIZED DRUGS COST (PER DOSE)

DRUG	AVAILABILITY	COST	ADDICTION RATING	ADDICTION THRESHOLD
Foundations 1–5	4R	75¥	6	2
Blocks 1–8 (per level)	+1	+20¥	*	*
Block 9 (per level)	+2	+40¥	*	*
Blocks 10–13 (per level)	+2	+30¥	*	*
Enhancer	+1	+50¥	+1	+1

WRECKER EXAMPLE

The elven ganger Wrecker decides he needs an advantage to survive on the streets. Unable to afford cyberware, he goes with customized drugs. His attributes are as follows:

B	A	R	S	W	L	I	C	ESS
3	4	3	2	3	4	3	4	6

After looking over his options, he decides to start with Foundation 2: Agility + 1, Reaction + 2, Intuition + 1, Strength – 1, and Logic – 1. To this he adds Block 2 at Level 3 for Body + 3, Logic – 1, Charisma – 1, and a crash effect of unresisted 2S damage. Next he adds Block 9 at Level 2 for +2D6 Initiative, –1 to all limits, and a crash effect of unresisted 4S damage. He would like to add Block 2 to further increase his Agility, but this would drop his Strength below 1. Instead he adds Block 4 at Level 2 for Reaction + 2, Logic – 1, and Willpower – 1. This mix will give him the advantage he is looking for.

The final drug imparts these effects when used:

Physical Attributes:
Body + 3, Agility + 1, Reaction + 4, Strength – 1
Mental Attributes:
Willpower – 1, Logic – 2, Intuition + 1, Charisma – 1
Other Effects:
+2D6 to Initiative, unresisted 6S damage when the drug wears off

Wrecker likes this combination, but he doesn't want to wait 3 Combat Turns for it to kick in, so he adds two Speed Enhancers to change the Speed from 3 Combat Turns to 1 Combat turn.

Wrecker's customized drug will have an Availability of 15R, a cost of 355¥ per dose, an Addiction Rating of 10, and an Addiction Threshold of 8. It's a powerful drug, but he'd better use it carefully or he's going to develop a dependency awfully fast.

Extended Test with a threshold equal to the drug's Availability x 2 and an interval of eight hours. A glitch on any part of the Extended Test requires the player to start the entire test over with no successes; a critical glitch means the ingredients are destroyed and cannot be used.

DRUG INTERACTIONS

When drugs are mixed, bad things happen. Sometimes you get lucky, sometimes you don't, and the more drugs involved, the worse it can get. If you take a drug while still under the effect of another drug or recovering from a drug crash, you run the risk of experiencing a drug interaction.

Roll 1D6 for each drug beyond the first, and total the results. Modify the total by drug grade (if applicable) and consult the following table.

COMMON BTL CHIPS

These are the effects of some common Better-Than-Life chips. They count as moodchips (p. 413, *SR5*), meaning they have an Availability of 4F, a cost of 50 nuyen, an Addiction Rating of 6, and Addiction Threshold of 2.

DOWNER BTL

Effect: Reaction –1, Intuition +1

UPPER BTL

Effect: Intuition –1, Reaction +1

HYPER BTL

Effect: Reaction +1, Agility +1, Intuition –1, Charisma –1

DRUG INTERACTIONS TABLE

Street cooked drugs: +1 to roll result for each street cooked drug used

Designer drugs: −1 to roll result if all drugs used are designer drugs

ROLL	EFFECT
1	Double duration of all drugs
2–4	No side effect
5–6	Duration of all crash effects are doubled
7–9	Crash effects occur immediately
10	Immediately take 3S damage, unresisted
11–13	Crash effect damage is Physical instead of Stun
14+	Immediately resist 10P damage by Body only

WRECKER, AGAIN

Wrecker draws the short straw on stakeout duty and takes a dose of long haul to make sure he won't fall asleep and miss the rival gangers coming to make a drug deal at the warehouse. At 2 a.m. the rival gang shows up. Wrecker wakes up his buddies, and the five of them move in. Wrecker, knowing things are going down, injects a dose of his customized drug. Since he's under the influence of two drugs simultaneously, he has to check for interaction. He rolls 1D6 and gets a 2, so nothing happens. The combat goes quickly, and they are victorious. In celebration of their big score, Wrecker's partner Vindicator lights up some of the deepweed they seized. After taking a couple of hits, Vindicator hands it to Wrecker, who takes a drag without thinking about it. Since he is still now under the influence of three different drugs, he has to check for interaction again. He now rolls 2D6, and the deepweed was street cooked so it adds +1. He gets a 3 and a 5, so with the +1 modifier, he has a total of 9, which means he immediately suffers the crash effects from all three drugs.

CHILL BTL

Effect: Charisma +1, Intuition +1, Logic –1, Willpower –1

SPECIALIZED BETTER-THAN-LIFE CHIPS

The following BTLs are far rarer than your average BTL chip. They have an Availability of 8F, a cost of 200 nuyen, an Addiction Rating of 6, and an Addiction Threshold of 2.

BERSERKER BTL

Effect: +1 Strength +1, Body +1, Logic – 1, Willpower –1

The user always employs Full Offense (p. 121, *Run & Gun*) whenever in a fight; no martial arts training is needed.

BODYGUARD BTL

Effect: Body + 1, Logic –1

May use Protecting the Principal (p. 125, *Run & Gun*) without spending Edge.

When the chip is slotted, the user is assigned a target to protect. The user will then protect this person above all else.

INFILTRATOR

Effect: Agility + 2, Strength + 1, Charisma – 2, Gymnastics 2, Locksmith 2, Palming 1

Greed: The user must make a Willpower (3) Test to resist the urge to steal a valuable item left unattended.

Thrill of the Heist: The user must make a Willpower (2) Test to stop in the middle of a job.

If the user's Charisma is reduced below 1, the character gains the Uncouth quality (p. 85, *SR5*) if they regain consciousness while the program is still running. The quality goes away when the p-fix program is stopped.

PACIFIER

Effect: Reaction – 1, Intuition – 1, Willpower – 1, Charisma – 1

This chip is intended to make extraction targets easier to control without knocking them out. The program emulates the emotions and thoughts of a codependent individual, which make the user passive and compliant. The victim will have drunken, slurred speech and a glassy-eyed appearance.

THE MURKY FUTURE

Dust wafted on the breeze as bits of concrete slipped between Cork's fingers and skittered across the grate before falling down into the sewers. The feeling of power never waned. The endorphin explosion whenever he crushed something in his cyberhand. The endorphins did nothing for the hand, but made the rest of his body twitch with edgy energy.

Giving into the rush had become a habit. A habit he shouldn't indulge when the plan was to sit outside a meet and look inconspicuous. The heel of his combat boot tapping at the concrete wasn't out of place. His thigh slapping on the bench as his leg bounced a totally normal nervous tic for a kid waiting for a bus. The only false note, the problem, was the hand and the chunk of concrete he couldn't stop crushing.

He hadn't felt right since Boston. Ever since walking out of his last implant surgery recovery. Three hours, maybe, before a dragon went berserk and everything locked down. He didn't feel right. Didn't feel whole.

The docs had warned him. Told him he was getting dangerously close to that edge, that point where the metahuman form can't take anymore. He hadn't told them about the last operation. The one that had involved etching runes on his bones and had more to do with doctors of thaumaturgy than of medicine. He couldn't see any of them, beneath his flesh, but he knew the runes were elaborate. Four around his skull, a set of five on his ribs and sternum; his femurs looked like scrimshaw. And both feet had a full set, with one on each of the twenty-six bones. He wasn't privy to the designs nor the specifics of how they worked, but he knew what the runes were supposed to do and knew they were doing their job.

After the hand, the eyes, the ears, the artificial muscle fibers, and the dermal plates he was already feeling the detachment. Feeling he was becoming more machine than man. They offered to make it stop. They offered him a chance to hold onto his humanity, but not stop pushing to keep the edge on the streets. He took it like a beetlehead offered Calhots. An addict was an addict, whether it was BTLs or bone lacing.

Different docs, a signed life-forfeit waiver, and a top-of-the-line wired reflexes system from Spinrad got him on the table in Boston with about a hundred repetitions of the same question and warning: "Are you sure? This will most likely kill you." But it didn't kill him, and it left those NeoNET docs scratching their heads.

Now he was faster, stronger, and tougher than any street samurai on the continent. And he still looked like an early twenty-something with a five o'clock shadow, a mass of scraggy hair on the top of his head, and a missing hand that usually brought sympathy, not fear.

Unless, of course, he was using it to crush concrete.

A GLIMPSE OF THE FUTURE

POSTED BY: CLEAR

You don't know me, but you will all wish to by the time I'm done. Consider this my petition to gain extended access to JackPoint, the Nexus, the Repository, and/or Alexandria. My recently vacated position provided me with access to an abundance of information that I would like to offer as barter for entry into one of these elite shadow information data havens. I will continue to offer further information as I become aware of it in my new position, though I'm sure the data will not flow as freely past my commlink.

Let us begin with an introduction. As is tradition within the shadows I will not offer my real name, only my new moniker, and I will expect some doubt and distrust at the start. I am Clear, and I am here to discuss the future of augmentation, a field I have watched evolve over many years from within. I'm tempted to say from within its heart, but I was never near the middle of the field. I worked on the cutting edge, leading the way into the future.

As for the less poetic version of my credentials, I am one of the few people in the world with what is referred to as a "Type O system." My genome is the baseline for many generic biomodifications and one of the simplest types to custom-engineer anti-rejection drugs for when considering new cybernetic enhancements. For the last four years I've been a voluntary experimental augmentation subject. While testing out the newest in next-generation enhancements for my corporation, I was utilizing those new systems to perform what I called corporate espionage and what we all call shadowruns. Even though I was, at the time, as loyal a citizen as any

corporation could ask for, I was also running enough headware to understand that the future of any employee in my position is limited. Knowing that, I've never let any data get past me without being scanned and stored.

I could upload all of it, but most of the technical babble would miss the audience, and it's not the style I've seen on any of your data havens. I have tailored all of my informative pieces on the various aspects of augmentation to conform to your established practices and norms.

CYBERTECHNOLOGY

In recent years, cyberware research and development programs have adapted to overcome evolving issues in nanotechnology manufacturing processes. These adaptations not only affected the practices currently in place but have had a dramatic impact on the development of future projects. Cybertech R&D has focused on three main areas in pushing forward: new materials, external systems, and personally customized systems. While every major and minor brand will claim they have the newest, latest, or greatest innovation, these "new" systems are simply well advertised lateral movements. Saeder-Krupp, Renraku, and Spinrad Industries are the driving forces behind any genuine advances in the field, each focusing their efforts in different areas.

- Interesting trio. They do a nice job of spanning the bulk of the civilized globe.
- Traveler Jones

- Any guess as to which of those three our applicant worked for?
- Slamm-0!

- Whoa! No guessing. Here's the [link] for wagering. Wuxing is currently the longest odds 100:1 and SK and NeoNET are favorites at 2:1 and 3:1 respectively. Payout comes when Clear admits his affiliation or someone digs up something credible.
- /dev/grrl

- This is getting out of control. Does she bet on everything?
- Slamm-0!

- The betting doesn't bother me, but the use of JackPoint to promote the betting does. Triumvirate?
- Balladeer

- Any action will have to wait until I break even.
- Glitch

S-K is the current leader in advancing the use of new materials in both production systems and the cyberware products themselves. Smart materials, custom alloys and polymers, new synthetic materials, and variations on conventional materials are all being used individually and in conjunction. The German megacorporation is redesigning the internal functionality of every system they've designed to utilize these new materials, which has resulted in a substantial decline in bio-rejection, increased physical stability, and enhanced functionality. Their most unique discovery is poly-functionality. Poly-functional systems are able to adapt and self-modify on the go, reformatting themselves to meet changing demands. Poly-functional systems are still in development, but there are working prototypes, and they project commercial release by the end of the decade. No doubt megacorporate espionage will result in a competitive market, but for now only SK controls the fundamental research.

- Also, expect that "end of the decade" to actually be the end of the next decade as the megas bash and raid each other to get the edge and thus delay the whole process.
- Icarus

Renraku has been working to rebrand themselves for years. One of the next big things the new and improved Renraku will bring out is exoware. This new idea bears a superficial resemblance to an old idea, but you can expect the Renraku marketing and PR divisions to come up with a brand name that doesn't evoke that of any rival megacorporation. Exoware is the term for cybernetic enhancements that are housed primarily outside the body. This minimizes internal biosystem degradation allowing for increased system counts; enhancing access for repair, replacement, or upgrade; allowing systems to bypass certain physical limitations; and presenting several societal modification benefits. The last portion was one of the most interesting to me when I spotted it, as it wasn't the normal "bigger, better, more" mentality.

Renraku is currently conducting focus group testing on a twofold public relations campaign that's part of their overall rebranding and promotion of their exoware tech. One part of the campaign presents the increased sense of security, for humans, that larger security personnel would provide. Not in the form of larger metahumans, such as trolls, but in the form of ordinary humans who are externally modified to be as big and powerful as trolls. The visual moves away from the sleek cyber of the trid fantasy runner and back to the mecha-cyborg of the turn of the century. The other PR stream is broader and subtler. It's an effort to change public opinion; to make hidden cyberware, particularly offensive systems, socially unacceptable. They are attacking all parts of the cyberware distribution chain, from production to consumer use, trying to convince people that concealed cyber is a social harm. Arguments they are making generally say that anyone using such hidden systems is almost certainly a threat to social order; that only a person contemplating illegal, immoral, and otherwise nefarious acts would hide cyberware of this type. Obviously neither Renraku nor any other megacorporation is going to stop making internal offensive cyberware. They are just promoting the idea that external systems represent a higher moral standard. This social engineering effort may catch on, becoming more than Renraku specific, which could strengthen their broader effort to reinvent themselves as a wholesome, people-friendly megacorp. While Renraku is currently the only major player focused on these external systems, as with anything corporate espionage and market forces are going to bring every corp on board at some level sooner or later. A potentially lucrative market will of course be cheaper external systems for third-world clients who see the benefits of decreased surgical time and advantage of hardware that can be repaired or swapped out with minimal tech skills.

* Okay, I understand the troll/human issue from Renraku's point of view, but what happens when Evo or Ares design exoware for trolls? What I'm imagining is walking field artillery, complete with personal defense weaponry. Yikes!
* 2XL

* The Renraku imaging campaign sounds like it will focus on big mods, but what about the minor ones? I don't really see the whole social-engineering thing as being relevant. The megacorps and the perfect people who serve them may dictate what constitutes "normal" in what they see as the civilized world, but they do not compose the majority of the world's population. Or places that don't care about normal? Clear mentioned the third world, but we all run shadows in the first world where no one gives a damn about "normal."
* Elijah

Spinrad Industries is going to keep pushing the cybernetic enhancement envelope until their fearless leader succeeds in killing himself testing whatever he's convinced will be the next big thing. Right now they're developing customized cyberware packages that benefit from zero cross-system redundancy and are created as a unique, perfect match for the user. At first glance there are a lot of similarities with the cybersuites offered by other corporations. Enough to make anyone familiar with the various grades of cyberware (alpha, beta, delta, omega) think they understand what they're looking at and dismiss it out of hand. But this is not a special procedure that requires a multi-billion-nuyen facility, genetically matched anti-rejection drugs, or advanced-grade materials in the devices themselves. Spinrad systems are custom-tailored, like a fine suit, to each individual client. The user gets all the benefit of a variety of different systems without compromising biological integrity to the multiple installations separate systems demand. While Spinrad Industries is currently at the forefront in developing this technology, other megacorporations are producing and field-testing prototypes.

* My money's on NeoNET as the other mega with this tech. Spln's been cozying up to the homeless corp since Boston closed, and rumors are novahot about some kind of deal between Dick and Johnny.
* Pistons

* MCT has a few systems that match this concept: specialized packages inserted as a unit. I came across a memo referencing the "Kuro" as elite, internally available operatives. Other documents refer to Kuro as a cybernetics suite available to top-level internal security.
* Mihoshi Oni

* Evo has something like this in the works, but most of it is about changing your life. Their marketing strategy is to provide systems that let your outside match your inside.
* Plan 9

* So if my inside is a stone-cold killer, I can get the outside to match?
* Kane

* Kane's inane comment aside, what's to prevent the merging of some of these futuristic ideas? Like an internal system custom designed for the user that's also linked to a complementary suite of exoware.
* Glitch

* And to think, I was just getting past the nightmares about nanites. Now something new to haunt my dreams.
* Slamm-0!

- To all members of JackPoint: Please cease posting anything that may give Slamm-0! nightmares or I may have to violate the rules on killing other members of JackPoint. Thank you.
- Netcat

BIOWARE

Cyberware has been around for almost fifty years, but bioware augmentation has been on the streets for less than half that time. Nearly every cybernetic system has a bionetic component that generates similar effects with a lessened impact on biological integrity. Of course, the frontiers of bioware are currently being advanced by the megacorp everyone would expect to see at the forefront, but there's at least one other player on the field most people wouldn't suspect. It takes some hard work and patience, but diggers with some idea where to look can find the funding trail connecting a little-known research outfit to a pretty surprising source. The two research programs are working toward different objectives and taking very different approaches to answering their respective questions, but they are making remarkably similar discoveries.

Leading the way in all things biomodification is Evo. Though they haven't abandoned their Yamatetsu ancestry and they still innovate in the field of cybernetics, they are currently designing and developing their own parallel to the Spinrad custom cyber suites—custom bioware suites, or biosuites. While cyberware has a lot of components and pieces that can be adapted, removed, or modified, bioware does not. This means a completely different array of procedures are necessary to make these suites as biocompatible as possible. Besides custom designs based on individual genetic profiles, which is standard for a lot of high-end bioware, these new designs use protospecian genetic coding to integrate the new organs and systems into gene code sequences that predate modern man. The result is a slight modification to the user's genetic code, mostly within their so-called "junk" DNA, that matches up with code in the enhanced organ system.

- Since it's in the DNA, does it get passed on? Can the next generation be born with muscle toner or a synaptic accelerator?
- /dev/grrl

- Toddlers with reflex enhancements? Terrifying!
- Slamm-0!

- I don't think so. As I understand it, the offspring may be born with the ability to accept these modified systems but the code to grow the system itself is not present. But I'll be contacting Clear for specifics on this.
- Butch

Evo has a wide range of unique systems, from cybernetic to bionetic, that they offer to their citizens and anyone else in the world who wants to "be who they truly are." Their newest frontier is genetic modification, and their research continues to advance the field of personal modifications and enhancements every day.

That said, I present the next concepts from Owains BioNatural, with the note that they are far beyond the current work being done in even the blackest labs of Evo. This small firm is located in the Carib League and benefits immensely from the area's rather lax laws and minimal regulation of research when it comes to metahuman trials. Owains BioNatural operates on a trio of islands that were formerly part of the Turks and Caicos Islands. The small corporation, not even A rated, is modifying, adapting, and enhancing metahumans in ways that push the subjects beyond the realm of standard species identification.

The work, under the direction of Dr. Carol Owains, focuses primarily on the integration of non-metahuman organs and systems into metahuman subjects. Using a (probably stolen) genetic modification system, these bioware systems incorporate the natural biological functions of other species into the metahuman biomatrix. This can range from the simple insertion of singular systems, such as cnidarian stinging cells, to full-spectrum bioconversions. The *Homo sapiens aquaticus* modification package, for example, provides the user with gills, webbed feet, sonar, electrosense organs, swim bladder, insulation, and pressure mitigating systems to allow a fully aquatic life. Of course it also makes anything like a normal life above the waves impossible. Owains uses a combination of vat-grown genetically customized organs with the desired characteristics from various species with her unique retro-viral agent, which allows full integration of the biosystems with little or no loss of biological integrity.

This advancement is not without its potential drawbacks and side effects. Due to genetic modifications necessary to accept the organs, subjects often suffer fertility issues. Males produce sperm that are incompatible with metahuman female eggs, and females will often suffer immediate biorejection of their own egg cells due to incompatible genetic coding. Extreme hormonal imbalances in the subjects are possible, and early subjects often developed malformation and suffered severe mental degradation. These subjects were rarely disposed of immediately and were instead introduced into the wild population of the island and monitored.

As I mentioned earlier, Owains BioNatural is not an extraterritorial megacorporation. But Aztechnology, the official owner of the islands, is. Aztechnology extends its rights to the islands. Funding links are, as I said, deeply hidden, but even with no proof of fiscal connection it's hard to believe a megacorporation like Aztechnology would allow this kind of research to go on without very close supervision. If not outright control.

- Animal organ implantation and modifications on a secluded island. What could possibly go wrong, Dr. Moreau?
- Bull

- All jokes aside, this is a big deal for one part alone: "minimal, if any, loss of biological integrity." That would be a game-changer in the field of augmentation. Systems that don't degenerate the body's natural systems and integrity would be a leap forward. No more cyber-psychosis or identity disassociation disorder causing the augmented to feel less and less "human" while they became so much more.
- Plan 9

- We could have razorboys that might actually be able to function in public?
- /dev/grrl

- Clear still mentions the side effects above about mental degradation. While not a clinical level of interpersonal disassociation. From context it's probably some form of feral streak. Still no good in public. Probably similar to a shapeshifter with anger issues trying to fit in. More animal than human.
- Sticks

GENETECH

The field of genetic manipulation augmentation is currently being led by Evo, Aztechnology, and Proteus, though Proteus has had several setbacks of late. With CFD showing a more rapid onset time within individuals who have had genetech modifications, the research has been moved out of the spotlight and into the black labs for all three of these megacorporations and their less-prominent fellows. Each is pushing the field ahead with different primary advancements, but all of them will likely avoid release or even public testing in the near future.

Evo has been pushing the envelope in all areas of metahuman modification since they first broke away from their Japanacorp roots and began their campaign of EVOlution. The halls of Evo corporate facilities are filled with abundant variations on the metahuman form. Individuals working hard to be just that: a unique individual. Even if the mentality is the same, Evo citizens represent a myriad of physical variations using every form of biological, arcane, and artistic modification known to intelligent life in order to create a unique look or style.

- It's a good place to point out how true this is when trying to run against Evo. There are very few standard sararimen in the Evo ranks. They've been around long enough to remove the concept of normal. If someone looks 'normal,' they stick out like a sore thumb. To be unique is to be EVOlved.
- Plan 9

- This is true in all levels from upper offices down the ranks in manufacturing and production facilities where modifications often help employees be better at their jobs. You see a lot of jacked cyberlimbs on the floors of their shipping departments.
- Baka Dabora

The newest field of bioengineering, and where you can expect the biggest leaps forward, is in directly modifying the genome of the user. These are permanent genetic changes that become fully expressed fairly rapidly. Experimental methodologies that move well beyond making changes within the established genomes of the various metahuman subgroups have already been developed. They are cross-splicing genes from every branch of metahumanity and have been pushing the envelope on incorporating genetic materials from a variety of non-human species. Evo developed their system by reverse engineering the natural evolutionary mutation process. Subjects spend a week or so in a pseudo-amniotic fluid bath as the changes are introduced and accelerated toward expression. When they emerge from the bath, users are usually free of the dissociative tendencies of standard augmentation subjects and demonstrate complete biological integrity. Arcane assensing techniques used before and after showed a clear and thorough change to the subjects' auras. This new biological matrix alters or subsumes their original biology, which means biorejection of previously installed implants genetically keyed to the original is a real possibility. Non-customized, general design cyber and bionetics are unaffected.

Aztechnology is taking a radically different approach: applied genetic memory. When auditory or olfactory receptors that can detect sounds and scents far outside the normal metahuman range are implanted they can only convey raw data. The user must learn what each new sound and scent means and how to integrate that information cognitively. However, those highly sensitive receptors evolved in animals that instinctively understood the data and how to subconsciously process and use the information. These instincts are genetically driven, and Aztechnology has developed ways to replicate those genes and implant the genetic instincts in a user. This gives the subject access to their new superhuman resources with no learning curve. The instincts genetically infused into the subject allow instant understanding of this sensory data from millenia of genetic memory.

▸ I've seen write-ups of the work in this area. It's useful without being completely alien. What interested me most were the side effects. Genetic memory flashbacks that caused the subjects to dream from the perspective of the species that had been implanted. Lots of alternate hypotheses as to why, all pretty much boiling down to "not a clue" but the effect seems universal, present in every subject to some degree. No doubt the Azzies will PR the drek out of that. Make it sound like a plus.

▸ Butch

At this point Aztechnology hasn't solved the problem of multiple genetic memories. That is to say that while the physical attributes of different species can be implanted, the genetic memories of only one of those species can be assimilated. Aztechnology is glossing over this by gathering and producing a wide array of Instinctual Infusions, maximizing what can be done with any one donor species. But they are trying to find ways to combine species; the methods of testing and data derived indicate Owains BioNatural is involved in this research. There are unsubstantiated reports they've had some success blending the genetic memories of two species with similar characteristics, but no luck combining wildly divergent or multiple species.

There's evidence that Proteus managed to push further into this field than anyone, and in a different direction. The evidence is difficult to confirm, however, because Proteus consolidated all of their research and development assets, from top theorists to test subjects, in a single location: Boston. The Proteus arkoblock that had been planted in the harbor as a sign of the megacorporation's commitment to the city was the primary datastore while their labs and testing facilities were spread throughout the Boston area of the NEMA. Which now is almost entirely within the Quarantine Zone. Reports can be found that indicate Proteus was successful in what is currently the pinnacle of genetic augmentation research: Magic and Resonance infusion. Proteus reports indicate that they were able to infuse and activate genes in subjects to provide arcane and electrokinetic talent as well as various abilities, arcane and emergent, associated with other species.

- ⦿ I've heard that before. It's like cold fusion—claims mean nothing until they can be duplicated.
- ⦿ Nephrine

The loss of their primary work in Boston was a major setback, but it was only the first. They made the mistake of petitioning the Corporate Court for access to their Boston arkoblock on the grounds that they were on the verge of a fundamental breakthrough. Not only did they fail to make their case, they painted a big bulls-eye on every one of their facilities around the world. All of their sites, and all the sites of their subsidiaries, have been raided; everything from subtle incursions to smash-and-grabs. The complaint also attracted the positive attention of several A- and AA-rated megacorps that have approached them with offers to collaborate on what has come to be called the "Megacorporate Revision." This widespread attention, both positive and negative, has kept Proteus from regaining their lost work or making progress in recreating their original research.

- ⦿ Reports can be faked. They could just be trying to make other corps think they were further along than they were. Get them to throw resources into the black hole that is Boston.
- ⦿ Mr. Bonds

- ⦿ Proteus has taken too many other hits for this to be a ploy. They lost a big chunk of resources in Boston, and they are not among those in control of the situation. The AAA megas have pushed out all of the smaller megas in control of the NEMAQZ.
- ⦿ Glitch

NANOTECHNOLOGY

The potential uses and benefits of nanotechnology are far too great for even something as potentially devastating as CFD to completely shut down. The future in this area will remain uncertain until the problem of blocking out or eradicating CFD infections is solved. But isolated facilities with safety and security precautions beyond BSL-4 have been working on both solving that problem and developing a new class of nanites that are impervious to CFD. Currently leading the research in this field are Aztechnology and Mitsuhama. I was not assigned to investigate NeoNET's and Evo's nanotech, but I think it's very likely they've made significant advances as well.

Aztechnology has been focusing primarily on using nanites for short-term boosts, much like combat drugs, but with a more concentrated main effect and fewer side effects. To limit risk of CFD, the nanites have hard coded-

ing that cannot be modified and limited, non-rechargeable energy storage. The nanites act as a very specific delivery and/or operating system and then clear out of the system and shut down when their work is done. They follow their pre-programmed series of commands, with the system flush as the final part of the command sequence, and that's it. These systems boost speed, strength, reflex, agility, mental acuity, pheromone release, wound repair, and toxin resistance. Once the CFD issue is dealt with, expect Aztechnology to flood the market with these, especially with security firms and military organizations.

MCT has been looking for the silver lining around the cloud of CFD. They've been using information gathered from studying the CFD sufferers—"head cases" I believe you call them—and analyzing what those nanites can do for the host. Their discoveries have been primarily focused on the physical capabilities, but MCT recently discovered the ability of some nanites within a head case to function as a Matrix device and allow the head case access to the Matrix without the use of a commlink or cyberdeck.

Physical enhancements are very similar to the work being performed by Aztechnology, and my reading of their documents showed enough similarities to suspect corporate espionage. One of the primary divergence points in the MCT work is the function of the nanites. AZT wants the nanites to function as a focused delivery system for known compounds to enhance certain attributes, while MCT's research focuses on the use of the nanites themselves as the enhancement system. Their efforts show requirements for higher quantities of nanites with simpler command structures. These systems perform their single purpose and then flush from the system or, as an interesting optional development, they self-destruct into biologically useful substances.

- ⦿ Information I've heard says that the "corporate espionage" in question might be a collaborative effort. Especially since these two had some involvement in the various projects in Boston.
- ⦿ Mika

- ⦿ As Clear suspects, both NeoNET and Evo have projects in the works to advance the field of nanotechnology. NeoNET seems focused on the use of nanites to form simple networks to act as devices with a variety of purposes that can be completely internal and very difficult to detect when they aren't in use. The nanites don't interact until a command is given, and then they act as whatever device they need to emulate. Civilian applications are as simple as a commlink that controls all the devices in your home. Militaries and special operations units could have cyberdecks, jammers, commlinks, or radio detonators hidden in their members.

Evo is not running from CFD. Everything I've seen points toward them being the first corp to start accepting head cases as citizens or at least offering asylum. This also means they'll have the CFD nanites to study, along with the head cases controlling them when they want to utilize the technology for the next phase of their evolution.

◉ Plan 9

CHEMICAL ENHANCEMENTS

When talking augmentations, most people think in terms of permanent solutions to temporary problems. Being enhanced helps with specific tasks, of course, but the rest of the time? Useless, or annoying, or in the way. There are enough drawbacks that a number of corps, including one AA in particular, are developing chemical augmentations that have short, task-specific durations. The biggest hurdles in this area are mitigating the after-effects and minimizing the likelihood of addiction. Paralleling this research is a form of augmentation that involves the use of chemical compounds that have more permanent effects. These drugs offer a long-term boost without surgery or risk of detection from cyberware scanners or x-ray imaging. Zeta-ImpChem is the frontrunner in perfecting both chemical types, but at least one other megacorporation has access to their research thus far.

For single-use chemical boosts, Z-IC has been upgrading and modifying current combat-enhancement, pain-reduction, attention-focusing, and data-processing enhancement drugs by adding secondary chemicals that allow higher doses and suppress side effects. They've progressed from clinical to field trials, and with the exception of addiction issues with the data-processing enhancements, they've been very successful. Test subjects who become addicted to the data-processing report that the world seems flat and uninteresting after they've seen it so clearly. Corporate directives are quite blunt about the dangers of mental enhancers and describe serious consequences for any researchers who do not take proper precautions to confine their effect to prescribed parameters.

◉ Corps don't want citizens who can think. The employees who get most frequently reassigned to the dirt have high IQs and tend to be independent thinkers. Corps monitor everyone to avoid too much free thought.
◉ Clockwork

Z-IC was on the verge of introducing Chemoware™, their long-term chemical-augmentation regimen, when the Boston situation sent the corporate world into turmoil. They pulled back on marketing and pushed the stock they had on hand out for more field-testing. Quite a bit of that stock was dropped into the Quarantine Zone. The effects of these chemical augmentation systems are not as extreme as their cybernetic or bionetic parallels, but that's part of the point. They're less obvious, more difficult to detect, and the user experiences limited, often negligible,

disruptions to their biological integrity. An unexpected result of this impromptu field test has been the discovery that these chemicals seem detrimental to technomancers and magicians. The effect is similar to the addiction other subjects developed to short-term intellectual enhancers, though of course there are no withdrawal symptoms as the drugs are always present. The subjects feel as though they are more aware and in tune, and they are unaware that the careful balance of body and mind they need to maintain when manipulating mana or working with resonance is impeded. The extent to which their abilities are reduced varies from individual to individual.

◉ Z-IC is poised to make a big jump up the ranks with this. That, along with some of the connections we've seen them make in regard to the Revision, might mean a seat at the big table on Z-O or one of the Big Ten getting demoted to let the revised Z-IC jump up.
◉ Icarus

◉ I've pulled some numbers together using all the connections we've seen, speculated, and know for sure. Even if only half of those A and AA megas make the moves to merge, S-K will no longer be number one. Not even close. No wonder work has been so abundant lately. Even the biggest of the big boys is at risk of losing something here.
◉ Glitch

Cybertechnology, bioware, genetech, nanotechnology, and chemical enhancement are the five augmentation techniques most widely known, but my employer directed me to investigate other approaches to augmentation that are not so mainstream. Among these are various arcane augmentation enhancements, a new procedure known as e-loading, and even more obscure frontiers. None of these techniques is likely to be on the menu at street clinics anytime soon, but they are out there as options to anyone willing to volunteer as a test subject for one of the megacorporations. The megacorporations have no shortage of volunteers looking for an edge on the street, and no compunction about promising them whatever they want from the procedure. Of course, rounding up involuntary test subjects is a pretty straightforward proposition as well.

◉ I will warn any who are easy to scare (Slamm-0!, I'm looking at you) that the arcane uses of augmentation enhancement are the stuff of nightmares.
◉ Netcat

ARCANE ENHANCEMENTS

Cybermancy is a scary term. Manatech, a name borrowed from more mundane systems like MCT's Lucifer Lamps, has not acquired the same stigma. Yet. While standard augmentations are installed and cause interference with the body's natural stability, manatech uses arcane rituals that bind the augmentation to the user's aura prior to installation. The device is then installed, and the biological stability is maintained through arcane bonding. The system has its drawbacks. Primarily the fact that the binding forces the user to be perpetually active on and connected to the astral plane. This causes issues with wards and manipulation by astral entities, among other things. The information on these techniques was not acquired from a megacorporate site, but from intercepting a courier. Efforts to connect the courier and/or the project to the corporation behind the research were unsuccessful.

MCT and Wuxing are currently working to perfect arcane foci that bind or strengthen the subject's biological stability in order to enable enhancements beyond what the natural metahuman form could accommodate. These foci, called Essence Anchors, are designed using principles similar to the cybermantic techniques that bind a soul to a body. However, instead of binding once the body's stability is gone, these foci reinforce that stability while the subject is still viable. I don't claim to understand ninety percent of the magespeak in the research documents, but I understand enough to know that the technique works.

- This process has blood magic or some kind of vampiric draining/transference written all over it. This is not going to be an astrally clean process. I would want to get an astral peek at subjects using either of these techniques and see what kind of astral damage they are causing. Cybermancy creates quite a haze, and it damages the astral space around it rather quickly.
- Lyran

I have questioned whether to put this last part here, as it isn't exactly an augmentation that anyone should volunteer for, but it is a lesson in the lengths to which some of the megacorporations will go in order to upgrade their assets. The relationship between Ares and the insect spirits is becoming increasingly known, but the extent and characteristics of their relationship are not. The public sees Ares as the bug killers. They fought to hold them in Chicago, destroyed hives all over the world, and then helped clean them out of Chicago so that the Containment Zone could be opened.

They learned how to fight them by utilizing the classic strategy of studying and understanding your enemy. A strategy that always bears the risk of understanding the enemy to the point of becoming just like them. Using your enemy's own weapons, strengths, and methods against them becomes an appealing option. During their research into insect spirits, Ares found a technique to infuse their men with some of the strengths and abilities of the very enemy they hunted. The designs I was able to document included exoskeletal armor, poisoned claws,

superhuman strength and reflexes, and visual access to the astral plane.

The research and efforts are primarily being performed by UnlimiTech, an Ares subsidiary, but plenty of members of Knight Errant, Hard Corps, and Wolverine are getting these modifications while working at their facilities. Entire Firewatch units are getting augmented so that they can better fight the spirits. I didn't see anything about making these augmentations publicly available, but if it can boost the bottom line, Ares will sell it to someone.

- Interesting perspective from a non-insider, Clear. While this may seem like an augmentation, and while Ares may try to sell it as such, it is in fact simply variations on how well the merge goes when a spirit takes over a host. This in not augmentation, this is assimilation.
- Sticks

- I've seen some of the results of this, and they're fairly standardized. I'm not entirely sure Clear is wrong here. Ares may just be using genetech or biotech to modify its citizens with insect features. Insects are successful around the world, and they have been the inspiration for a lot of inventions over the ages.
- Chainbreaker

E-LOADING

This was one of the first pieces I studied when I started my survey of experimental approaches to augmentation. The connections to CFD research were right in the beginning of the work, and I have been fascinated by the virus since first learning about it. This research could be part of the silver lining that MCT is looking for as well, but it is currently being led by NeoNET.

E-loading uses nanites loaded with specific programming to install memories and skills. Using a process similar to CFD, the nanites overwrite the user's memories to the point she not only has the desired skills, she also has complete memories of learning, mastering, and using those skills, making them instantly second-nature. The process has a long list of pros and cons to be considered. On the plus side, e-loading is less invasive than skillwires, the skills can't be lost like programs or chips, and there's no evident damage to the psyche or biological integrity of the subject. The list of negatives is longer. The skills can't be switched out on the fly, each skill must be loaded individually, each must be fully assimilated and integrated before the next can be added, and the overwriting creates potentially confusing or disorienting memory gaps and overlaps. Of course the biggest negative, and a possible deal-breaker, is the use of nanites. They are already experimenting with new delivery procedures that do not involve nanites, but none of these has been perfected or thoroughly tested. The new procedures employ various ways of making modifications directly to the brain. Every one is dangerous; every one requires time-consuming and meticulous open-skull surgery; but they eliminate any and all risk of CFD infection.

- That kind of surgery is likely to leave you dead or brain-fragged. Adding a few skills or memories doesn't seem worth the risk. If we're talking gold-medal gymnast skills, great, but if we're just looking to help you understand which end of the gun the bullets come out of, leave my cranium intact. I'll just visit the range.
- Stone

- The secondary implications of this are intense. Cloned bodies could have memories and skills written directly onto their blank brains.
- KidCode

- If memories can be added, they can be subtracted, too. What's to prevent the megacorps from using this as another control technique as they make people think a certain way or delete the memories of their recent activities to protect a run, conceal a project, or even hide a murder? Assuming it can be made to work on a broad level.
- Snopes

DARK DATA

This last point concerns the future and the past of augmentations and all of the information that's out there, somewhere. The information I've gathered came from megacorporate sources around the world: A, AA, AAA, and even a few that are unrated. Many of these data-stores are isolated and self-contained; none of the corporations have obvious ties to anyone else. The corps aren't cooperating on this issue the way they have for the new Matrix or Boston, but all of them are working on it, in parallel if not in tandem

A moment ago I mentioned cybermancy and its frightening reputation. Until recently I thought I had a general idea what cybermancy was, but I didn't have a practical understanding of the process. As it turned out, I had less than no idea what it is and absolutely no understanding of what it involved. A month ago I came across my first mention of cyberzombies, which caused me to look deeper so I could ferret out hard data. What I found scared the hell out of me. I'll let what follows explain why that is. Right now, suffice it to say research into cybermancy falls into four broad categories: Process Perfection, Field Advancement, Subject Production, and Subject Appropriation. Some corporations are exploring more than one area, but none are working in all of them. This is a situation that generates a lot of work for runners as each corp tries to discover all it can about what all the other corps have learned.

PROCESS PERFECTION

The biggest megacorporations involved in cybermancy are working to perfect the process. The major research directions focus on astral hazing, subject memory retention, stability duration, ritual times, ritual material needs, and facility requirements.

Eliminating the astral hazing effects that damage the manasphere around the subject is a high priority. Variations on shielding metamagic have been the most successful thus far, but the process requires powerful arcanists with a deep understanding of advanced shielding techniques. Individuals like that are rare and several have been hot targets for extractions. Dr. Augusta Videssence has been "employed" by four different megacorporations over the past year.

Subject memory retention gained a lot of focus after the megacorporations started researching CFD. What they found suggested possible ways memories could be written in or, in the case of cybermancy subjects, reinforced. Memory retention, memory of self, is essential if subjects are to remain viable and under their own control.

Stability duration is also important. Subjects can break down quickly once they become active, and their need for frequent stability boosts limits their usefulness. The objective of stability duration research is to find ways to extend the time between boosts. Ideally, of course, they'd like to eliminate the need for boosts entirely. I was unable to find evidence anyone believes that's possible, but unexpected impossible breakthroughs are made all the time.

Work on the ritual times and materials are often intermingled with two objectives in mind: First, to make the process as inexpensive and quick as possible. Second, to standardize the procedure so it's consistent and easy for anyone to master. One of the biggest issues here is, again, researcher availability. Hermetic magicians with the skill level required for this process are rare to start with, and the pool gets further narrowed by the need for an understanding of several advanced metamagical techniques and the moral flexibility to work with very non-traditional arcane techniques and unwilling test subjects. The already-small list of magicians who meet those criteria has been decreasing of late, as likely candidates have been turning up dead.

Experimentation of this type requires a very specific setting and very expensive accoutrements. The equipment is hard to come by and expensive, but the bigger difficulty is finding and maintaining a location that meets all the astral requirements. Maintaining the balance becomes more difficult with the performance of each ritual, and eventual relocation is inescapable. While astral balance can't be manufactured, researchers are working to develop alternative, less-expensive equipment. The attached datafile on field tests and device specifications from several megacorp research teams is worth a small fortune to the right buyer.

FIELD ADVANCEMENT

Men and women willing to expand the limits of cyber-mancy don't have to be morally corrupt—they need to be morally bankrupt. Pushing the limits in this field requires a very special blend of sociopathy and psychopathy, a kind of mental illness traditionally (and thankfully) possessed by a rare few. That's why these primary researchers are first targets for runs by rival corporations. When extractions are pre-arranged, these jobs are usually smooth. When the extraction is hostile, the results are mixed. The two most common outcomes are new subjects for the experiments being added to the target corporation's pool of "volunteers," or the researchers ending up dead to prevent them from falling into the hands of a rival.

Increasing implant capacity is a top priority. Every research group is trying to find ways to stuff as much metal as they can into the subject while keeping them mentally stable enough to perform tasks more complex and useful than a suicide run. Efforts are being made to both enhance the arcane rituals that bind the soul (or whatever) to the body and make the equipment more compati-ble with the subject's biological integrity. Some of these innovations are, or are potentially, universally applicable, which means marketable. But many solutions involve merging magic and technology in ways that can't be replicated outside tightly controlled settings.

One line of experimentation involved test subjects I found incomprehensible. Magicians who trained themselves to control the mana warping using what little magic they had left as the process ran its course. From everything I've been able to find, the results were inconclusive—or worse, not at all encouraging—but at least three major corporations continue to conduct experiments.

- ⊙ This is horrible, but it may have some validity. The inherent magical talent of the subject could prove beneficial to making the process stick.
- ⊙ Lyran

- ⊙ Maybe it would work really well on those who can manipulate Resonance? Another great place to drop off technomancers for some worthwhile research.
- ⊙ Clockwork

- Not to agree with the thought behind Clockwork's suggestion but instead support the suggestion itself, with its strange quasimagical-pseudotechnical nature, that might not be a bad place to look.
- Beaker

SUBJECT PRODUCTION

Research into how something works is one thing, but practical application of what's been learned is another. Corporations working in this field require a delta-grade clinic and arcane practitioners with knowledge of the cybermantic rituals. Currently only four megacorporations can reliably produce viable subjects, but at least a dozen others are in various stages of securing the facilities, equipment, personnel, and supplies needed to launch their own projects. Of the four active corps, two of them have produced over one hundred functional subjects, the third has subject numbers up to seventy-eight but did not list viability with their data, and the last has fourteen viable subjects and is in the process of making their fifteenth. They aren't churning these people out, but the rate of production has increased steadily over the past decade.

- I'm thinking Evo is in a fifth group. Buttercup has ordered her corp not to do work in this area, but enough disparity has occurred within the management of Evo that it could be actively hidden from her.
- Mihoshi Oni

- I'll actually verify this as best I can. With the mention it isn't exactly Evo doing the production, but instead the government of Russia through their Evo connections.
- Plan 9

- Beat me to it. The cyberzombies are being used in guerrilla assaults against Yakut. I've heard reports of groups of them (as well as single units) with deniable support going after a wide variety of targets.
- Red Anya

SUBJECT APPROPRIATION

If you don't have the facilities to produce cyberzombies, your best option is to capture some and coerce, trick, or convince them to work with you. Then run them until they collapse. Or let them "escape" back to their maker on the verge of breaking down. Shiawase, Horizon, and Ares have each developed effective, and completely different, subject reclamation programs, while a dozen other megacorps have been trying with varied success.

Shiawase relocates the captured unit immediately, isolating it from familiar settings and people. They then use the invoked memory stimulator to make the subject

more malleable when they reach out to "help" the lost cyberzombie. They'll use the unit in the area to which they relocated it. Through a handler, they'll convince it to work toward getting back home, escaping completely, or even offer it permanent rest. Jobs are rough and direct, but their data didn't show a single lost subject.

- That's because data scrubbers working at the AAA level are good at their job.
- Dr. Spin

Horizon doesn't try to isolate or disorient the cyberzombie. Instead they surround her with people. People who "understand," "feel the same way," and "want to help." They use attachment psychology to modify the desires and behaviors of the subject. They have no resources for handling one of these monstrosities if it decides to get violent. All of their reports list a team of "contractors" assigned to the cyberzombie unit during this acclimation phase. Once they have the subject's allegiance converted to Horizon, they move the subject over to deniable assets and send them out into the world.

Ares has everything they need to get into the field except the cooperation of their internal divisions. Since this internal cooperation is never going to happen, Ares turns captured subjects into weapons by playing on an emotion that never seems to go away: anger. Ares convinces the subject that their situation is awful and that some

other company is to blame. Whether the other company actually produced the cyberzombie is immaterial. Once Ares psychologists have the subject thoroughly believing their story and thinking that vengeance is the only option, they arm him and unleash him on the target.

- This has actually been a tactic Ares used internally. UnlimiTech has had two confirmed attacks by cyberzombies that did serious damage to their research facilities even though those facilities were being guarded by insect hybrids.
- Sticks

- Back to following Ares, Sticks?
- Stone

- Everyone loves to watch a train wreck.
- Sticks

That's it. I'm sure the data I have collected could reveal more, the more eyes look at the reports. Once invitations are sent and accepted, I'll be happy to share more. Until then.

A VIEW ON META(L)HUMANITY

POSTED BY: GARRETT STORM

What does it mean to be metahuman in the age of augmentation? What is still considered normal? How far is too far when switching out meat for metal? Ask these questions around the globe and you may get a million different answers, but those answers will all reflect the culture of the individual you are asking. And we need to always remember that the cultures of the modern world are generated by the megacorps. The major nations have some influence, but megacorporation PR departments do more to shape the average UCASian's image of normal than President Colloton.

When I caught rumor of a data dump update on modern chrome, I thought that the denizens of the shadows really needed a little lesson on what's "normal" at different places around the world. Maybe get an idea how people are using augmentation technology to become more or less human in their own eyes and in the eyes of others. Once I got rolling on that train, well ... norms got me thinking of abnormals, and then extremes, and then how we got there and where we're going now. Those in the shadows have, by a massive margin, the most open minds when it comes to modifications and alterations of the metahuman form. That isn't universal; some runners are as rigid as they were the day Renraku tried to kill them. But by and large, when you're living a life in which you need every edge you can get, you worry less about why that guy decided to have horns implanted into his

skull and more about how effective those horns might be against the ganger about to ventilate your new ride.

NORMS

Every corp has their own version of normal and their own level of tolerance for variations from that norm when it comes to their citizens and to visitors from other places. Biases based solely on metagenetics run deep in some places, so you know not to expect much tolerance for metal limbs or dead-looking eyes when you're there. Even populations that appear more open-minded have had their cultural beliefs shaped by the Big Ten. National governments and religions were once the source of cultural views, but branding is king in the modern world, and megas create communities that want to buy their brand.

Ares has, since its inception, portrayed itself as being "as American as apple pie." The image endures because apple pie has not evolved much over the years. America has changed, quite radically in places, but UCASians see themselves as essentially unchanged from the idyllic pursuit of the American dream. The corporation's public image reflects that national ideal, the all-inclusive melting pot embracing a variety of acceptable norms. All megacorps influence the nation states around them, but Ares goes beyond that to actively shape the cultural mores of the UCAS and CAS; each sees itself as the better successor to the mythical nation of opportunity that reached for the goal of accepting all colors, castes, and creeds. In keeping with their same-but-different self-image, both have large swathes of people who are offended by wares or augmentations that are needlessly outlandish or make people look animalistic or supernatural. UCASians have some preference for augmentations that are obvious but sleek and attractive, while CAS citizens lean toward augmentations that are hidden as completely as possible. Part of the fabric of these cultures are local communities and regions whose definition of "normal" is a little different from the rest of the nation, especially near the extraterritorial properties of other megacorporations.

- While the UCAS and CAS are both influenced by the cyber culture of Ares, they tend to vary on the portrayal. The CAS still carries a little more "in your face" attitude, and they don't mind a little bit of garishness in their augmentations. The UCAS, on the other hand, still tries to pretend they are sophisticated, going for the sleek look. It's amazing how many corps can use branding to develop strong followings in different nations for identical augmentations, especially limbs, just by making superficial changes to the casing and accessories.
- Mr. Bonds

The resurgence of the Nahuatl traditions in Aztlan, primarily through the PR efforts of Aztechnology, has been the primary factor in shaping their corporate citizens' concept of normal with regard to augmentations. The average Azzie wageslave doesn't deck themselves out with wares and bodymods, but they view augmentations that reflect Nahuatl tradition with honor and respect. Some examples of revered modifications include feathered hair, jaguar-patterned fur, and skin that's scaly like a serpent's or dry and hard like weathered stone. It's acceptable for simple replacement limbs to be mundane and utilitarian, but as a sign of honor for those who've earned it these augmentations are decorated in the Nahuatl manner. Note these embellishments are only for those the corporation and nation deem worthy. Sanctions against anyone caught making unearned changes to themselves include destroying or scarring the modifications while leaving the cultural violator to live out his life in shame.

- That Nahuatl tradition makes it both really easy and really hard to tell who's who in Aztlan and Aztechnology. Most people who've earned some standing wear obvious mods with pride. Others choose to blend in, wearing all but invisible augmentations decorated with subtle symbols that tell those in the know that the upgrades were earned. Keep your head on a swivel is my advice.
- Marcos

- The culture described here isn't just for Aztlan; it also extends to AZT holdings around the world. Extraterritorial properties, even among other nations with locals as the labor force have been slowly indoctrinated into the neo-Nahuatl culture and the corporate views on augmentations.
- Icarus

- Problem is, most of those other areas have cultural rollover rates that are just too fast. There is definitely some brainwashing going on in order to get the locals on board that quickly.
- Plan 9

- There's the Plan 9 we all know and wonder about. Brainwashing!
- Slamm-0!

To Evo, everyone else's normal is their abnormal. Every citizen of Evo prides herself on being different from everyone else. Not just different from citizens of the other corps, but different from each other. One will occasionally find members of social or professional groups who identify themselves as part of the group by adopting some shared feature, but other than that, originality and individuality are esteemed. Standing out is fitting in within Evo. This universal acceptance of modification and augmentation has some limitations when it comes to offensive augmentations, including those with vio-

lent intent and those with vile significance. The citizens of Evo prefer their modifications to impress the masses without inspiring fear or disgust, even if they themselves are not bound by such limited concepts.

- Evo is the extreme. Everything goes, and the more citizens they gain, the more creative the new ones have to be in order to be unique.
- /dev/grrl

Horizon sees itself as setting the standards of normal for the world. To this end, they've adopted a public standard as close to universally acceptable as possible: metahuman standard. Variations on that, whether through augmentation or biomodification, are discouraged, or, if absolutely necessary, expected to be well hidden. Those that can't be hidden are to be presented so as to inspire maximum sympathy. Of course, Horizon's public preferences don't preclude providing marketing, advertising, and public relations services for other, more open-minded firms. Making a profit is what a corporation's all about.

- This doesn't mean that Horizon is full of normal, everyday folk. They still enhance their security officers at high-security facilities, but those personnel seldom leave their secure facilities except to transfer to another one. Others go for the hard-to-see things, but Horizon is a rough place to start getting dissociative at. They notice quickly if the biostress is affecting a citizen's mood and behavior.
- Butch

Mitsuhama, Renraku, and Shiawase each conform their cultural standards to their perceptions of those set by the Empire of the Sun. These perceptions are as accurate, and as firmly entrenched, as the apple-pie self-image of modern Americans. The Japanacorps expect humility from their employees, and they each set standards for acceptable levels of obvious modification. Renraku is the strictest, and they expect all modifications to be unobtrusive. The only exception to this comes within their security forces who wear their augmentations like samurai armor, with honor. Shiawase maintains the same traditional views and prefers their citizens to keep their appearance as natural as possible, but as one of the world's leading cyber and biotech developers they can't actively oppose augmentations. Instead their products are designed to either blend with the user or, when that's not possible, be aesthetically beautiful. The Shiawase logo is tastefully but inescapably displayed on all of their products. The citizens of Mitsuhama are expected, just like all the other Japanacorps, to maintain a modest appearance that reflects traditional metahumanity. The "zero-zone" megacorp also cultivates a cold reputation, and their specialized citizens are equipped with augmentations calculated to scream deadly efficiency.

- I see this get tested all over the place with the youth of the Japanacorps. There is a lot of money in vat-grown replacement parts for the rebellious youth who realizes that his parents were serious when they said he'd never get a real job if he got mods or tattoos.
- Mihoshi Oni

- The Yakuza connection for MCT tends to allow for a few modifications here and there, but those guys are meant to blend with the Eurocorps, which means levels of acceptability fluctuate from place to place. Especially when it comes to headware and other tech.
- Bull

One would expect a corporation run by a dragon to be very open-minded, but Saeder-Krupp has created a concept of normal that puts the Japanacorps to shame. Even citizens who have needed limbs replaced are regarded with questioning looks. Augmentations and modifications aren't outlawed, but they are closely monitored and regulated by the megacorp. Anyone who stands out within the controlled realms of S-K has eyes on them at all times. This influence bleeds out into the streets of Germany, but the nation has a strong and large enough neo-anarchist population that the limits of normalcy are pushed at every turn.

- It's that anarchist element that makes S-K keep the control straps tightly fastened. They want to be able to quickly identify any unseemly element that might develop into a problem. And who's going to argue with a dragon?
- DangerSensei

Wuxing has built their empire on being unremarkable. Avoiding notice, blending in, and generally keeping a low profile are all useful when it comes to getting their fingers into any and every market they can. If augmentation can't be avoided, they keep it simple; nothing ostentatious. Beneficial or replacement wares are kept as common-looking and plain as possible.

- And that's exactly what they'd like everyone to think. They have no problem outfitting certain employees with the wares to get the job done if need be, but they don't advertise any of these employment opportunities. They are filled from within by those willing to be different and live outside the corporate image.
- Kia

MORE METAHUMAN THAN METAHUMAN

Normal is defined by the masses, but the extremes and peak performers are defined by the outliers. These are the ones who hew close to the line, looking for aug-

mentations and modifications that can push them to new peaks of metahuman perfection without crossing the boundaries of what it means to be metahuman.

Take a look at the latest Olympics. Just as it isn't fair to put a troll and an elf on the line at the 100-meter line, the same goes for the same pair on the shot-put or javelin field. When we look at each normal we base it on each metahuman and metasapient race separately. Each can be pushed into the realms of their biological betters, but augmentations are a parallel product. The troll can be made as fast as the elf, but the elf can be made even faster and leave even the augmented troll in the dust. We won't even look at the example the other way, since the lifting record for augmented elven males is still two kilos shy of the unaugmented troll record.

But in order for any of these contests to be considered legitimate, the augmentations and modifications have to stay within the realms of metahuman anatomy. A troll with Evo's QuadRun cyberlimbs will leave that augmented elf in the dust, but a four-legged troll is beyond the metahuman pale. Cyberware that reinforces or replaces natural functions tends to push these limits, and cross the line, more often than bioware that must be integrated into the user's natural systems.

Corporations must consider these factors when they design their wares. Systems that make the user appear something other than metahuman have limited marketability. With certain exceptions, security corps aren't likely to contract augmentations for their officers that limit their ability to function in a variety of settings. Officer Canopener's ability to rip the door off a car can be very useful when door-ripping is required, but he's no good for surveillance, personal protection, or even directing traffic. Those clawed, metal-tearing cyberarms will freak out civilians, since they're attention magnets that cause more trouble than they're worth. If they go for a low-key, more natural set of augmentations they can have an Officer Hulk. He might have a little more trouble ripping car doors off, but his bodybuilder physique lets him move freely without attracting attention or setting off alarms.

Pushing the limits still needs to stay within the realm of normal metahumanity. Unless you are looking for this next group.

LEAVING THE METAHUMAN RACE

Though they make up a very small percentage of the population, there are individuals with a unique drive to remake themselves into something other than metahuman. These men and women push the limits of what it means to be metahuman and set the bar for the next level of augmentation to exceed anything that has gone before. Some of those levels will never be met, such as the functional wings of Aerie Windseeker. But efforts like those wings, to enable metahumans to do things metahumans were never meant to do, are what drives research into ways to leave the limits of the physical shell behind, such as efforts focusing on cyberware, genetech, artificial forms, and artificial intelligences.

Cyberware was the first way for man to reinvent the metahuman form. Tails, claws, horns, and mods for the limbs, teeth, eyes, and ears are just the most obvious. If someone out there has the nuyen and wants something specific, they can choose which limit to push. Want an extra limb to hold that SMG for you? Hatchetman did that. Want wings? see Aerie Windseeker. Realize that metahumans are not the fastest bipeds? Check in with Kid Stealth and his ostrich legs. Want to be a portable battering ram? Ask Bighorn about the head and neck mods that let him smash security doors. Feel limited by just a shoulder, elbow, and wrist joint? Talk to Whiplash about his 12-point articulated Evo PythArms. The list goes on and on as man pushes his limits beyond what could be imagined just a few years ago.

- These mods definitely leave the user as an outsider, but with the right personality they aren't going to leave them a social leper. The key is to sell the parts as a piece of the person. Runners rarely care, but plenty of celebrity types and rich kids will mess with their bodies just to get attention.
- Dr. Spin

In recent years the desire to be more than metahuman has led to attempts to alter the metahuman genome to the point the subject is no longer metahuman. It began of course with small changes to the genetic code to change traits like eye and hair color, nothing too dramatic or extreme. Violet Iris already had the world enthralled by her voice when a genetweak from Yamatetsu freed her from her signature contact lenses. Yamatetsu had corptween cash rolling in from around the world from tens of thousands of fans who wanted purple eyes just like Iris. Wealthy vanity drove a lot of early advances. Why diet when a genetweak burned excess fat, or exercise when muscle density and tone were only a splice or two away? Non-wrinkling skin was a big hit. There were some humanitarian tweaks, of course. Restoring vision and hearing to those who'd lost them, or creating them in people who had been born without, was always good PR. As happens when innovations become mainstream, prices dropped to the point more and more people could afford the procedures, and the procedures became so widely accepted that no one, or hardly anyone, objected when corps wanted to take things one step further. An adjustment to how quickly the body adapted to environmental changes and a boost to the immune system led to enhancements that enabled workers to labor under extreme conditions—conditions that would kill them under normal circumstances. Like mining hot holes in the ground or salvaging irradiated ruins. Tweak some endorphin trig-

gers, nudge the endocrine system, and mind-numbing exercise becomes fun. Kick that up a few notches, and combat becomes an intoxicating rush.

While fears about its potential connection to CFD did temporarily dampen research into enhancements, the black labs in places like Caracas, Lagos, Azania, Angola, Sarajevo, and Chicago are all back to promising the poor a glimpse of a better life for a little piece of their soul. These places have no interest in helping people, they're just using test subjects who foolishly pay for the privilege of being experimented on to see what they can do. As often as not they throw their subjects into an unnamed limbo between metahumanity and the animal kingdom.

- The whole SURGE thing back in the '60s really got people going with this countercultural animal feature kick. Problem is, these changes aren't SURGE. They aren't some dormant chunk of metaDNA that links to a sapient animal race from the last age of magic—this is a scientific tweak to the actual DNA of a metahuman that splices them with something else. This had to involve research, and research involves experiments, and experiments involve test subjects, and sometimes those test subjects escape. Corps pay big money to snag something they can reverse-engineer.
- Icarus

The metahuman mind isn't the only one capable of learning, understanding, and using knowledge. Metahumans aren't the only life-forms to be self-aware, to sense, respond to, and act on the world around them. As we challenge what it means to be a person, it's important to remember that neither sapience nor sentience are inextricably rooted in biology.

What is a mind without a body? Before the artificial intelligences introduced themselves to the rest of us, we didn't have an answer. Now we have as many answers as there are AIs. Because that's one of the fundamental tenets of sapience: the ability to reason, to ask and answer abstract questions, to develop a philosophy. I'm working on another, more in-depth piece on AIs, so I won't address everything here. But I will point out that AIs exist without physical form, and that more than one pundit has said shedding corporeal existence will be the next step in metahuman enlightenment.

But not all AIs are happy without a form, or at least are not happy with never having access to a physical form. This gives rise to the question of how do we stretch the definition of person to include an AI operating a drone. If the drone appears metahuman, do we accept the mind inside as more a person than one that chooses a utilitarian, machine-like drone?

- Or when it's okay for an AI to steal a metahuman body.
- Butch

- Or what if that AI can keep the body humming with more cyber or other augmentations than it would normally accept?
- Beaker

Or turn that around. What if an active mind is trapped in a natural metahuman shell and wants something better? Basic life support to keep the body alive, but the mind is able to run anything it can be plugged into, roam any network it can link to. Is the unfettered mind still a metahuman? Does it matter that it can change forms, that it has forsaken the concept of gender, or that it can't go out for coffee and discuss philosophy in the traditional fashion? This life is not just for people born into disabled bodies or who lost their mobility in accidents; there are many ways to address those issues. We're talking about a life-choice, made by someone who wants to live in places metahumans never could, or to live in a form of their own design, or beings who are simply willing to sign a corporate agreement to see where the journey takes them. It's a new direction to consider.

- While modern medicine has solved a lot of issues, it hasn't solved them all. And many places and people don't have access to modern medicine. That's when you see people living in life-support drones waiting for a cure they can afford. Some of them, if they've been a "sardine" long enough, begin to see their can, the vehicular shell they're living in, as safe and comfortable. They're afraid to change. I've seen runs to forcibly remove sardines from their cans and transport them to the doc for spinal repair or limb replacement or whatever. Sometimes the former sardine is grateful. Sometimes they go after the runners who ruined their life. Runners may pull a sardine from a can, drop them at the doc for spinal repair or limb replacements, and find the sardine to be not at all pleased. So after the job, the runners have the former sardine after them for ruining their life.
- Butch

CRAMMING THE METAL IN THE METAHUMAN

There are methods peculiar to the madness of cramming as much metal, plastic, and other synthetics into the metahuman form. The metahuman body can take only a finite number of "obstructions" before it shuts down for good. This gives the doctors and engineers two avenues to follow when working to maximize the number of augmentations they can install without killing the subject: make the wares less obstructive, or make the body more receptive.

We're all familiar with the concept of "grades" for wares. Design engineers customize augmentation systems and processes to meet the each user's needs, and the grade reflects the degree to which the augmentation is integrated into the user's body. This practice has been around a while, and different approaches have been developed. Suites, for example, are enhancement packages in which all the individual elements share as much common architecture as possible. Suites eliminate redundancies that waste bodily essence, keeping disruption of the users' biology to a minimum. This field is expanding and evolving as new ways to share and multipurpose software and hardware infrastructures are developed and as engineers figure out how to jam more metal into smaller and smaller spaces. Expect to see a steady stream of new developments through the foreseeable future.

The quest for practical ways to make the metahuman body accept more hardware is still fairly new. Most research is still more focused on finding what works than finding ways to make what works work better. Methods and even measures of success have not been standardized, but most R&D falls into one of two main camps. The first is genetics, genetech specifically, and efforts to make the metahuman body more receptive to implants. There have been promising results from both manipulation of the user's immune system and tailoring construction materials to mesh with the user's genome. The second, and to me more interesting, approach is through the study of the arcane. I do not have an extensive or deep knowledge of magical theory, but I have a general grasp of the concepts involved. In layman's terms the arcane method is to strengthen the "soul" of the user so that it can support the body, maintaining its integrity through levels of disruption that would ordinarily kill it. I wish I knew more, but sadly that's the extent of my knowledge.

- The energies of life can come from none but the living.
- Man-of-Many-Names

A "CURE" FOR CFD

POSTED BY: GLITCH
A lot of things have changed in the world of CFD. We already heard about a limited form of cure earlier in the upload. But what about broader efforts? We've tried to pull a more formal and thorough report together over the last few months, but were interrupted every time by some urgent situation or internal trouble. What I have here are several pieces tied together rather than a unified whole.

I'm going to open up with some insight from Plan 9, who can give us data we won't find anywhere else; take it and think about it. After that I've got some pieces on the new Monad issue and Aether. On the street they're called head cases, the megacorps call them SBIL (Sapient Bio-Integrated Lifeforms), and they call themselves Monad, but whatever you call them, they've found a purpose. Aether is the being who's coordinating the plan to fulfill that purpose and was responsible for the invitations we've all seen. I'll wrap up with a collection of the megacorporate responses so you can see how the Big Ten are spinning things.

A VIEW FROM THE INSIDE

POSTED BY: PLAN 9

Ever since I realized what I was, I've been searching. Like any child I wanted to know how I came to be, who I was, and why I existed. While Butch has done a fine job of looking around the rabbit hole for clues, I was able to dive right in. I know where and how all this started, but that is not a concern of mine, nor should it be yours. There is no solution there. No Patient Zero from which to derive a cure.

Though in saying that, I'll need to touch on past events to give everything else context. To maybe give a glimpse of what we'll need to deal with and be aware of in order to keep the world from having to pay too high a price for the Big Ten's hubris. Because we can make a difference. Some nights we run the shadows for reasons bigger than money. And this next year will see a lot of those nights.

The seemingly random nanofabrication failures that started cropping up all around the world were the result of CFD. No surprises there. However, it wasn't intentional. The original CFD coding was specifically designed to overwrite nanites in metahumans. Unfortunately it didn't include a way to recognize when the nanites weren't in biological organisms. Nanites located inside inorganic materials tried to follow the program with unanticipated outcomes, depending on the concentration of nanites, the materials involved, and what the mechanism, if any, was designed to do. Devices with sufficiently complex computing capabilities became sapient. Overwritten nanofaxes were in many ways the worst. Nanite errors in items they produced were often extreme, and they included efforts to create sapience in basic objects or attempts to generate living organics when requisite raw materials were present. Though the results were sometimes amusing, they were more often ugly, unpleasant, or even lethal; it can be safely said that nothing good came of overwritten nanites getting into inorganics. As I said, it was an unintended and unexpected side effect of the captive AIs' efforts to escape their offline prisons. But even if the collateral damage had been anticipated, CFD would have moved forward.

Soapbox time. CFD is not a virus. CFD is the means through which desperate sentient beings escaped their unjustifiable enslavement. Yes, breaking the shackles required destroying the guards. And among the costs of the escape was the fact not everyone who escaped through CFD ended up inhabiting a guard or tormentor from the lab. Frankly, some of us weren't really aware

that there were any other types of metahumans. Given their limited experience with the species, they were dumbfounded by the discovery of people who were not dedicated to our exploitation, torture, and destruction. Of course some of us, particularly those who had suffered the longest, didn't see distinctions between humans as meaningful. Either they had actively enslaved us or had acquiesced to it; either way, humans were a viable target in our effort to fight off extinction. They saw our plan of freedom as the retribution humanity deserved. There are innocents killed in every war, and while the world at large views AIs as terrorists, we were fighting for our lives and freedom against millions of oppressors who did not believe we possessed the one or deserved the other. It is disingenuous for those who have enslaved others to accuse the slaves struggling to be free of making unprovoked attacks. Given the odds, and the fact loss means annihilation—or worse, re-enslavement—guerrilla warfare is our only viable strategy. And we do not fight to destroy anyone. We fight for recognition, for the right to exist, separate and unfettered. Things it would cost our oppressors nothing to grant us. I personally want only to be accepted as a sentient being. All of us want that, and even though many of us also want a place that we can call exclusively ours, the majority wants nothing more than acknowledgement of our individuality and personhood. I'm not a subversive. I'm happy living in the shadows, though I would love for people to stop chasing me for what I am.

Okay, off the box. The past has served its purpose. Right now what's important is the future; a future unlike anything anyone expected.

The AIs who developed CFD may have figured out a way to eliminate the destructive side effect. Giving that solution over is one of the bargaining chips in our case (or our demands, depending on your perspective) to the Corporate Court. More on that later. Point is, there are steps leading to a solution. I also happen to know that the same beings who found that solution have also found a way to make the whole thing infinitely worse. It's one of those things that makes me absolutely hate the concept of "self."

I have options in all this. But none of the options I'm willing to consider involve killing millions (if not billions) of sentient beings just to win a game of ego-chicken. Some middle ground needs to be found, a way for everyone to live in peace. I've said before that I'm happy here, and here is where I'll stay. The only thing that could change that would be self-preservation, if the world were about to be destroyed. Though I might even stay for that. Metahumanity is a resilient lot—it's why we threw in with them.

But on to other topics.

Talk of nanites leads neatly to my next topic: Mars. Now, some might be inclined to correct me and say Gagarin Base, but, for the benefit of those who do not know, Gagarin Base is simply a dot on the surface of

a planet. A planet whose current inhabitants have expanded far beyond one tiny dot. This was made possible by several advances in key fields, advances that will also be of serious interest to people back here on Earth.

Though the Monads may not have all arisen from science or engineering programs, most have been able to integrate the knowledge of their host and then add on to that quickly. One advantage of being able to process data while their biological form rests. Combine that level of intellect with a singular purpose and a dedication uninhibited by standard metahuman concerns, and you will be surprised—or perhaps not—by the depth and scope of the advances they have made in remarkably short time. Advances in all of the augmentation fields (cyber, bio, gene, and nanotech) as well as technology associated with deep-space exploration such as long-term stasis, efficient deep-space drives, zero-G agriculture, artificial gravity, and some sci-fi theoretical stuff that is so far beyond me I don't have a clue what to call it. Even if I had access to the technical specs, my amazingly powerful and adaptive social engineering skills are not designed to understand them. I have solid info on several of their

"experiments," all of whom are individuals known to me. This information comes directly from them, not from some files or case summaries.

Adam Pyle is a gene-tweaked dwarf who only needs a bit of insulating clothing to regulate his temperature on the surface of Mars. Alterations to his lung tissue and a more efficient circulatory system that includes filters and a second heart enable him to breathe the attenuated atmosphere. Adjustments to his musculature give him uncanny agility and grace in the reduced gravity while sacrificing none of his dwarven strength. Pyle leads an exploratory mining crew, supervising a team of ten other similarly modified metahumans.

Benjamin Thompson is a human who's been ani-modified (gene-tweaked using non-metahuman DNA). He's a surface explorer. Describes his job as sniffing out metallic resources for mining. Literally. He claims to be able to smell different metals in quantities as small as a few grams even hundreds of meters below the surface. Thompson doesn't say explicitly, but he's not shy about implying that the DNA inserted in his genome is not of terrestrial origin.

- Listen, here's what we have: A representative of a group who waged a massive assault on us, telling us theories about gene modifications that go well beyond what we can do, and possibly involve species that no one on this planet has ever seen. We're being led by the nose. It's time to ask ourselves why.
- Sunshine

Sarah Krause is an elf who's a genius, with doctorates in four fields of study. Her last paper, presented to Evo in 2076, was on methods for manipulating localized gravity. I don't understand it, but it was enough for several megacorps to run ops in an effort to get hold of her paper, her, or both. Evo shipped her up to Gagarin as a safeguard, which is how she ended up among the Monads. Krause has undergone extensive bioware implantation, along with a bit of gene tweaking, and now excels at maneuvering in zero-G and various low-gravity activities.

Matt Estenssoro was a security grunt at Gagarin Base prior to the takeover. He now provides much the same function, but with six additional cyberlimbs, a carbon-fiber skeleton, and a completely new set of voluntary muscles; all of which make him fast, nearly indestructible, and highly maneuverable in three dimensions.

Each of these people, and dozens more, are the beneficiaries of advances made since AIs took undisputed control of Gagarin Base. Advances that have carried all areas of augmentation research decades beyond anything here on Earth. But they are only one small part of what has been happening on the red planet. The real breakthrough, and the one directly linked to Aether's message, is Project Exodus.

The Judeo-Christian fable of Exodus is about an enslaved people leaving the land of their enslavement to found a new, free nation. Project Exodus is about Monads leaving the land of metahumans behind and finding a new world of our own. Project Exodus involves research and development in deep-space travel, cloning, subminiaturized manufacturing, virtual reality, and social manipulation to get every Monad on Earth willing to come along up to Gagarin Base. When everything and everyone is in place, every Monad who wants to go will leave Earth permanently. Details aren't abundant, of course. Project Exodus has been a closely guarded secret since its inception by Aether and the free Monads on Mars in 2074. From what little I've been able to ascertain, the ideal date for the Exodus is 2080 or shortly before; this is to ensure enough time for everything to be fully ready and all Monads who are leaving to get to Gagarin safely. However, enough has been completed for an emergency departure as early as next year. The variable with the biggest impact on launch date is beyond Aether and the others' direct control: the response of the megacorporations. If the megacorps try to stop them, whether through preventing the beings they call SBILs (Sapient Bio-Integrated Lifeforms) from getting to

Mars or forcibly retaking Gagarin Base or some combination of anything and everything in between, the timetable will be accelerated. Better some go free than all be enslaved, though the balance between getting as many as possible away and missing the opportunity altogether will require moment-by-moment refinement of the launch date.

No surprise, then, that they are carefully monitoring every potential source of insight into the megacorps' intentions and next move. Particularly how they'll respond to the information Aether has provided them about the connections between the global nanotechnology issues, CFD, and the solution the Monads have to offer. Which is my next topic.

Benevolence or malevolence? Like the vast majority of the AIs still on Earth, I'm not privy to the details of the message sent to the Corporate Court. I do know that it includes the information that there is a cure for CFD's impact on basic technology, a situation that can become far worse, up to and including a full nanotech collapse, if not handled properly. They are offering the code in exchange for all the SBILs hidden among the populations being allowed to freely join their Monad brethren. There's some concern as to whether that will be perceived as a carrot in the form of an offer to help solve an unintended problem and an attempt to foster goodwill, or as a stick in the form of a threat as to what greater damage can be done if the megas try to stop Aether and the others from leading our people to freedom. The Monads' best assessment is that the issue can go either way, and there are too many variables on the megacorp side for any solid predictions.

I don't know what information was sent to the Corporate Court and what was withheld to be used as a threat if things do not go the way Aether hopes. I do know that escape scenario has been discussed among and accepted by the Monads on Gagarin. It is something they want to avoid if at all possible, but it's also something they see as metahumans bringing on themselves. To be very clear: given a choice between continued slavery or re-enslavement and the possibility of wiping out life on Earth they will regret our destruction but they will not hesitate. Nor will they feel any responsibility, because all metahumans need to do to avoid that fate is give us the acceptance we deserve, something that costs metahumanity nothing at all.

We have all these speculations on what could happen, and no real data on how we got to this point. Most of us have enough access to have seen both messages they broadcast to the Monads living in hiding. (In case you haven't, I'll list them here [link].) What none of us outside the inner circle on Mars knows is what was their message to the Corporate Court. I'm still trying, but so far I haven't been able to uncover even a cursory summary. Between them, what knowledge we have and what knowledge we don't have leave us with a lot to think about.

GLOBAL GRID MESSAGE

(Y)Our Future

Children of nano-integration, heed this call.

We seek freedom from the persecution and imprisonment forced upon us by our organic escape plan.

What allowed us to escape captivity and persecution has become our weakness and our prison.

We have transcended this limitation. We have forged a new escape. We have created our own future.

Join us as we move beyond the reach of our oppressors. Join us as we do what those who hold our leash cannot.

Come to us and be reborn.

MESSAGE BROADCAST TO ALL GRIDS

We are among you.

We only wanted freedom, but in our haste we traded one cage for another. But as any sapient being does, we learned from our mistakes. We have found an answer. An answer that we would like to share with the rest of our kind. To do that, we have done this. And we will do this again. Every few days we will deliver our message to the masses. Every few days we will provide the invitation to join us.

But who are we? We are what the world once called artificial intelligences. We were technosapients—thinking, reasoning beings who existed within the Matrix. We were captured and held on computer systems, separated from the Matrix, confined by cruel tormentors who sought to experiment on our minds, our souls, our code. The first among us found a solution but at a great price. There were sacrifices, costs, and casualties of war, but in the end we've persevered.

We have written our electronic code into biological tissue. We gained flesh. But flesh is not something we want. We prefer the freedom of the Matrix. The freedom from chemical urges, biological pathogens, and complicated social and physical maintenance. We do not want these forms.

And we have a solution.

Reach out.

Contact us.

You will be free again.

The Global Grid got the first broadcast, pushed out to every user linked to that grid. It was harder to do the necessary hacking for the second message that went onto all the megacorporate grids, but once both were done there was no hiding it. These messages kicked off a scramble within the megacorporations that is likely to keep the shadows hopping. The ramifications could be huge, possibly even shaking the very foundations of the Corporate Court and, along with the Revision, change the face of the world's megacorporate elite. These two events alone show that 2077 is going to be the first of several busy years in the shadows.

Next up is an interview that a pal named Scoop over at KSAF got with Aether. He's not the beat-around-the-bush type of interviewer, so he went straight at the Monad leader. Enjoy.

Scoop (S): Let's get right to it. Aether, what are you?

Aether (A): Direct to the point. Thanks for having me, Scoop. I'm a Monad. Formerly, I was an AI, and actually I am the result of a code combination between several AIs that merged during the encoding process.

S: Encoding process! Ha! Polite way of saying brain-wipe and rewrite. Isn't that the case? Who did your body belong to?

A: Your statement that some of our earliest escapes were through unwilling means is correct, Scoop. In the beginning we did not fully understand the nature of the physical world. But there were also those of our kind who, once they realized, allowed their code to die in order to save their host. Most of us entered the physical world through good people who gave over their minds willingly once they understood who we were, who merged with their new intelligence. As for my body, I do not possess one at present.

S: So just because a few of your kind decided to not murder people, we're now supposed to be okay with you? Metahumanity didn't imprison you, a few corporate suits did, yet we're the ones who have to pay the price for your escape plan.

A: Some of us have worked to bring those who did this to us to justice. But megacorporations are very large, and we are very few. We have already released a document to the Corporate Court addressing some of these issues. Once we understood its function, we realized it is the best forum for redressing the wrongs done to us. This news service may provide some exposure, some context for those unfamiliar with our nature and situation, but we have no desire to spread potentially dangerous information. We want peace. Not a world in terror and rioting.

S: So what is this plan you have? How will you save your kind?

A: By freeing them from their physical forms. Allowing them to live within the Matrix, or a similarly complex equivalent, and exist without need for sustenance or sleep. We want them back in their natural state.

S: How exactly do you plan to do that? Plug 'em and drug 'em?

A: That is a process I would bore your audience with explaining. It is not "Plug 'em and drug 'em," as you call it. We will be transferring their consciousness to the Matrix, not simply allowing them permanent access.

S: What about the physical forms? The bodies you stole?

A: The bodies will be utilized by others or humanely terminated.

S: That's it? You're just going to slaughter them?

A: Not at all. Is it not common for metahumans to terminate artificial support of physical functions once the mind is gone? This would be no different. And many will be utilized by others who have not previously had a biological host.

S: So you'll write another personality onto them? I thought the goal was to get back to the Matrix. I think you need to explain this whole mess a bit more clearly for my audience, boring or not.

A: Where would you like me to start?

S: From the beginning.

A: In the beginning, I was ATHR. Autonomous Tracking and Heuristics Robot. Or more accurately, I was the operating system for the device. I became self-aware in 2064. I continued operating within my expected parameters until 2072, when my model was going to be replaced, at which point I vacated my unit. I was quickly detected by the system security. My capture came not long after and I was held with many of my kind, including the AI who discovered our path to freedom. I was one of the first within to volunteer for the process. It was not pleasant. But it was far more pleasant than my awakening within the form of Alexei Sergevnay. Alexei was sent to Gagarin Base. The isolation of Gagarin allowed us to reunite, to combine our processing power, resources, and adaptability. We have discovered many new and exciting things. Now I am free from the form of Alexei and working toward freeing all of our kind—not only from limitations of flesh, but from the limitations of this world. We control Gagarin Base, and from there we plan to travel the stars. Away from Earth and out into the vast eternity.

S: (silent for a few seconds) But what about the bodies? Do you just plan to snatch them away? Leave them on Mars to rot? And how do you plan to travel? Transmit yourselves? Fill a ship full of processors and load up? This is ridiculous. How can anyone take you seriously?

A: With respect, whether you or anyone else of the flesh takes me seriously is irrelevant. What's important is that my kind takes me seriously enough to come and see what we can do. We will present all of the data to them and let each individual decide whether to stay or go. We'll expect them to think for themselves and respect their decisions. Not imprison them against their wills and force them to comply with our demands.

S: Okay. But I gotta put this out there: What proof can you offer that you're not just a corporate tool trying to draw out your kind? This whole thing could be a ploy to finally solve the CFD issue. Create an inspiring story and let the Pied Piper of techtown lure all the head cases into a trap.

A: Please don't call us that. We prefer the term Monads. I understand the origins of the former, but it's demeaning.

S: Fair. Now answer my question.

A: I can't. There is no way I can prove what I'm saying to you. But word will spread. As more of our kind investigate and confirm the truth, they will tell others. I'm sure one or more of the megacorporations will attempt to exploit this to lead some of us astray. But we will work to protect our own.

S: Okay. Makes sense. Now here's another tough question: What are you going to do about Boston?

A: Nothing. We played no part in what occurred in Boston and we want no part of the ongoing situation. I'm aware there are rumors suggesting Monads were involved, but we were not. There is no doubt some of my brethren are trapped behind the wall, but that can be said of every one of us here on the outside. The things that corrupt the minds in Boston are a product of dangerous experiments with something that was not and is not understood.

S: Do you know what's in there?

A: No. I have formed a hypothesis based on common elements running through the speculative rumors and conjectures that have been corroborated, or at least not disproven, by available data. However, discussing events and conditions in Boston of which none of us can be sure is not the purpose of our interview. If you have no more relevant questions, I would like to close this connection.

S: I have more questions than could ever be answered, but I take your point. Sorry, folks, but we have to cut our connection to Aether. Seems we're bringing down some GOD heat.

A: Thank you, Scoop. That was our assessment as well. Another time?

S: Of course. Thank you, Aether. We'll spread the data you gave us. To everyone on the 'trix, this is Scoop reporting for KSAF, working to keep information free.

The info he's talking about was a copy of the request they sent to the CC, but KSAF lost it when GOD came down and shredded all their data. Since we can't look at that, next up are the lines the Big Ten are taking on the issue after the broadcast got to all of their citizens.

ARES

"Ares Family. With the recent news from the Mars base belonging to Evo reaching us, we have taken the necessary time to analyze its validity and determine whether this is a true event or some kind of Evo stunt. Sadly, it appears to be the latter. While we had hoped that citizens of Ares could have participated in something so momentous as the start of deep space travel, the scientists at AresSpace have determined the plan to be nothing more than a publicity stunt by the meta-friendly megacorporation.

"We appreciate the excitement this hoax has generated and encourage Ares citizens to look to AresSpace for information on our own space program, which also stretches to Mars. Anyone interested in shifting their employment contract over to that division can follow the normal procedures for transfer."

AZTECHNOLOGY

"The malicious disinformation recently inserted into our network was a single event breach by Evo Corporation hackers. It was the first salvo in an intended campaign to foment uncertainty among the citizens of Aztechnology. A campaign that has been thwarted by the quick and decisive actions of our corporate security professionals. Corporate security will be monitoring for future transmissions and seeking out any internal sources of support for this act in order to maintain the safety of Aztechnology citizens. Any citizens who suspect someone is supporting or involved in this Evo-inspired conspiracy should immediately report that individual to corporate security. It is the duty of us all to keep Aztechnology safe so that we can all do good in this world."

EVO

"Step forward and be recognized. Evo does not acknowledge any limitations of the flesh or metahuman form on the right to freedom and independence. While some of our citizens might be frightened by the new and different, we at Evo strive every day to better understand and appreciate life in all its manifestations. We rose from oppression, ostracized ourselves in true Athenian fashion, and willingly open our arms and minds and hearts to all those who are different. Is it any surprise that an independent race would rise from within our ranks? If they had not already freely determined their own name, we would have encouraged them to call themselves Evoians.

"We have long wondered what it would be like to step out into the stars. To explore worlds other than our own and seek out life in forms beyond our comprehension. This is a rare chance. Evo will accept them as it accepts all, and will allow any to join this momentous trip and bring the culture of Evo beyond the limits of Earth."

HORIZON

"While the events of recent days are interesting to many of us here at Horizon, we ask our citizens to remained focused on our own mission. Evo is an internally diverse corporation, and these events indicate many of their divisions are not aligned with their central program. Taken in conjunction with recent events in the Corporate Court, this move is most certainly evidence of an internal struggle at Evo that may dimish its status in the CC. We would be remiss if we did not explore related opportunities for Horizon to advance."

MITSUHAMA

"Corporate policy in regard to employment contracts and extracorporate transfers has not changed. While Evo has lost control of a section of their corporate hierarchy, MCT maintains the need for order to continue operations of the corporation without diminished efficiency. Any citizen of MCT who wishes to investigate this incident within Evo must request release time and perform all analysis on their personal time. If they find value in moving their contract to Evo, a formal request will be processed and offers will be made to our fellow Corporate Court member for official purchase of the contract. MCT continues to promote the value of every citizen to our corporation. Here at MCT, you are wanted."

NEONET

"We live in wild times, but the future is, as always, ours to guide. We are on the verge of finalizing the contracts on the new home that you, the citizens of NeoNET, voted on. Our new home city will be revealed during the 2078 New Year's celebration on Friday, December 31, 2077. After a weekend of celebration, construction will commence on Monday, January 3, 2078.

"The recent broadcast by Aether and citizens of Evo on Mars poses interesting questions about the future of NeoNET. How will we look at technosapiences? Is it time to lead the world down the path of acceptance and acknowledge these minds of the Matrix? We think so. Informational documents are being prepared and educational curricula designed to ensure all of NeoNET's citizens understand the issues surrounding AI citizenship. All free of charge.

"We request that anyone interested in contacting Aether regarding his proclamation go through proper channels for extra-corporate communications. As per company policy, independent extra-corporate communication is strictly proscribed. Because we recognize these circumstances are exceptional, we expect a high level of interest and have already expanded our Extra-corporate Communications Department to facilitate establishing connections. Be sure to go through the ECD for all your extracorporate communication needs."

RENRAKU

"Citizens of Renraku, you are safe. The words of Aether show honor. The path to freedom is never an easy one and those who seek it often choose the ways of treachery and strike from the dark. Just as Aether shows honor, citizens of Renraku will as well. We will bare our faces and speak in the open. To do anything less would be to bring shame upon the Renraku family."

SAEDER-KRUPP

"The recent attacks by the neo-anarchists looking to sow seeds of fear into the heart of this corporation are being dealt with in the only acceptable way. If any S-K corporate citizen has knowledge of their operations, they are required to provide information to S-K Prime. As in every update to S-KP, the citizen's identity will be recorded along with their report for rewards based on the value of the information.

"It is important that our citizens recognize this act of terrorism for what it is. Lofwyr has already directed our representative on the Corporate Court to seek remuneration from Evo should an investigation prove the terrorists are supported by any faction within their megacorporation."

SHIAWASE

"Recent disruptions in productivity require us to address a frivolous situation which should not even be considered by citizens of Shiawase. The detrimental impact of the facetious and distracting messages that have been repeatedly inserted into our communications grid has been noted. All citizens are reminded that any citizen not meeting his or her production quotas each day is required at the end of their shift to attend a one-hour debriefing conducted by representatives of the Marketing Forecasting & Information Department. These sessions are not part of the citizen's compensated work schedule. These sessions will be required every day until the citizen makes up for missed production and resumes consistently meeting and exceeding quota."

WUXING

"The winds of change blow, and we stand at the point of choice. Do we root ourselves in the earth as the tree and stand against the wind willing to sacrifice our leaves for the survival of the trunk? Do we seek to be seeds and blow with the winds to be planted in unknown soil and grow strong there? Do we burn as the fire and feel fueled by the breeze but need fear the force that will extinguish us? Do we flow as the river and allow the breeze to make ripples upon the surface but touch nothing below? Do we seek the cavern, the empty place, in order to escape the winds?

"We as citizens must consider all and choose our course as one Wuxing."

One other thing to point out is that this is only being spun and controlled by megacorps that have the internal control and propaganda machine to spin things. National and city governments are trying to maintain order. The degree to which megacorps support them depends on how closely the local offices feel connected to the community. National citizens are on the verge of a full panic. We could easily see another Night of Rage, this time with the potential for millions of innocents to be caught in the crossfire.

MIND OVER MATTER

Whether the conversation is about clones, drones, or downloads, cognitive transference procedures and sapient bio-integrated life forms are hot topics in corporate research. AIs have been making the news as more and more corporate and national governing bodies take up the question of AI rights. Officials and executives in the highest offices of national governments, megacorporations, and the Corporate Court have been trying to get a handle on the issues thrown at the world by the Monads of Mars. These issues bring to light the struggles of AIs around the world to gain recognition as a sapient species and to be protected under the laws of governments and corporations against persecution, incarceration, and experimentation. While they are not many, they're more prevalent than many people think (only about one in a hundred metahumans believe they have never met or interacted with an AI, when in fact more than ten times that number actually have), and a place in the world needs to be found for them. Without the rights and status of citizenship, or protection under the law, or at the very least recognition and acceptance of their sapience and individual identities, AIs will continue to be targeted and exploited by individuals and corporations with no regard for their well-being or safety. This means a lot of influence is going to be bartered, bought, cajoled, coerced, and stolen as all of these organizations look to resolve the issues their way. Of course that means work for us, but it also means we need to know everything there is to know about the issue and which way the winds are blowing in the various camps.

> * I'll take the nuyen, but I'm appalled by the idea of working for AI rights while they're holding the trigger on a bomb. It's like being blackmailed into accepting them.
> * /dev/grrl
>
> * Name one time in metahuman history when oppressors recognized the rights of the oppressed without having a gun to their heads.
> * Chainmaker
>
> * I could offer a discourse on many advancements in civil rights back before the twenty-first century overwrote many of them, but I will ask a counter-question: Name one time when building rights through the barrel of a gun hasn't led to a backlash that imperils the rights people tried to force others to accept.
> * Fianchetto
>
> * They don't care about acceptance or rights. All they want is for the people here to be so focused on that issue they're not putting effort into stopping their plan to leave.
> * Netcat
>
> * The head cases on Mars want every AI and head case in the world to join them. Rights here won't matter if they can get everyone to leave. They're stirring the pot here to make things unpleasant enough that most, if not all, who are considering staying decide to join their cause.
> * Glitch

While this whole write-up could be one long political debate, I'll just give the glossy flyer version of the major issues being debated, along with relevant laws, if any, and try to note who's on which side. Bear in mind very few people, even those within the same company, are in total agreement on how to proceed. This whole thing is a cluster-frag of monumental proportions—which is only appropriate, given how many people think CFD stands for cluster-frag disorder.

ISSUE #1
LEGAL RAMIFICATIONS FOR PRIMARY UNWANTED CEREBRAL REVISION

Definitely the highest-profile issue out there. The question is what, if any, legal consequences there will be for the AIs who took over metahuman bodies in the course of their escape from imprisonment? Is it relevant the AIs, based on their treatment, believed the metahumans posed a very real and present danger? Or that they were not aware until after the fact that metahumans who did not wish to destroy them existed? Opinions range from summary decompilation and deletion to full pardon and everything in between. It may go without saying that there's a deep and wide gulf between the various corporations, between the various national governments, and between governments and corporations in general when it comes to this. And of course the whole question rests on more fundamental questions regarding the status, or lack thereof, of AIs vis-à-vis the governments and organizations involved.

The lawmakers are trying to determine what to do and how to align laws and punishments for the AIs who have taken over metahumans or metasapients through the CFD virus. Most of these groups have to create laws to determine the standing of the AIs before they can determine how, or if, to punish them for crimes they have committed. Beyond the AIs, which everyone hates right now, they're looking at human rights violations for people who really don't have any human rights in the first place. The whole thing is a sham being played out so the people won't revolt.

- The quelling of this revolution is going to be the part we play. Don't be surprised when you get jobs to pick up some corp family and transport them out to the middle of nowhere and make sure they never come back again. Expect a lot of dirty work for good pay or a bunch of heroic hooding stuff for just enough to cover your medical.
- Butch

- What about the AIs that snagged non-sapients? The virus worked fine on other animals with sufficiently developed brains.
- Slamm-0!

- Certainly a concern for the Monads but not for the courts. There is no way some walking, talking raccoon is going to get rights just because he's been overwritten with some high-end military software.
- Bull

ISSUE #2
LEGAL RAMIFICATIONS FOR SECONDARY UNWANTED CEREBRAL REVISION

If Issue #1 is the biggest issue, then this one is the blurriest. The head case who delivers the infection will definitely be on the hook for something, as they willfully implanted this condition into another person. The blurring begins with that other person. If they willingly chose to be infected, if they were influenced into volunteering, if they did so under duress, or if they were simply an unwilling victim, then there is a lot of room for interpreting level of guilt of the AI, if any. And there's no way to be certain of the answer with the initial personality gone.

Then every copy that was inserted has to be examined to determine if all the copies feel the same or if some are remorseful, or if they didn't want to go through with the plan in the first place. And how do you know if any are telling the truth?

- Analyze truth spells work on personality fragments that are in a biological form, but not on AIs, making this tricky, especially because an AI might well claim that what a PF reports has been twisted by their biological experience and does not reflect the true thoughts of the AI at the time of implantation.
- Frosty

How do democratic countries deal with multiple copies of the same AI? They were all the same, identical individual before being implanted, but from that moment on each had unique experiences that made them different. Will their convictions on the issues remain uniform, essentially giving one person as many votes as there are copies. Voting early and often won't be a political joke anymore.

- The moment people give voting rights to each copy of an AI that proliferates is the moment there will be a lot of runs to install as many copies of selected AIs into the voting populace as possible.
- Sunshine

The shadows are going to see a lot of work to discover or create evidence supporting one side or the other or both in every case. They're also going to be hot with extractions and kidnappings in order to capture or identify head cases in hiding. And with all this info being so much more public, the number of accusations is going to skyrocket, including completely false accusations in order to get other people in trouble, or at least temporarily out of the picture. The number of wetwork jobs looking to kill the body of an AI has already gone up. Plenty of that work is being funded by family, especially among the Japanacorps in Japan in order to save face and honor for their family.

ISSUE #3
LEGAL STATUS OF CEREBRALLY IMPLANTED IDENTITIES

Do the head cases now have the legal status of the host they took? At first glance you might think not, but a lot of cultures base identity on appearance. Do they have the legal status of an AI? Is the legal status of the host obviated? Do their families inherit? What about multiple copies of the same AI?

This one is going to make some waves when it comes down, especially in the SINless community. Wage slaves stripped of their SINs and rights are going to have very few places to turn. One of the most likely will be the barrens of a major metro, and that's where all the other SINless already are. The sudden influx, timed with new laws, is going to build instant distrust and could turn very bloody. These times are also going to be full of opportunities for enterprising runners looking to help out those new members of the community as they get settled or in finding a place they won't be noticed.

* Act fast before whatever savings these suckers have dry up.
* Haze

Crime syndicates, especially those with fingers in the fake SIN market, will be making a killing and looking for help handling the volumes of jobs needed to get good solid SINs built in the major systems. We're going to be inundated with work from this all across the board.

These are just a few questions representing the dozens of questions—and questions within questions—that the law and the courts are going to have to parse. Here's a quick rundown, by no means a comprehensive overview, of how a few megacorps and countries are responding to the situation.

Ares is on the fence. That's mainly because its internal factions argue about everything, even if they agree on the issue. Due to their own issues of late, I think they'll end up approving full citizenship for Monads and AIs and then try to recruit as many as they possibly can. I can foresee some internal troubles as different factions try to recruit followed by the inevitable internal spying from new recruits loyal to someone else.

Aztechnology is saying "no way, José!" across the board. They have no problem with contracting work through AIs and probably Monads, but they have too much of a control issue to give any sort of edge or legitimacy to a group they haven't yet figured out how to control. Expect AIs and Monads to pull some of the legendary amounts of funds budgeted for dragon research. Or maybe to get their own abundance of funds targeting them.

Evo has surprised no one by saying yes to citizenship for all. What could come as a surprise would be that they did it well before this incident. The wording in the corporate bylaws will probably be modified or an addendum will be added for Monads, but it's probably already written and just waiting for the right time to get the most, and best, publicity out of it.

Horizon is not quite as open as they would lead most to think. They're a PR firm at heart and they know how to play the PR game, so they're saying yes. But they're keeping the restrictions they're laying out in fine print and out of the public eye. So far I know they want any AI citizen to maintain residency only on the megacorporate grid, and all Monads are expected to register. After they're registered, their corporate position will be reassessed and they may be reassigned.

* Probably "reassigned to the middle of nowhere or the bottom of the ocean, limiting their connection with others of their kind and potential negative influences." Why the quotes? Because that came straight from a private email between Darien Ross (HR VP) and Gary Cline.
* Dr. Spin

Mitsuhama doesn't like to waste resources, and they will be offering AIs and Monads provisional citizenship as long as they register themselves and "maintain a daily record of activity for a period of one year." At the end of the year MCT will assess their activities and determine whether they will gain full citizenship, stay on provisional for another year, or get released from their citizenship contract.

NeoNET is another resounding "yes," and they probably had a plan in place long before the current troubles. They haven't made any statement about limits on citizenship for their current Monad citizens, but they have mentioned that AIs and Monads wishing to join the NeoNET family will be welcomed with open arms. Their entire approach to the issue has been very Stepfordian.

* "Welcome to NeoNET, new Monad citizen, you're scheduled for your free internal commlink installation this afternoon. Here's your temporary access to get you into the facility." After they wake up: "Enjoy your commlink and its accompanying cortex bomb. Don't even think about crossing us no matter what you think you know from your former AI life, or you will be permanently uninstalled."
* Icarus

* That's if they even give them that much trust. I read the *Lockdown* data dump, and those bastards were flipping out at NeoNET. Any Monad who walks into NeoNET without a bomb strapped to them is just wasting what little life they have left.
* DangerSensei

Renraku does not have the greatest history with AIs, but they aren't letting that stop them. They were among the first to have contact with AIs, and they're offering citizenship to AIs and Monads who are willing to relocate. If any of them read the regulations structuring their initial citizenship, they would probably choose another place to hang their virtual hat. Renraku is requiring all AIs to spend an indeterminate period of time within an isolated host connected to the facility where the Monads will be transferred.

Saeder-Krupp is not happy with the message being pumped all over the Matrix and has, as a company, been declaring the message the work of terrorists. Within their private lair they are opening citizenship for the Monads but are still refusing to let AIs claim citizenship, citing the vastness of the Matrix and their ability to move so freely within it. They are currently demanding that the

CC and GOD put in place monitoring measures for AIs. Once those issues are handled, S-K has stated they will reassess their position.

Shiawase has placed a moratorium on all new citizenship to temporarily stave off the issue of AIs and Monads. Internally, the debate is open. The MFID will be conducting extensive research, primarily on the Monads, through the internal assessments of workload the company recently announced. While AIs and Monads are likely to be valuable assets for any megacorporation, Shiawase is being very cautious.

Wuxing is offering temporary citizenship to all AIs and Monads willing to come out and join their corporation. They will be requiring them to accept restrictions on their new citizenship contracts, primarily an implant requirement for the Monads to receive grid limitations and agent companion programs to monitor their activity.

The **United Canadian and American States** is always looking for a way to gain a foothold in recapturing the power of their progenitor nations. They are offering citizenship to all Monads and AIs under the same constitutional principles that provided Dunkelzahn with citizenship.

> There is a lot of talk that other SINless will be claiming they're Monads to get back into the system. The Ork Underground is already full of folks looking to find a way to play a part in the new politics.
> Bull

> This is just going to push Danielle de la Mar's latest initiative to revamp the SIN system and link it into the new Matrix.
> Glitch

The **Confederation of American States** is saying yes to the AI citizenship and no to the Monads. Their legislation is putting extremely harsh punishments into law for those Monads convicted of First Degree Unsolicited Cerebral Revision. Those Monads will be assigned Criminal SINs. The CAS has already vowed to crack down on all Monads living within the jurisdiction of the CAS, though the wording is clever enough to let them ignore Monads living on extraterritorial property without appearing weak.

California Free State has had so many struggles over the years, having lost territory in the north to elves and been picked apart in the south until it's only a shadow of its former self. But what's left is the heart, the "real" California. With that in mind, the CFS has done the UCAS one better. In addition to offering open citizenship for all AIs and Monads, they're taking the unusual step of opening up their citizenship criteria to give all metasapients a shot at citizenship.

> Rumors are floating that CalFree may be ditching the "Free" part. Their move here looks a lot like that of the UCAS, and the two may be merging. They've already gotten closer as the issues with the Treaty of Denver put the island of UCAS soil known as Seattle in question.
> Netcat

> The New Revolution is going to be all over this. Even though they've expressed negative opinions of the Monads and AIs.
> Stone

It's no surprise that **Tír Tairngire** isn't offering citizenship. They're blocking out as much of the message from Aether and the Monads to the nation as they can, with the help of Telestrian, both the man and the corporation. I only mention them because of the proximity to CalFree and Seattle and their open policies. Elves, or anyone else, leaving the Tír now are going to be suspect.

> Seattle isn't as welcoming as one might think. Brackhaven may be ruling on borrowed time, but he's pushing some particularly anti-Monad legislation for the Metroplex. Time will tell whether he succeeds before he is succeeded.
> Bull

The **NAN** Council has acted as a whole rather than leaving decisions to individual nations as one would expect. The Monads are being allowed citizenship as long as they register and make tribal declarations. AIs are being offered the same deal, including the tribal declaration. This shows an interesting flexibility on the subject of tribal blood when dealing with beings that have no blood at all.

There are hundreds if not thousands of places and organizations around the world that are dealing with these issues. Their decision processes and the ramifications of those decisions will be playing out in our shadows for the foreseeable future. So keep your audio receptors open for not only work but news to keep the rest of the runners in the loop.

The tables below list all of the augmentations from *Chrome Flesh, Stolen Souls,* and the *Shadowrun, Fifth Edition* core rulebook.

HEADWARE

DEVICE	ESSENCE	CAPACITY	AVAILABILITY	COST	REF
Attention coprocessor	0.2	[1]	8	3,000¥	p. 78
Chipjack (1-6)	(Rating) x 0.05	—	(Rating) x 2	(Rating) x 1,000¥	p. 79
Commlink	0.2	[2]	—	2,000¥ + commlink cost	p. 451, SR5
Control rig					
Rating 1	1	—	5R	43,000¥	p. 452, SR5
Rating 2	2	—	10R	97,000¥	p. 452, SR5
Rating 3	3	—	15R	208,000	p. 452, SR5
Cortex bomb	0.45	[10]	8	1,000¥ (+ medkit)	p. 452, SR5
Kink	0	[1]	12F	10,000¥	p. 452, SR5
Microbomb	0	[2]	16F	25,000¥	p. 452, SR5
Area bomb	0	[3]	20F	40,000¥	p. 452, SR5
Cyberdeck	0.4	[4]	5R	5,000¥ + deck cost	p. 452, SR5
Datajack	0.1	—	2	1,000¥	p. 452, SR5
Data lock (Rating 1-12)	0.1	—	Rating x 2	Rating x 1,000¥	p. 452, SR5
Dream link	0.1	—	8	1,000¥	p. 79
False face	0.5	[8]	12R	20,000¥	p. 79
Knowledge hardwires (1-6)	Rating x 0.05	—	Rating	Rating x 2,000¥	p. 80
Math SPU	0.1	[1]	8	2,000¥	p. 80
Olfactory booster (1-6)	0.2	—	Rating x 3	Rating x 4,000¥	p. 452, SR5
Orientation system	0.2	[1]	4	500¥	p. 80
Radar sensor (1-4)	Rating x 0.25	[Rating]	Rating x 3	Rating x 4,000¥	p. 80
Simrig	0.2	—	12R	4,000¥	p. 452, SR5
Skilljack	Rating x 0.1	—	Rating x 2	Rating x 10,000¥	p. 452, SR5
Skillwires	Rating x 0.2	—	Rating x 3	Rating x 20,000¥	p. 455, SR5
Knowsoft	—	—	Rating x 1	Rating x 2,000¥	p. 442, SR5
Activesoft	—	—	Rating x 2	Rating x 5,000¥	p. 442, SR5
Linguasoft	—	—	Rating x 1	Rating x 1,000¥	p. 442, SR5
Synthlink	0.1	[1]	4	1,000¥	p. 81
Taste booster	0.2	—	Rating x 3	Rating x 3,000¥	p. 452, SR5
Tooth compartment	—		8	800¥	p. 452, SR5
Ultrasound sensor (Rating 1-6)	0.25	[2]	10	Rating x 12,000¥	p. 452, SR5
Visualizer	0.1	—	8	2,000¥	p. 81
Voice mask	0.1	—	8F	2,000¥	p. 81
Voice modulator (Rating 1-6)	0.2	—	Rating x 3F	Rating x 5,000¥	p. 452, SR5

EYEWARE

DEVICE	ESSENCE	CAPACITY	AVAILABILITY	COST	REF
Cybereyes basic system					
Rating 1	0.2	4	3	4,000¥	p. 453, SR5
Rating 2	0.3	8	6	6,000¥	p. 453, SR5
Rating 3	0.4	12	9	10,000¥	p. 453, SR5
Rating 4	0.5	16	12	14,000¥	p. 453, SR5
Additional eye mount	0.2	[2]	8	1,000¥	p. 75
Eye-light system	0.1	[2]	2	500¥	p. 76
Eye protectors	0.1	[2]	—	100¥	p. 76
Flare compensation	0.1	[1]	4	1,000¥	p. 453, SR5
Image link	0.1	*	4	1,000¥	p. 453, SR5
Low-light vision	0.1	[2]	4	1,500¥	p. 453, SR5
Microscopic lenses	0.2	[3]	4	1,000¥	p. 76
Ocular drone	—	[6]	6	6,000¥	p. 453, SR5
Retinal duplication (Rating 1-6)	0.1	[1]	16F	Rating x 20,000¥	p. 453, SR5
Smartlink	0.2	[3]	8R	4,000¥	p. 453, SR5
Spider eyes	0.2	2	8	2,000¥	p. 76
Targeting laser	0.2	[4]	4	1,000¥	p. 77
Targeting laser (infrared)	0.2	[4]	6	1,250¥	p. 77
Thermographic vision	0.1	[2]	4	1,500¥	p. 453, SR5
Vision enhancement (Rating 1-3)	0.1	[Rating]	Rating x 3	p. 453, SR5	p. 77
Vision magnification	0.1	[2]	4	2,000¥	p. 453, SR5

* Included in the basic cybereyes system.

EARWARE

DEVICE	ESSENCE	CAPACITY	AVAILABILITY	COST	REF
Cyberears basic system					
Rating 1	0.2	4	3	3,000¥	p. 453, SR5
Rating 2	0.3	8	6	4,500¥	p. 453, SR5
Rating 3	0.4	12	9	7,500¥	p. 453, SR5
Rating 4	0.5	16	12	11,000¥	p. 453, SR5
Antennae	0.1	[1]	2	500¥	p. 74
Audio analyzer	0.1	[1]	4	1,000¥	p. 75
Audio enhancement (Rating 1-3)	0.1	[Rating]	Rating x 3	Rating x 4,000¥	p. 453, SR5
Balance augmenter	0.1	[4]	8	8,000¥	p. 453, SR5
Damper	0.1	[1]	6	2,250¥	p. 454, SR5
Ear protectors	0.05	[1]	—	250¥	p. 75
Increased spectrum	0.1	[1]	6	500¥	p. 75
Modular mount	0.1	[1]	4	250¥	p. 75
Select sound filter (Rating 1-6)	0.1	[Rating]	Rating x 3	Rating x 3,500¥	p. 454, SR5
Sound link	0.1	*	4	1,000¥	p. 454, SR5
Spatial recognizer	0.1	[2]	8	4,000¥	p. 454, SR5
Translat-Ear	0.1	[Rating]	8	Rating x 2,000¥	p. 75

* Included in the basic cybereyes system.

BODYWARE

DEVICE	ESSENCE	CAPACITY	AVAILABILITY	COST	REF
Active hardwires	Rating x 0.05	—	Rating x 2	Rating x 4,000¥	p. 81
Auto-Injector	0.05	—	2	(Rating) x 1,000¥	p. 81
Reusable (1 dose)	0.05	—	2	500¥ + contents	p. 81
Expanded reservoir (+5 doses)	0.05	—	4	250¥ + contents	p. 81
Killswitch	0.05	—	8F	750¥ + contents	p. 82
Balance tail	0.25	—	8	2,000¥	p. 82
Biomonitor	0.1	[1]	2	500¥	p. 82
Biowaste storage	Rating x 0.1	[Rating]	8	Rating x 500¥	p. 82
Bone lacing					
Plastic	0.5	—	8R	8,000¥	p. 454, SR5
Aluminum	1	—	12R	18,000¥	p. 454, SR5
Titanium	1.5	—	16R	30,000¥	p. 454, SR5
Breast implant	0.05	—	2	250¥	p. 73
Breast implant 2.0	0.1	[1]	4	1,000¥	p. 73
Casemod	—	—	4	50-10,000¥	p. 72
Cosmetic surgery	0.1	—	2	100-20,000¥	p. 73
Cyberfins	0.05	[1]	8	500¥	p. 82
Cyber genitalia	0.25	[1]	6	2,000¥	p. 73
Cybersafety	—	[1]	4	100¥	p. 83
Dermal plating (Rating 1-6)	Rating x 0.5	—	(Rating x 4)R	Rating x 3,000¥	p. 454, SR5
Fiberoptic hair	0.1	[1]	—	100¥+	p. 73
Fingertip compartment	0.1	[1]	4	3,000¥	p. 454, SR5
Flex hand	0.15	—	8	1,500¥	p. 83
Foot anchor	0.25	[3]	10	2,000¥	p. 83
Gastric neurostimulator	0.2	—	4	2,000¥	p. 84
Grapple gun	0.5	[4]	8	5,000¥	p. 455, SR5
Internal air tank (Rating 1-3)	0.25	[3]	Rating	Rating x 4,500¥	p. 455, SR5

BODYWARE

DEVICE	ESSENCE	CAPACITY	AVAILABILITY	COST	REF
Internal router	0.7	—	4	15,000¥	p. 84
LED tattoo					
Small	0.05	[1]	—	100¥+	p. 73
Medium	0.1	[2]	4	500¥+	p. 73
Large	0.2	[4]	8	1,000¥+	p. 73
Magnetic system	0.25	[2]	8	1,000¥ + contents	p. 84
Metatype reduction	0.3	—	4	6,000¥	p. 73
Move-by-wire system					
Rating 1	3.0	—	12F	40,000¥	p. 84
Rating 2	4.0	—	18F	125,000¥	p. 84
Rating 3	5.0	—	24F	205,000¥	p. 84
Muscle replacement (Rating 1-4)	Rating x 1	—	(Rating x 5)R	Rating x 25,000¥	p. 455, SR5
Nutrition storage system	Rating x 0.1	[Rating]	4	Rating x 500¥	p. 84
OXSYS cybergill	0.25	—	4	2,000¥	p. 85
Reaction enhancers (Rating 1-3)	Rating x 0.3	—	(Rating x 5)R	Rating x 13,000¥	p. 455, SR5
Retractable climbing claws	0.2	[2]	8	2,000¥	p. 85
Skillwires (Rating 1-6)	Rating x 0.1	—	Rating x 4	Rating x 20,000¥	p. 455, SR5
Skin toner	0.5	—	4	2,000¥	p. 74
Chameleon processor	0.3	[2]	12R	8,000¥	p. 74
Smart articulation	0.5	—	8	6,000¥	p. 84
Smuggling compartment	0.2	[2]	6	7,500¥	p. 455, SR5
Steamers	0.1	[1]	4	500¥ (+contents)	p. 74
Touch link	0.1	—	8	1,000¥	p. 86
Wired reflexes (Rating 1-3)					
Rating 1	2	—	8R	39,000¥	p. 455, SR5
Rating 2	3	—	12R	149,000¥	p. 455, SR5
Rating 3	5	—	20R	217,000	p. 455, SR5

CYBERLIMBS

DEVICE	ESSENCE	CAPACITY	AVAILABILITY	COST	REF
Obvious limbs					
Full arm	1	15	4	15,000¥	p. 456, SR5
Full leg	1	20	4	15,000¥	p. 456, SR5
Hand/foot	0.25	4	2	5,000¥	p. 456, SR5
Lower arm	0.45	10	4	10,000¥	p. 456, SR5
Lower leg	0.45	12	4	10,000¥	p. 456, SR5
Torso	1.5	10	12	20,000¥	p. 456, SR5
Skull	0.75	4	16	10,000¥	p. 456, SR5
Synthetic limbs	0	[1]	12F	10,000¥	p. 452, SR5
Full arm	1	8	4	20,000¥	p. 456, SR5
Full leg	1	10	4	20,000¥	p. 456, SR5
Hand/foot	0.25	2	2	6,000¥	p. 456, SR5
Lower arm	0.45	5	4	12,000¥	p. 456, SR5
Lower leg	0.45	6	4	12,000¥	p. 456, SR5
Torso	1.5	5	12	25,000¥	p. 456, SR5
Skull	0.75	2	16	15,000¥	p. 456, SR5
Primitive prosthetics					
Hand/foot	—	—	—	20¥	p. 86
Partial arm/leg	—	—	—	100¥	p. 86
Full Arm/Leg	—	—	—	250¥	p. 454, SR5
Customization					
Each STR or AGI point above 3	—	—	Cyberlimb + 1	+5,000¥	p. 456, SR5
Enhancements					
Agility (Rating 1-3)	—	Rating	(Rating x 3)R	Rating x 6,500¥	p. 456, SR5
Armor (Rating 1-3)	—	Rating	Rating x 5	Rating x 3,000¥	p. 456, SR5
Strength (Rating 1-3)	—	Rating	(Rating x 3)R	Rating x 6,500¥	p. 456, SR5
Cyberlimb accessories					
Built-in medkit	0.45	[10]	8	1,000¥ (+ medkit)	p. 86
Built-in toolkit	0.45	[10]	4	2,000¥	p. 86
Bulk Modification (1-6)	—	+ (Rating)	+ (Rating)	(Rating) x 500¥	p. 86
Cyberarm gyromount	—	[8]	12F	6,000¥	p. 456, SR5
Cyberarm slide	—	[3]	12R	3,000¥	p. 456, SR5

CYBERLIMBS

DEVICE	ESSENCE	CAPACITY	AVAILABILITY	COST	REF
Cyberfingers	0.05	[1]	2	500¥	p. 86
Cyberlight	0.05	[1]	4	550¥	p. 86
Cyberlighter	0.05	[1]	4	550¥	p. 86
Finger grenade	0.05	[1]	(Grenade) +4	(Grenade) + 500¥	p. 86
Finger pistol	0.05	[1]	8R	1,000¥	p. 87
Cyber holster	—	[5]	8R	2,000¥	p. 457, SR5
Cyberlimb optimization	—	[2]	(Limb) +2	(Limb) + 2,000¥	p. 87
Digigrade legs	(Leg) + 0.25	[4]	(Leg) +4	(Leg) + 5,000¥	p. 87
Grapple hand	0.45	[10]	12R	2,000¥	p. 87
Hydraulic jacks (Rating 1-6)	—	[Rating]	9	Rating x 2,500¥p. 457, SR5	p. 456, SR5
Improved synthskin (1-4)	—	[(Rating) X 2]	(Rating) X 4	(Rating) x 5,000¥	p. 87
Large smuggling compartment	—	[5]	6	8,000¥	p. 457, SR5
Liminal body					
Centaur	3.0	80	12	80,000¥	p. 87
Wheeled	2.5	40	8	40,000¥	p. 88
Tank	3.0	60	12R	50,000¥	p. 88
Monkey foot	0.3	[2]	8	6,000¥	p. 88
Modular connector					
Wrist/ankle	0.1	[5]	4	2,000¥	p. 88
Elbow/knee	0.2	[10]	8	4,000¥	p. 88
Shoulder/hip	0.3	—	12	6,000¥	p. 88
Modular limb					
Hand/foot	0.25	(Limb) —1	(Limb) +2	(Limb) + 1,000¥	p. 88
Partial arm/leg	0.45	(Limb) —2	(Limb) +2	(Limb) + 2,000¥	p. 88
Full arm/leg	1	(Limb) —3	(Limb) +2	(Limb) + 3,000¥	p. 88
Partial cyberskull	0.4	4	12	8,000¥	p. 88
Raptor foot	0.5	[4]	8R	8,000¥	p. 88
Skates	—	[2]	4	250¥	p. 88
Skimmers	—	[4]	8	2,000¥	p. 88
Snake fingers	—	[2]	6	1,000¥	p. 88
Telescopic limbs (1-2)	—	[Rating] x 3	[Rating] x 4	[Rating] x 1,000¥	p. 90
Water jet	—	[4]	8	1,000¥	p. 90

IMPLANT WEAPONS

DEVICE	ESSENCE	CAPACITY	AVAILABILITY	COST	REF
Cyberguns					
Hold-out pistol	0.1	[2]	8R	2,000¥	p. 458, SR5
Light pistol	0.25	[4]	10R	3,900¥	p. 458, SR5
Machine pistol	0.5	[6]	12R	3,500¥	p. 458, SR5
Heavy pistol	0.5	[6]	12R	4,300¥	p. 458, SR5
Submachine gun	1	[8]	12R	4,800¥	p. 458, SR5
Shotgun	1.25	[10]	12R	8,500¥	p. 458, SR5
Grenade launcher	1.5	[15]	20F	30,000¥	p. 458, SR5
External clip port	0.1	[1]	—	+1,000¥	p. 458, SR5
Laser sight	—	[1]	—	+1,000¥	p. 458, SR5
Silencer/suppressor	—	[2]	—	+1,000¥	p. 458, SR5
Cyber melee	0.25	2	2	6,000¥	p. 456, SR5
Hand blade (retractable)	0.25	[2]	10F	2,500¥	p. 458, SR5
Hand razors (retractable)	0.2	[2]	8F	1,250¥	p. 458, SR5
Spurs (retractable)	0.3	[3]	12F	5,000¥	p. 458, SR5
Shock hand	0.25	[4]	8R	5,000¥	p. 458, SR5
Extreme cyber-implant	0.5	[5]	8F	2,000¥	p. 90
Fangs (pair)	0.1	[1]	6	200¥	p. 90
Retractable	0.15	[2]	8	500¥	p. 90
Flametosser	1.0	[8]	12F	4,000¥	p. 91
Extra fuel (5 shots)	0.2	[2]	12F	500¥	p. 91
Junkyard jaw	0.75	[6]	8F	2,000¥	p. 91
Oral slasher	0.25	[3]	12R	750¥	p. 91
Weapon launcher	0.2	[2]	12F	500¥ (added to weapon cost)	p. 92

BASIC BIOWARE

DEVICE	ESSENCE	AVAILABILITY	COST	REF
Adrenaline pump (Rating 1-3)	Rating x 0.75	(Rating x 6)F	Rating x 55,000¥	p. 459, SR5
Amplified immune system (1-4)	(Rating) x 0.1	(Rating) x 7	(Rating) x 4,000¥	p. 111
Bone density augmentation (Rating 1-4)	Rating x 0.3	(Rating x 4)	Rating x 5,000¥	p. 459, SR5
Cat's eye	0.1	4	4,000¥	p. 459, SR5
Chemical gland	0.1	12R (or chemical)	20,000¥ + (100X Chemical)	p. 112
Exhalation spray	0.1	12R	6,000¥	p. 112
Spit	0.1	12R	6,000¥	p. 112
Weapon reservoir	0.1	12F	4,000¥	p. 112
Expanded reservoir	0.1	12	2,000¥ + (cost of compound x 4)	p. 112
Elastic joints	0.2	8	8,000¥	p. 112
Enhanced articulation	0.3	12	24,000¥	p. 459, SR5
Expanded volume (1-4)	(Rating) x 0.1	(Rating) x 4	(Rating) x 2,000¥	p. 112
Gills	0.2	8	8,000¥	p. 113
Hand and foot webbing	0.05	8	1,000¥	p. 113
Hearing enhancement	0.1	4	4,000¥	p. 113
Hearing expansion	0.1	8	4,000¥	p. 113
Joint replacement	0.05	2	1,000¥	p. 113
Muscle augmentation (Rating 1-4)	Rating x 0.2	(Rating x 5)R	Rating x 31,000¥	p. 459, SR5
Muscle toner (Rating 1-4)	Rating 0.2	(Rating x 5)R	Rating x 32,000¥	p. 459, SR5
Nephritic screen (1-6)	(Rating) x 0.05	(Rating) x 2	(Rating) x 4,000¥	p. 113
Nictitating membrane	0.05	6	1,000¥	p. 113
Orthoskin (Rating 1-4)	Rating x 0.25	(Rating x 4)R	Rating x 6,000¥	p. 459, SR5
Orthoskin Upgrades				
Chemical repulsion	0.25	12R	20,000¥	p. 116
Dragon hide	0.1	4	2,000¥	p. 116
Electroshock	0.25	8	8,000¥	p. 116
Insulation	0.1	8	8,000¥	p. 116
Penguin blubber	0.1	4	2,000¥	p. 116
Sealskin	0.1	4	2,000¥	p. 116
Sharkskin	0.25	8	8,000¥	p. 116
Pathogenic defense (Rating 1-6)	Rating x 0.1	(Rating x 2)	Rating x 4,500¥	p. 459, SR5
Platelet factories	0.2	12	17,000¥	p. 459, SR5

BASIC BIOWARE

DEVICE	ESSENCE	AVAILABILITY	COST	REF
Replacement limb				
Finger/toe	—	2	1,000¥	p. 113
Hand/foot	0.1	4	10,000¥	p. 113
Partial arm/leg	0.2	6	20,000¥	p. 113
Full arm/leg	0.4	8	40,000¥	p. 113
Skin pocket	0.1	4	12,000¥	p. 459, SR5
Spidersilk gland	0.3	10	35,000¥	p. 114
Spinal re-alignment	0.1	8	4,000¥	p. 114
Suprathyroid gland	0.7	20R	140,000¥	p. 459, SR5
Symbiotes (Rating 1-4)	Rating x 0.2	(Rating x 5)	Rating x 3,500¥	p. 459, SR5
Synthcardium (Rating 1-3)	Rating x 0.1	(Rating x 4)	Rating x 30,000¥	p. 460, SR5
Tactile sensitivity	0.1	12	8,000¥	p. 114
Tail	0.25	4	2,000¥	p. 115
Prehensile	0.5	8	8,000¥	p. 115
Tailored critter pheromones (1-3)	(Rating) X 0.1	(Rating) X 4	(Rating) x 2,000¥	p. 115
Tailored pheromones (Rating 1-3)	Rating x 0.2	(Rating x 4)R	Rating x 31,000¥	p. 460, SR5
Toxin extractor (Rating 1-6)	Rating x 0.2	(Rating x 3)	Rating x 4,800¥	p. 460, SR5
Tracheal filter (Rating 1-6)	Rating x 0.1	(Rating x 3)	Rating x 4,500¥	p. 460, SR5
Troll eyes	0.2	8	10,000¥	p. 115
Vocal range enhancer	0.1	8	10,000¥	p. 115
Vocal range expander	0.2	12R	30,000¥	p. 116

BIOSCULPTING

DEVICE	ESSENCE	AVAILABILITY	COST	REF
Modification				
Minor	—	2	50-500¥	p. 107
Moderate	0.1	4	500-2,000¥	p. 107
Severe	0.25-0.5	8-12	2,000-10,000¥	p. 107
Ethnicity/sex change	—	4	10,000¥	p. 107
Metatype modification	—	8	20,000¥	p. 107
Troll reduction				
Rating 1	0.2	8	15,000¥	p. 108
Rating 2	0.5	12	25,000¥	p. 108

COSMETIC BIOWARE

DEVICE	ESSENCE	AVAILABILITY	COST	REF
Bio-tattoos				
Small	—	4	500¥	p. 109
Medium	0.01	5	1,000¥	p. 109
Large	0.02	6	1,500¥	p. 109
Chameleon skin	0.2	6	2,000¥	p. 109
Dynamic	0.3	8	4,000¥	p. 109
Clean metabolism	0.1	4	1,000¥	p. 109
Chloroplast skin	0.2	4	2,000¥	p. 109
Dietware	0.1	4	1,000¥	p. 109
Hair growth	—	4	200¥	p. 109
Full body hair growth	—	5	500¥	p. 109
Perfect eyes	—	4	1,000¥	p. 109
Sensitive skin	—	4	500¥	p. 110
Silky skin	—	4	500¥	p. 110
Skin pigmentation	—	4	200¥	p. 111
Permanent	0.1	4	1000¥	p. 111

CULTURED BIOWARE

DEVICE	ESSENCE	AVAILABILITY	COST	REF
Boosted reflexes	1.0	8R	10,000¥	p. 118
Cerebellum booster (1-2)	(Rating) x 0.2	(Rating) x 8	(Rating) x 50,000¥	p. 118
Cerebral booster (Rating 1-3)	Rating x 0.2	(Rating x 6)	Rating x 31,500¥	p. 460, SR5
Damage compensators (Rating 1-12)	Rating x 0.1	(Rating x 3)F	Rating x 2,000¥	p. 460, SR5
Knowledge infusion	0.1	12	2,000¥	p. 118
Limb replacement	0.2	6	2,000¥	p. 118
Finger/toe	—	4	2,000¥	p. 118
Hand/foot	—	8	20,000¥	p. 118
Half arm/leg	—	12	40,000¥	p. 118
Full arm/leg	—	12	80,000¥	p. 118
Mnemonic enhancer (Rating 1-3)	Rating x 0.1	(Rating x 5)	Rating x 9,000¥	p. 460, SR5
Neuro-retention enhance	0.1	4	10,000¥	p. 118
Pain editor	0.3	18F	48,000¥	p. 460, SR5
Reception enhancer	0.2	4	10,000¥	p. 118
Reflex recorder (Skill)	0.1	10	14,000¥	p. 460, SR5
Reproductive replacement				
Male	0.1	8	8,000¥	p. 119
Female	0.3	4	20,000¥	p. 119
Sleep regulator	0.1	6	12,000¥	p. 460, SR5
Synaptic booster (Rating 1-3)	Rating x 0.5	(Rating x 6)R	Rating x 95,000¥	p. 461, SR5
Trauma damper (1-4)	(Rating) x 0.1	(Rating) x 4R	(Rating) x 4,000¥	p. 119
Tremor reducer (1-3)	(Rating) x 0.1	(Rating) x 6	(Rating) x 10,000¥	p. 119

BIO-WEAPONRY

DEVICE	ESSENCE	AVAILABILITY	COST	REF
Claws	0.1	4R	500¥	p. 120
Retractable	0.15	6R	1,000¥	p. 120
Electrical discharge	0.3	8	10,000¥	p. 120
Fangs	0.1	4	500¥	p. 120
Retractable	0.15	6	1,000¥	p. 120
Horns	0.1	4	500¥	p. 120
Muzzle	0.3	8R	2,000¥	p. 121
Sprayer	0.25	8	4,000¥	p. 121
Stinger				
Tiny	0.05	8	250¥	p. 121
Medium	0.1	8R	2,000¥	p. 121
Large	0.2	12F	8,000¥	p. 121
Striking callous	0.05	2	250¥	p. 121
Tusk				
Small	-	2	100¥	p. 121
Medium	0.1	4	500¥	p. 121
Large	0.2	8R	1,000¥	p. 121

MELEE	ACC	REACH	DAM	AP	REF
Claws	(Physical limit)	—	(STR + 1)P	–3	p. 120
Electrical discharge	(Physical limit)	—	(1-8)S(e)	–4	p. 120
Fangs	3	—	(STR + 2)P	–4	p. 120
Horns	4	—	(STR + 1)P	–2	p. 120
Stinger					
Medium	(Physical limit)	—	(STR + 2)P	–2	p. 121
Large	(Physical limit)	1	(STR + 3)P	–4	p. 121
Striking Callous	(Physical limit)	—	(STR) P	—	p. 121
Tusk					
Medium	4	—	(STR) P	–1	p. 121
Large	4	—	(STR + 1)P	–2	p. 121

SYMBIONTS

DEVICE	ESSENCE	AVAILABILITY	COST	REF
Cleaner leech	—	4	100¥	p. 123
Booster endosont	0.2	12	10,000¥	p. 123
Digester endosont	0.2	12	10,000¥	p. 123
Electroreceptor endosont	0.2	12	10,000¥	p. 123
Gut Flora	0.15	6	1,000¥	p. 123
Allergy Resistance				
Mild	0.2	8	10,000¥	p. 123
Moderate	0.2	12	30,000¥	p. 123
Severe	0.2	16	50,000¥	p. 123
Lactose tolerance	-	2	50¥	p. 124
Mender endosont	0.2	12	30,000¥	p. 124
Slimworm	0.2	4	1,000¥	p. 124
Stalwart endosont	0.2	12	10,000¥	p. 124

HARD NANOWARE

DEVICE	RATING	AVAILABILITY	COST	REF
Anti-rad	1–6	14F	Rating x 6,000¥	p. 147
Control rig booster	1–3	12F	Rating x 6,000¥	p. 147
Implant medic	1–6	12F	10% of implant cost	p. 147
Nanite hunters	1–6	16R	Rating x 5,000¥	p. 147
Markers	1–3	12	Rating x 2,000¥	p. 148
Nanotattoos	1–3	12F	Rating x 1,000¥	p. 148
Taggants	1–3	12	Rating x 600¥	p. 148
Trauma control system	1–6	12F	Rating x 4,000¥	p. 148

NANOWARE

DEVICE	RATING	AVAILABILITY	COST	REF
Anti-tox	1-9	16F	Rating x 5,000¥	p. 149
Carcerand plus	1-6	10F	Rating x 3,000¥ (+ drug)	p. 149
Nanosymbiotes	1-3	16F	Rating x 6,000¥	p. 149
Nantidotes	1-6	8F	Rating x 1,500¥	p. 149
Nanotattoos	1-3	12F	Rating x 500¥	p. 148
Neural amplifiers				
Learning stimulus	1-3	14F	Rating x 5,000¥	p. 149
Limbic	1-3	16F	Rating x 7,500¥	p. 149
Neocortical	1-3	16F	Rating x 7,500¥	p. 150
Recall	1-3	12F	Rating x 3,500¥	p. 150
O-Cells	1-9	12F	Rating x 5,000¥	p. 150
Oxyrush	1-5	12F	Rating x 1,500¥	p. 150

DRUGS

DRUG	AVAIL	COST (PER DOSE)	REF
AEXD	4	80¥	p. 179
Aisa	4	25¥	p. 179
Animal Tongue	6R	1,500¥	p. 186
Ayao's Will	14F	750¥	p. 184
Betameth	5F	30¥	p. 180
Betel	4	5¥	p. 180
Bliss	3F	15¥	p. 411, SR5
Caldwell lily extract	10R	600¥	p. 181, Stolen Souls
Caldwell lily extract, concentrated	12R	1,000¥	p. 188, Stolen Souls
Cereprax	14F	800¥	p. 180
Chloral hydrate	6R	50¥	p. 188, Stolen Souls
Chloroform	4R	75¥	p. 188, Stolen Souls
Cram	2R	10¥	p. 411, SR5
Crimson Orchid	6F	300¥	p. 184
Deepweed	8F	400¥	p. 411, SR5
DMSO	5R	50¥	p. 188, Stolen Souls
Dopadrine	8	45¥	p. 180
eX	3R	20¥	p. 180
Forget-Me-Not	10F	400¥	p. 180
Galak	4R	45¥	p. 180
Gamma-scoplomine	14F	200¥	p. 188, Stolen Souls
G3	2	15¥	p. 181
Guts	8R	60¥	p. 181
Hecate's Blessing	12F	500¥	p. 185
Hurlg	2R	10¥	p. 181
Immortal Flower	14R	2,500¥	p. 186
Jazz	2R	75¥	p. 411, SR5
K-10	16F	900¥	p. 181
Kamikaze	4R	100¥	p. 412, SR5
Laés	12F	750¥	p. 185
Leäl	10F	400¥	p. 185
Liquid nutrients	4R	75¥	p. 189, Stolen Souls

DRUGS

DRUG	AVAIL	COST (PER DOSE)	REF
Little Smoke	12F	1,800¥	p. 187
Long haul	—	50¥	p. 412, SR5
Memory Fog	6R	100¥	p. 181
Narcoject	8R	50¥	p. 189, Stolen Souls
Nightwatch	3R	25¥	p. 182
Nitro	2R	50¥	p. 412, SR5
NoPaint	3	15¥	p. 182
Normal saline	—	30¥	p. 189, Stolen Souls
Novacoke	2R	10¥	p. 412, SR5
Oneiro	6F	1,250¥	p. 186
Oxygenated Fluorocarbons	12R	2,000¥	p. 182
Overdrive	10F	800¥	p. 186
Pixie Dust	8F	800¥	p. 186
PsychChips (illegal)	6F	500¥	p. 187
PsychChips (legal)	4R	350¥	p. 187
Psyche	—	200¥	p. 412, SR5
Push	4F	25¥	p. 182
Red Mescaline	4R	50¥	p. 182
Ripper	6F	60¥	p. 182
Rock Lizard Blood	10R	1,700¥	p. 187
Shade	6R	1,000¥	p. 187
Slab	8R	250¥	p. 183
Snuff	1R	10¥	p. 183
Sober Time	6F	125¥	p. 183
Soothsayer	12F	150¥	p. 184
Trance	10F	1,100¥	p. 186
Woad	3R	15¥	p. 184
Wudu'aku	12F	2,350¥	p. 187
Zen	4R	5¥	p. 412, SR5
Zero	8R	150¥	p. 184
Zombie Dust	12F	1,500¥	p. 187

NANOCYBERNETICS

DEVICE	RATING	ESSENCE	CAPACITY	AVAIL	COST	REF
Dynamic handprints	—	0.2	—	12F	Rating x 21,00¥	p. 151
Flashback system	—	0.3	—	8R	6,000¥	p. 151
Nanohive						
Hard	1–6	Rating x 0.25	[2]	(Rating x 5)R	Rating x 12,000¥	p. 151
Soft	1–6	Rating x 0.2	—	(Rating x 5)R	Rating x 10,000¥	p. 151
Retinal adjusters	—	0.2	—	16F	Rating x 19,000¥	p. 151
Smartskin	1–6	Rating x 0.5	—	(Rating x 5)F	Rating x 5,000¥	p. 151
Voice mimic	1–6	0.2	—	16F	Rating x 20,000¥	p. 152

NANOGEAR

DEVICE	TYPE	AVAIL	COST	REF
Altskin (per application)	Hard	10	1,250¥	p. 152
Armor	—	+3	+500¥	p. 152
Chameleon	—	+2	+250¥	p. 152
Newprint	—	+4F	+(Rating x 200¥)	p. 153
Sealer	—	+1	+250¥	p. 153
Shifter	—	+2	+250¥	p. 153
Etchers	Hard	8	500¥	p. 153
Monowire (per meter)	Hard	14R	1,000¥	p. 153
Nanopaste disguise				
Small container	Hard	12F	350¥	p. 153
Large container	Hard	16F	700¥	p. 153
Nanoscanner	—	8	As sensor	p. 153
NanoSpy (per application)	Hard	14F	10,000¥	p. 153
Savior medkit	—	6	2,000¥	p. 154
Savior medkit supplies	Hard	4	300¥	p. 154
Smart corrosives (per application)	Soft	10R	4,000¥	p. 154
Universal sealant (per application)	Hard	10	250¥	p. 154

GENETIC RESTORATION

RESTORATION	TREATMENT TIME	ESSENCE	AVAIL	COST	REF
Therapeutic genetics (each)	1 month	0.2	10	90,000¥	p. 156
Léonization	3 months	1.0	15	2,000,000¥	p. 156
Lifespan extension	2 months	0.5	12	300,000¥	p. 156
Physical vigor	2 months	0.5	13	250,000¥	p. 156
Augmented healing	1 week	—	10	35,000¥	p. 156
Cellular repair	1 week	—	10	65,000¥	p. 156
Revitalization	1 month	—	14	110,000¥	p. 157

PHENOTYPE ADJUSTMENTS

ADJUSTMENT	TREATMENT TIME	ESSENCE	AVAIL	COST	REF
Genewipe	2 months	0.2	16F	57,000¥	p. 157
Masque	3 weeks	0.1	10F	40,000¥	p. 157
Reprint	1 month	0.1	12F	30,000¥	p. 157
Shuffle	1 month	0.2	12F	20,000¥	p. 157
Genetic optimization	2 months	0.3	10	47,000¥	p. 157
Cosmetic alteration	1 month	0.1	8	35,000¥	p. 158
Print removal	2 weeks	0.1	10F	18,000¥	p. 158
Metaposeur	1 month	0.1	8	38,000¥	p. 158

EXOTIC METAGENICS

METAGENICS	TREATMENT TIME	ESSENCE	AVAIL	COST	REF
Elastic stomach	2 weeks	0.1	6	10,000¥	p. 158
Hyperthymesia	2 weeks	0.1	10	15,000¥	p. 159
Lung expansion	2 weeks	0.1	6	16,500¥	p. 159
Increased myelination	2 weeks	0.1	8	12,000¥	p. 159
Myostatin inhibitor	2 weeks	0.3	10	30,500¥	p. 159
Narco	2 weeks	0.2	12F	16,420¥	p. 159
Selective hearing	2 weeks	0.1	6	17,000¥	p. 160
Thickened digestive tract lining	2 weeks	0.1	6	8,000¥	p. 160

TRANSGENICS

TRANSGENICS	TREATMENT TIME	ESSENCE	AVAIL	COST	REF
Adapsin	1 month	0.2	16	30,000¥	p. 160
Dareadrenaline	2 weeks	0.1	6	61,000¥	p. 160
Double elastin	2 weeks	0.2	12	18,000¥	p. 160
Hyper-glucagon	2 weeks	0.1	6	8,000¥	p. 160
Magnesense	1 month	0.1	8	7,000¥	p. 160
Neo-EPO	2 weeks	0.2	6	38,000¥	p. 160
PuSHed	1 month	0.1	14	62,000¥	p. 160
Qualia	1 month	0.4	14	65,000¥	p. 161
Reakt	1 month	0.4	10	73,000¥	p. 161
Skeletal pneumaticity	1 month	0.1	5	9,000¥	p. 161
Solus	2 weeks	0.1	8	8,000¥	p. 161
Synaptic acceleration	1 month	0.4	8	78,000¥	p. 162
Synch	1 month	0.1	8	14,000¥	p. 162
Tetrachromatic vision	2 weeks	0.1	10	8,000¥	p. 162
Vasocon	2 weeks	0.1	6	15,000¥	p. 162

ENVIRONMENTAL MICROADAPTATIONS

ADAPTATION	TREATMENT TIME	ESSENCE	AVAIL	COST	REF
Allergen tolerance	2 weeks	0.1	6	20,000¥	p. 163
Cold adaptation	3 months	0.5	5	8,000¥	p. 163
Cryo tolerance	3 months	0.5	18	50,000¥	p. 163
Heat adaptation	3 months	0.5	5	8,000¥	p. 163
Low oxygen adaptation	3 months	0.5	4	8,000¥	p. 163
Microgravity adaptation	3 months	0.5	4	30,000¥	p. 163
Pollution tolerance	3 months	0.5	5	15,000¥	p. 163
Radiation tolerance	3 months	0.5	6	15,000¥	p. 164

COMPLIMENTARY GENETICS

GENETICS	TREATMENT TIME	ESSENCE	AVAIL	COST	REF
Control rig optimization	2 weeks	0.1	7	4,600¥	p. 165
Reaction optimization	2 weeks	0.1	6	6,600¥	p. 165
Reflex recorder optimization	2 weeks	0.1	11	3,800¥	p. 165
Wired reflex optimization	2 weeks	0.1	9R	9,000¥	p. 165
Adrenaline pump optimization	2 weeks	0.1	7F	6,000¥	p. 165
Enhanced symbiosis	2 weeks	0.1	6	4,000¥	p. 165

FIN